SWORD ART ONLINE

GIRLS' OPS

004

ART: NEKO NEKOBYOU
ORIGINAL STORY: REKI KAWAHARA
CHARACTER DESIGN: abec

004

SWORD ART ONLINE
GIRLS' OPERATIONS

art: Neko Nekobyou
original story: Reki Kawahara
character design: abec

Contents

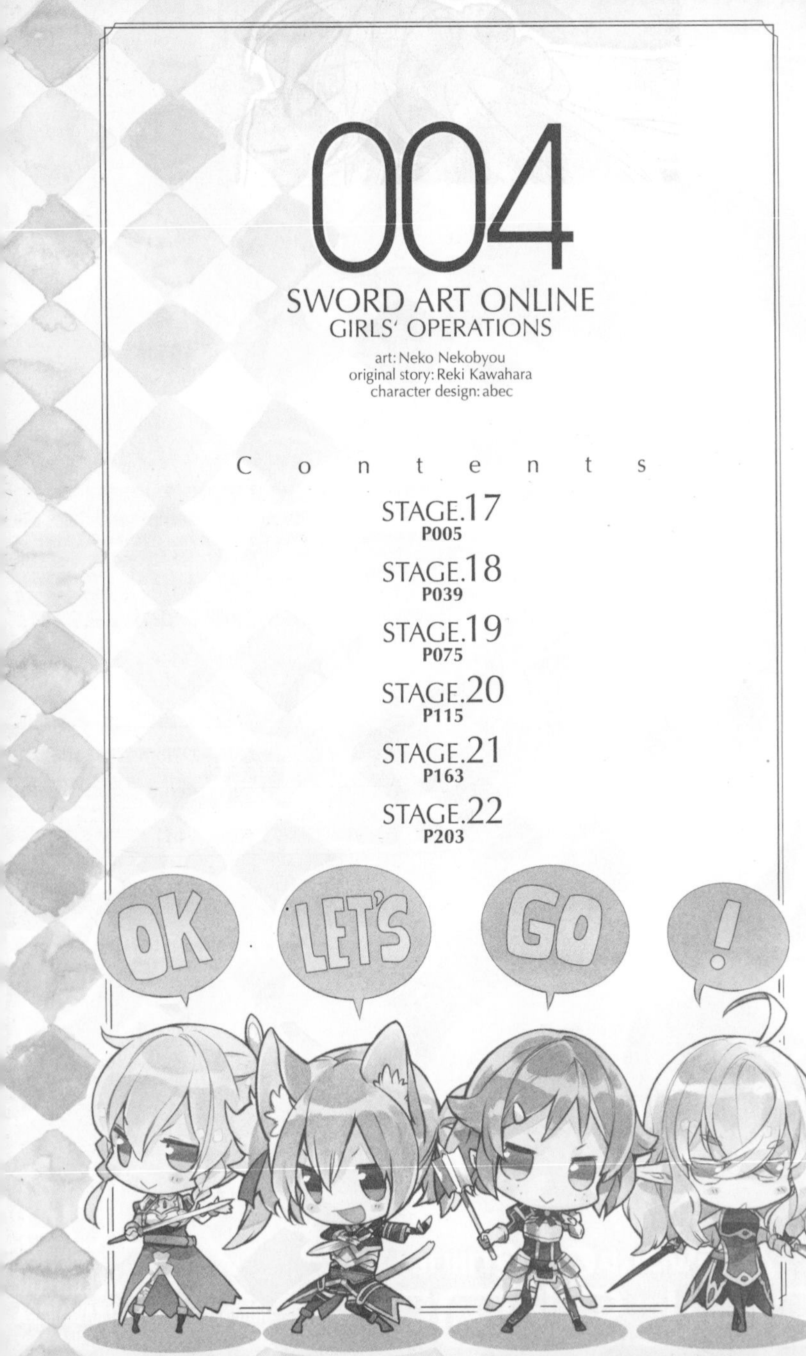
OK
LET'S
GO
!

SWORD ART ONLINE
GIRLS' OPS 004

SWORD ART ONLINE
GIRLS' OPERATIONS

ART: NEKO NEKOBYOU
ORIGINAL STORY: REKI KAWAHARA
CHARACTER DESIGN: abec

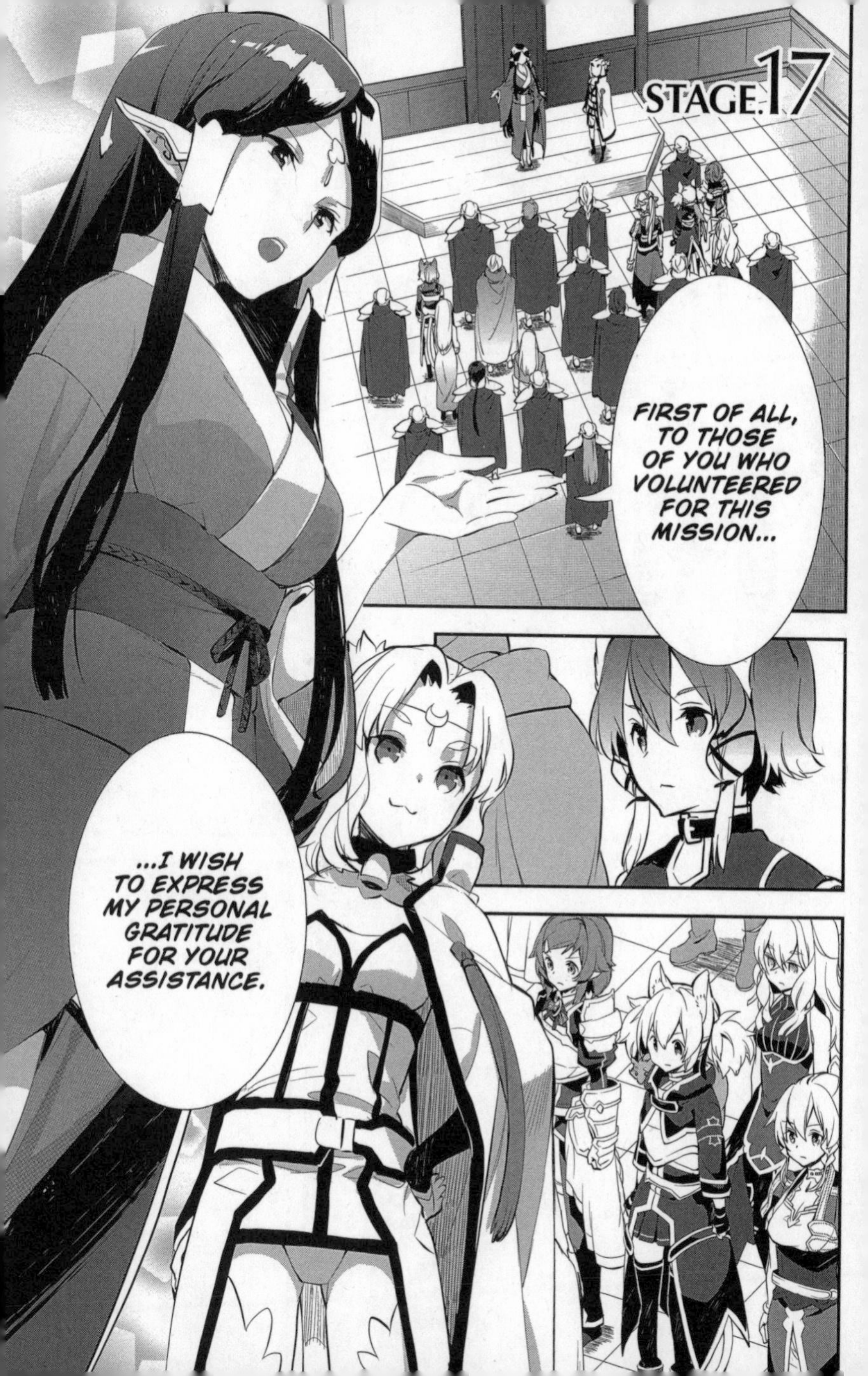
STAGE.17
FIRST OF ALL, TO THOSE OF YOU WHO VOLUNTEERED FOR THIS MISSION...
...I WISH TO EXPRESS MY PERSONAL GRATITUDE FOR YOUR ASSISTANCE.

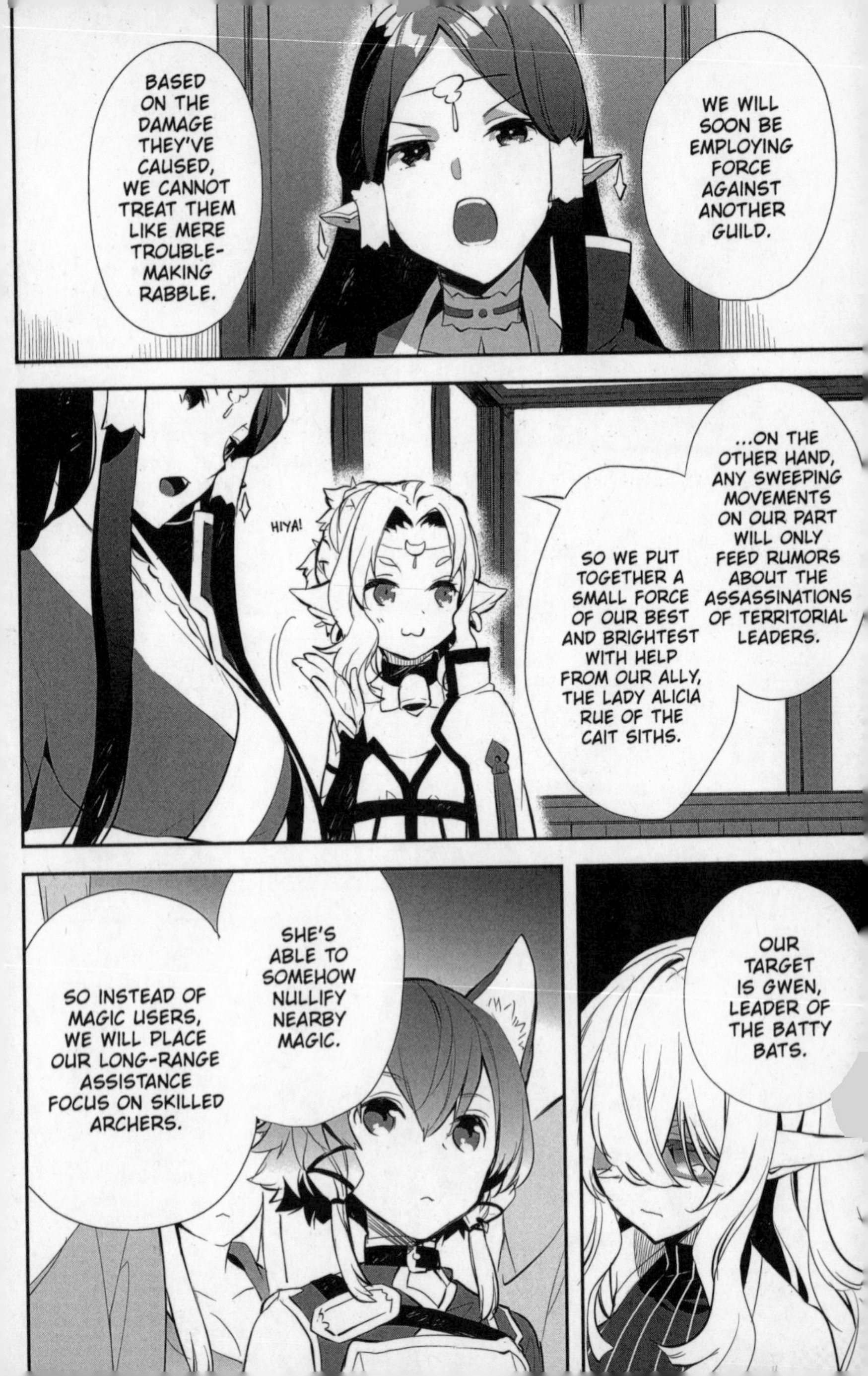
WE WILL SOON BE EMPLOYING FORCE AGAINST ANOTHER GUILD.
BASED ON THE DAMAGE THEY'VE CAUSED, WE CANNOT TREAT THEM LIKE MERE TROUBLE-MAKING RABBLE.
...ON THE OTHER HAND, ANY SWEEPING MOVEMENTS ON OUR PART WILL ONLY FEED RUMORS ABOUT THE ASSASSINATIONS OF TERRITORIAL LEADERS.
SO WE PUT TOGETHER A SMALL FORCE OF OUR BEST AND BRIGHTEST WITH HELP FROM OUR ALLY, THE LADY ALICIA RUE OF THE CAIT SITHS.
HIYA!
OUR TARGET IS GWEN, LEADER OF THE BATTY BATS.
SHE'S ABLE TO SOMEHOW NULLIFY NEARBY MAGIC.
SO INSTEAD OF MAGIC USERS, WE WILL PLACE OUR LONG-RANGE ASSISTANCE FOCUS ON SKILLED ARCHERS.

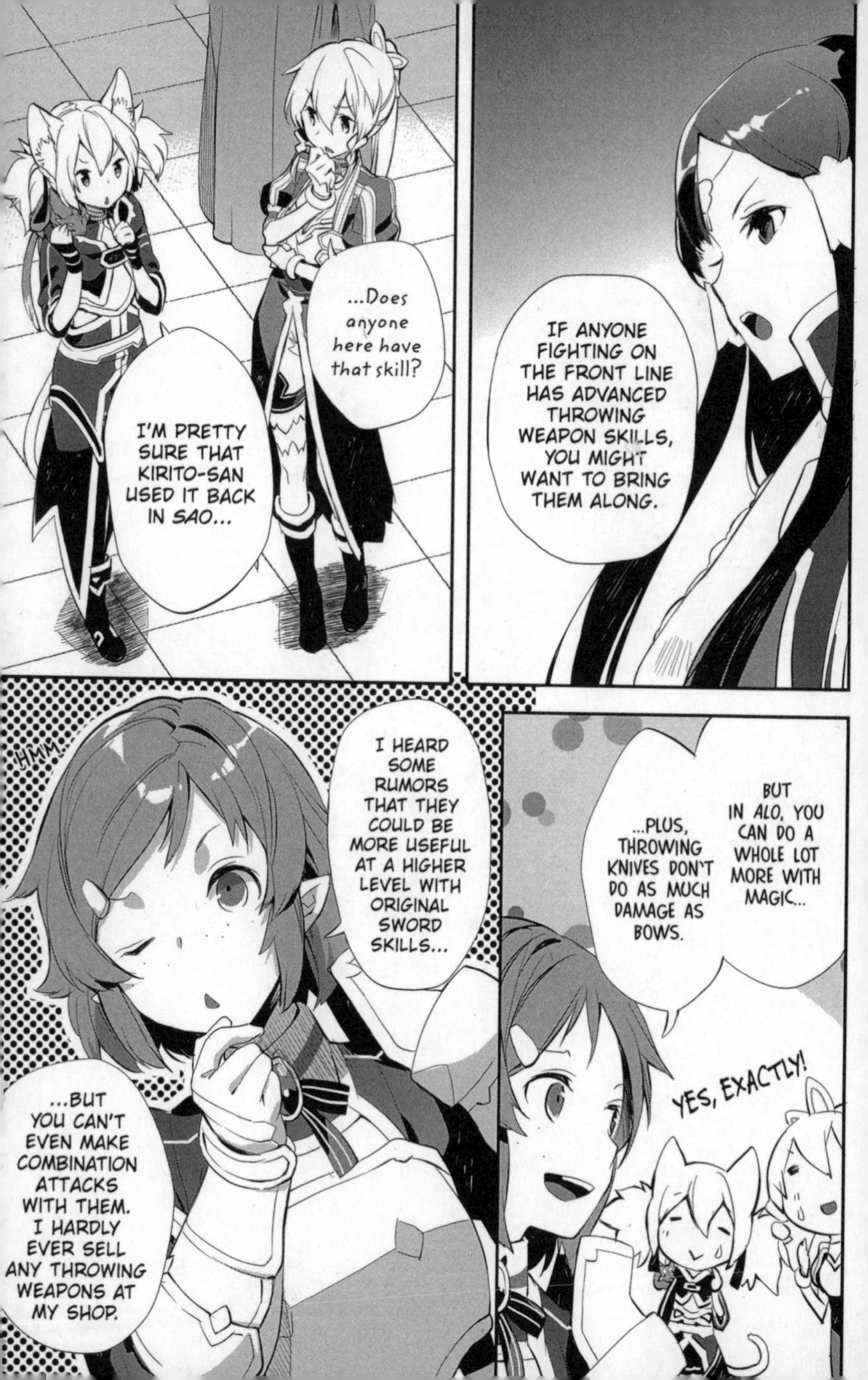
IF ANYONE FIGHTING ON THE FRONT LINE HAS ADVANCED THROWING WEAPON SKILLS, YOU MIGHT WANT TO BRING THEM ALONG.
...Does anyone here have that skill?
I'M PRETTY SURE THAT KIRITO-SAN USED IT BACK IN SAO...
BUT IN ALO, YOU CAN DO A WHOLE LOT MORE WITH MAGIC...
...PLUS, THROWING KNIVES DON'T DO AS MUCH DAMAGE AS BOWS.
YES, EXACTLY!
HMM...
I HEARD SOME RUMORS THAT THEY COULD BE MORE USEFUL AT A HIGHER LEVEL WITH ORIGINAL SWORD SKILLS...
...BUT YOU CAN'T EVEN MAKE COMBINATION ATTACKS WITH THEM. I HARDLY EVER SELL ANY THROWING WEAPONS AT MY SHOP.

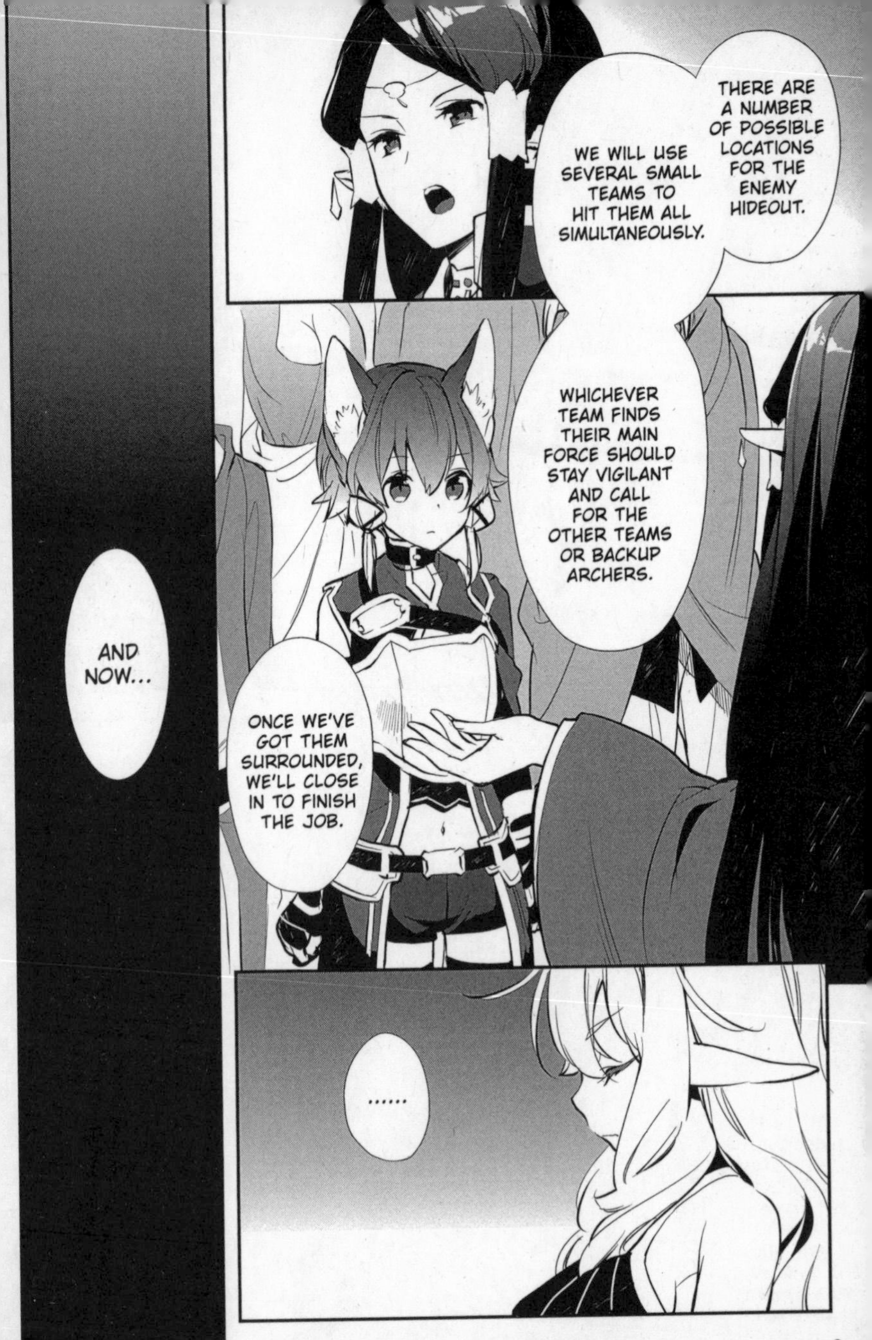
THERE ARE A NUMBER OF POSSIBLE LOCATIONS FOR THE ENEMY HIDEOUT.
WE WILL USE SEVERAL SMALL TEAMS TO HIT THEM ALL SIMULTANEOUSLY.
WHICHEVER TEAM FINDS THEIR MAIN FORCE SHOULD STAY VIGILANT AND CALL FOR THE OTHER TEAMS OR BACKUP ARCHERS.
ONCE WE'VE GOT THEM SURROUNDED, WE'LL CLOSE IN TO FINISH THE JOB.
AND NOW...
......

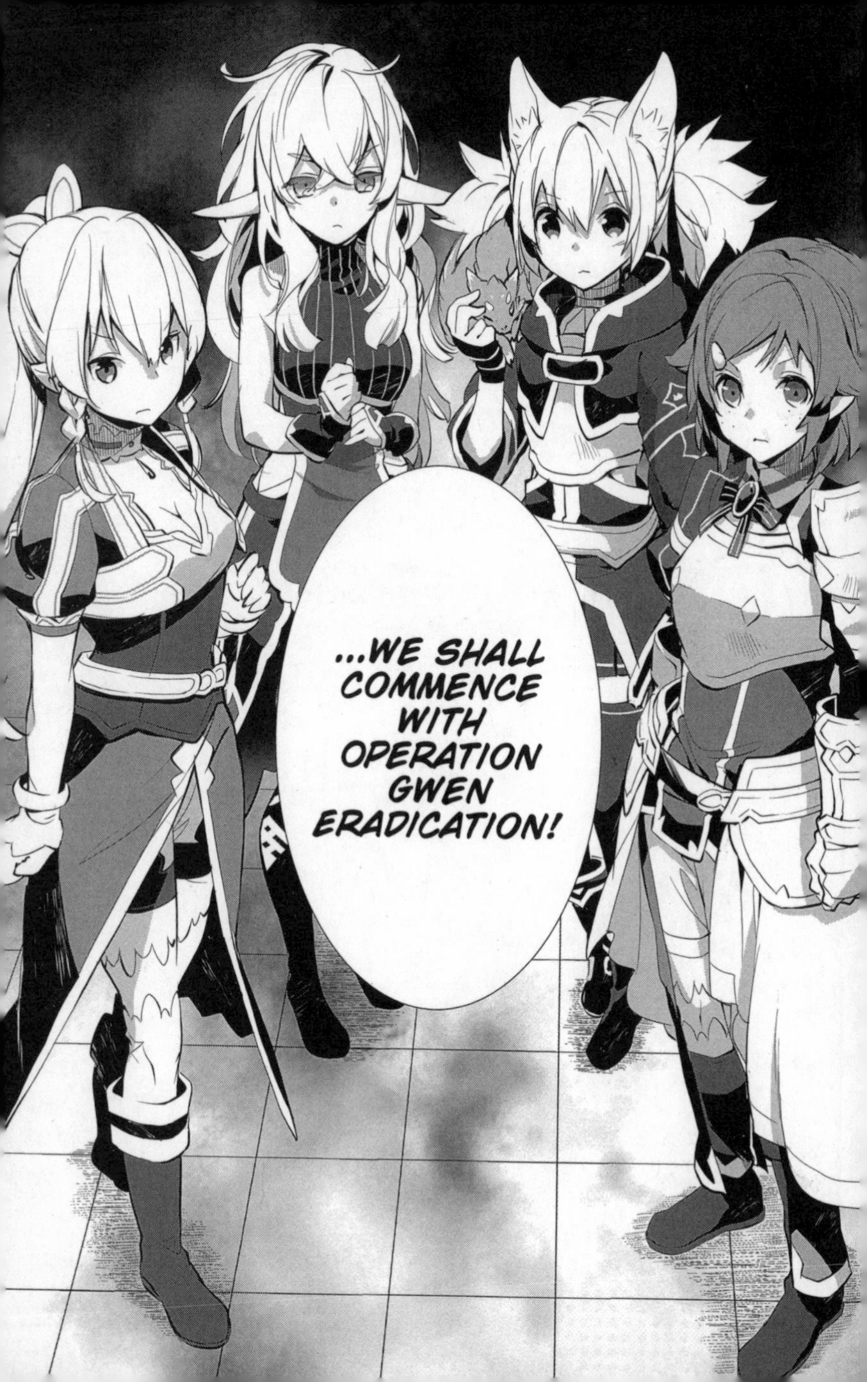
...WE SHALL COMMENCE WITH OPERATION GWEN ERADICATION!

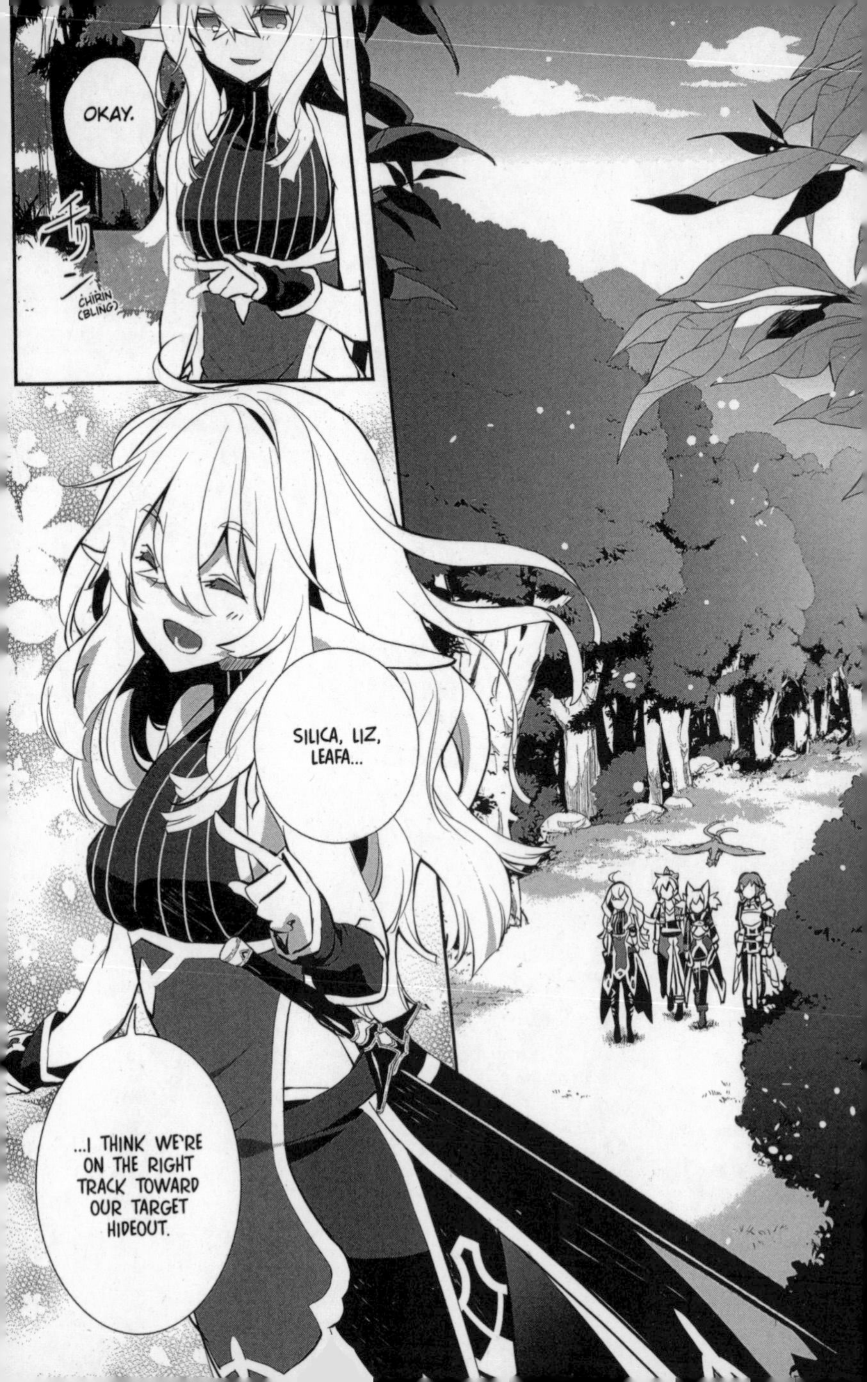
OKAY.
CHIRIN (BLING)
SILICA, LIZ, LEAFA...
...I THINK WE'RE ON THE RIGHT TRACK TOWARD OUR TARGET HIDEOUT.

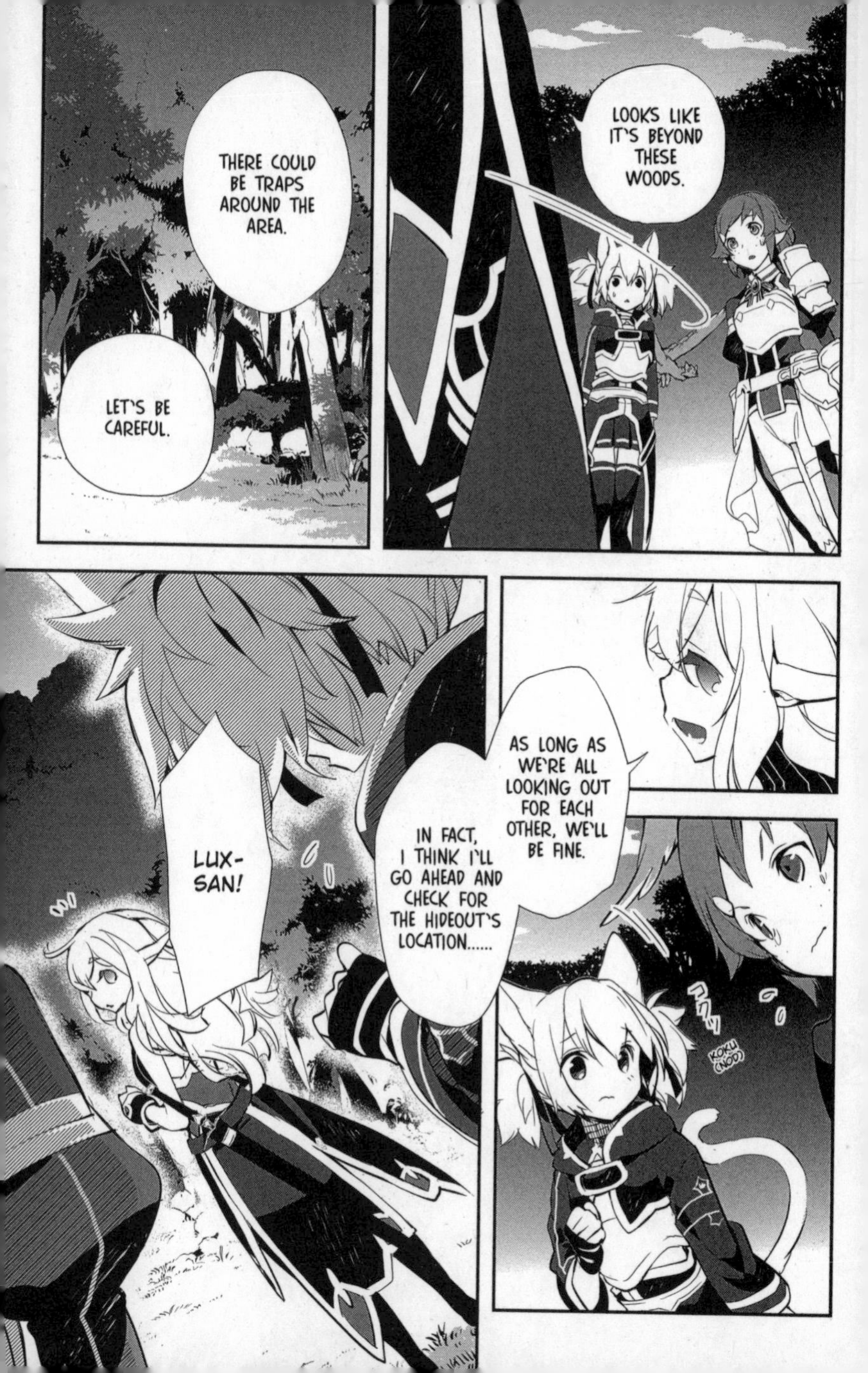
LOOKS LIKE IT'S BEYOND THESE WOODS.
THERE COULD BE TRAPS AROUND THE AREA.
LET'S BE CAREFUL.
AS LONG AS WE'RE ALL LOOKING OUT FOR EACH OTHER, WE'LL BE FINE.
KOKU (NOD)
IN FACT, I THINK I'LL GO AHEAD AND CHECK FOR THE HIDEOUT'S LOCATION......
LUX-SAN!

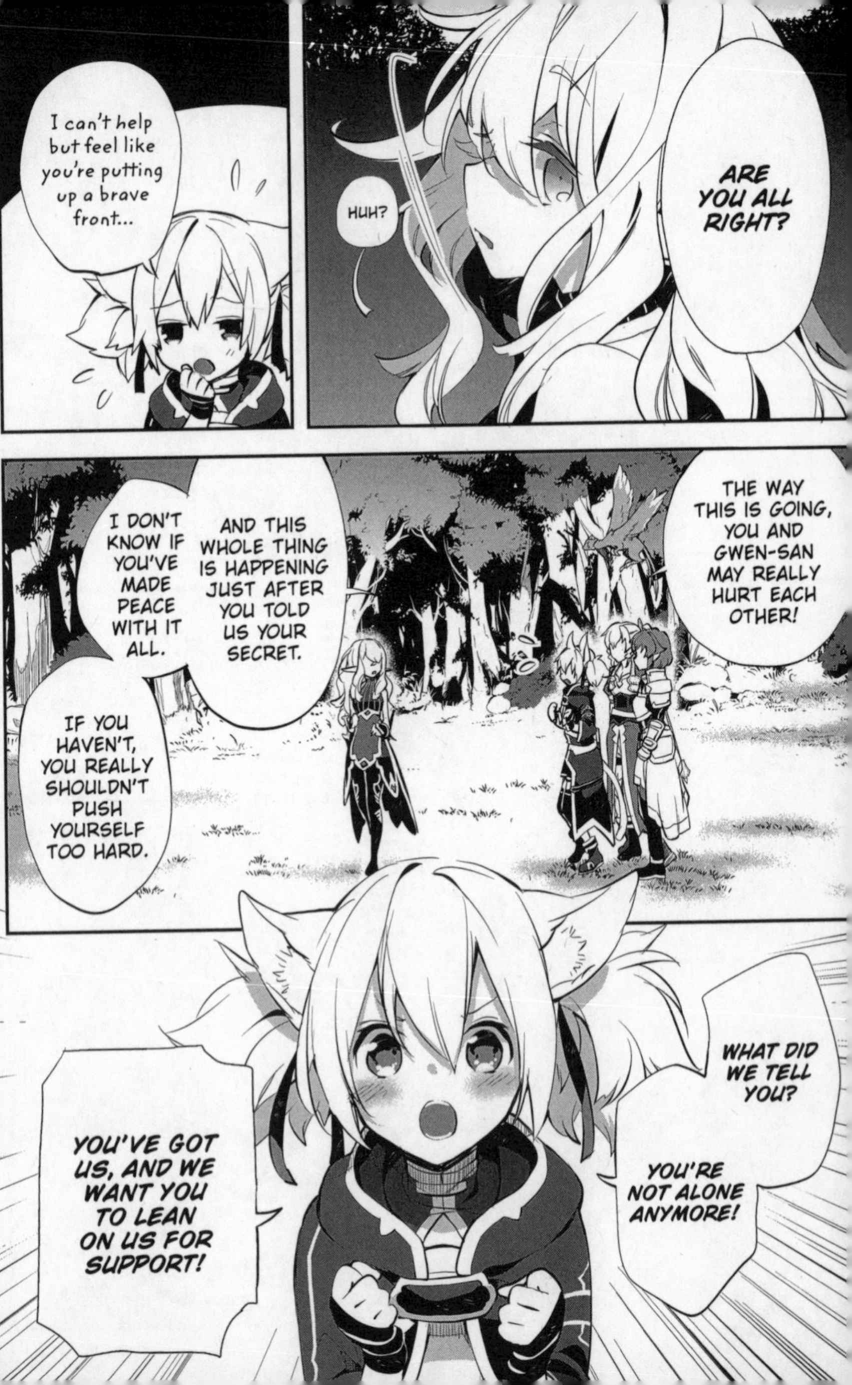
ARE YOU ALL RIGHT?
HUH?
I can't help but feel like you're putting up a brave front...
THE WAY THIS IS GOING, YOU AND GWEN-SAN MAY REALLY HURT EACH OTHER!
AND THIS WHOLE THING IS HAPPENING JUST AFTER YOU TOLD US YOUR SECRET.
I DON'T KNOW IF YOU'VE MADE PEACE WITH IT ALL.
IF YOU HAVEN'T, YOU REALLY SHOULDN'T PUSH YOURSELF TOO HARD.
WHAT DID WE TELL YOU?
YOU'RE NOT ALONE ANYMORE!
YOU'VE GOT US, AND WE WANT YOU TO LEAN ON US FOR SUPPORT!

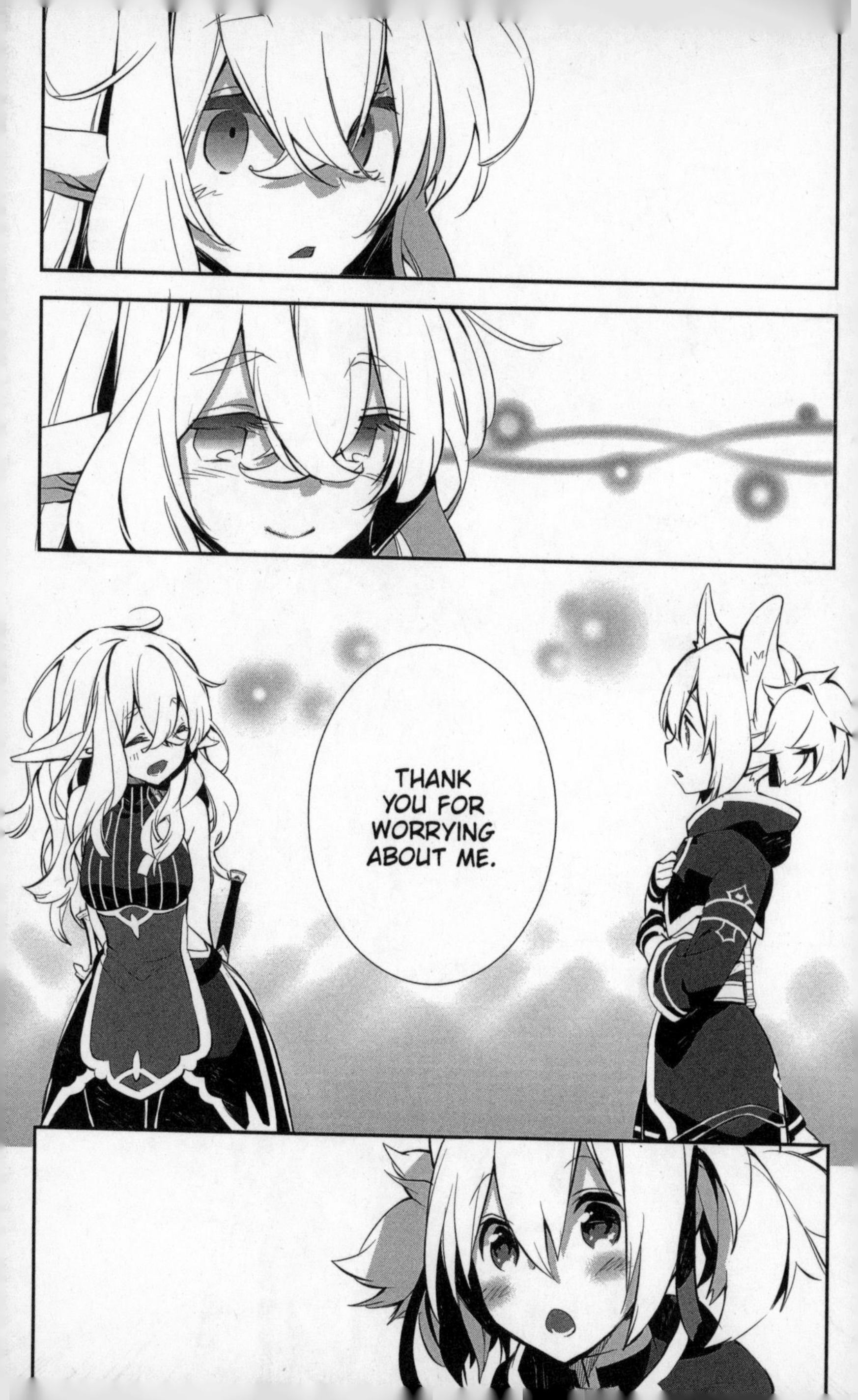
THANK YOU FOR WORRYING ABOUT ME.

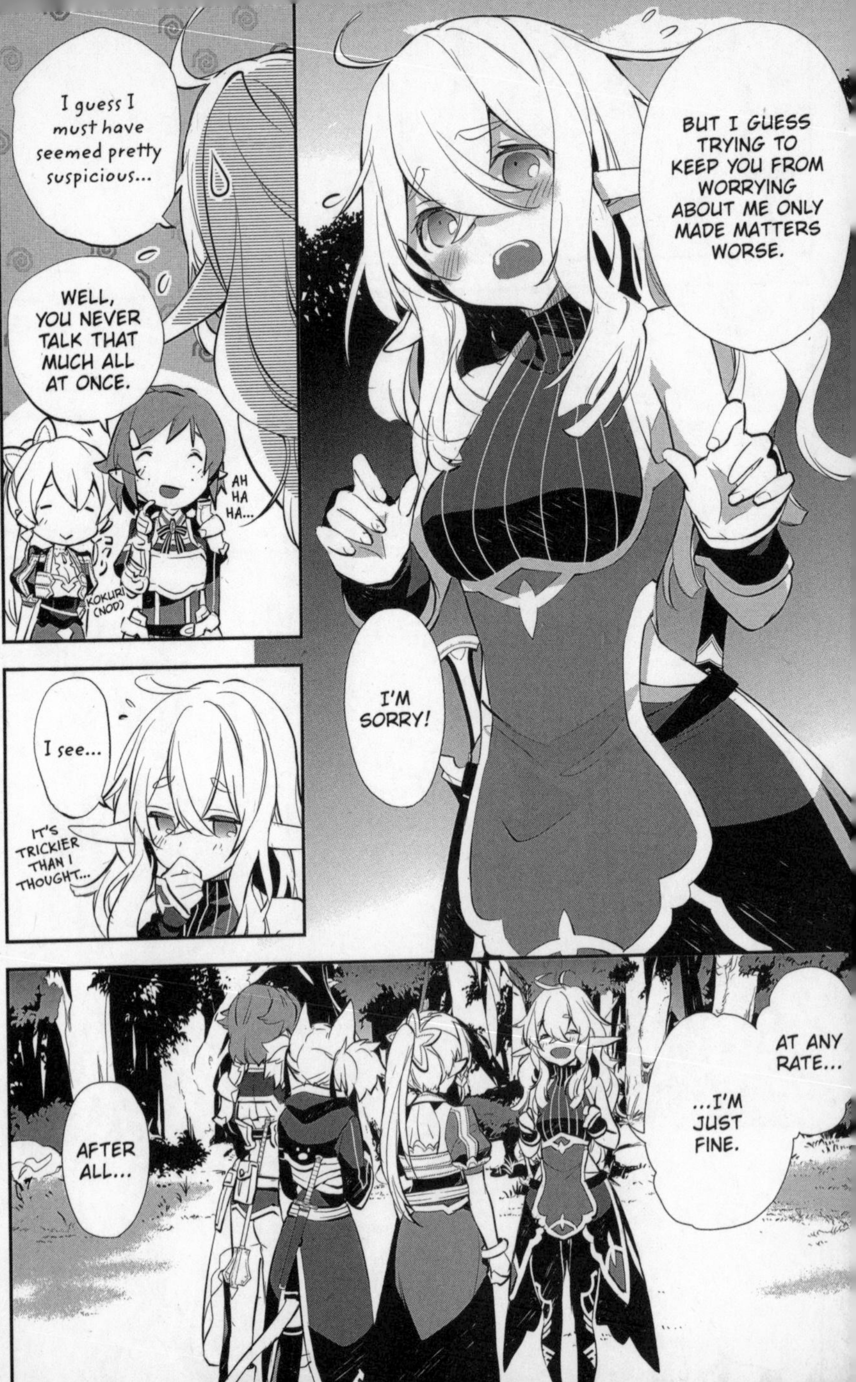
BUT I GUESS TRYING TO KEEP YOU FROM WORRYING ABOUT ME ONLY MADE MATTERS WORSE.
I'M SORRY!
I guess I must have seemed pretty suspicious...
WELL, YOU NEVER TALK THAT MUCH ALL AT ONCE.
AH HA HA...
KOKURI (NOD)
I see...
IT'S TRICKIER THAN I THOUGHT...
AT ANY RATE...
...I'M JUST FINE.
AFTER ALL...

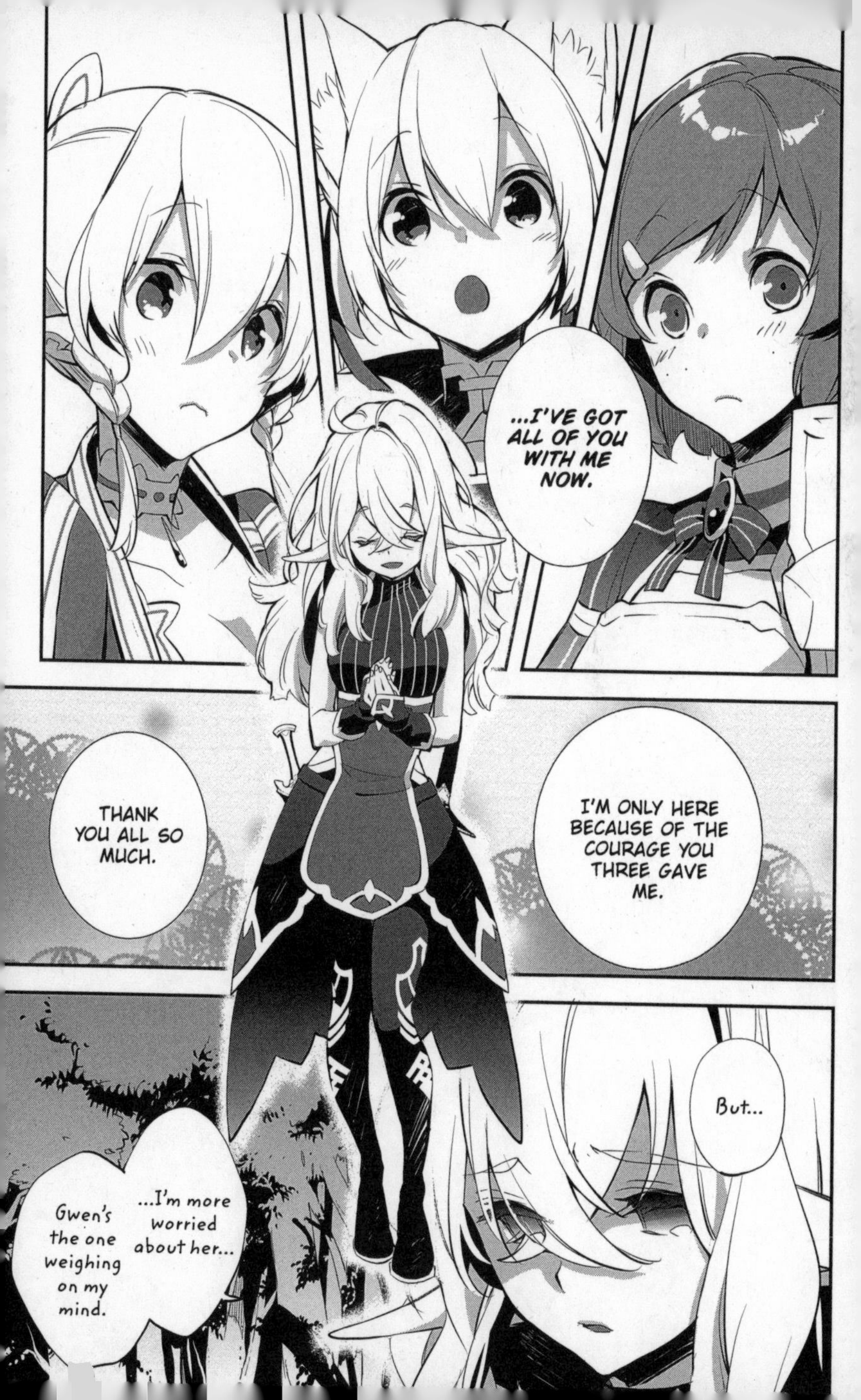
...I'VE GOT ALL OF YOU WITH ME NOW.
I'M ONLY HERE BECAUSE OF THE COURAGE YOU THREE GAVE ME.
THANK YOU ALL SO MUCH.
But...
...I'm more worried about her...
Gwen's the one weighing on my mind.

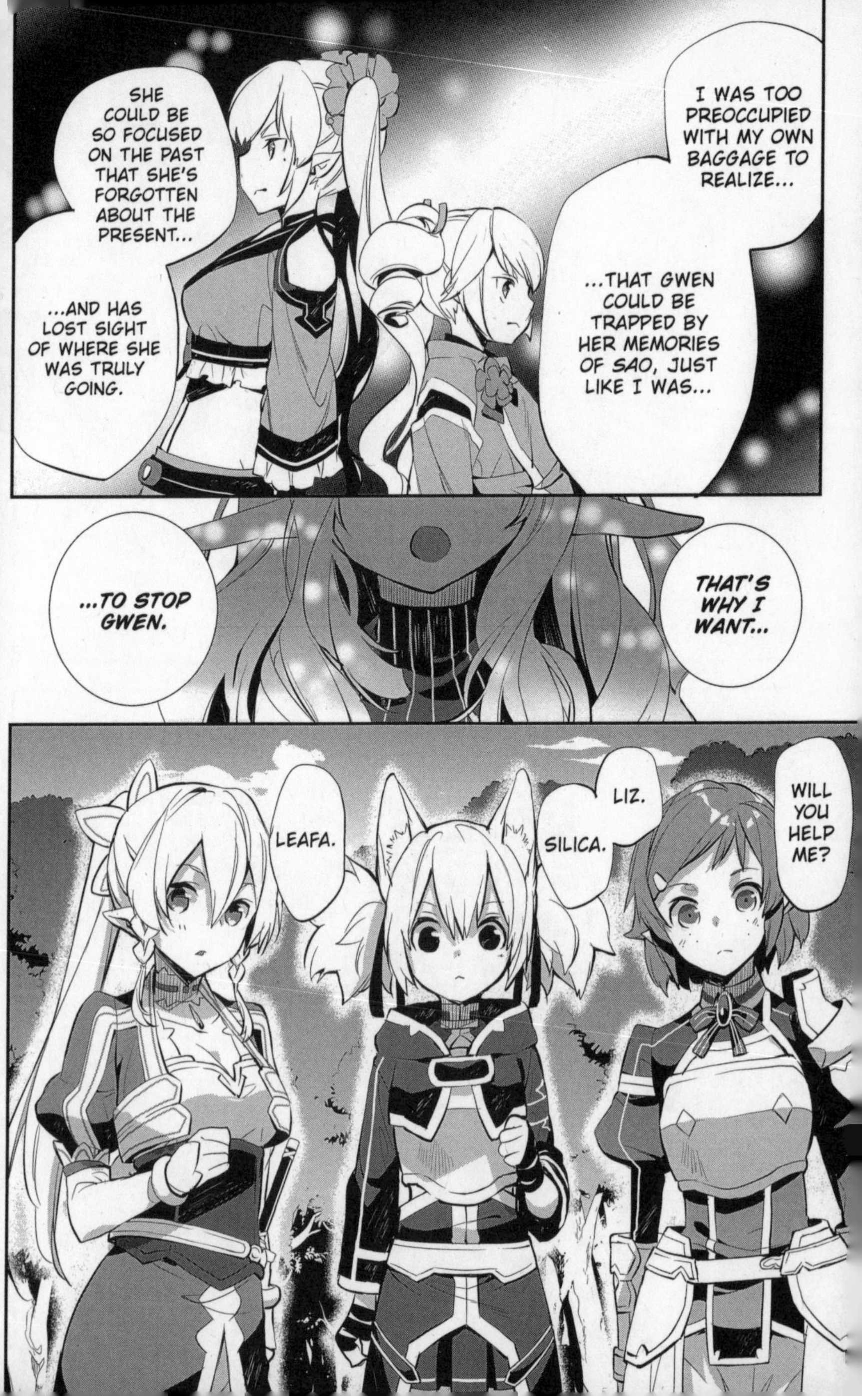
I WAS TOO PREOCCUPIED WITH MY OWN BAGGAGE TO REALIZE...
...THAT GWEN COULD BE TRAPPED BY HER MEMORIES OF SAO, JUST LIKE I WAS...
SHE COULD BE SO FOCUSED ON THE PAST THAT SHE'S FORGOTTEN ABOUT THE PRESENT...
...AND HAS LOST SIGHT OF WHERE SHE WAS TRULY GOING.
THAT'S WHY I WANT...
...TO STOP GWEN.
WILL YOU HELP ME?
LIZ.
SILICA.
LEAFA.

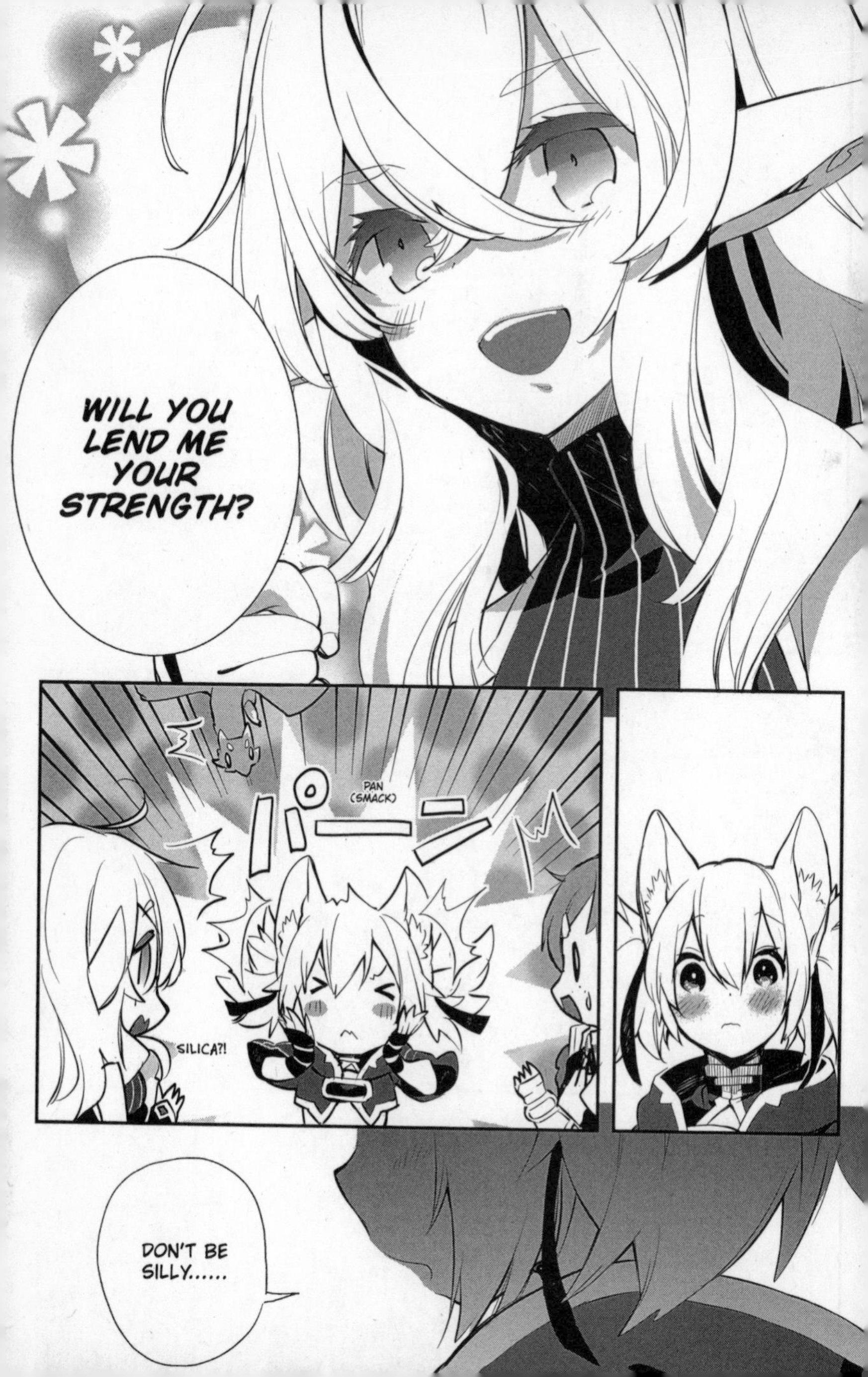
WILL YOU LEND ME YOUR STRENGTH?
PAN (SMACK)
SILICA?!
DON'T BE SILLY......

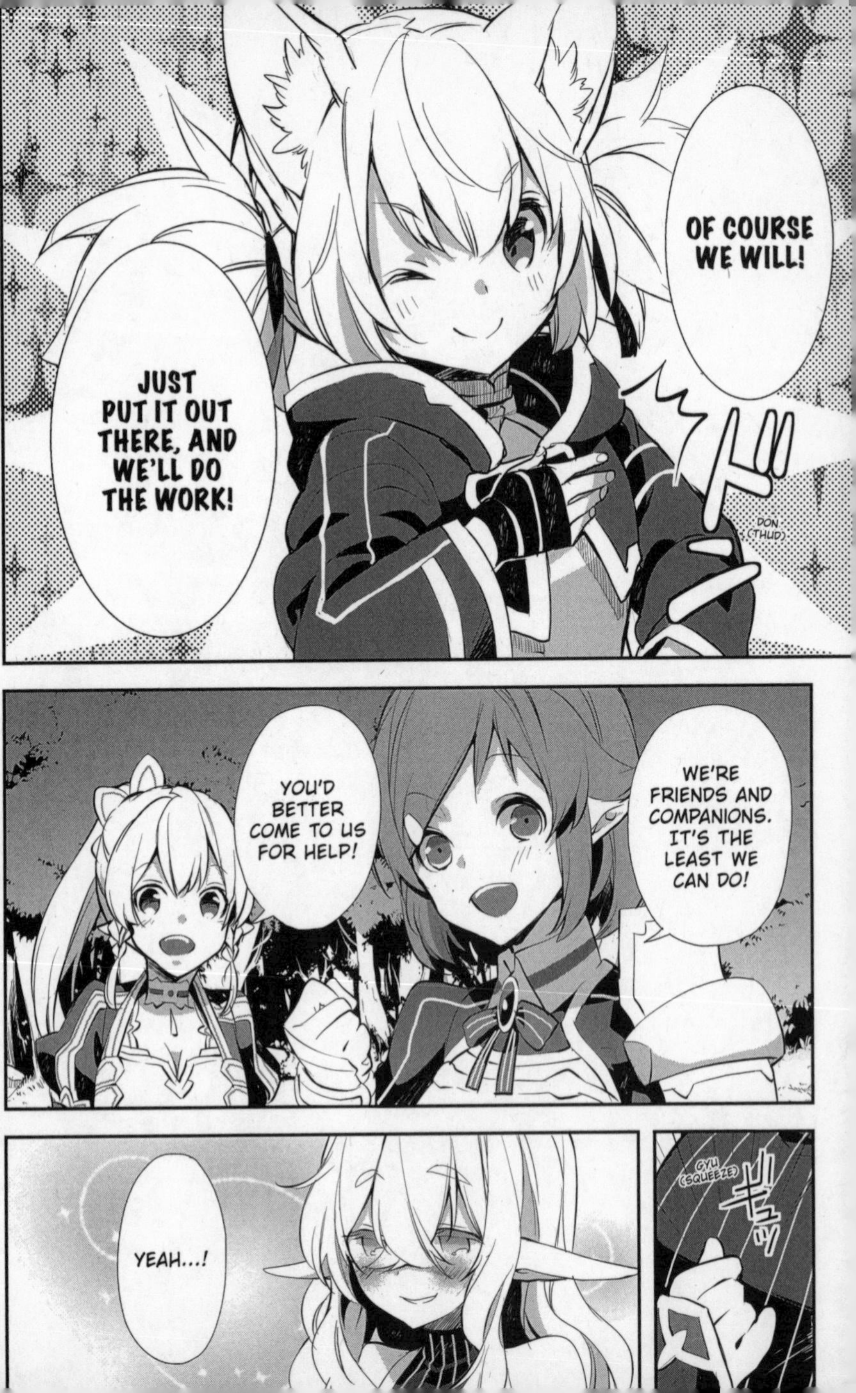
OF COURSE WE WILL!
JUST PUT IT OUT THERE, AND WE'LL DO THE WORK!
DON (THUD)
WE'RE FRIENDS AND COMPANIONS. IT'S THE LEAST WE CAN DO!
YOU'D BETTER COME TO US FOR HELP!
GYU (SQUEEZE)
YEAH...!

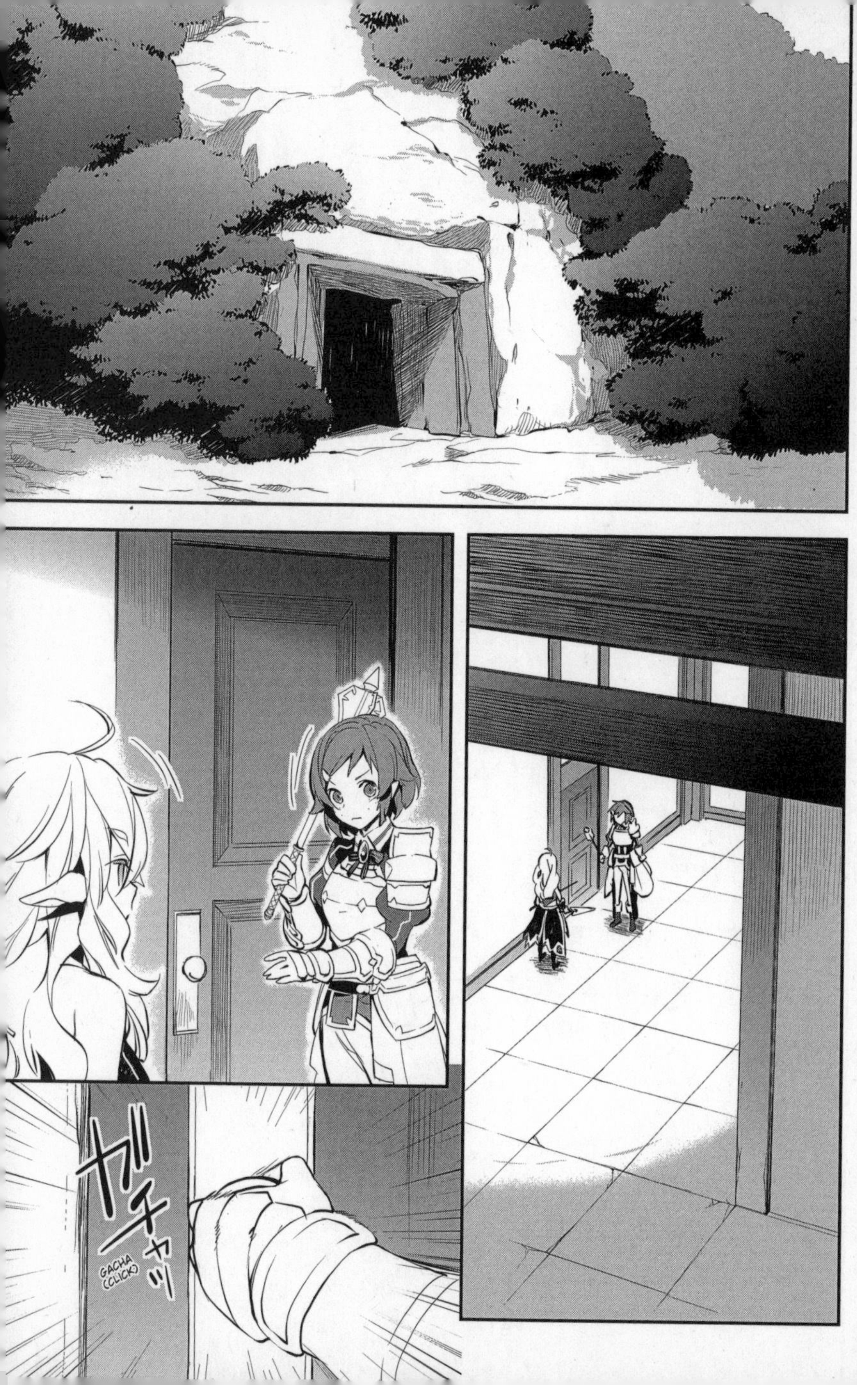
ガチャッ
GACHA (CLICK)

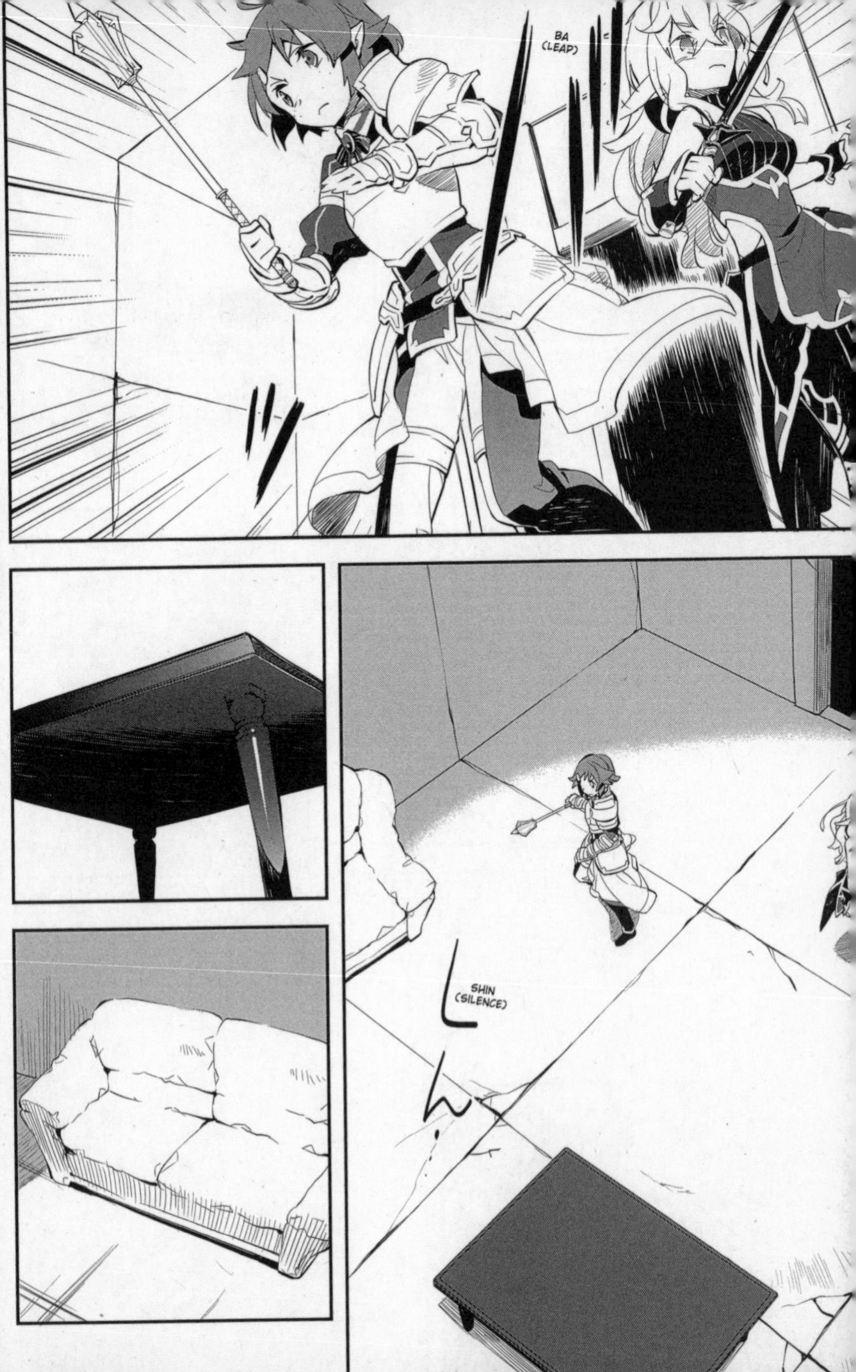
BA
(LEAP)
SHIN
(SILENCE)

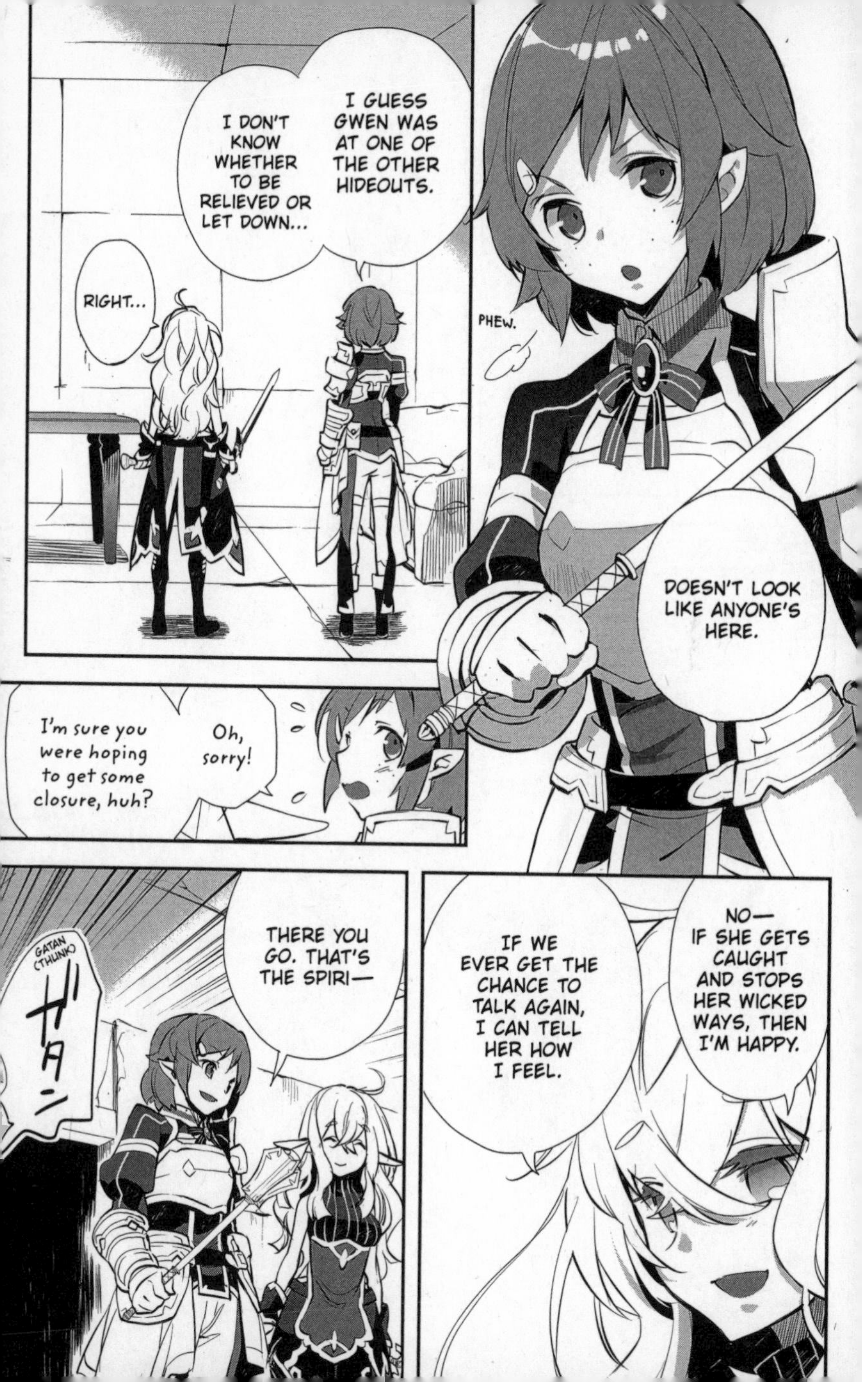
PHEW.
DOESN'T LOOK LIKE ANYONE'S HERE.
I GUESS GWEN WAS AT ONE OF THE OTHER HIDEOUTS.
I DON'T KNOW WHETHER TO BE RELIEVED OR LET DOWN...
RIGHT...
Oh, sorry!
I'm sure you were hoping to get some closure, huh?
NO— IF SHE GETS CAUGHT AND STOPS HER WICKED WAYS, THEN I'M HAPPY.
IF WE EVER GET THE CHANCE TO TALK AGAIN, I CAN TELL HER HOW I FEEL.
THERE YOU GO. THAT'S THE SPIRI—
GATAN (THUNK)
ガタン

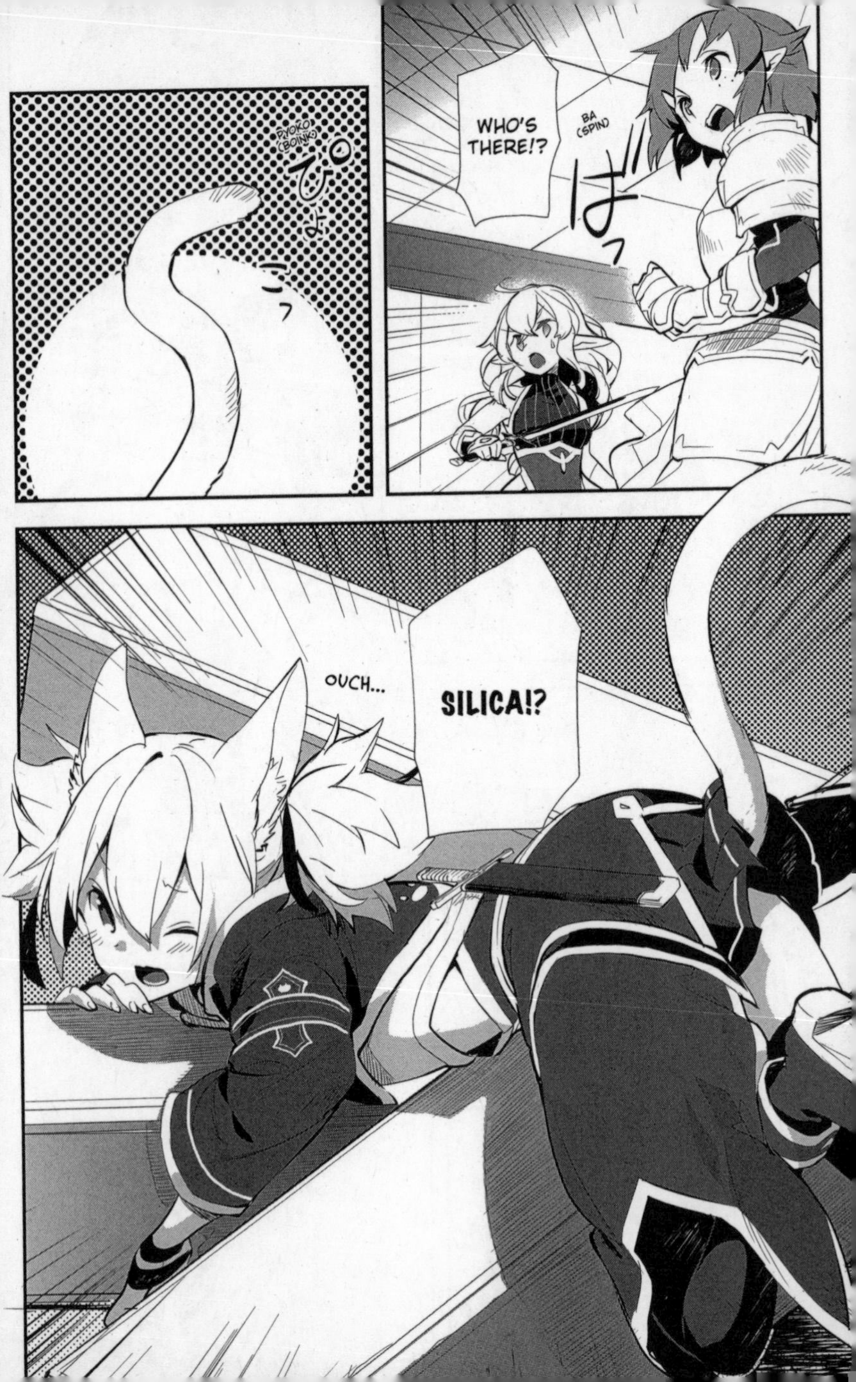
WHO'S THERE!?
BA (SPIN)
PYOKO (BOINK)
SILICA!?
OUCH...

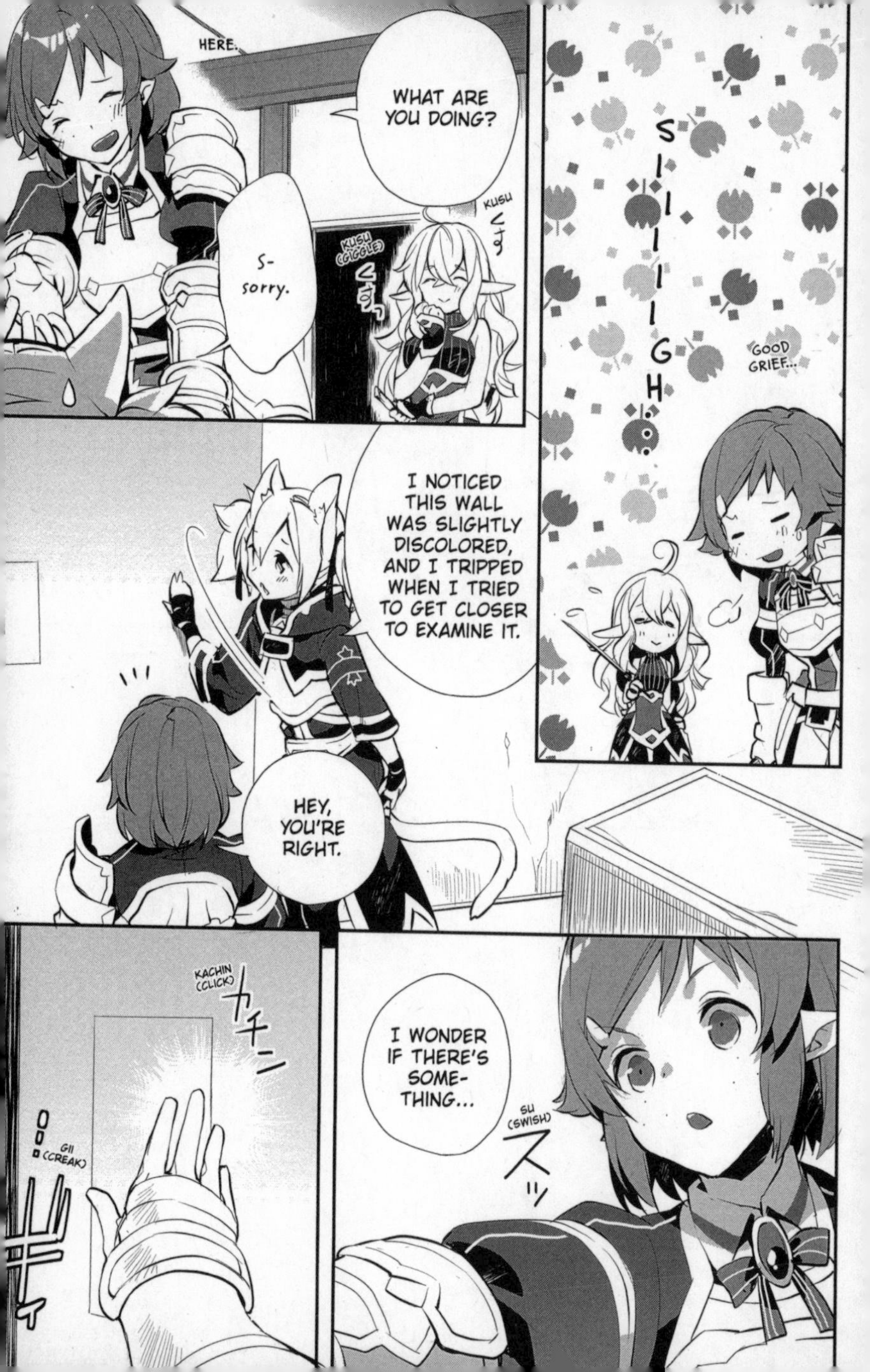
SIIIIIGH
GOOD GRIEF...
HERE.
WHAT ARE YOU DOING?
KUSU
KUSU (GIGGLE)
S-sorry.
I NOTICED THIS WALL WAS SLIGHTLY DISCOLORED, AND I TRIPPED WHEN I TRIED TO GET CLOSER TO EXAMINE IT.
HEY, YOU'RE RIGHT.
I WONDER IF THERE'S SOME-THING...
SU (SWISH)
KACHIN (CLICK)
GII (CREAK)

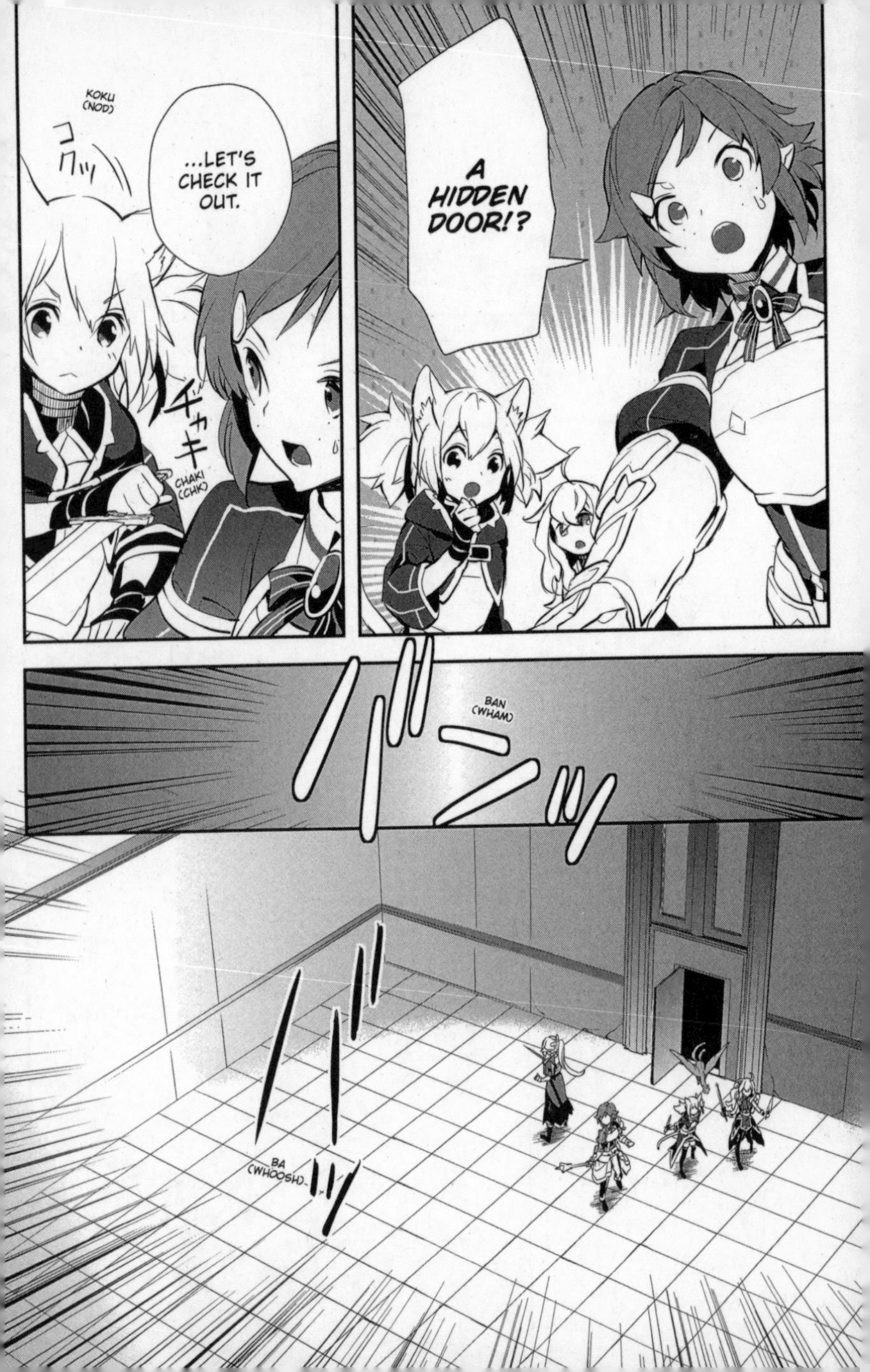
A HIDDEN DOOR!?
KOKU (NOD)
コクッ
...LET'S CHECK IT OUT.
チャキ
CHAKI (CHK)
BAN (WHAM)
バーンッ
BA (WHOOSH)
バッ

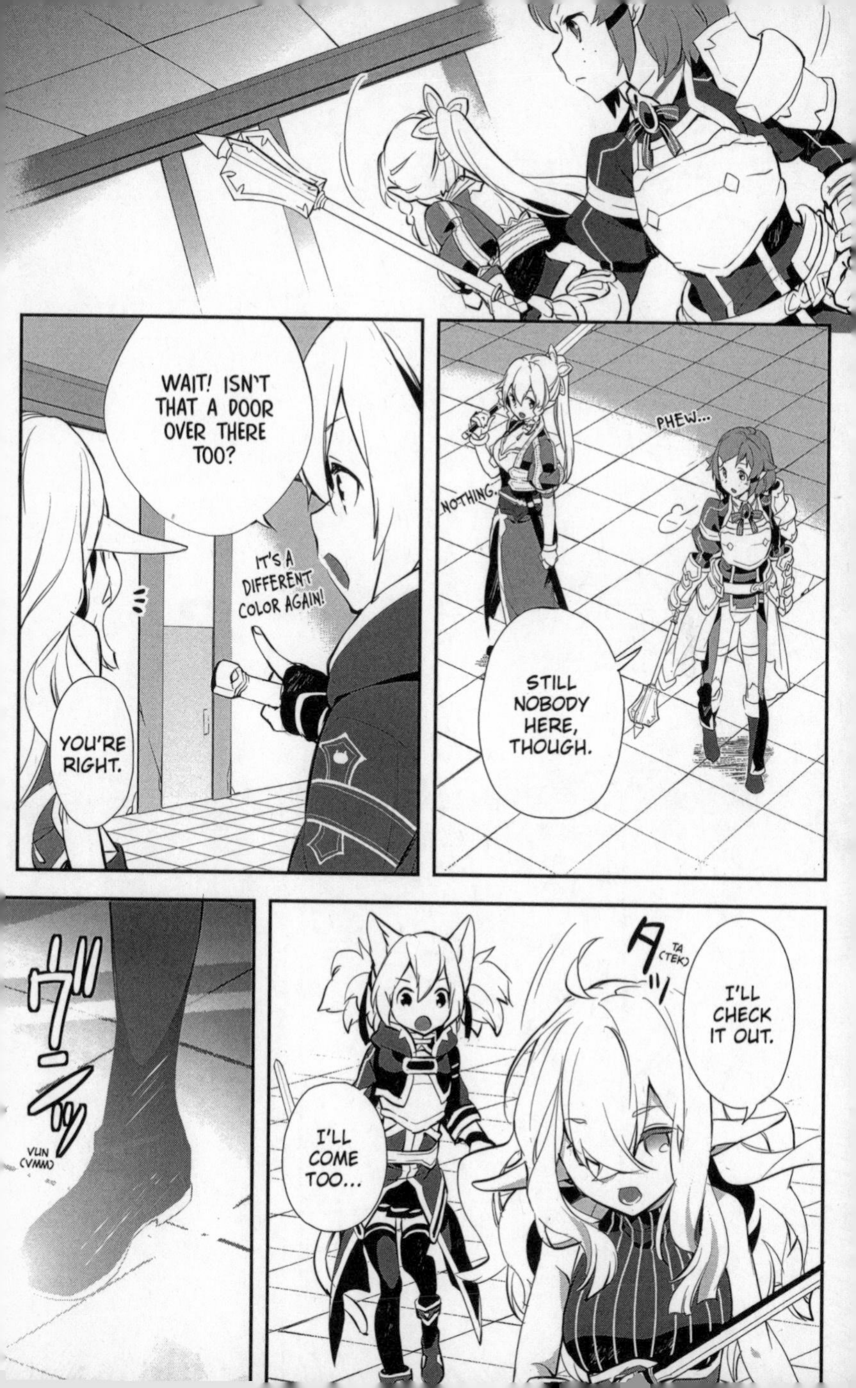
PHEW...
NOTHING.
STILL NOBODY HERE, THOUGH.
WAIT! ISN'T THAT A DOOR OVER THERE TOO?
IT'S A DIFFERENT COLOR AGAIN!
YOU'RE RIGHT.
TA (TEK)
I'LL CHECK IT OUT.
I'LL COME TOO...
VUN (VMM)

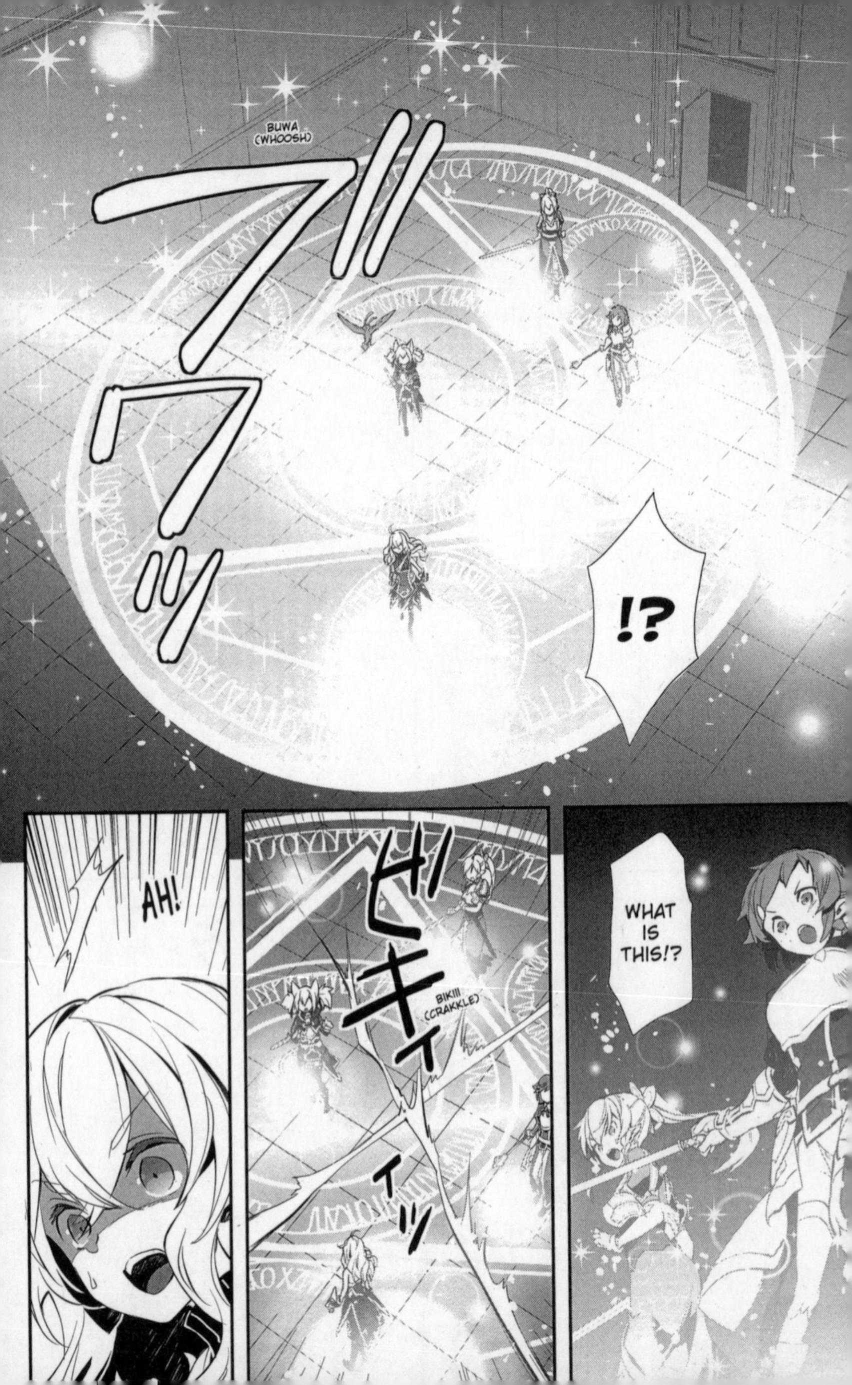
BUWA (WHOOSH)
!?
WHAT IS THIS!?
BIKIII (CRAKKLE)
AH!

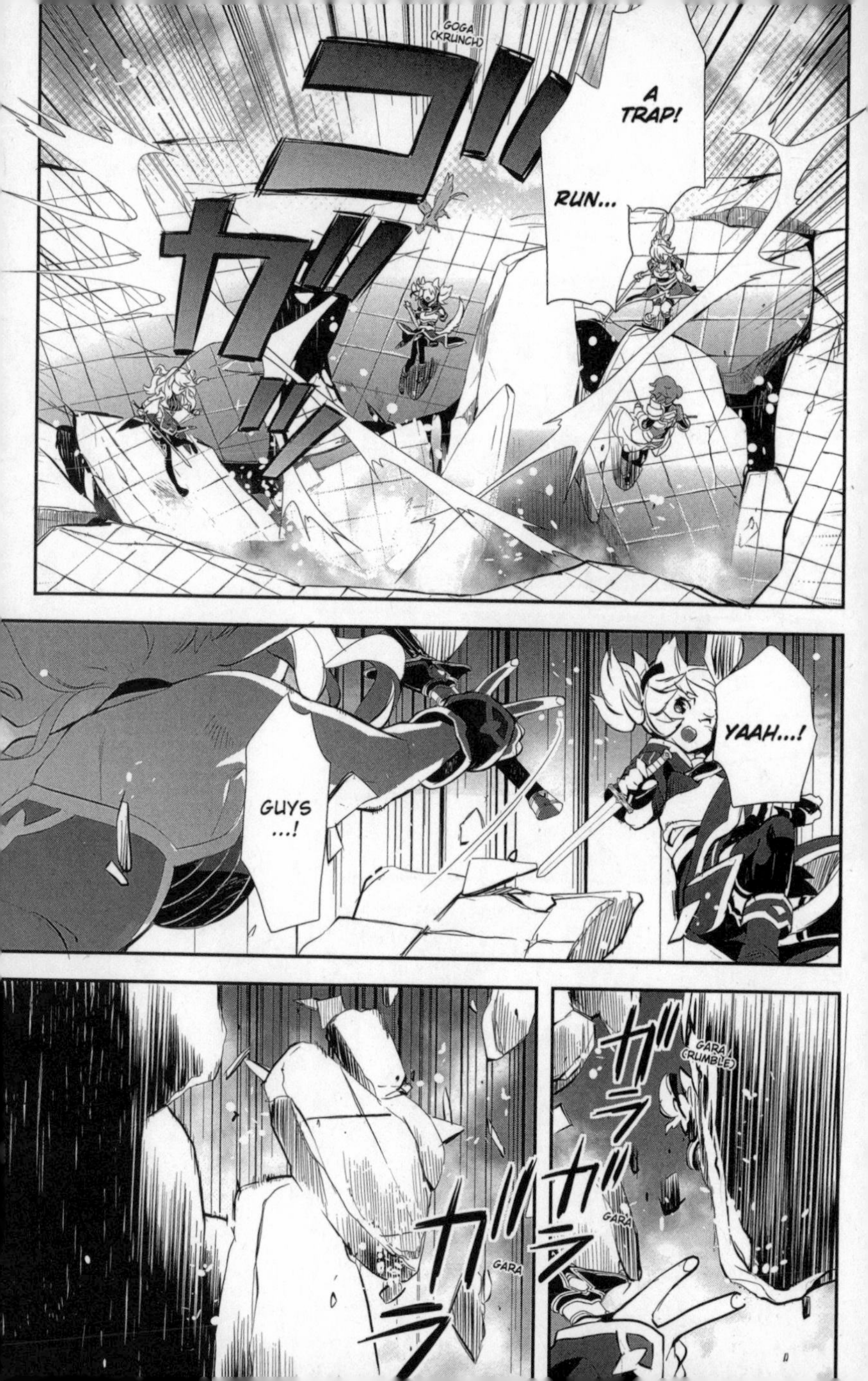
GOGA (KRUNCH)
A TRAP!
RUN...
YAAH...!
GUYS ...!
GARA (RUMBLE)
GARA
GARA

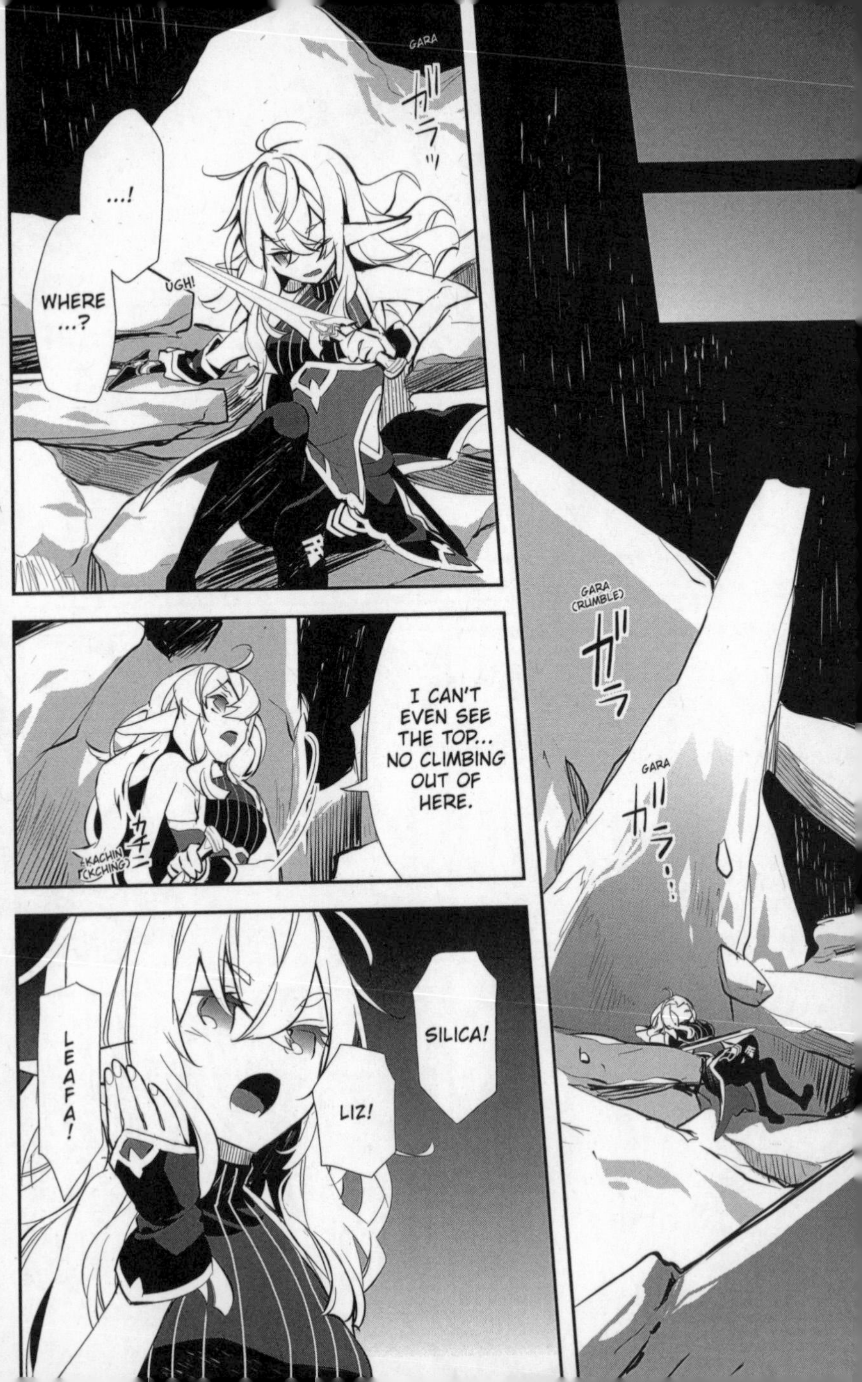
GARA
(RUMBLE)
GARA
GARA
...!
UGH!
WHERE ...?
I CAN'T EVEN SEE THE TOP... NO CLIMBING OUT OF HERE.
KACHIN
(KCHING)
SILICA!
LIZ!
LEAFA!

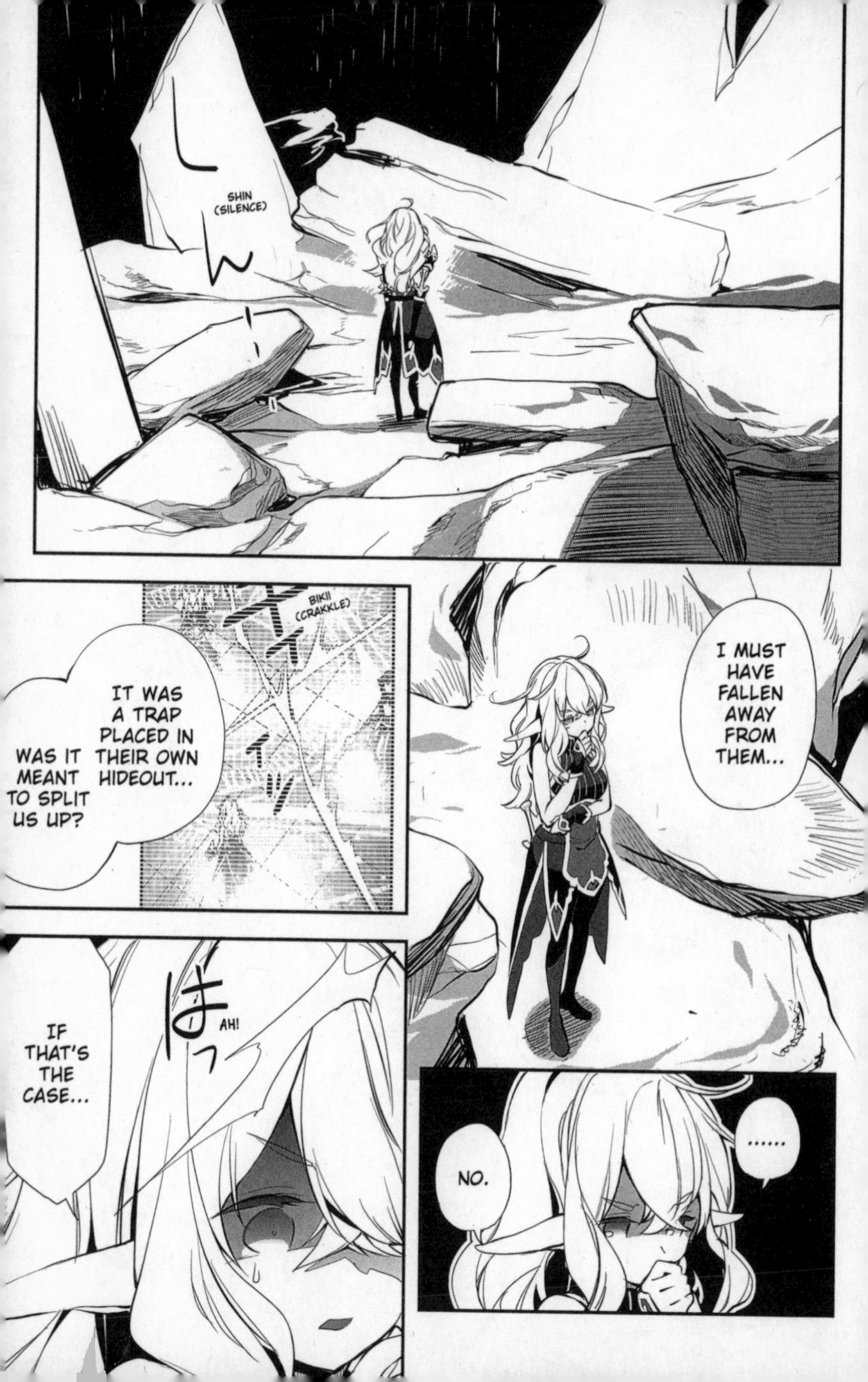
SHIN (SILENCE)
BIKII (CRAKKLE)
I MUST HAVE FALLEN AWAY FROM THEM...
IT WAS A TRAP PLACED IN THEIR OWN HIDEOUT...
WAS IT MEANT TO SPLIT US UP?
AH!
IF THAT'S THE CASE...
......
NO.

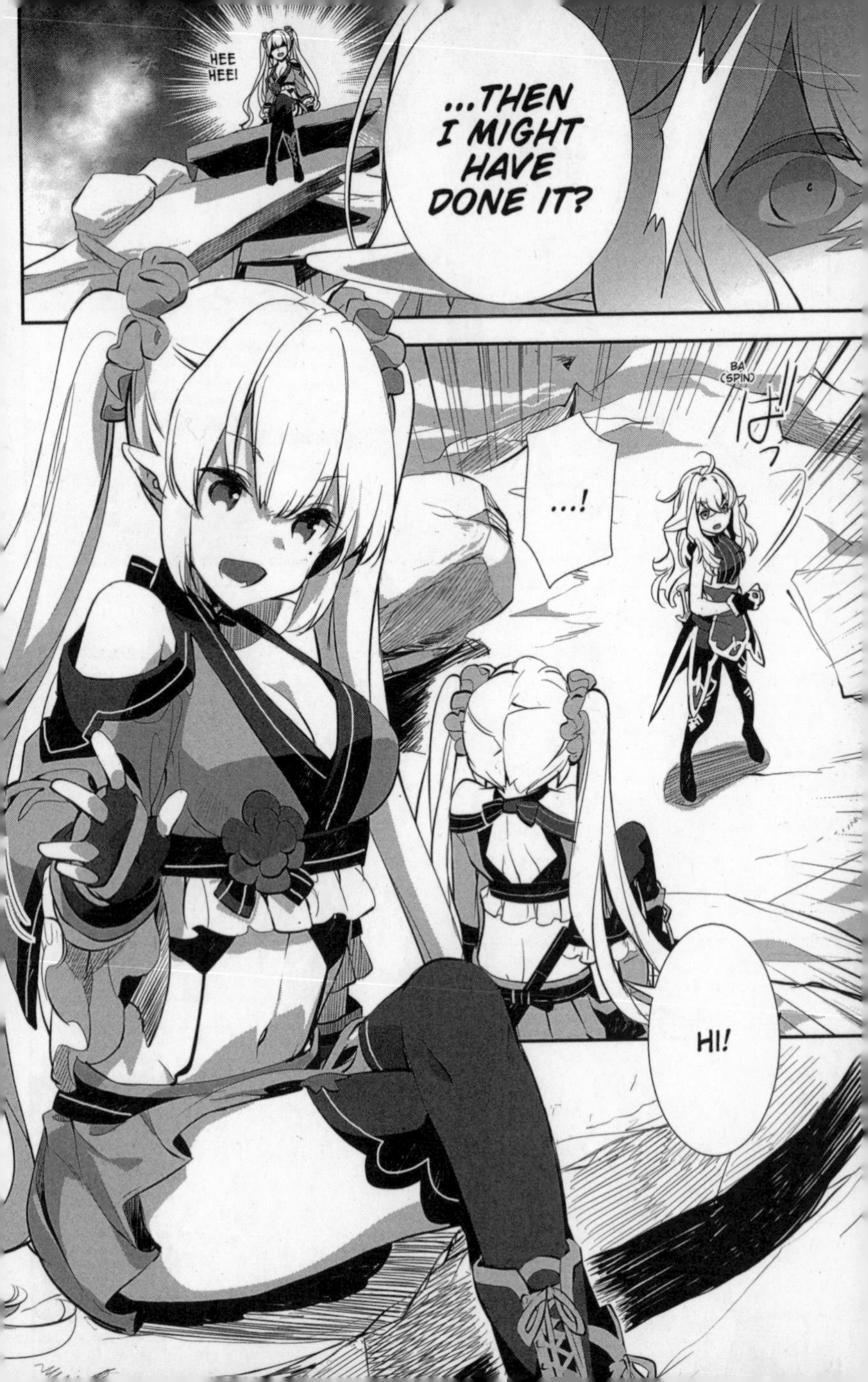
HEE HEE!
...THEN I MIGHT HAVE DONE IT?
BA (SPIN)
ばっ
...!
HI!

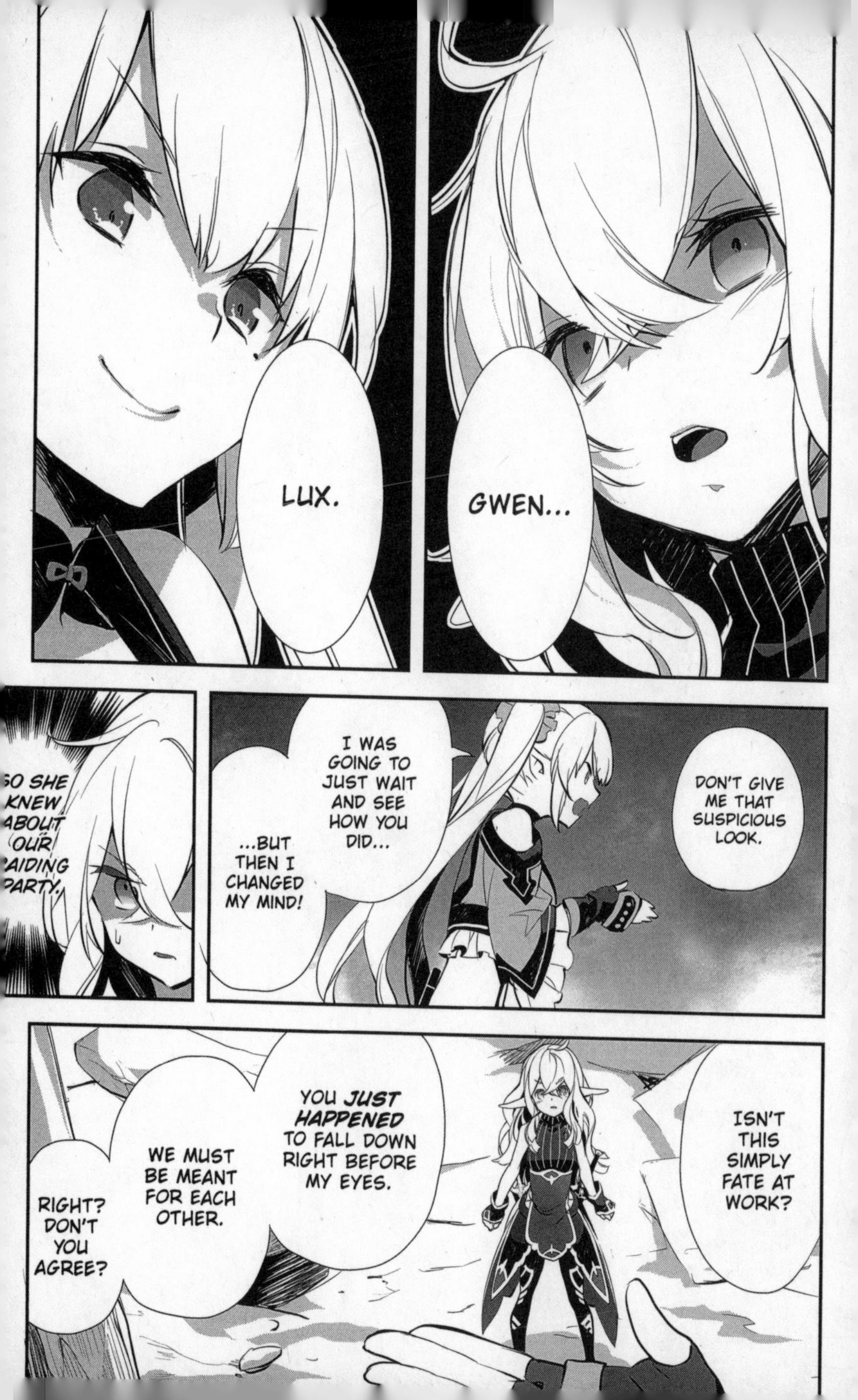
GWEN...
LUX.
DON'T GIVE ME THAT SUSPICIOUS LOOK.
I WAS GOING TO JUST WAIT AND SEE HOW YOU DID...
...BUT THEN I CHANGED MY MIND!
SO SHE KNEW ABOUT OUR RAIDING PARTY.
ISN'T THIS SIMPLY FATE AT WORK?
YOU ***JUST HAPPENED*** TO FALL DOWN RIGHT BEFORE MY EYES.
WE MUST BE MEANT FOR EACH OTHER.
RIGHT? DON'T YOU AGREE?

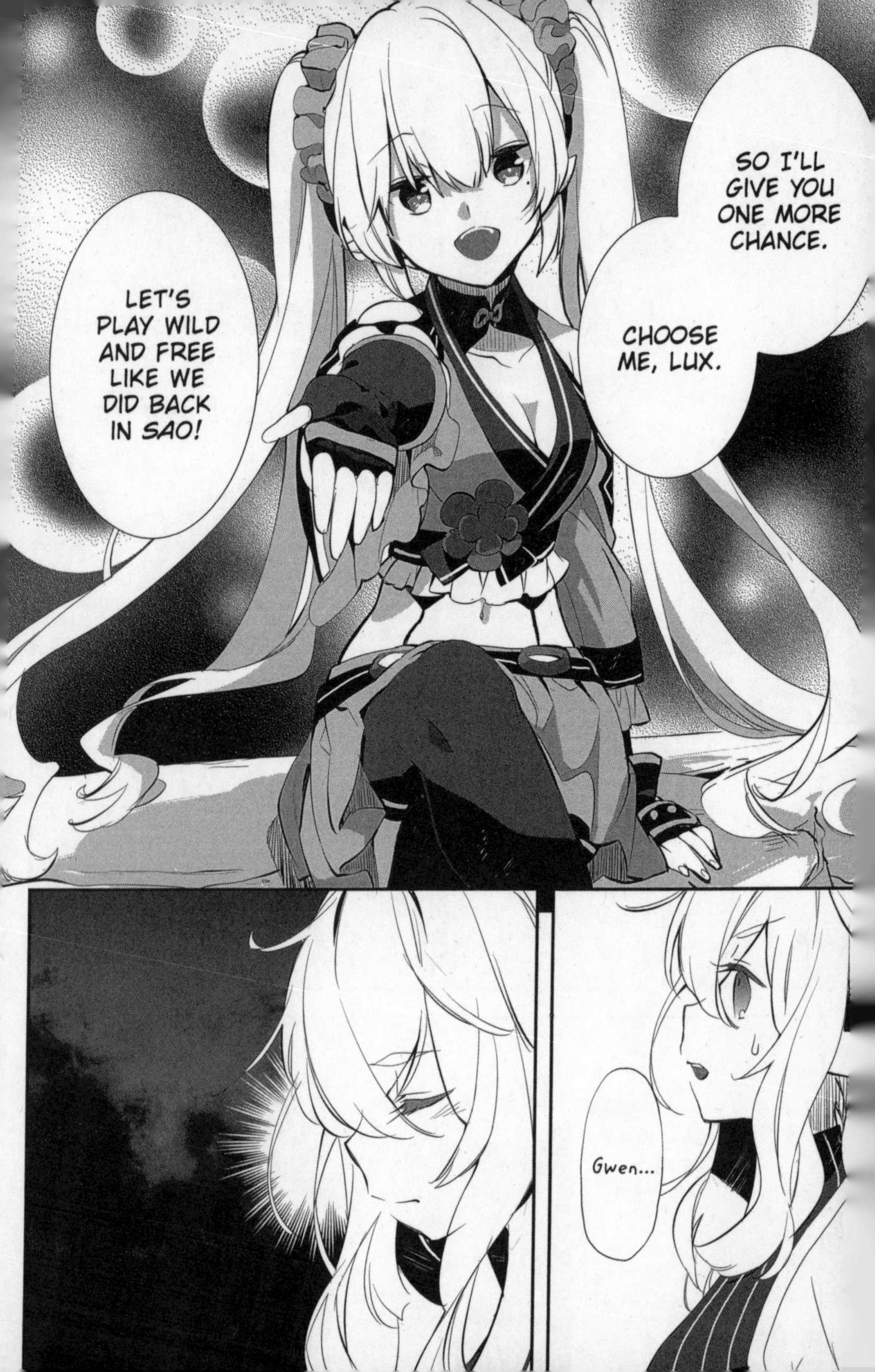
SO I'LL GIVE YOU ONE MORE CHANCE.
CHOOSE ME, LUX.
LET'S PLAY WILD AND FREE LIKE WE DID BACK IN SAO!
Gwen...

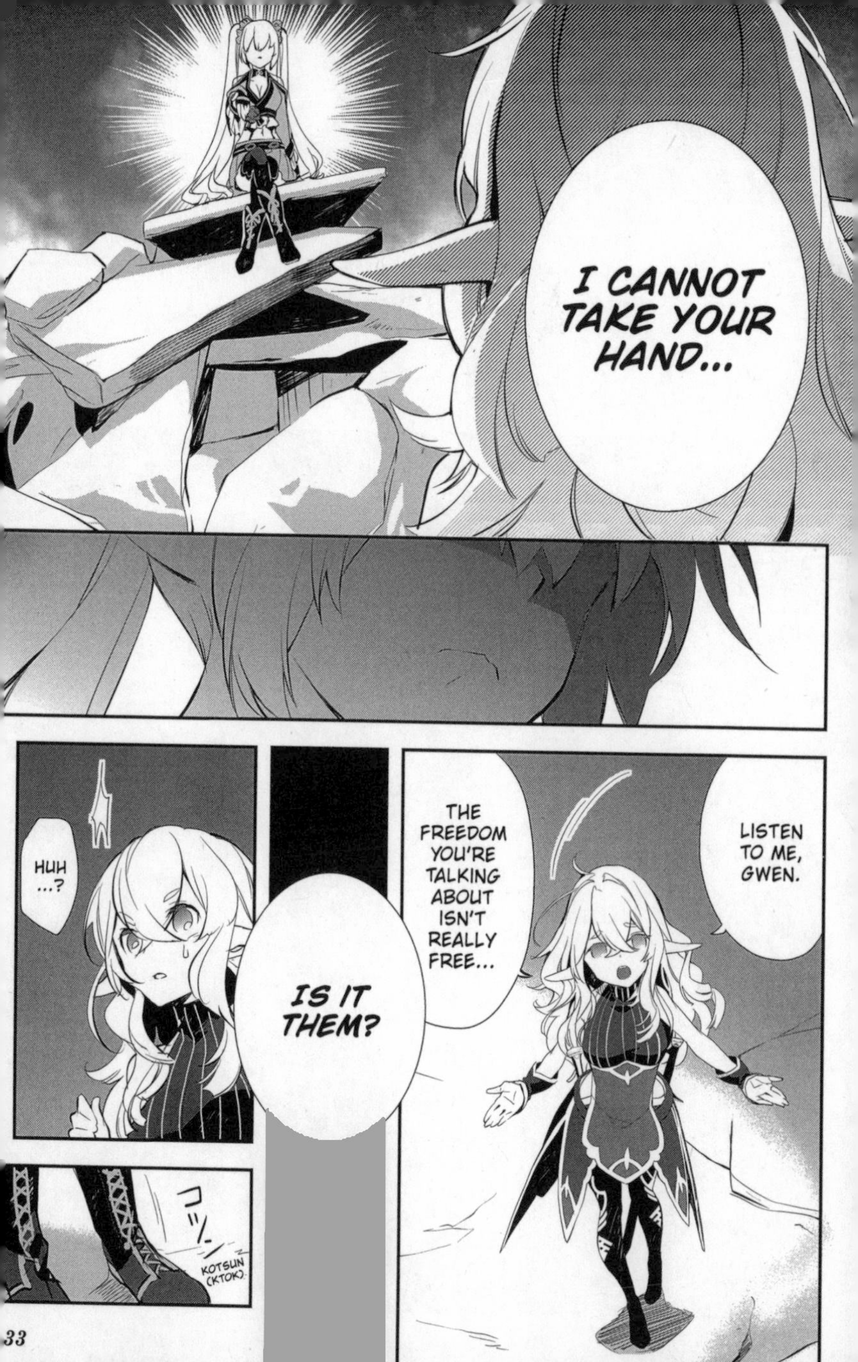

I CANNOT TAKE YOUR HAND...
LISTEN TO ME, GWEN.
THE FREEDOM YOU'RE TALKING ABOUT ISN'T REALLY FREE...
IS IT THEM?
HUH ...?
KOTSUN (KTOK)

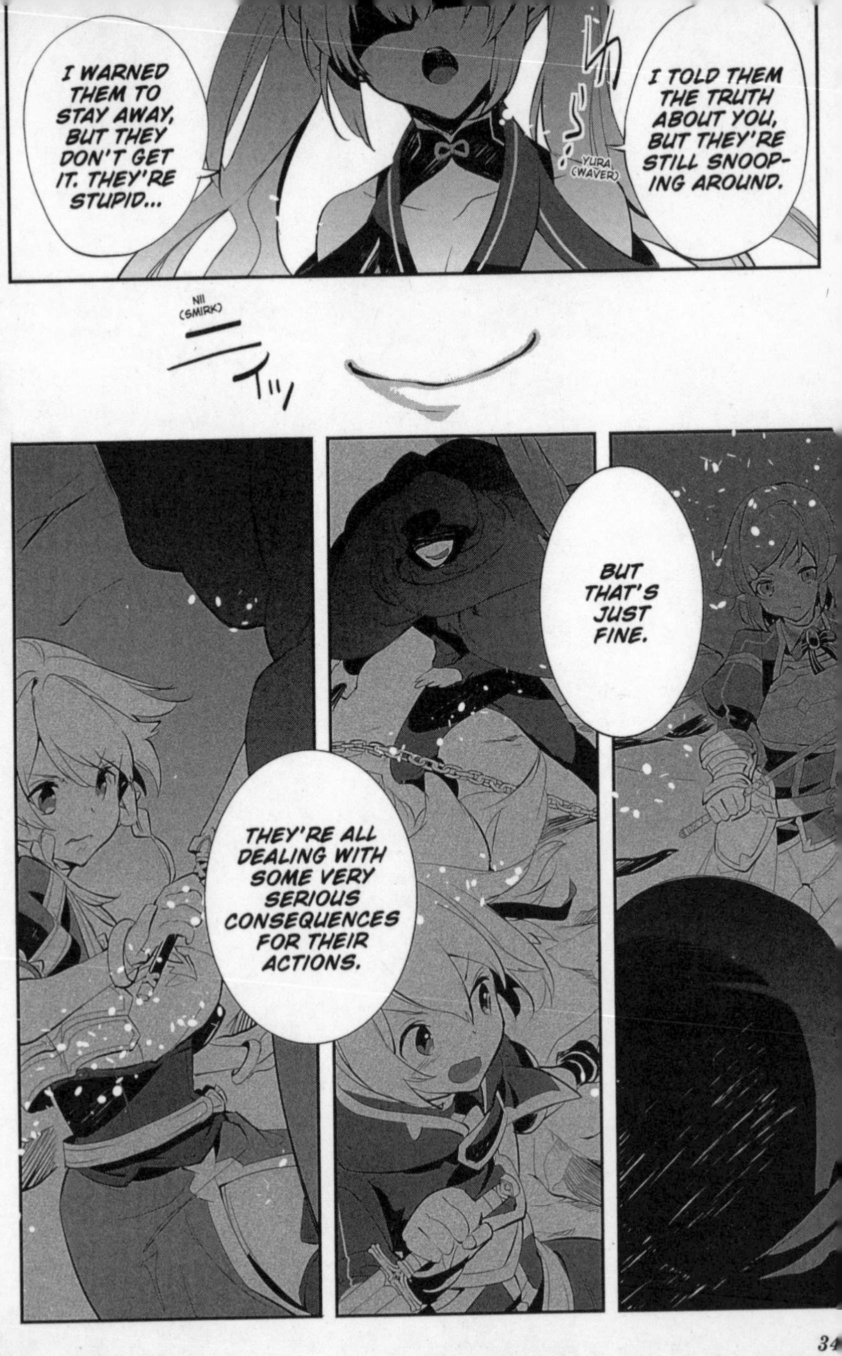
I TOLD THEM THE TRUTH ABOUT YOU, BUT THEY'RE STILL SNOOPING AROUND.
YURA (WAVER)
I WARNED THEM TO STAY AWAY, BUT THEY DON'T GET IT. THEY'RE STUPID...
NII (SMIRK)
BUT THAT'S JUST FINE.
THEY'RE ALL DEALING WITH SOME VERY SERIOUS CONSEQUENCES FOR THEIR ACTIONS.

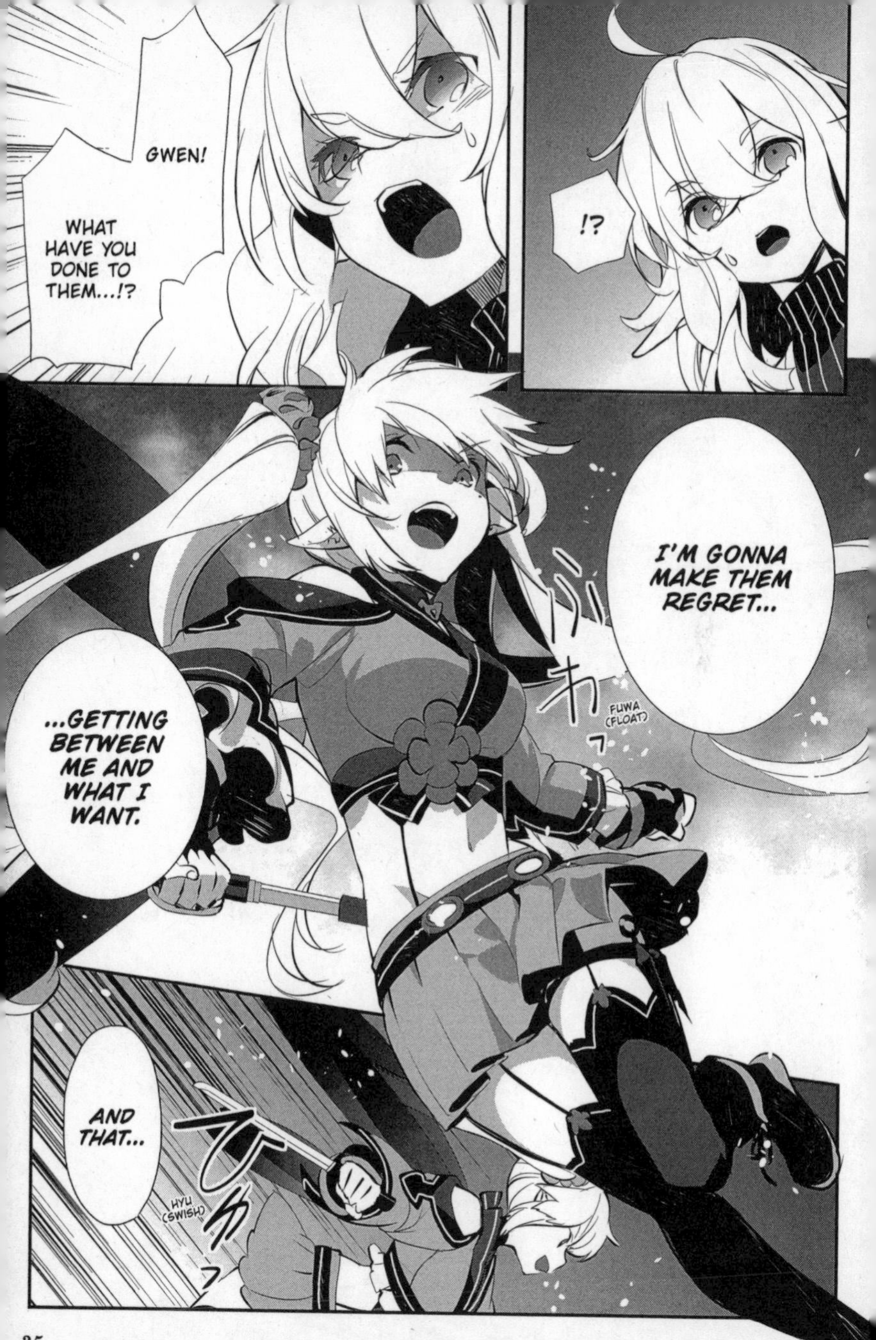
!?
GWEN!
WHAT HAVE YOU DONE TO THEM...!?
I'M GONNA MAKE THEM REGRET...
FUWA (FLOAT)
...GETTING BETWEEN ME AND WHAT I WANT.
AND THAT...
HYU (SWISH)

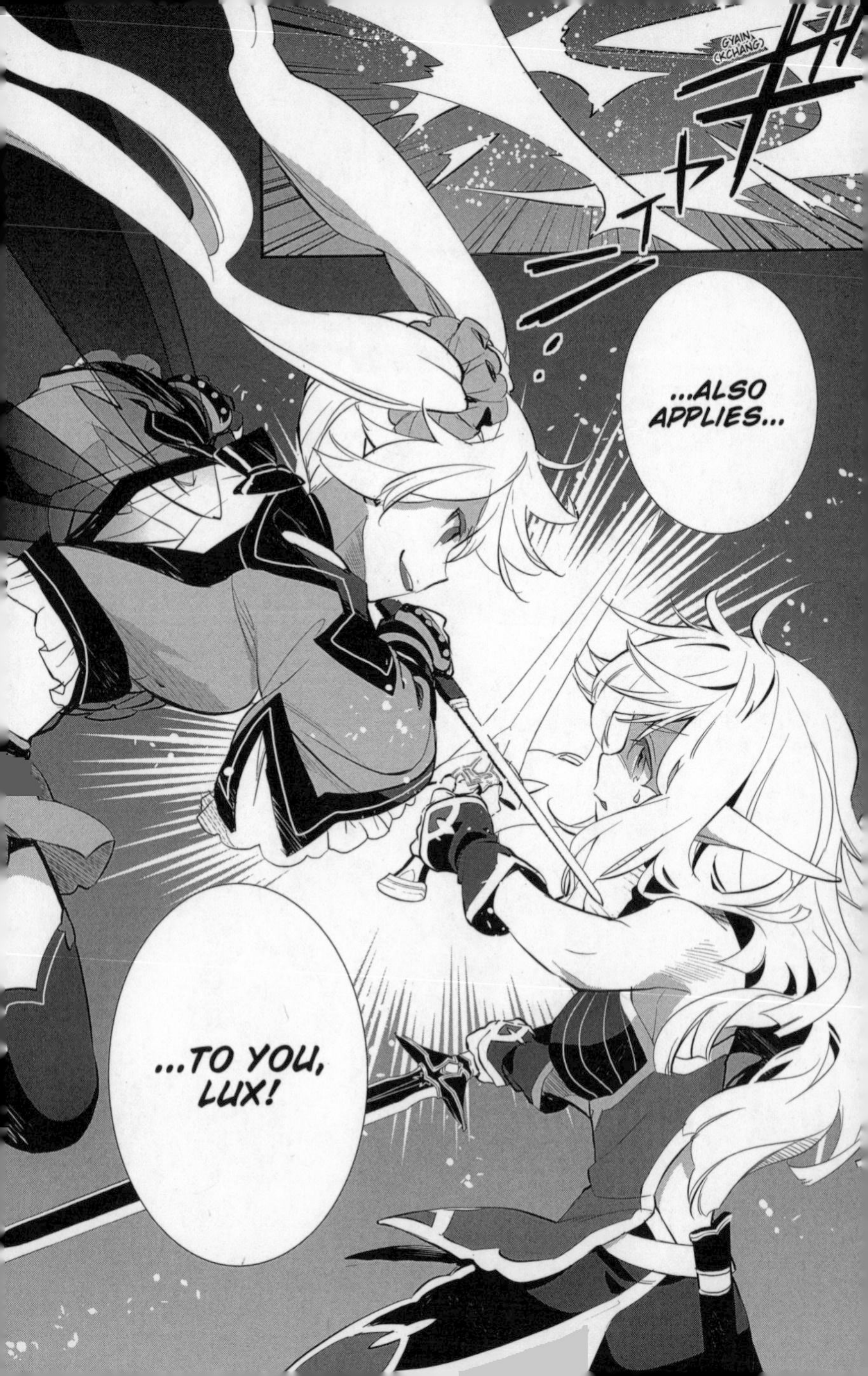
GYAIN (KCHANG)
ギャイン
...ALSO APPLIES...
...TO YOU, LUX!

SWORD ART ONLINE
GIRLS' OPS

SAO GIRLS
SLEEPING SERIES
KEIKO

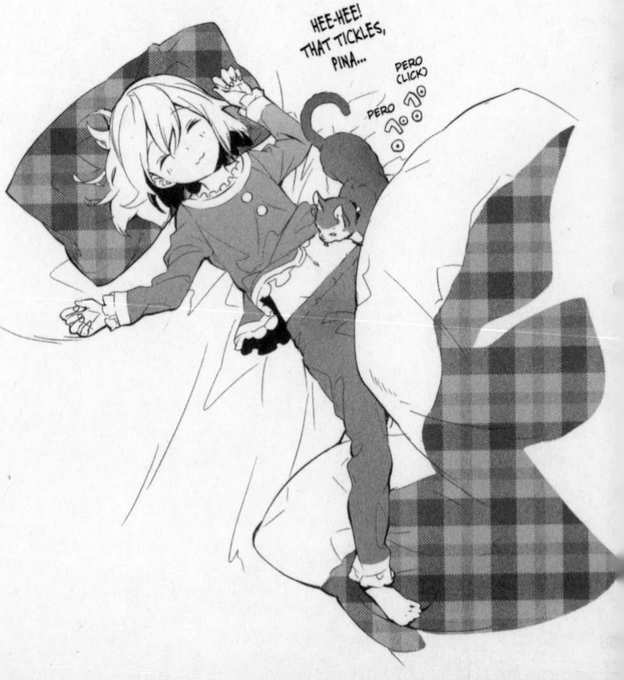
HEE-HEE! THAT TICKLES, PINA...
PERO (LICK)
PERO

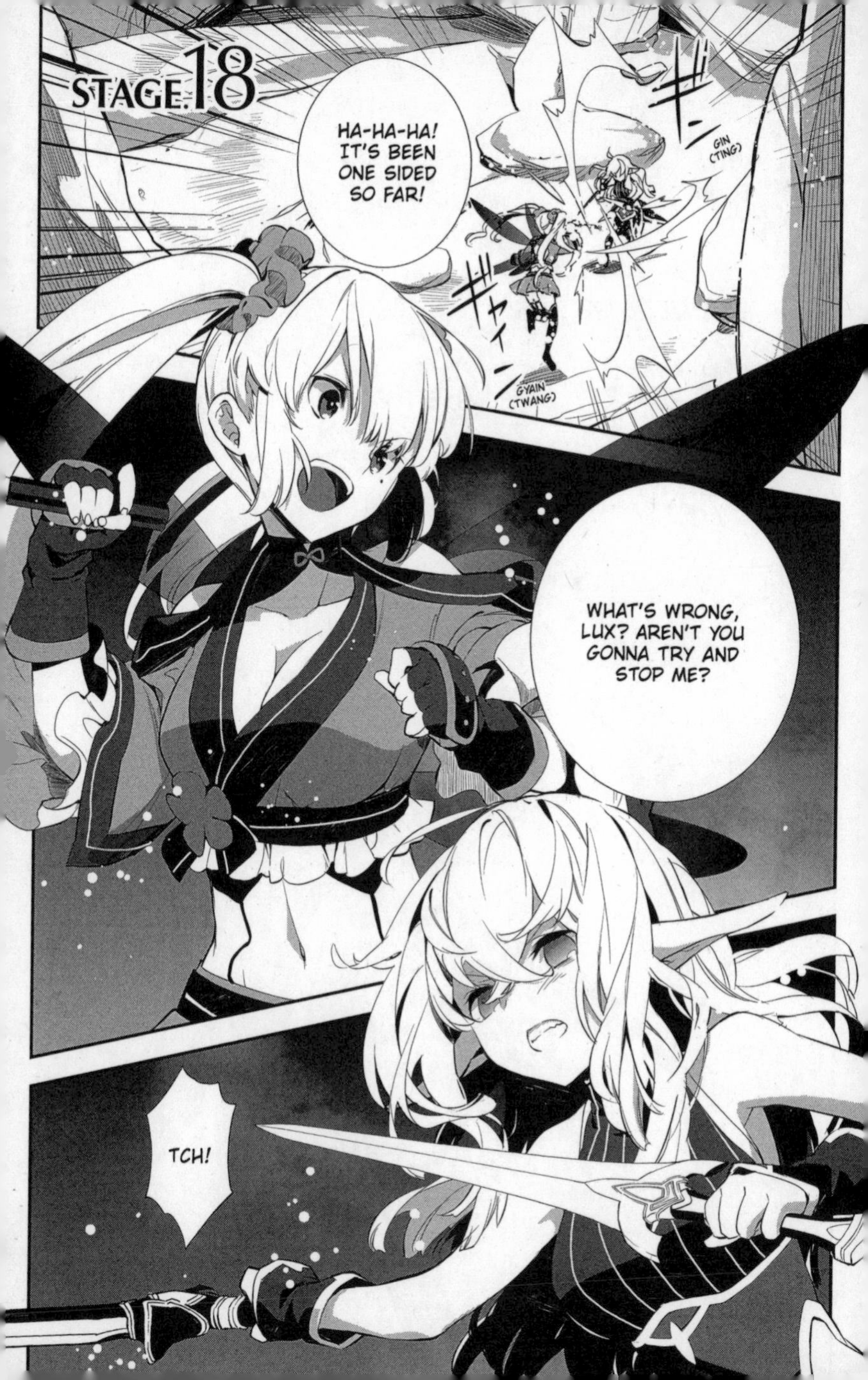
STAGE.18
HA-HA-HA! IT'S BEEN ONE SIDED SO FAR!
GIN (TING)
GYAIN (TWANG)
WHAT'S WRONG, LUX? AREN'T YOU GONNA TRY AND STOP ME?
TCH!

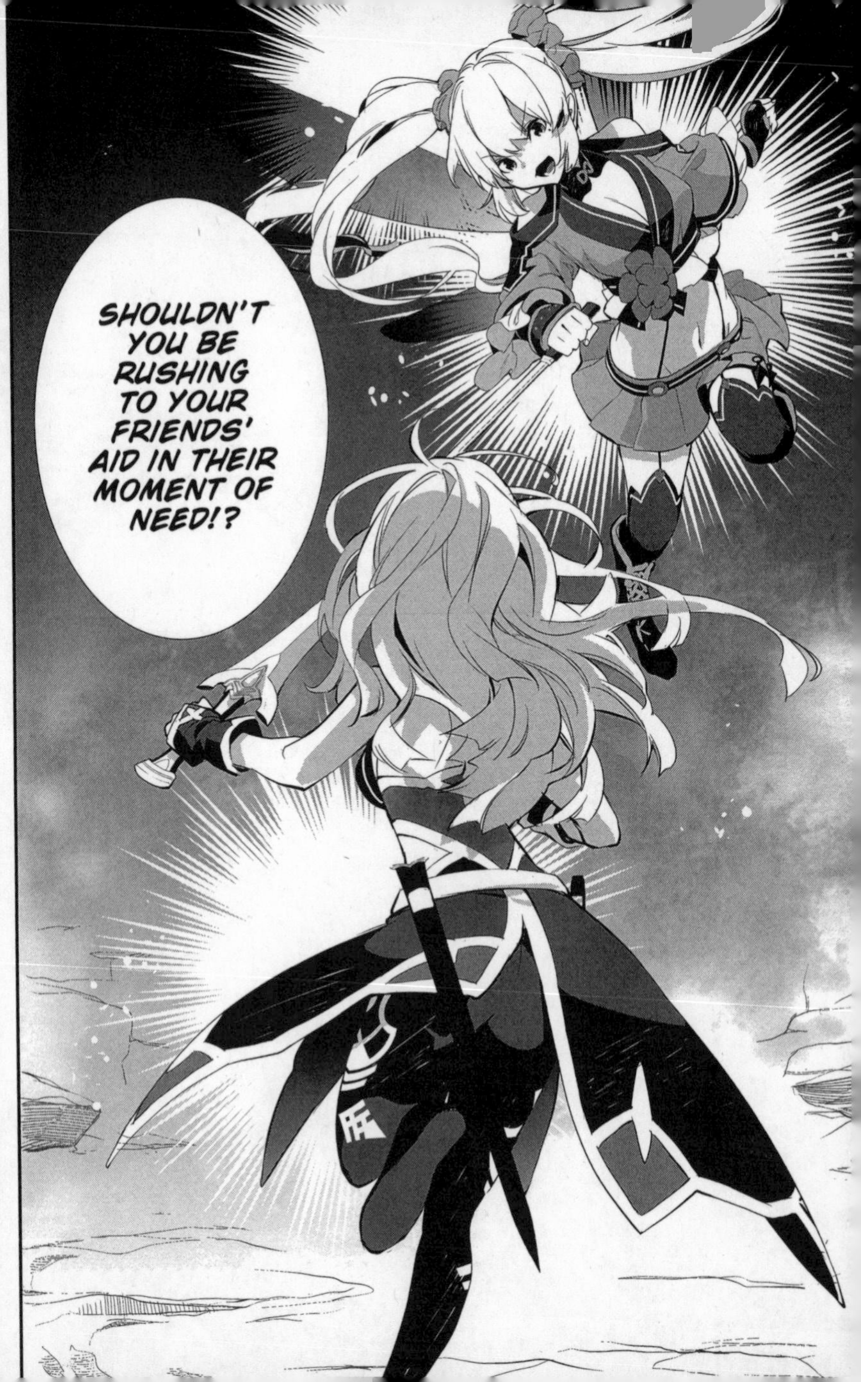
SHOULDN'T YOU BE RUSHING TO YOUR FRIENDS' AID IN THEIR MOMENT OF NEED!?

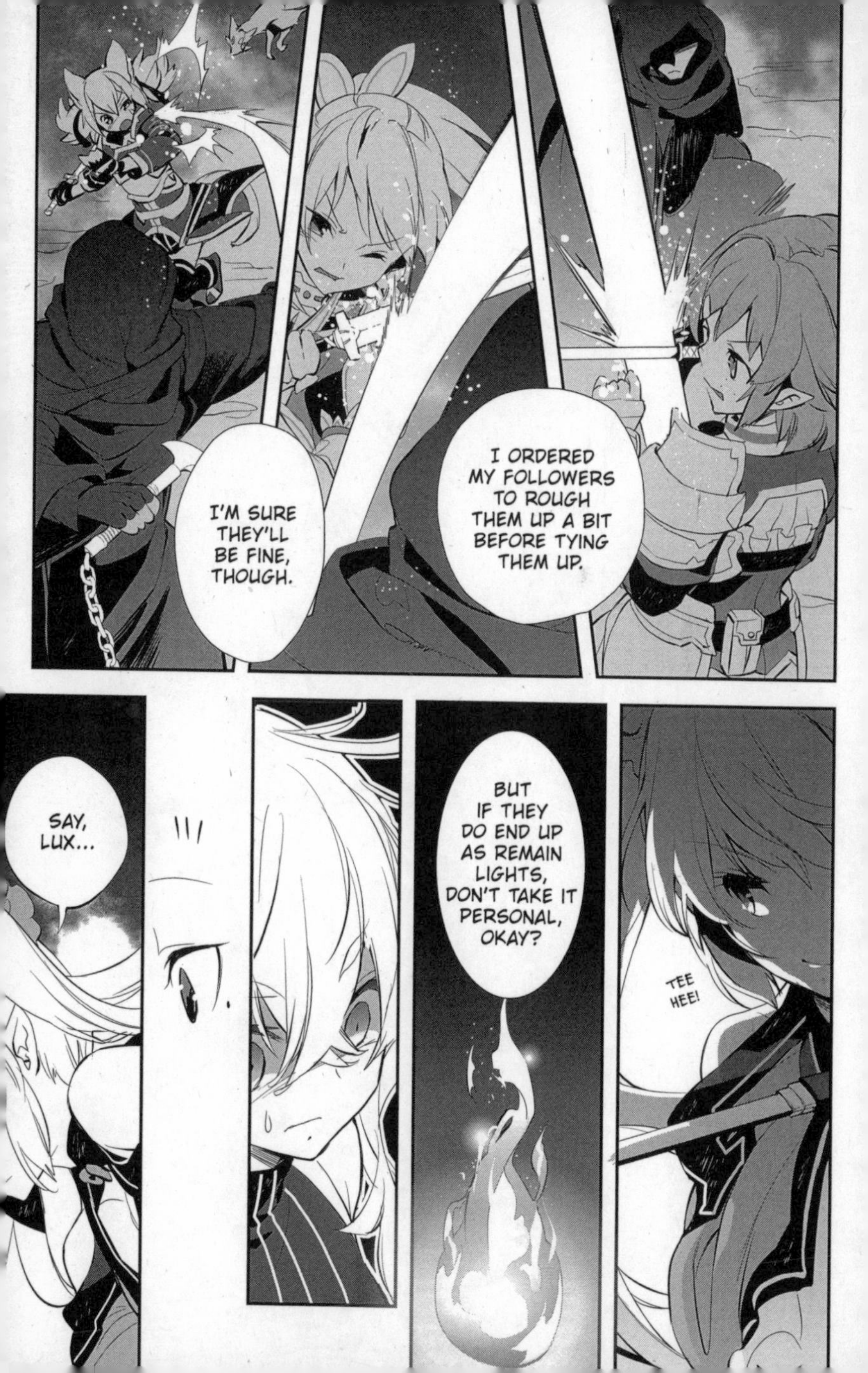
I ORDERED MY FOLLOWERS TO ROUGH THEM UP A BIT BEFORE TYING THEM UP.
I'M SURE THEY'LL BE FINE, THOUGH.
TEE HEE!
BUT IF THEY DO END UP AS REMAIN LIGHTS, DON'T TAKE IT PERSONAL, OKAY?
SAY, LUX...

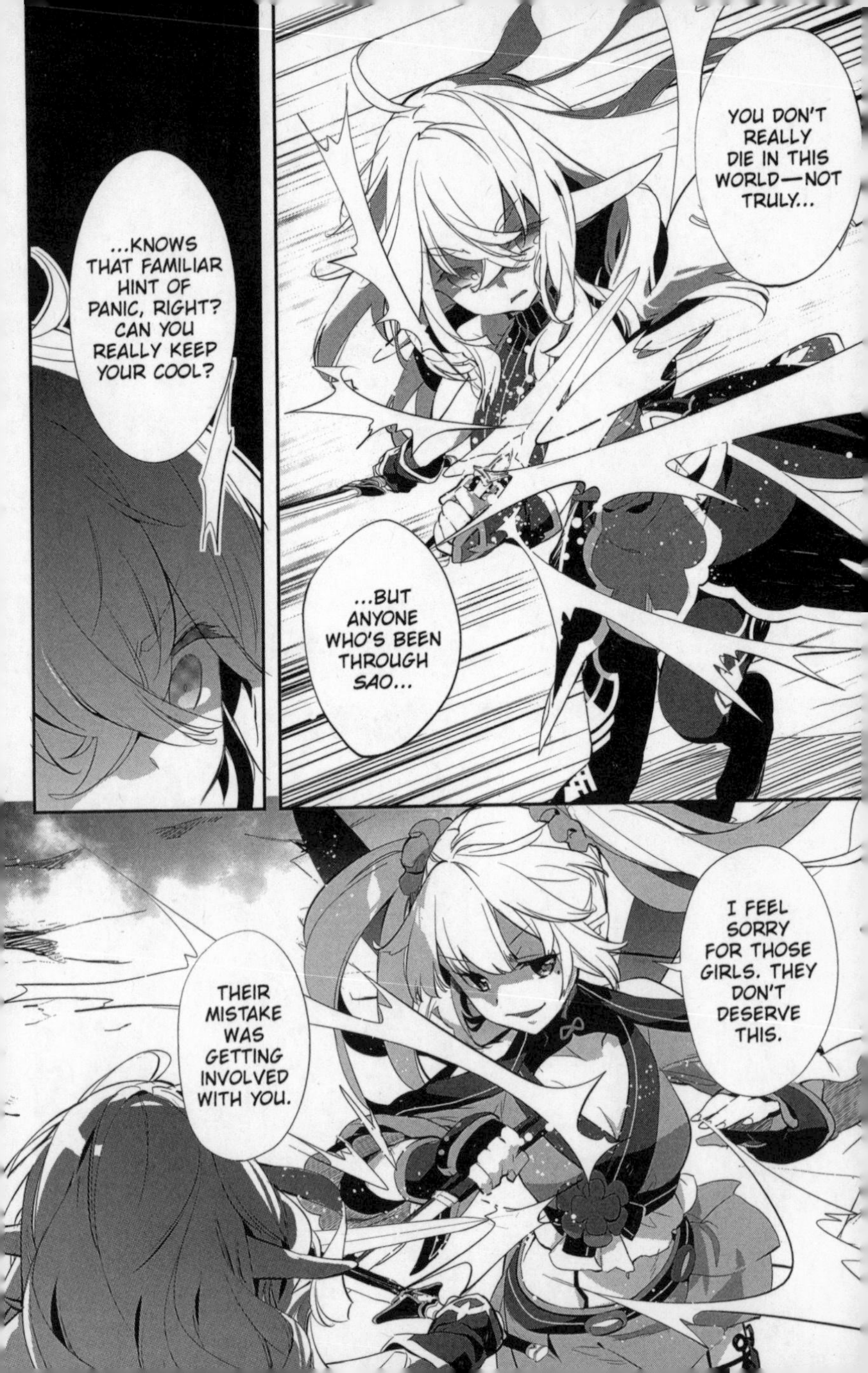
YOU DON'T REALLY DIE IN THIS WORLD—NOT TRULY...
...BUT ANYONE WHO'S BEEN THROUGH SAO...
...KNOWS THAT FAMILIAR HINT OF PANIC, RIGHT? CAN YOU REALLY KEEP YOUR COOL?
I FEEL SORRY FOR THOSE GIRLS. THEY DON'T DESERVE THIS.
THEIR MISTAKE WAS GETTING INVOLVED WITH YOU.

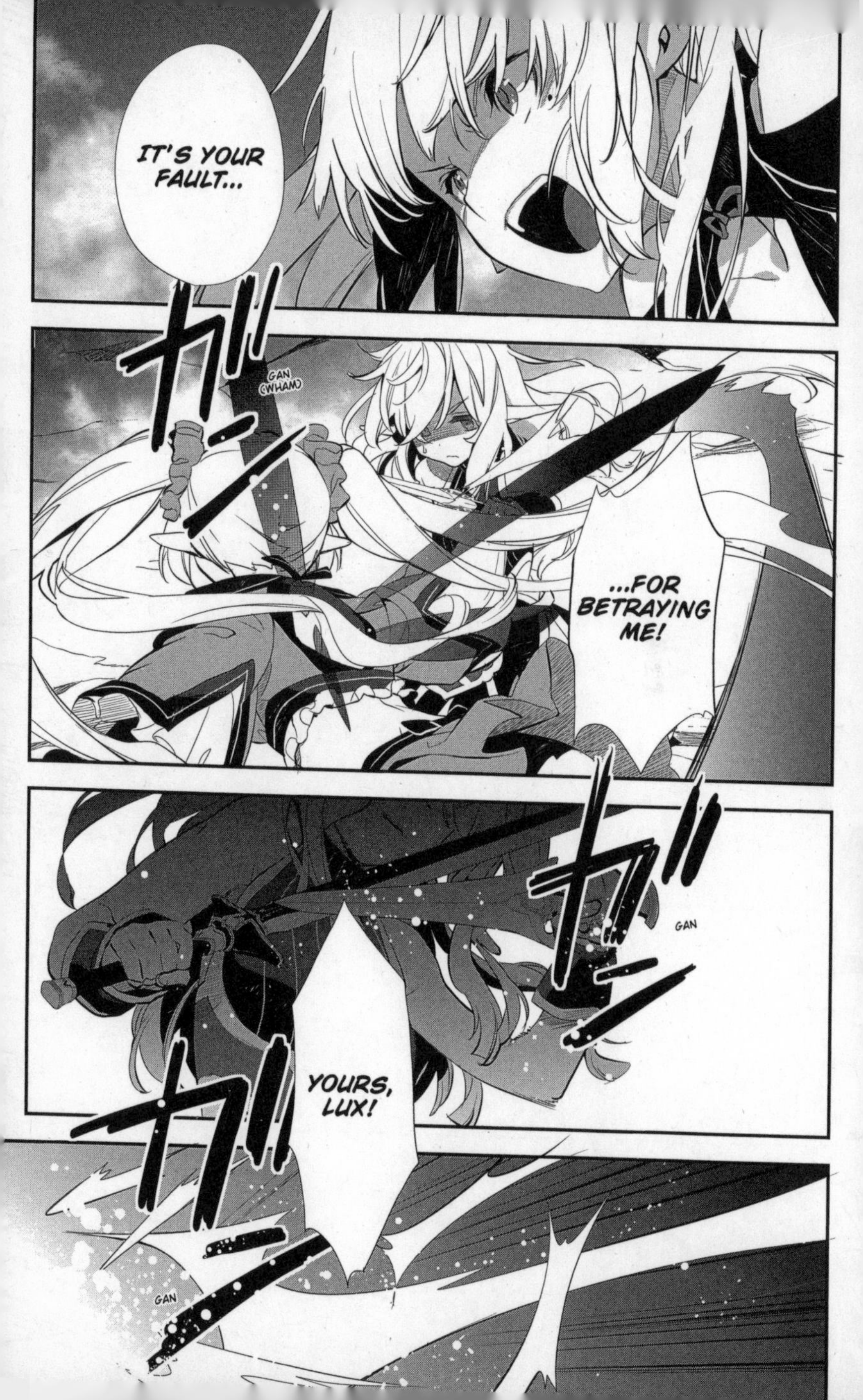
IT'S YOUR FAULT...
GAN (WHAM)
...FOR BETRAYING ME!
GAN
YOURS, LUX!
GAN

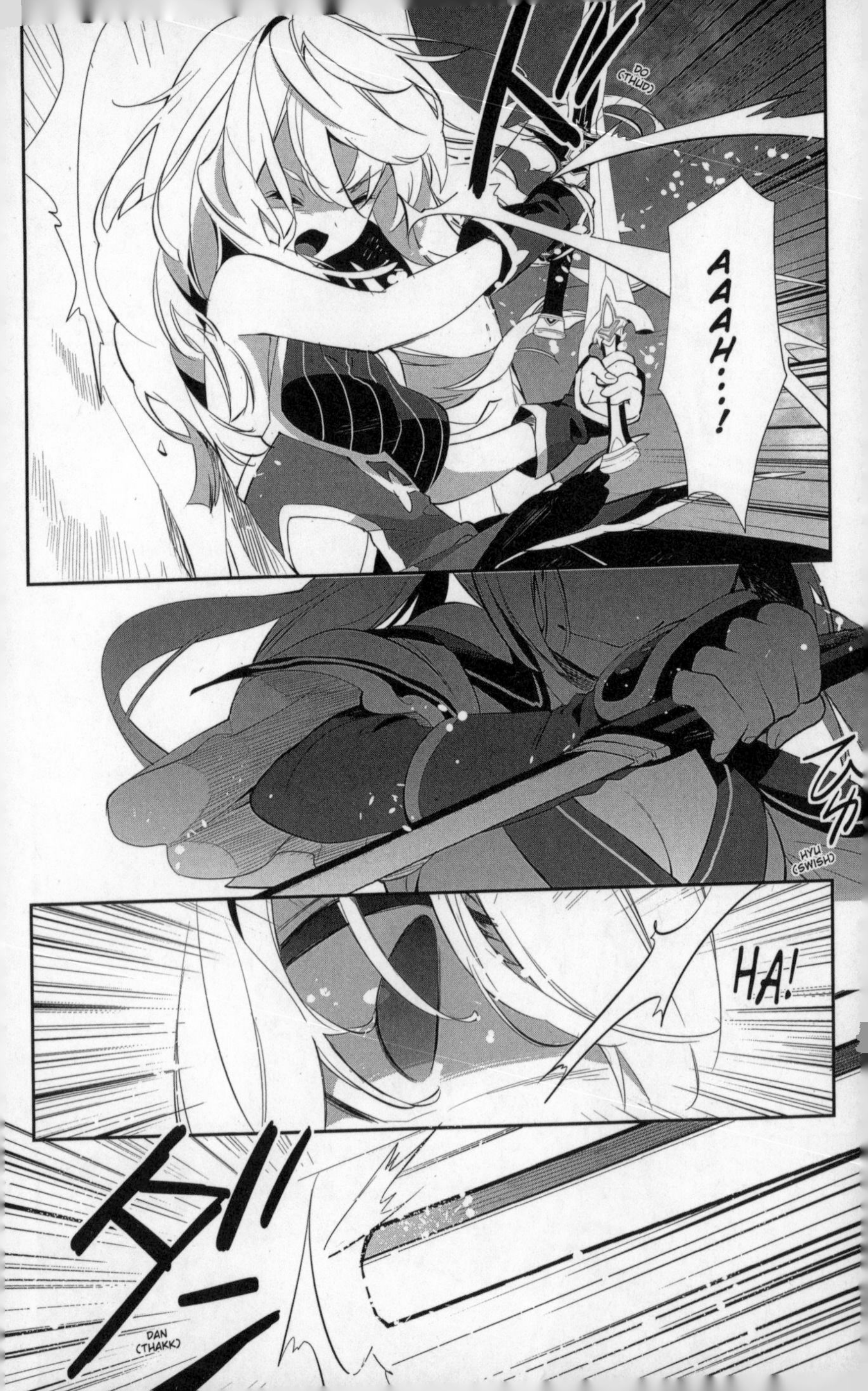
DO
(THUD)
AAAAH...!
HYU
(SWISH)
HA!
DAN
(THAKK)

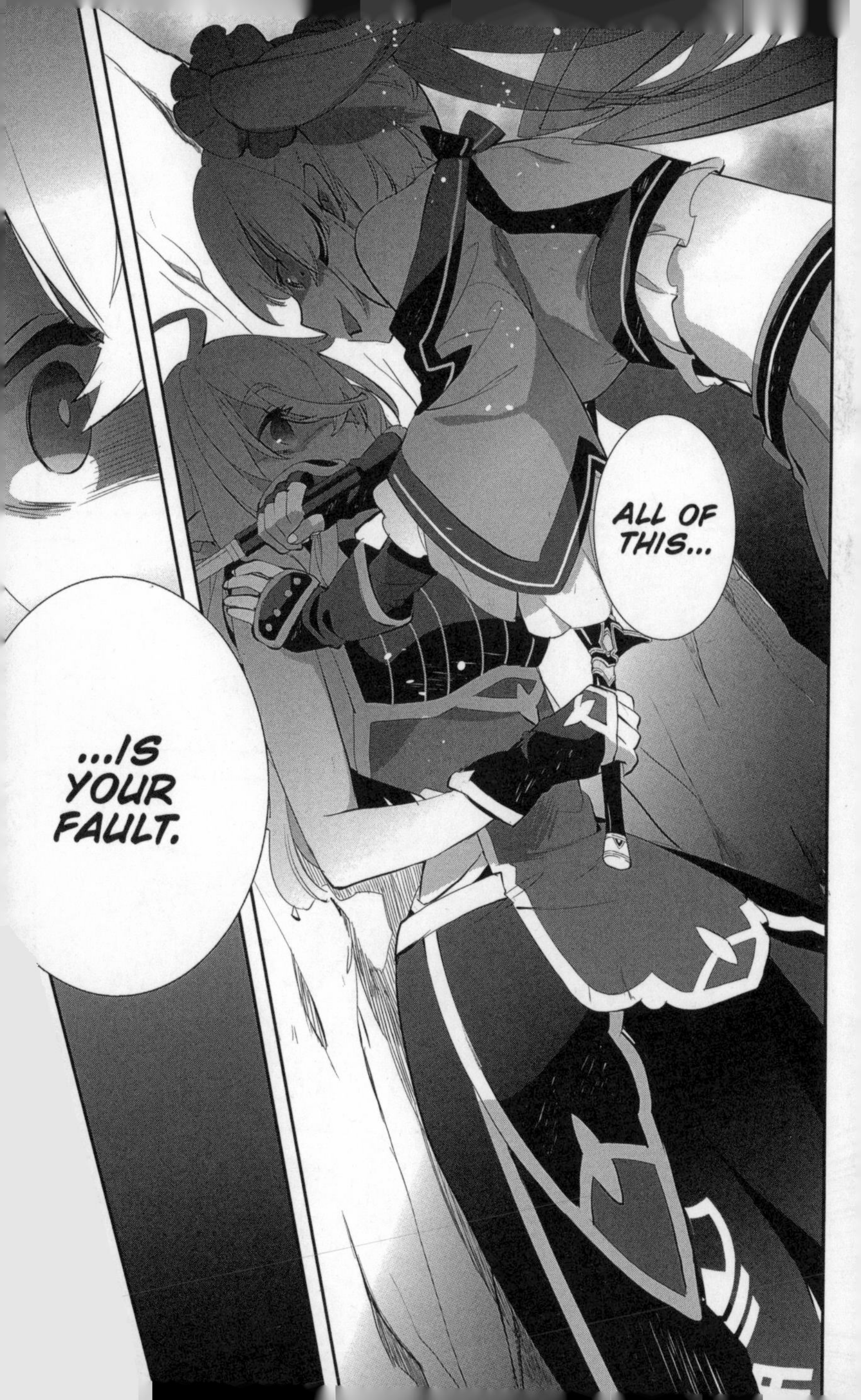
ALL OF THIS...
...IS YOUR FAULT.

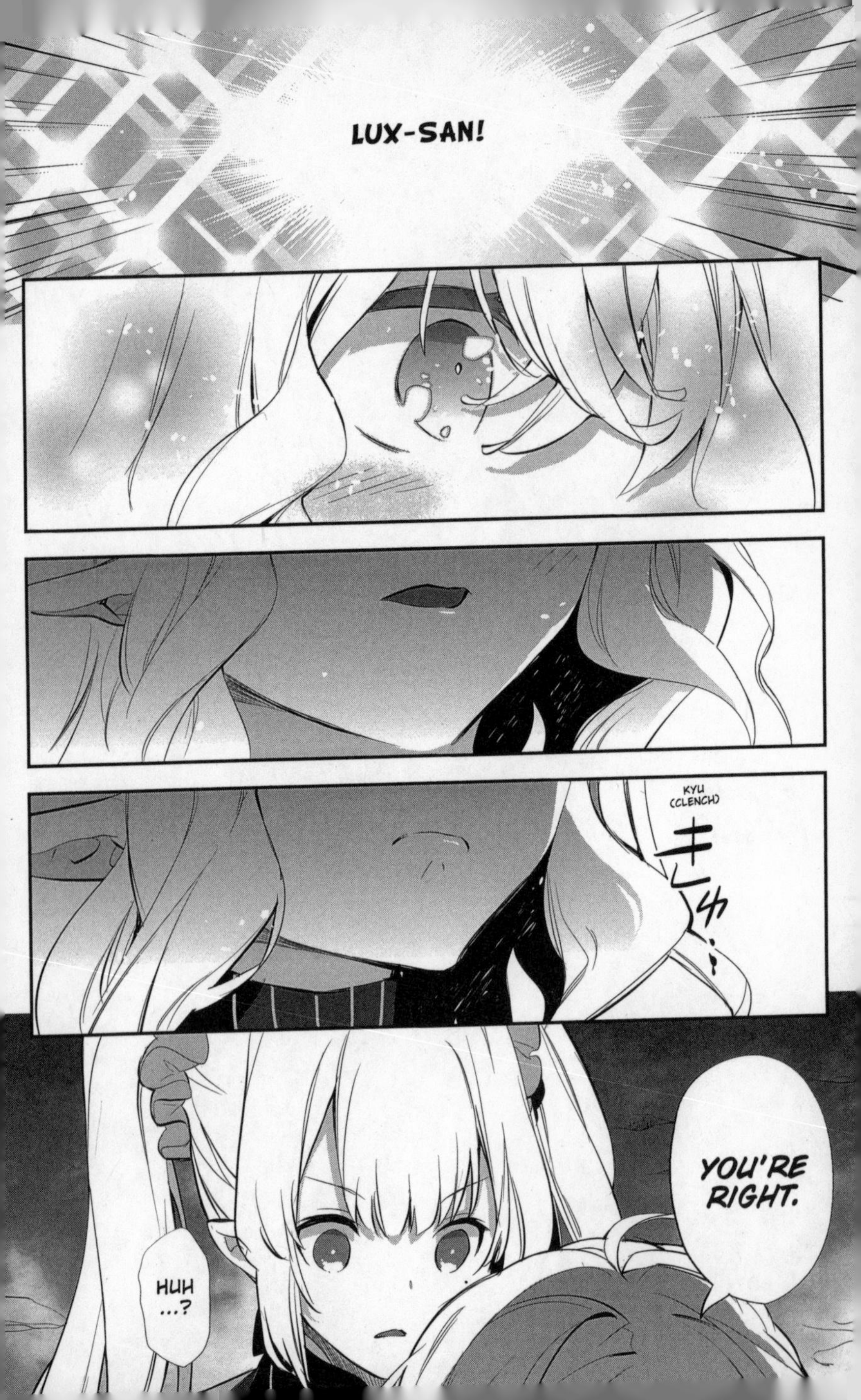
LUX-SAN!
KYU (CLENCH)
YOU'RE RIGHT.
HUH ...?

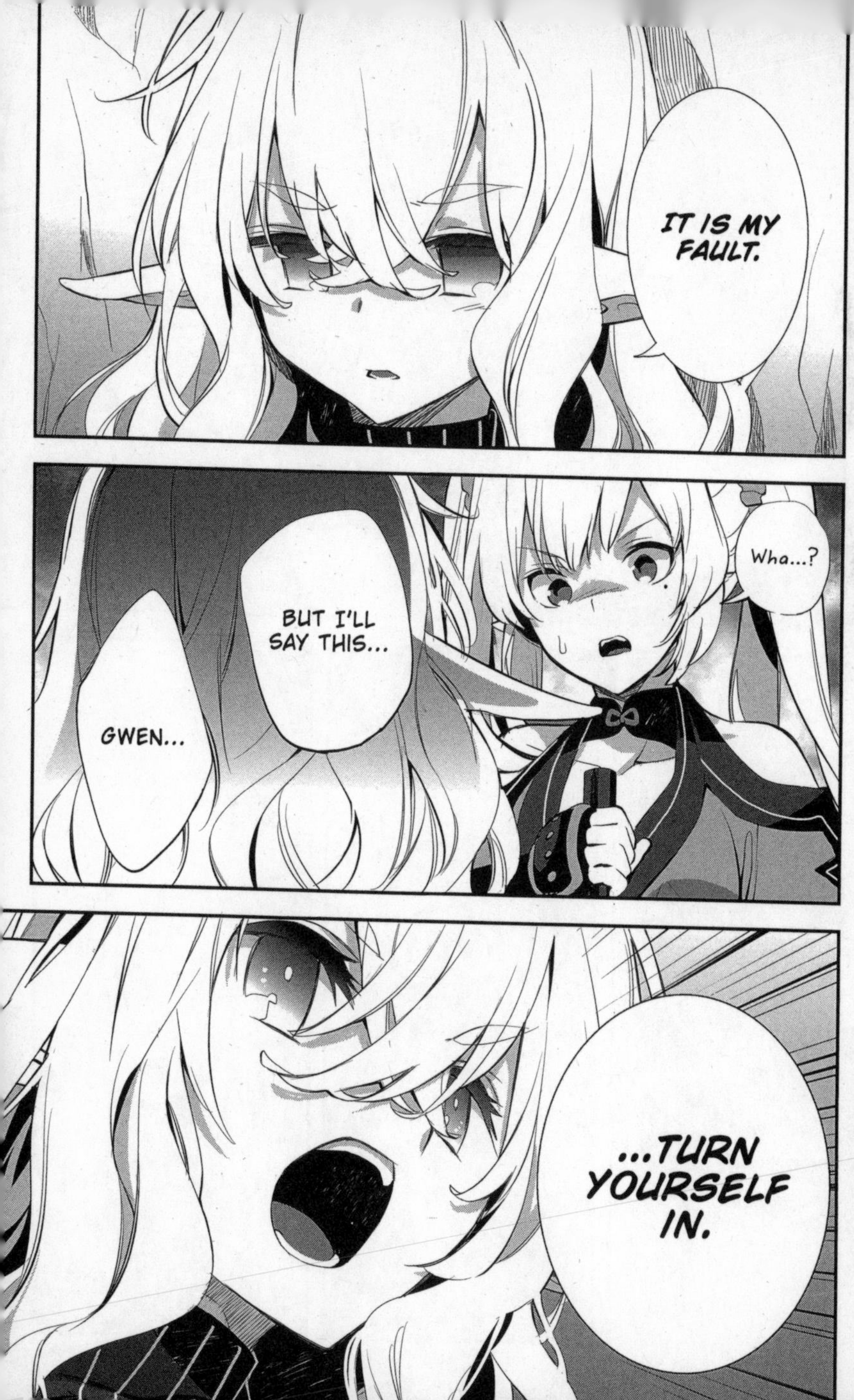
IT IS MY FAULT.
Wha...?
BUT I'LL SAY THIS...
GWEN...
...TURN YOURSELF IN.

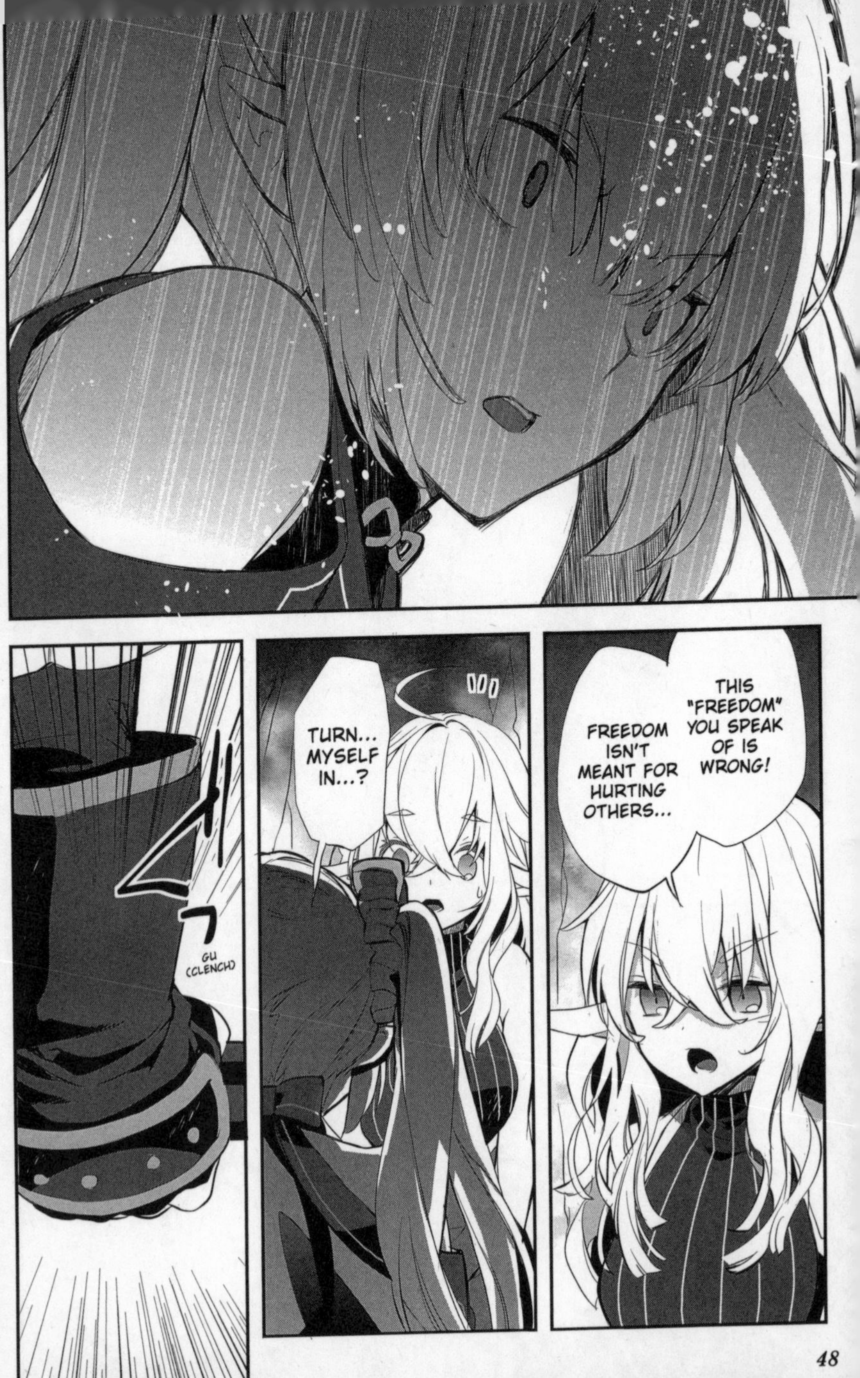
THIS "FREEDOM" YOU SPEAK OF IS WRONG!
FREEDOM ISN'T MEANT FOR HURTING OTHERS...
TURN... MYSELF IN...?
GU (CLENCH)

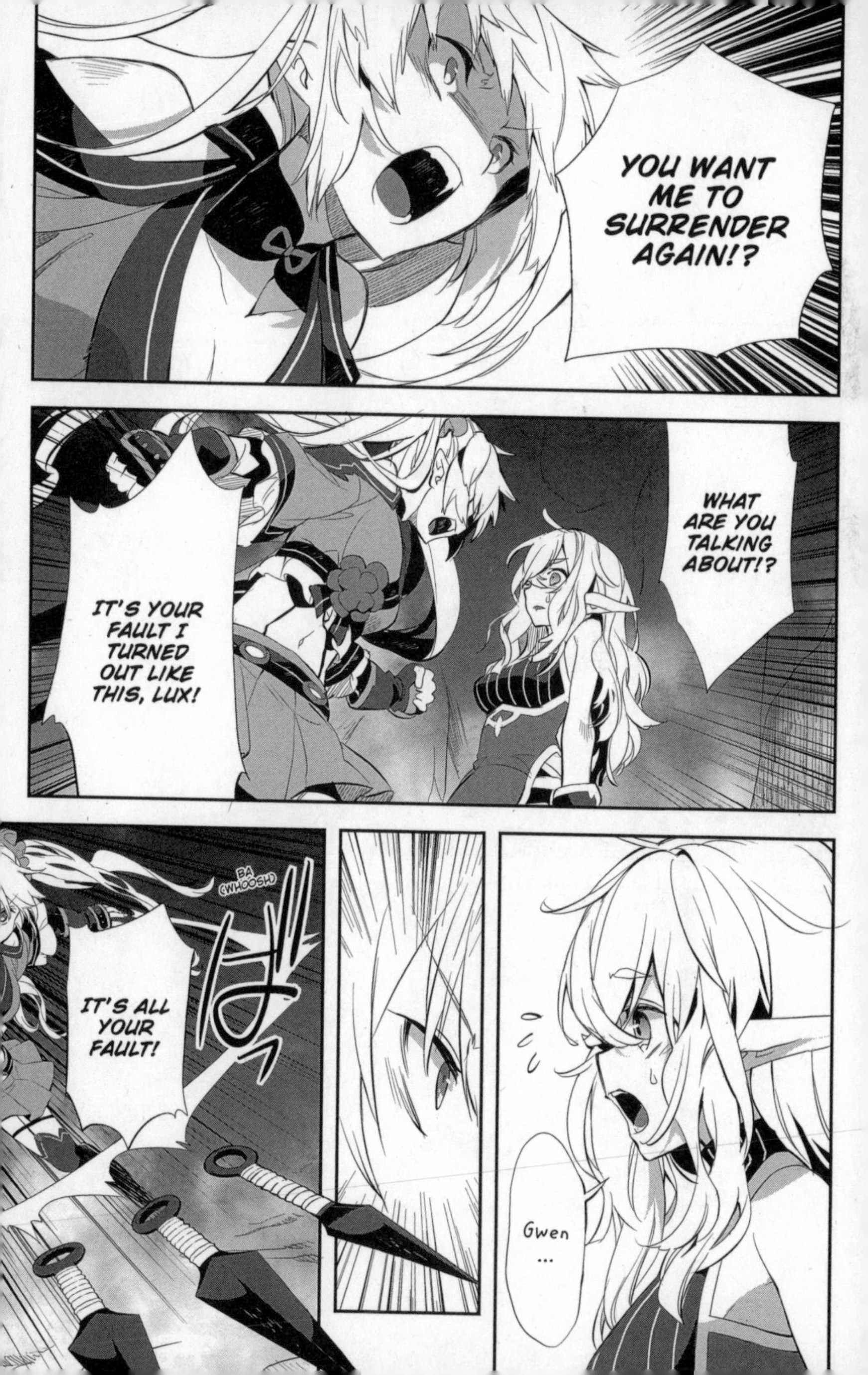
YOU WANT ME TO SURRENDER AGAIN!?
WHAT ARE YOU TALKING ABOUT!?
IT'S YOUR FAULT I TURNED OUT LIKE THIS, LUX!
BA (WHOOSH)
IT'S ALL YOUR FAULT!
Gwen ...

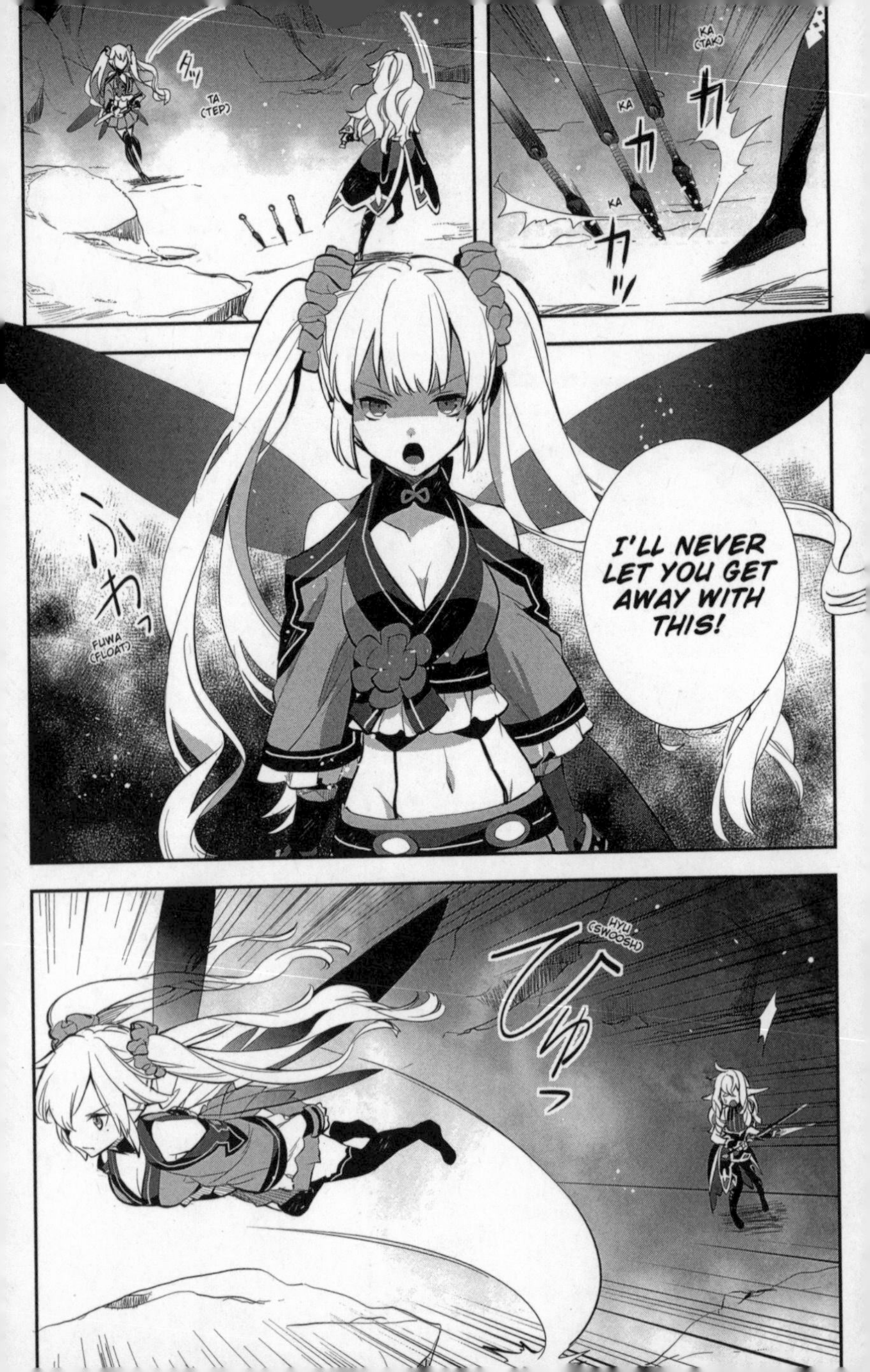

KA (TAK)
KA
KA
TA (TEP)
I'LL NEVER LET YOU GET AWAY WITH THIS!
FUWA (FLOAT)
HYU (SWOOSH)

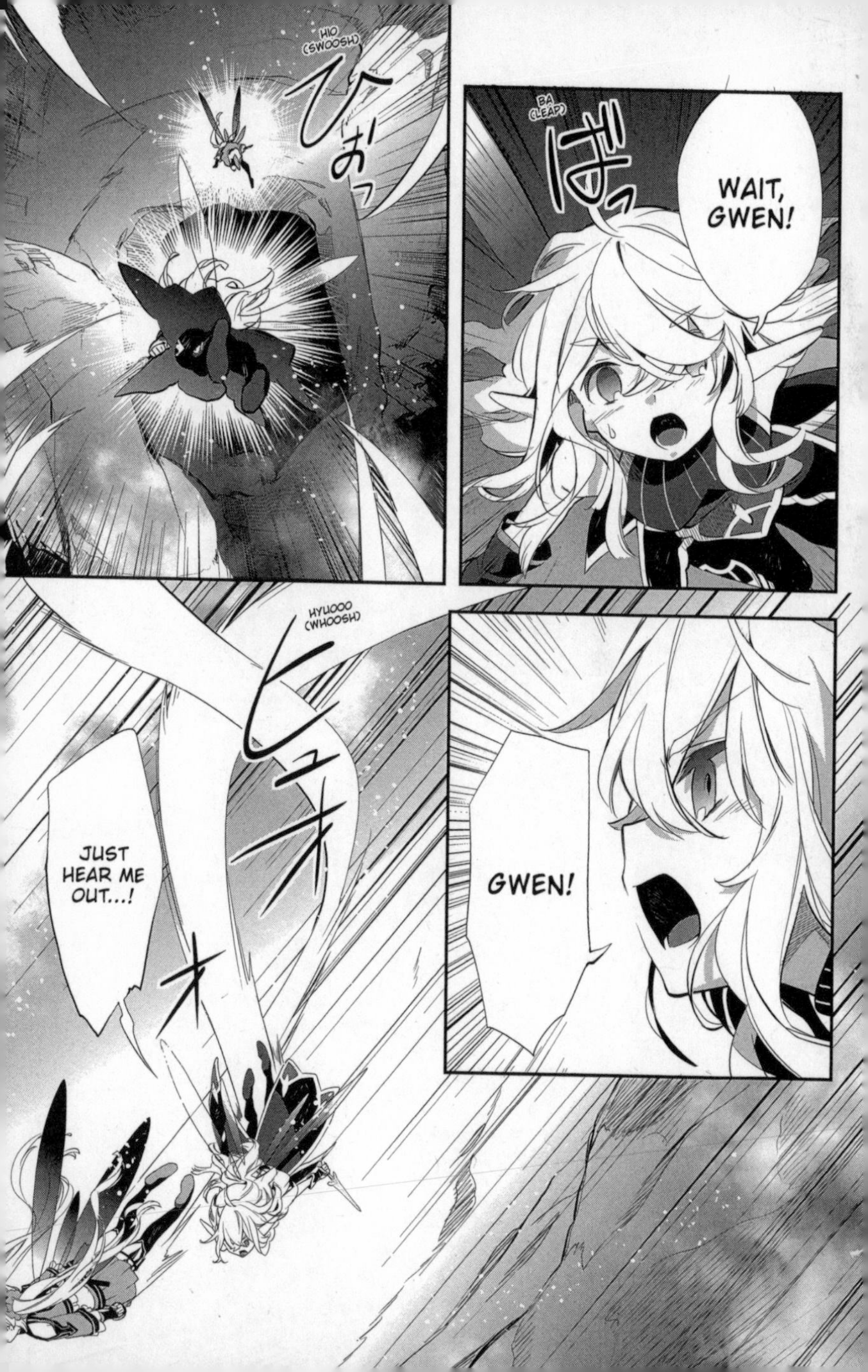

BA
(LEAP)
ばっ
WAIT, GWEN!
HIO
(SWOOSH)
ひおっ
GWEN!
HYUOOO
(WHOOSH)
ヒュオオ
JUST HEAR ME OUT...!

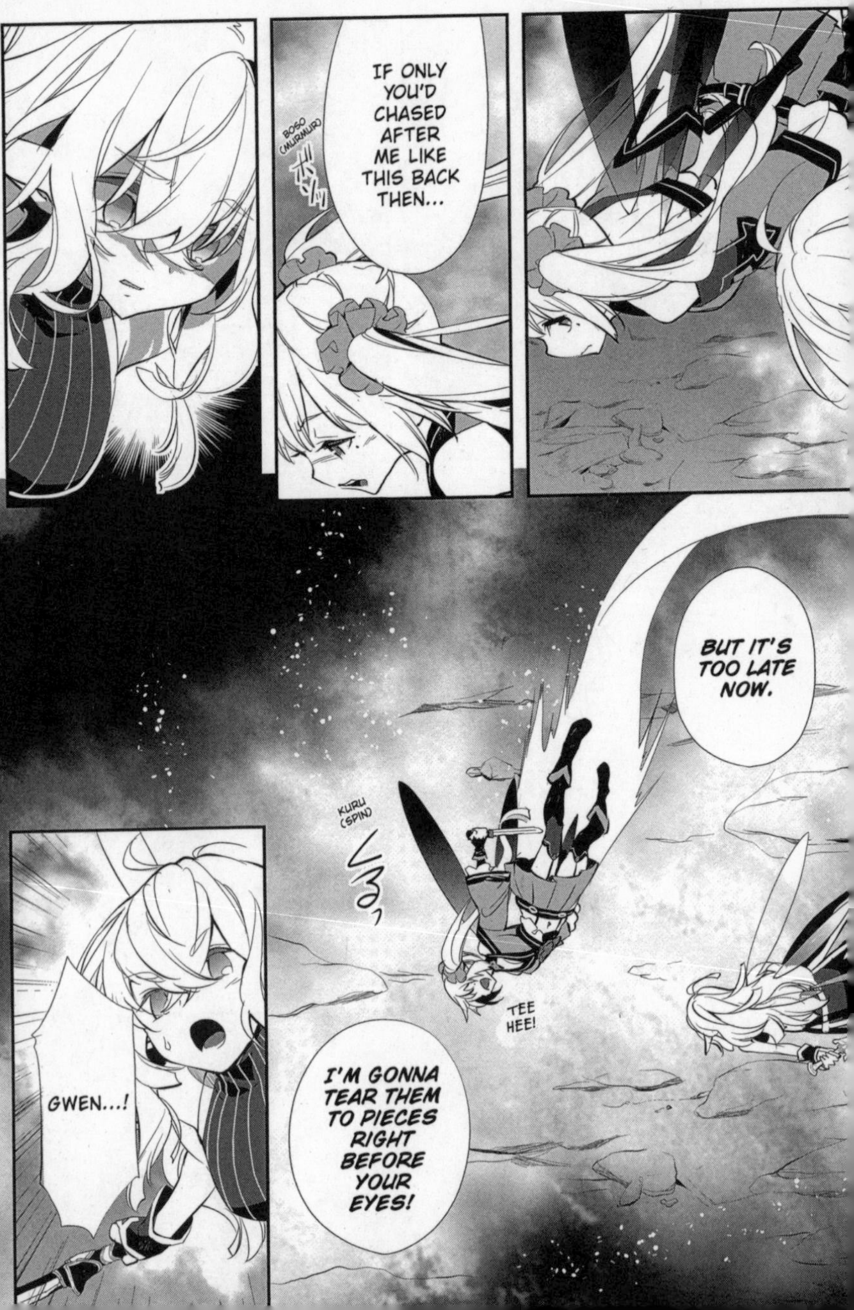

IF ONLY YOU'D CHASED AFTER ME LIKE THIS BACK THEN...
BOSO (MURMUR)
BUT IT'S TOO LATE NOW.
KURU (SPIN)
TEE HEE!
I'M GONNA TEAR THEM TO PIECES RIGHT BEFORE YOUR EYES!
GWEN...!

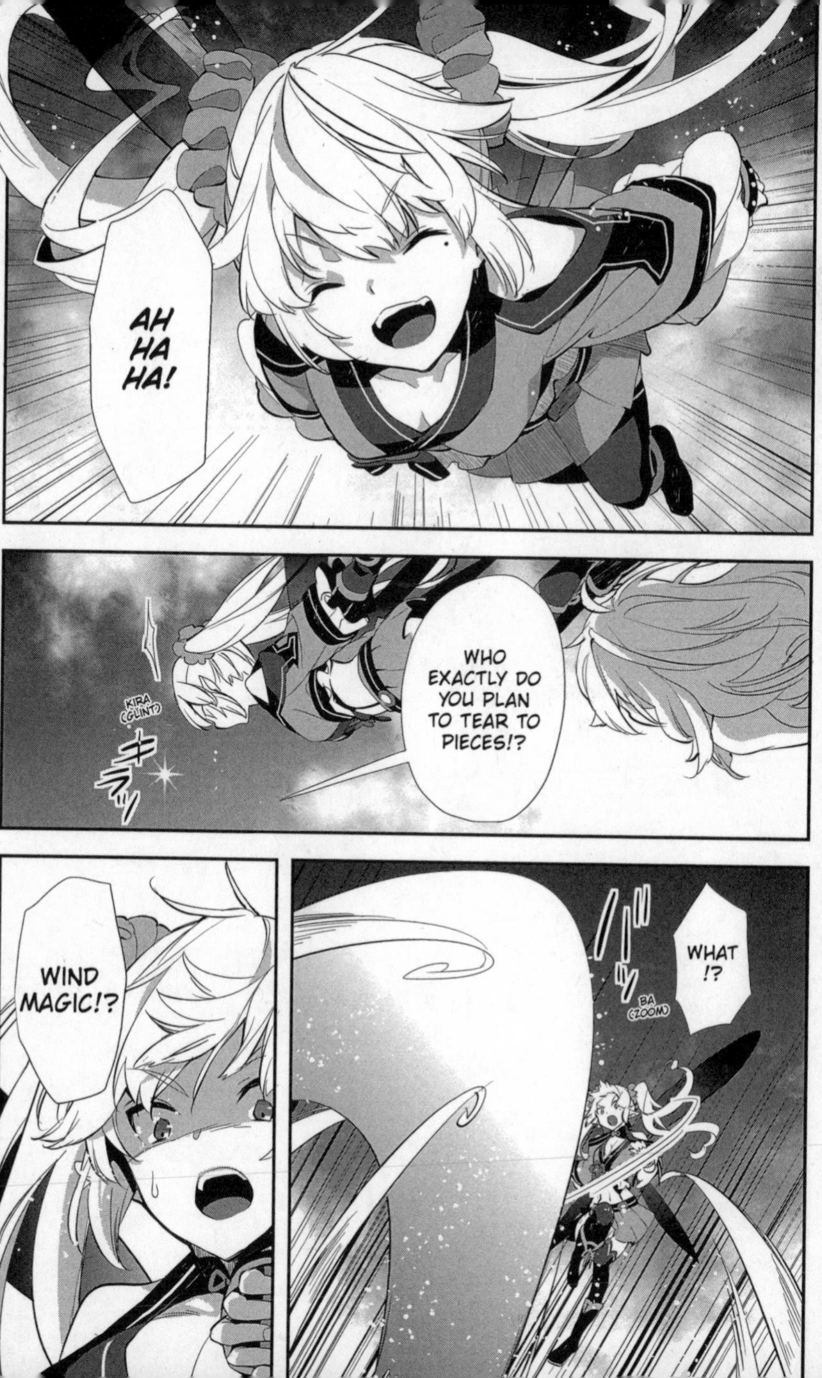

AH HA HA!
WHO EXACTLY DO YOU PLAN TO TEAR TO PIECES!?
KIRA (GLINT)
WHAT!?
BA (ZOOM)
WIND MAGIC!?

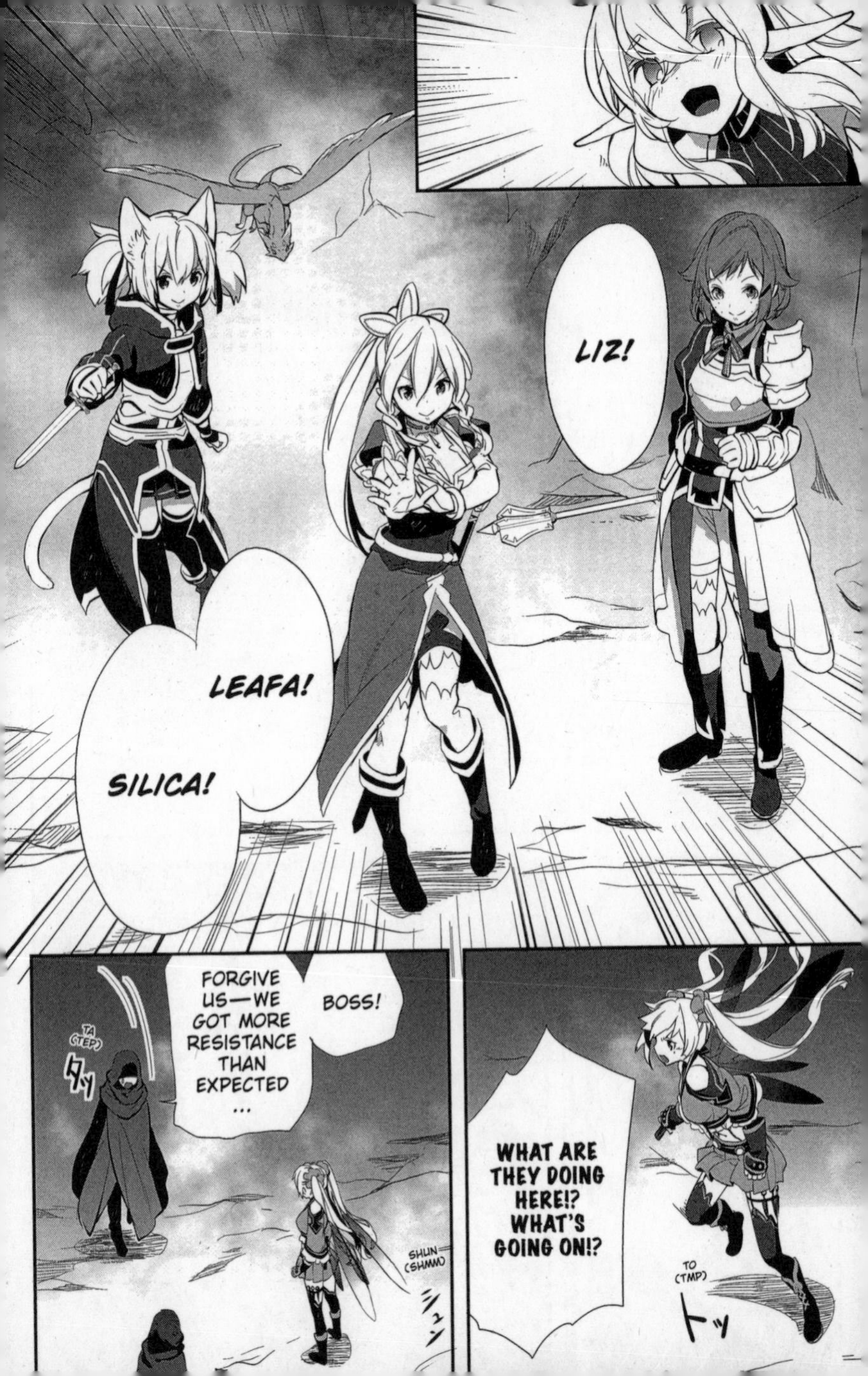
LIZ!
LEAFA!
SILICA!
WHAT ARE THEY DOING HERE!? WHAT'S GOING ON!?
TO (TMP)
トッ
BOSS!
FORGIVE US—WE GOT MORE RESISTANCE THAN EXPECTED...
TA (TEP)
タッ
SHUN (SHMM)

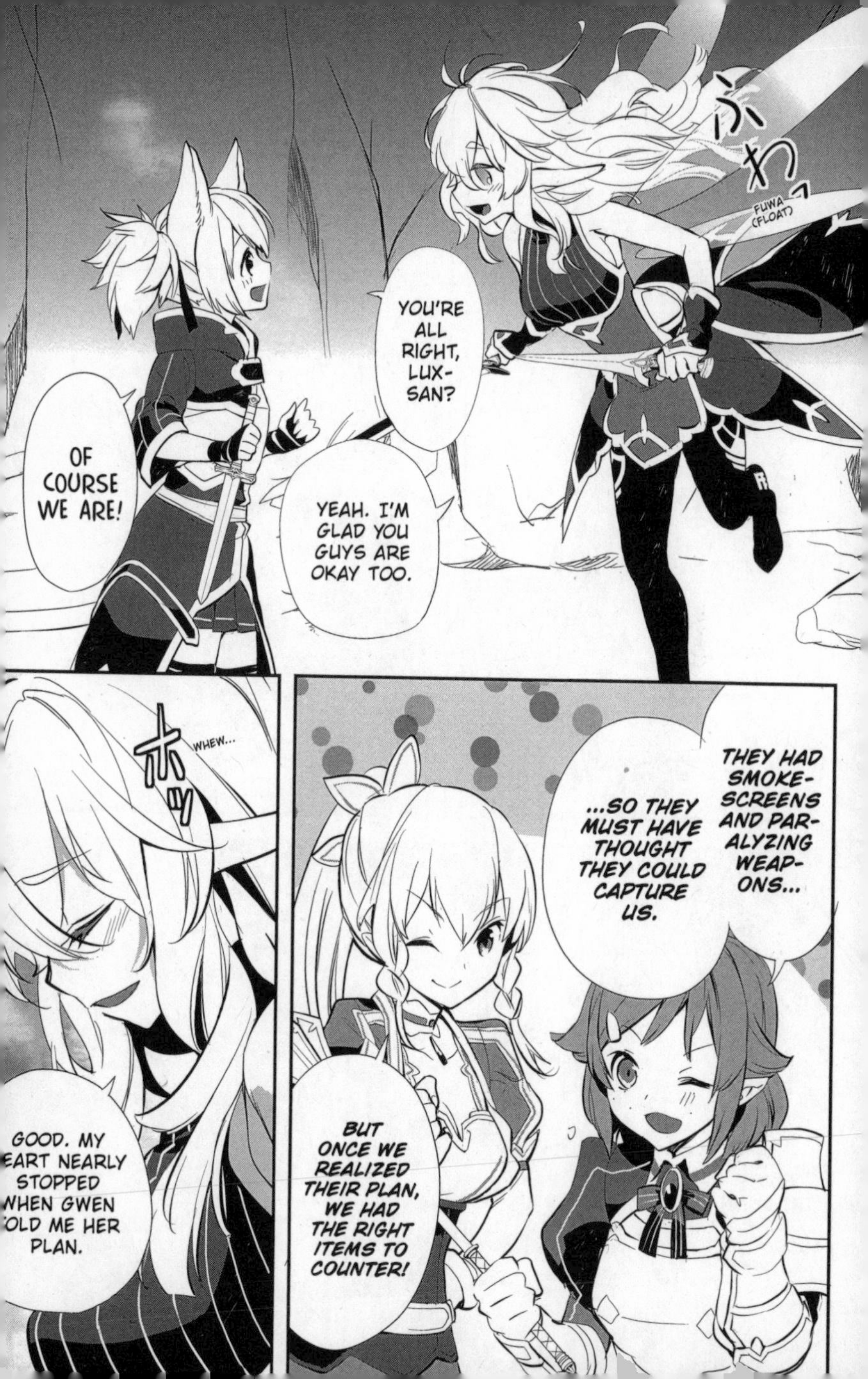
ふわっ
FUWA (FLOAT)
YOU'RE ALL RIGHT, LUX-SAN?
OF COURSE WE ARE!
YEAH. I'M GLAD YOU GUYS ARE OKAY TOO.
THEY HAD SMOKE-SCREENS AND PAR-ALYZING WEAP-ONS...
...SO THEY MUST HAVE THOUGHT THEY COULD CAPTURE US.
BUT ONCE WE REALIZED THEIR PLAN, WE HAD THE RIGHT ITEMS TO COUNTER!
ホッ
WHEW...
GOOD. MY EART NEARLY STOPPED HEN GWEN OLD ME HER PLAN.

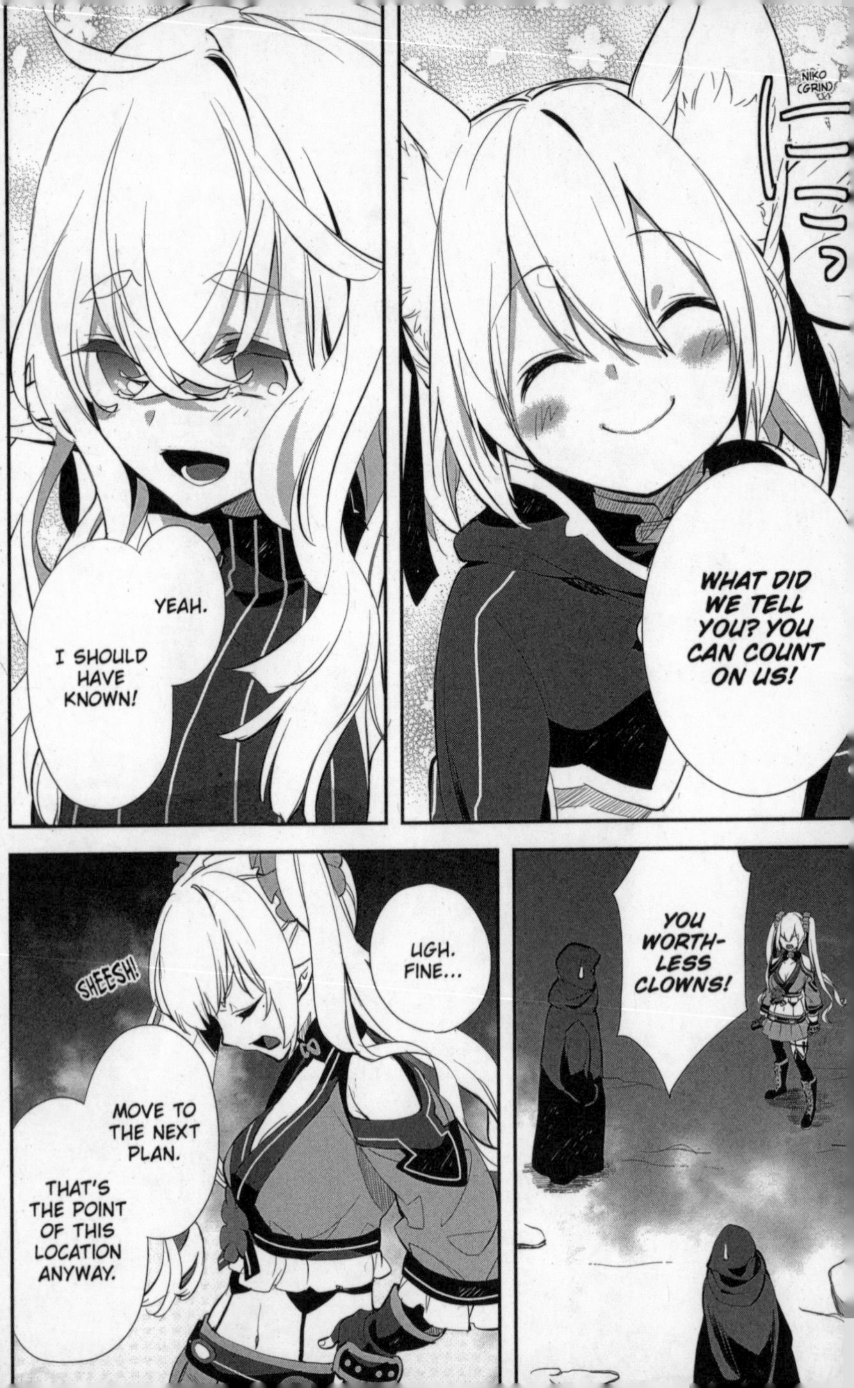
NIKO (GRIN)
ニコッ
WHAT DID WE TELL YOU? YOU CAN COUNT ON US!
YEAH.
I SHOULD HAVE KNOWN!
YOU WORTH-LESS CLOWNS!
UGH. FINE...
SHEESH!
MOVE TO THE NEXT PLAN.
THAT'S THE POINT OF THIS LOCATION ANYWAY.

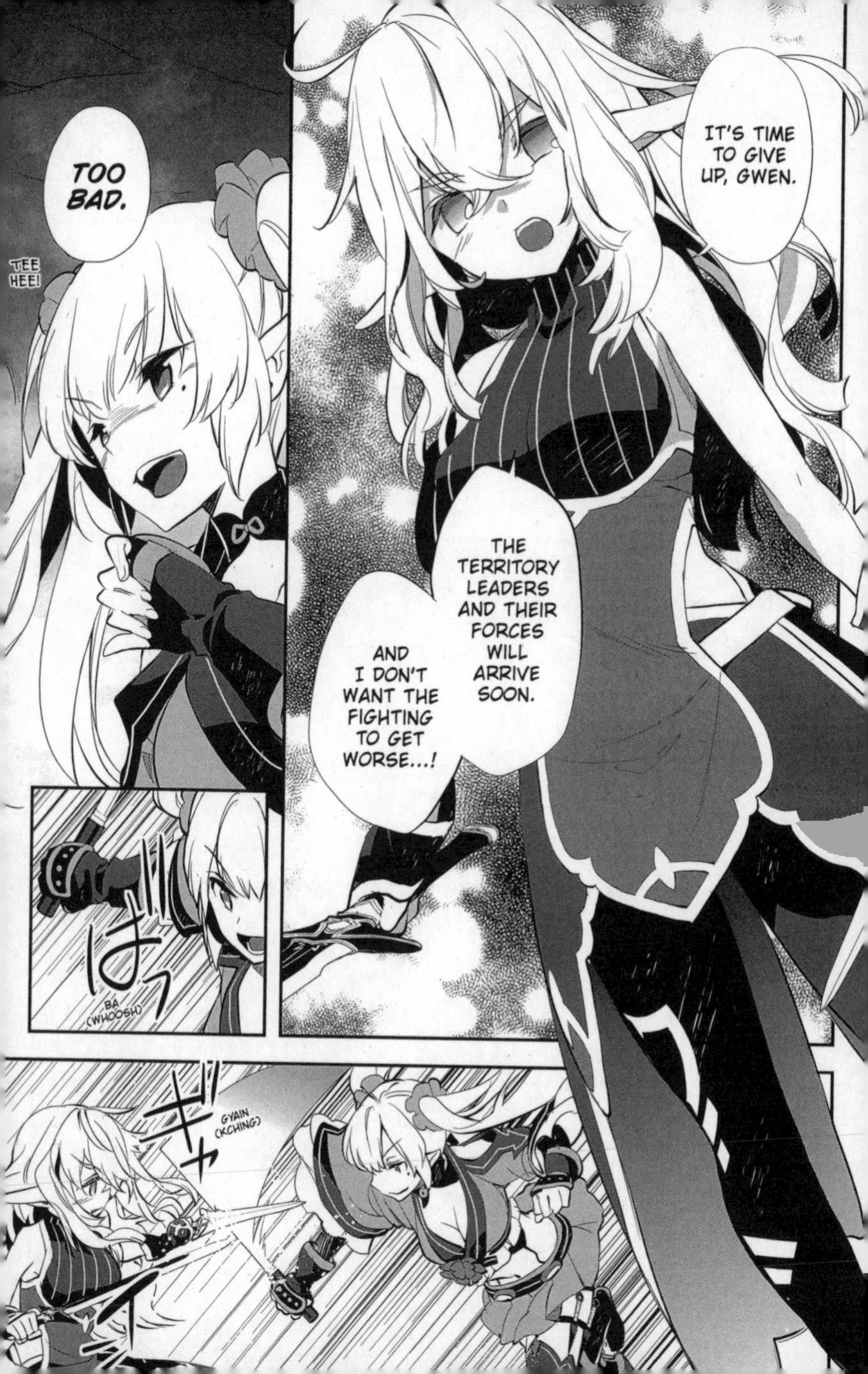
IT'S TIME TO GIVE UP, GWEN.
THE TERRITORY LEADERS AND THEIR FORCES WILL ARRIVE SOON.
AND I DON'T WANT THE FIGHTING TO GET WORSE...!
TOO BAD.
TEE HEE!
BA (WHOOSH)
GYAIN (KCHING)

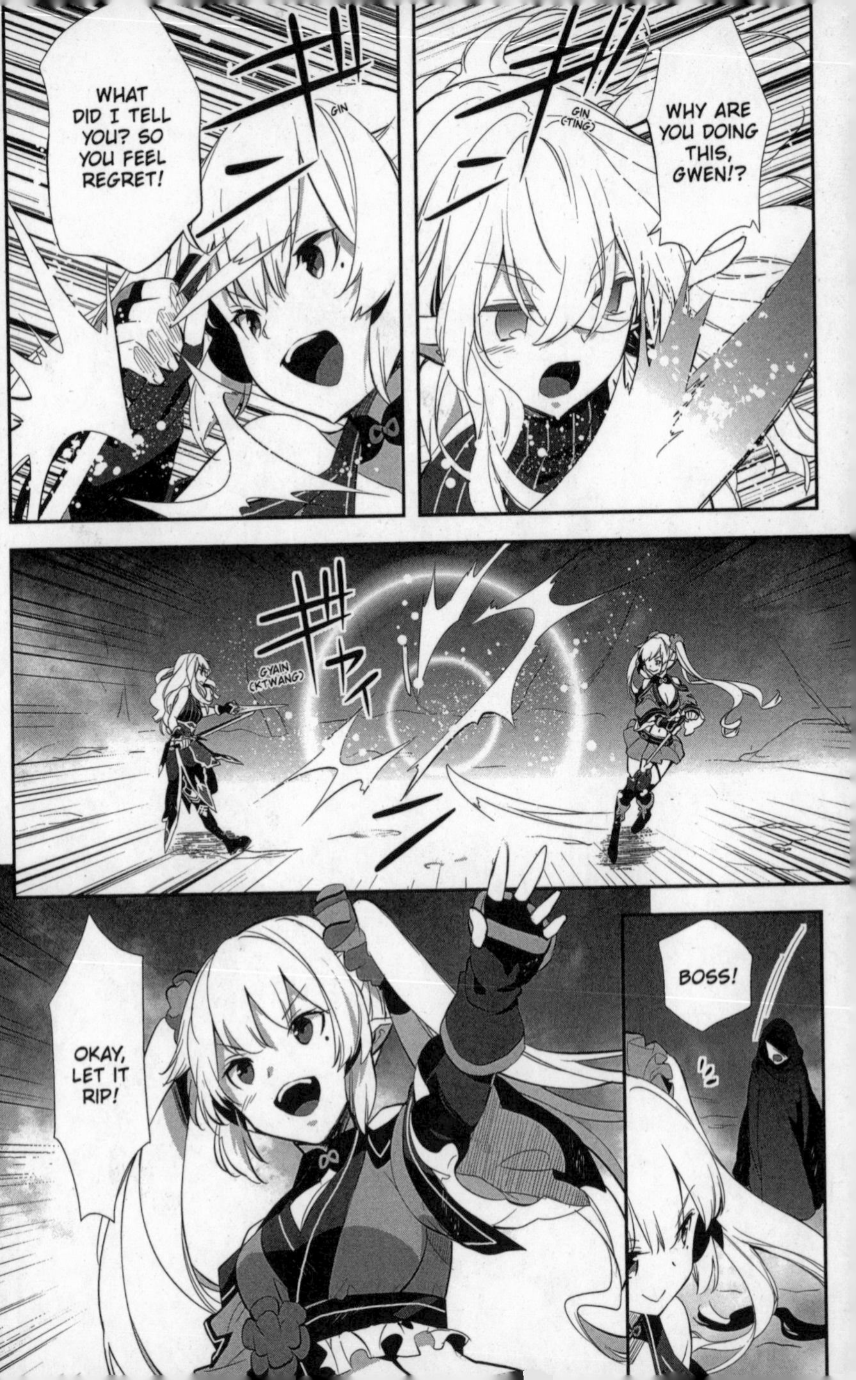

WHY ARE YOU DOING THIS, GWEN!?
GIN (TING)
WHAT DID I TELL YOU? SO YOU FEEL REGRET!
GIN
GYAIN (KTWANG)
BOSS!
OKAY, LET IT RIP!

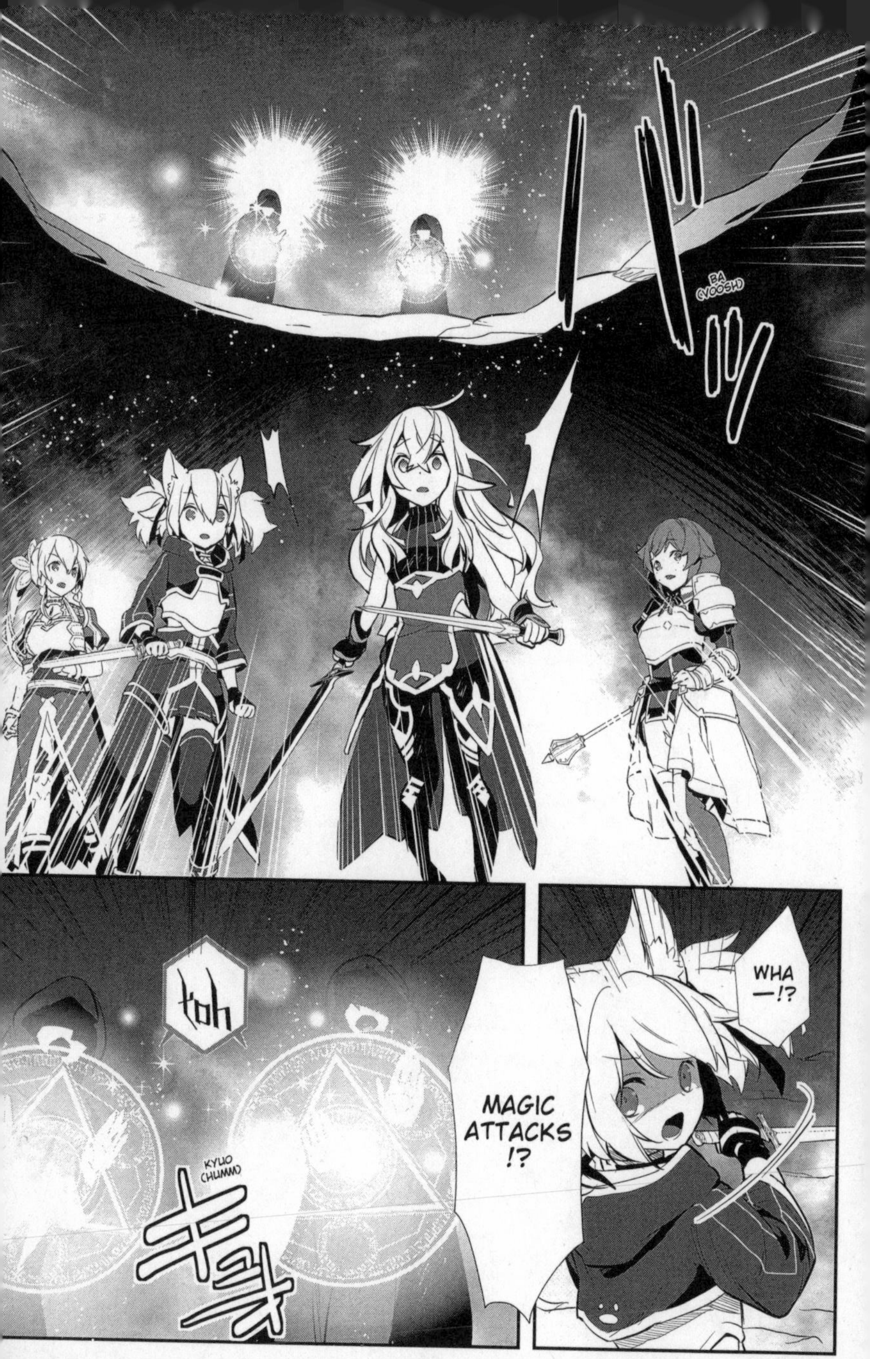
BA (VOOSH)
WHA—!?
MAGIC ATTACKS !?
toh
KYUO (HUMM)

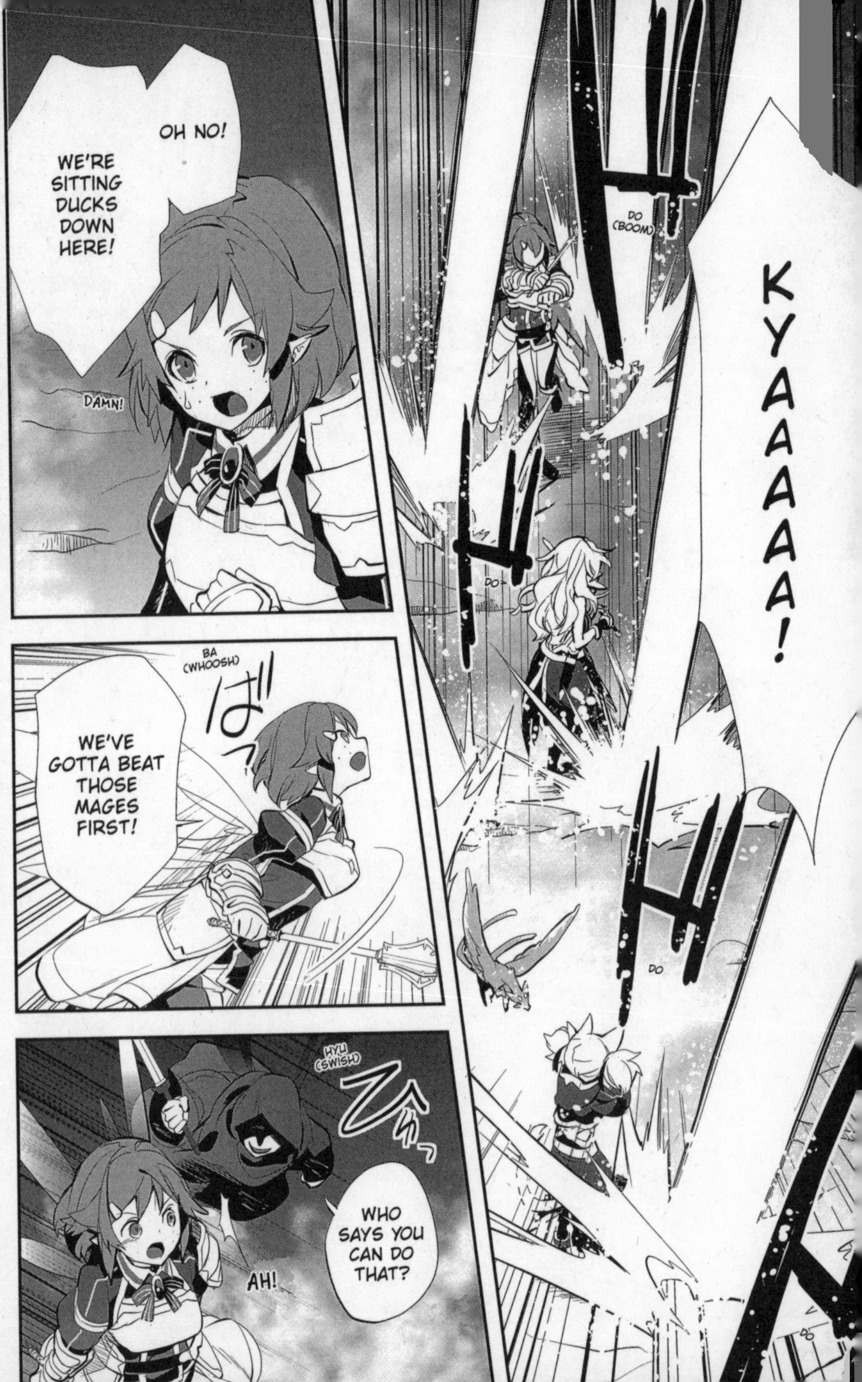
DO (BOOM)
DO
KYAAAAAA!
DO
DO
OH NO!
WE'RE SITTING DUCKS DOWN HERE!
DAMN!
BA (WHOOSH)
ばっ
WE'VE GOTTA BEAT THOSE MAGES FIRST!
HYU (SWISH)
ひゅっ
WHO SAYS YOU CAN DO THAT?
AH!

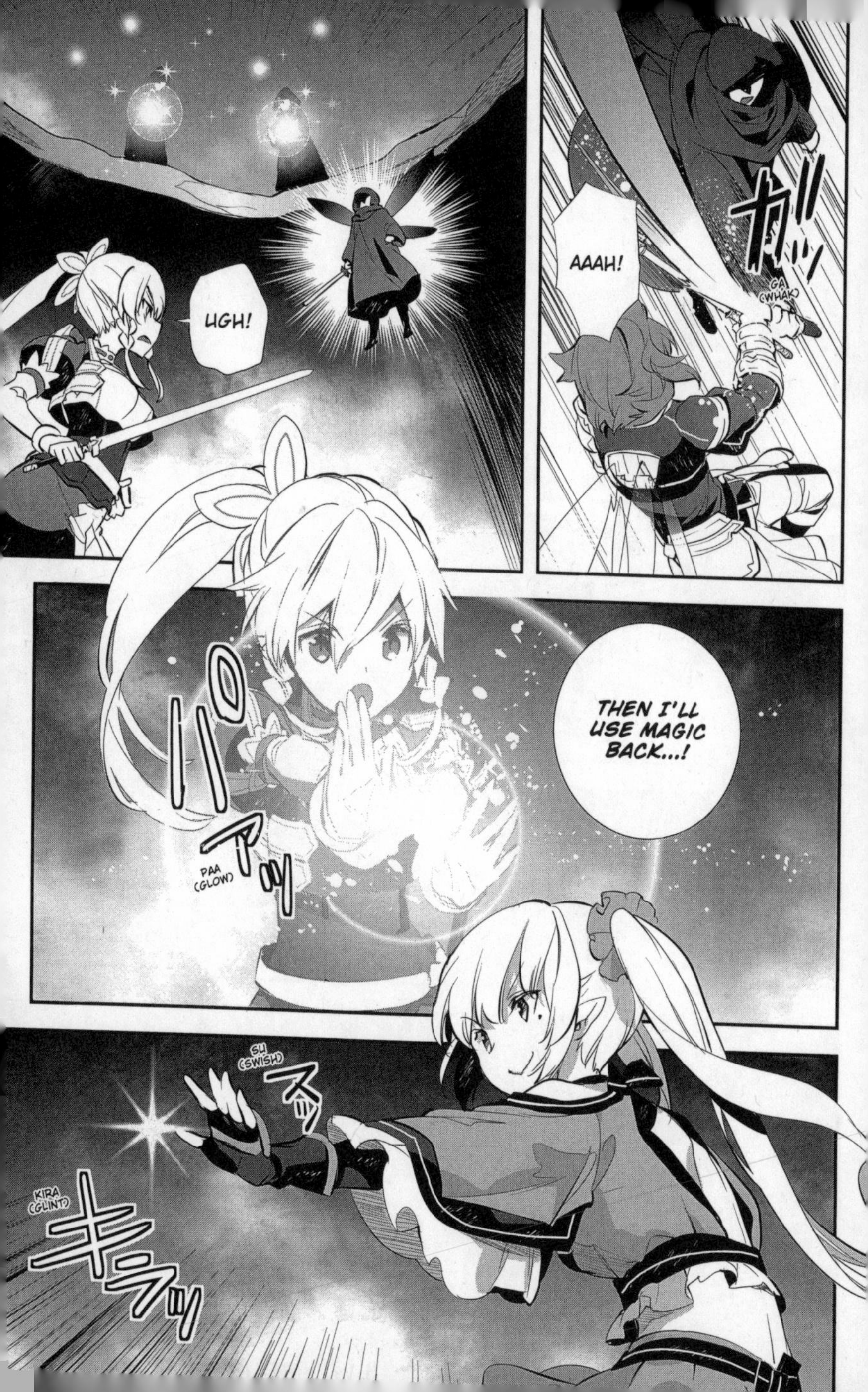
AAAH!
GA (WHAK)
UGH!
THEN I'LL USE MAGIC BACK...!
PAA (GLOW)
SU (SWISH)
KIRA (GLINT)

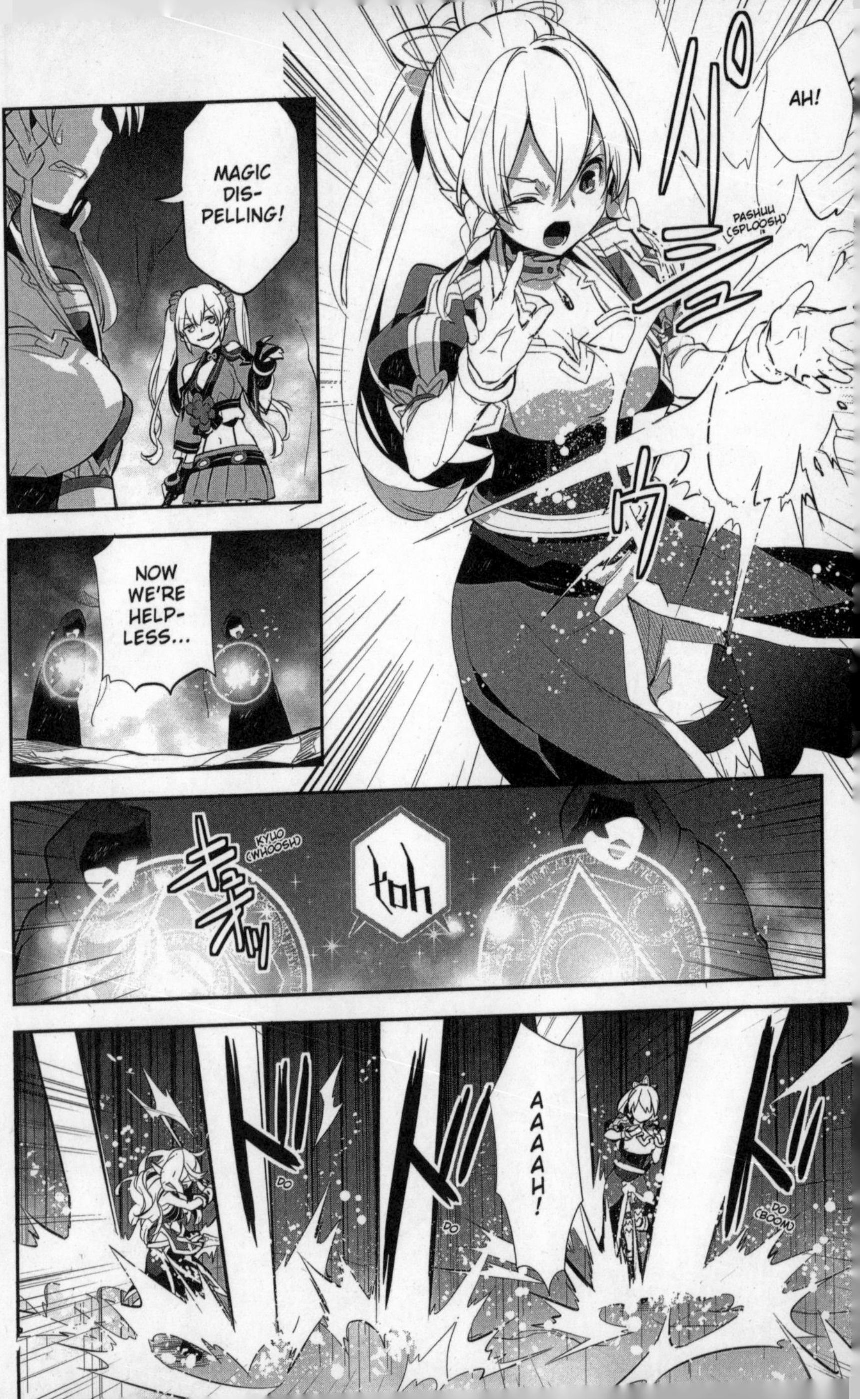
AH!
PASHUU (SPLOOSH)
MAGIC DISPELLING!
NOW WE'RE HELPLESS...
KYUO (WHOOSH)
koh
DO
DO
AAAAAH!
DO (BOOM)

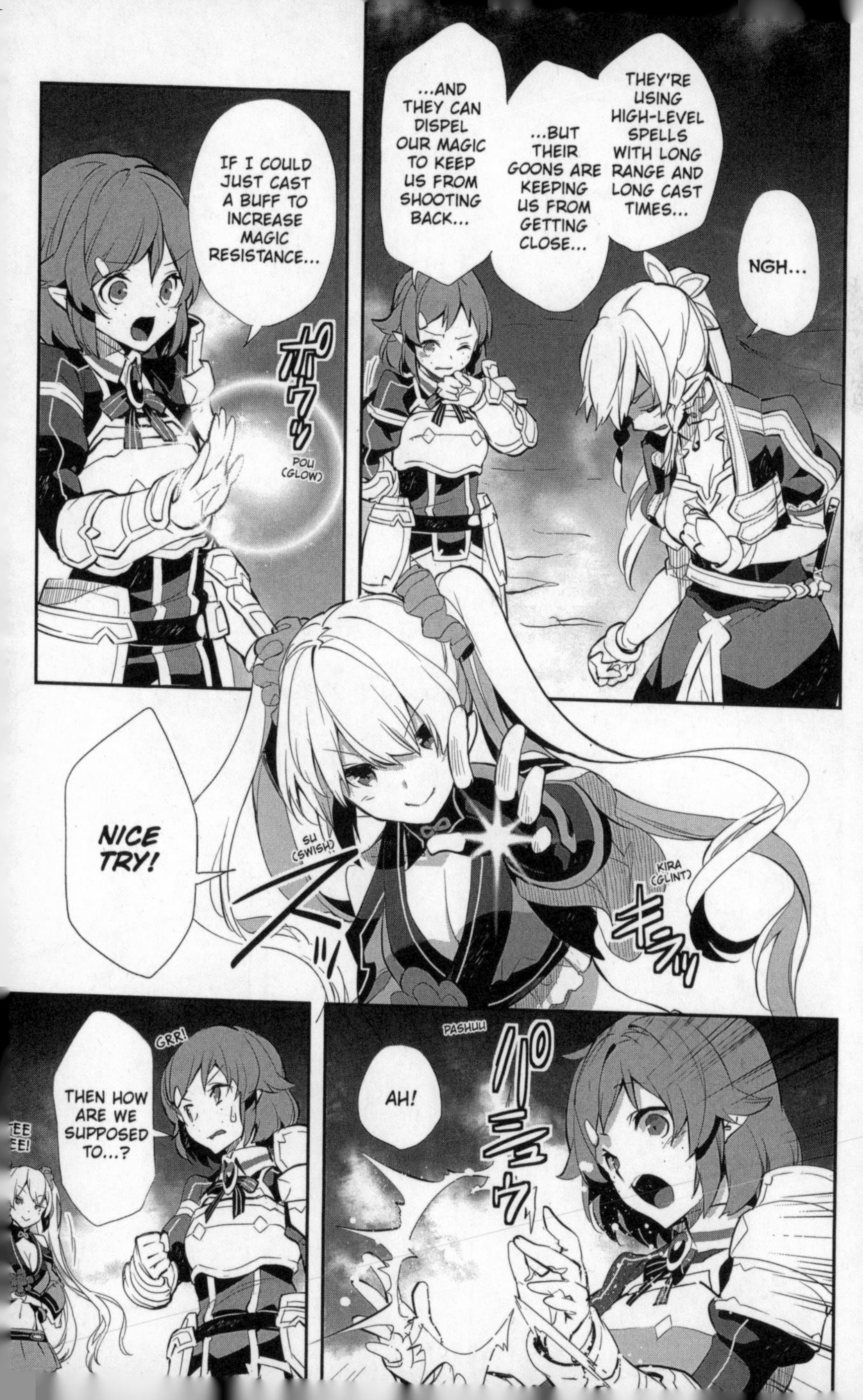
THEY'RE USING HIGH-LEVEL SPELLS WITH LONG RANGE AND LONG CAST TIMES...
...BUT THEIR GOONS ARE KEEPING US FROM GETTING CLOSE...
...AND THEY CAN DISPEL OUR MAGIC TO KEEP US FROM SHOOTING BACK...
NGH...
IF I COULD JUST CAST A BUFF TO INCREASE MAGIC RESISTANCE...
ポウッ
POU (GLOW)
キラッ
KIRA (GLINT)
ス
SU (SWISH)
NICE TRY!
パシュウ
PASHUU
AH!
GRR!
THEN HOW ARE WE SUPPOSED TO...?

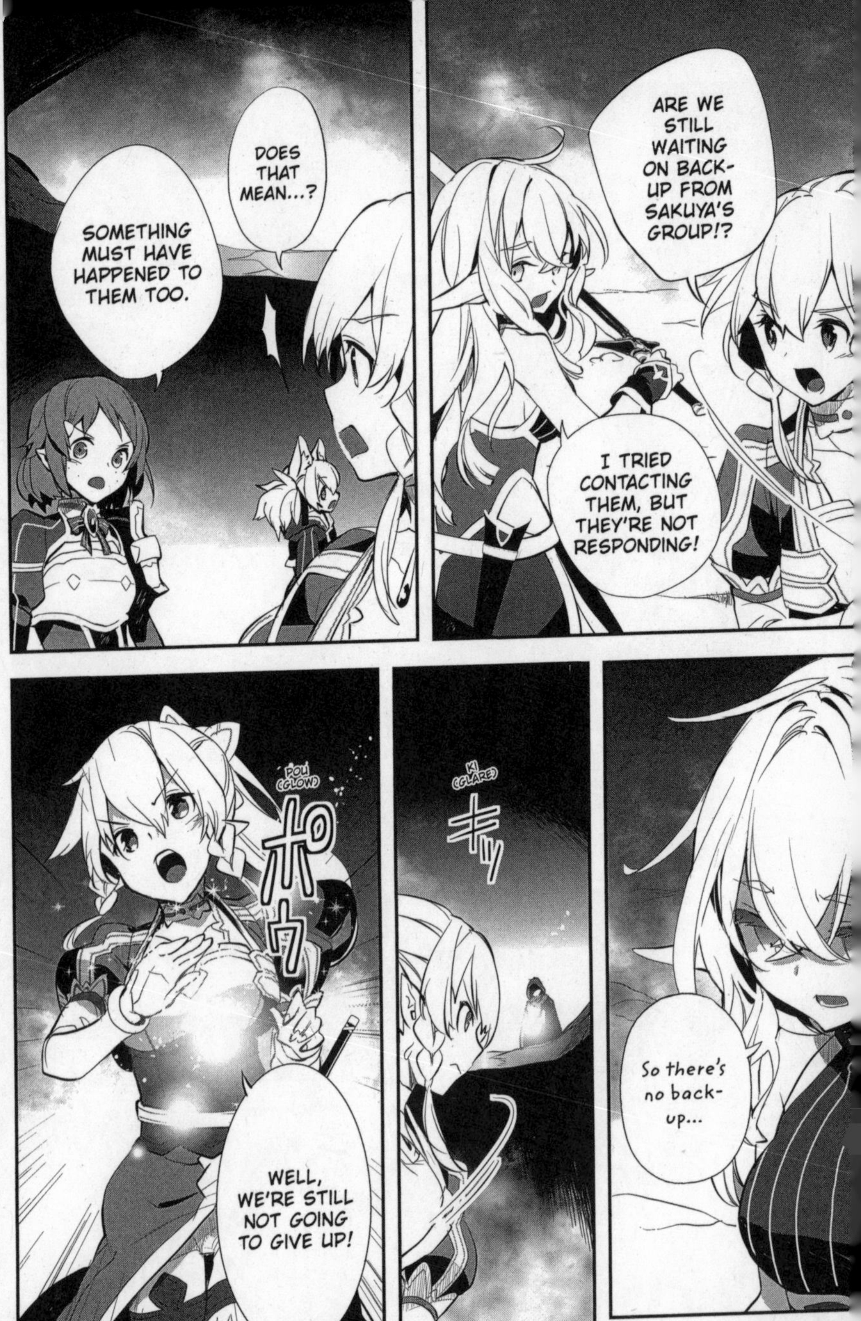
ARE WE STILL WAITING ON BACK-UP FROM SAKUYA'S GROUP!?
I TRIED CONTACTING THEM, BUT THEY'RE NOT RESPONDING!
DOES THAT MEAN...?
SOMETHING MUST HAVE HAPPENED TO THEM TOO.
So there's no back-up...
KI (GLARE)
キッ
POU (GLOW)
ポウ
WELL, WE'RE STILL NOT GOING TO GIVE UP!

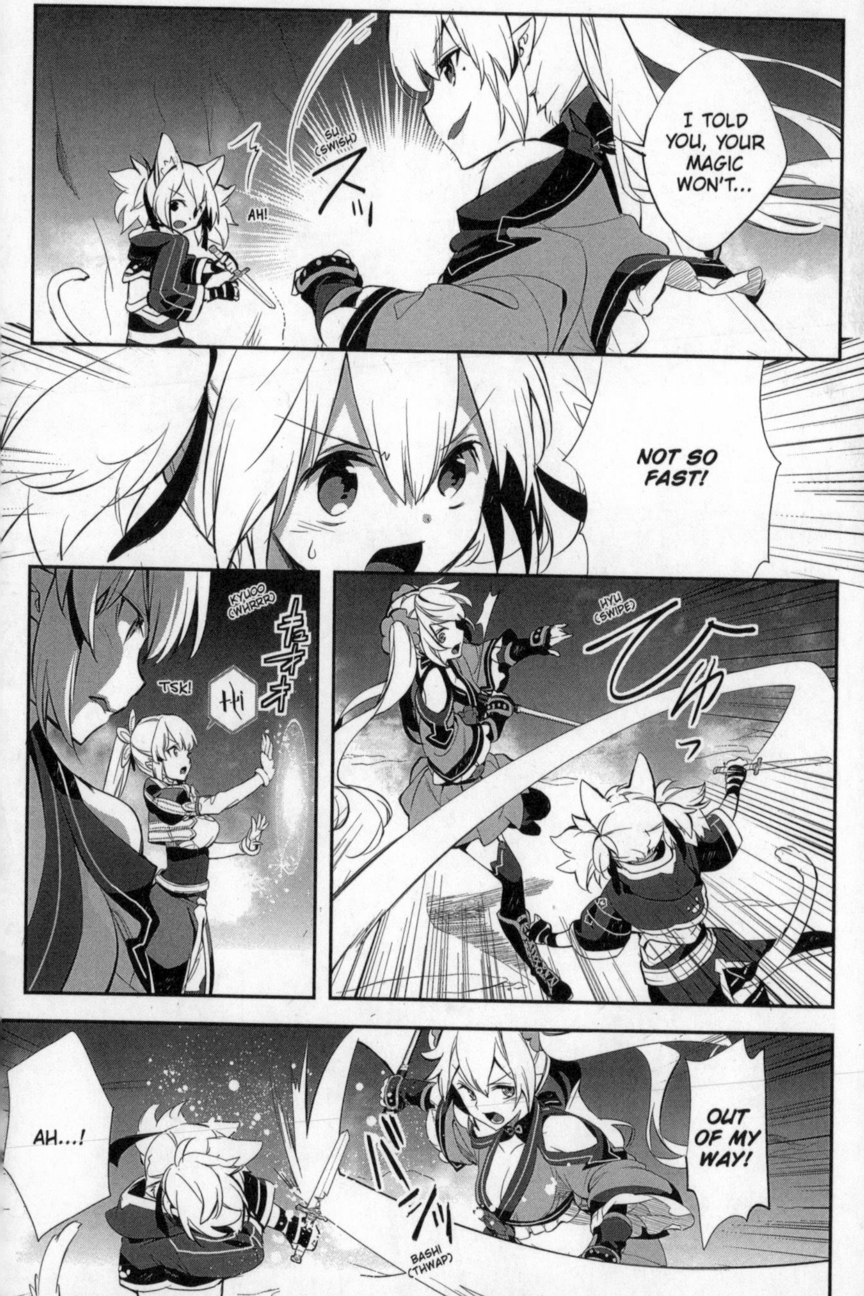
I TOLD YOU, YOUR MAGIC WON'T...
SU (SWISH)
AH!
NOT SO FAST!
HYU (SWIPE)
KYUOO (WHRRR)
TSK!
OUT OF MY WAY!
BASHI (THWAP)
AH...!

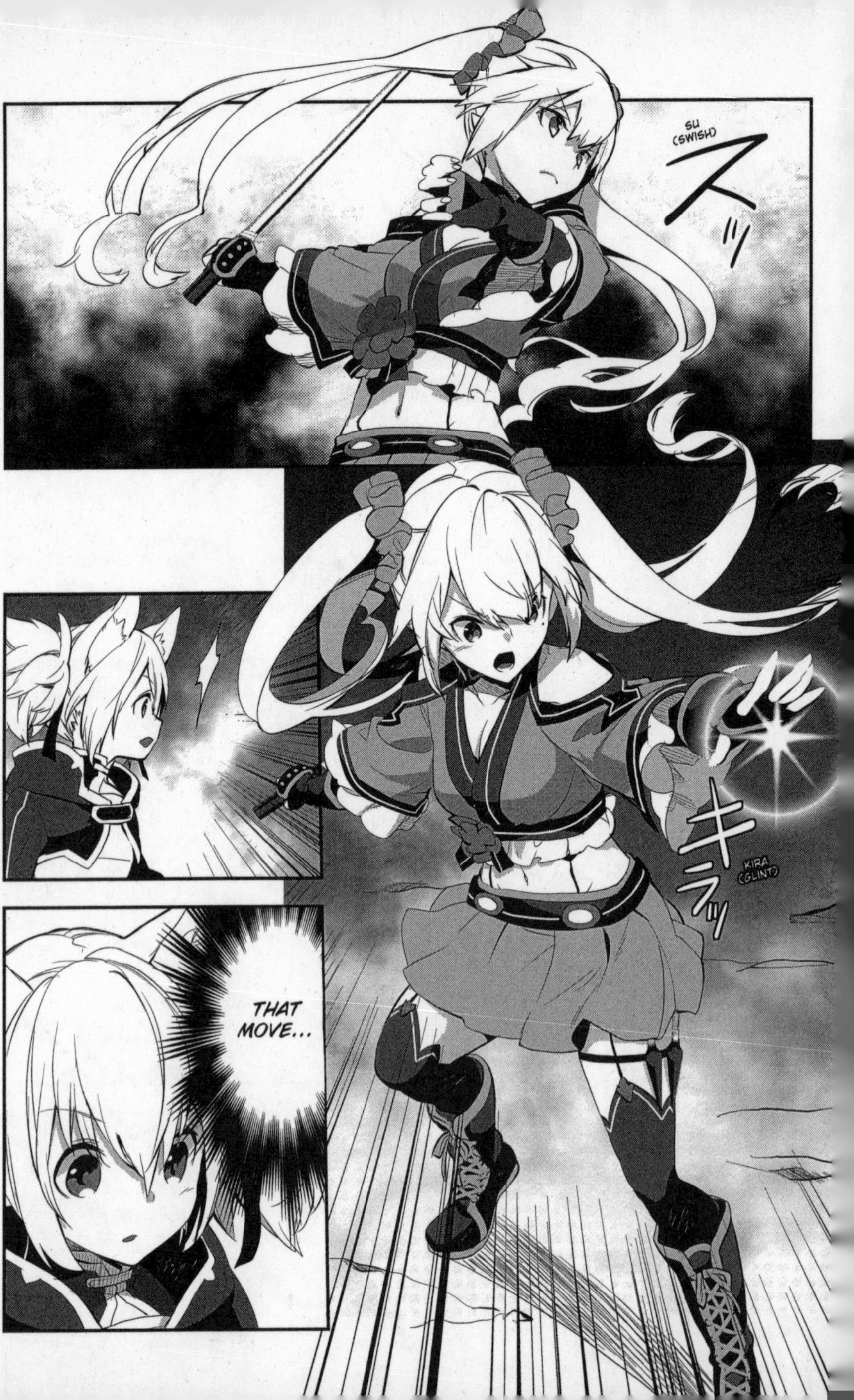
スッ
SU
(SWISH)
キラッ
KIRA
(GLINT)
THAT
MOVE...

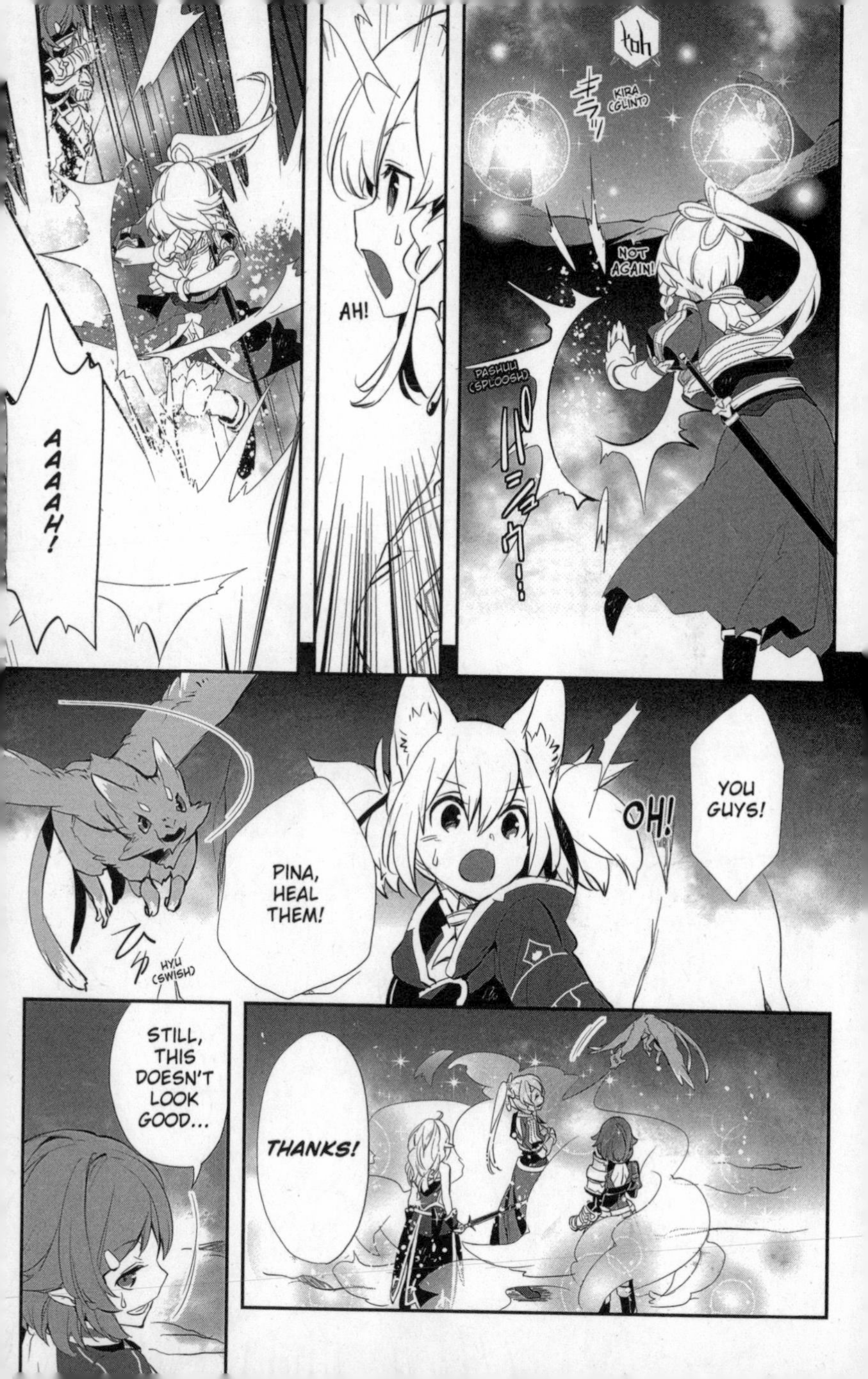

KIRA (GLINT)
NOT AGAIN!
PASHUU (SPLOOSH)
AH!
AAAAAH!
YOU GUYS!
OH!
PINA, HEAL THEM!
HYU (SWISH)
THANKS!
STILL, THIS DOESN'T LOOK GOOD...

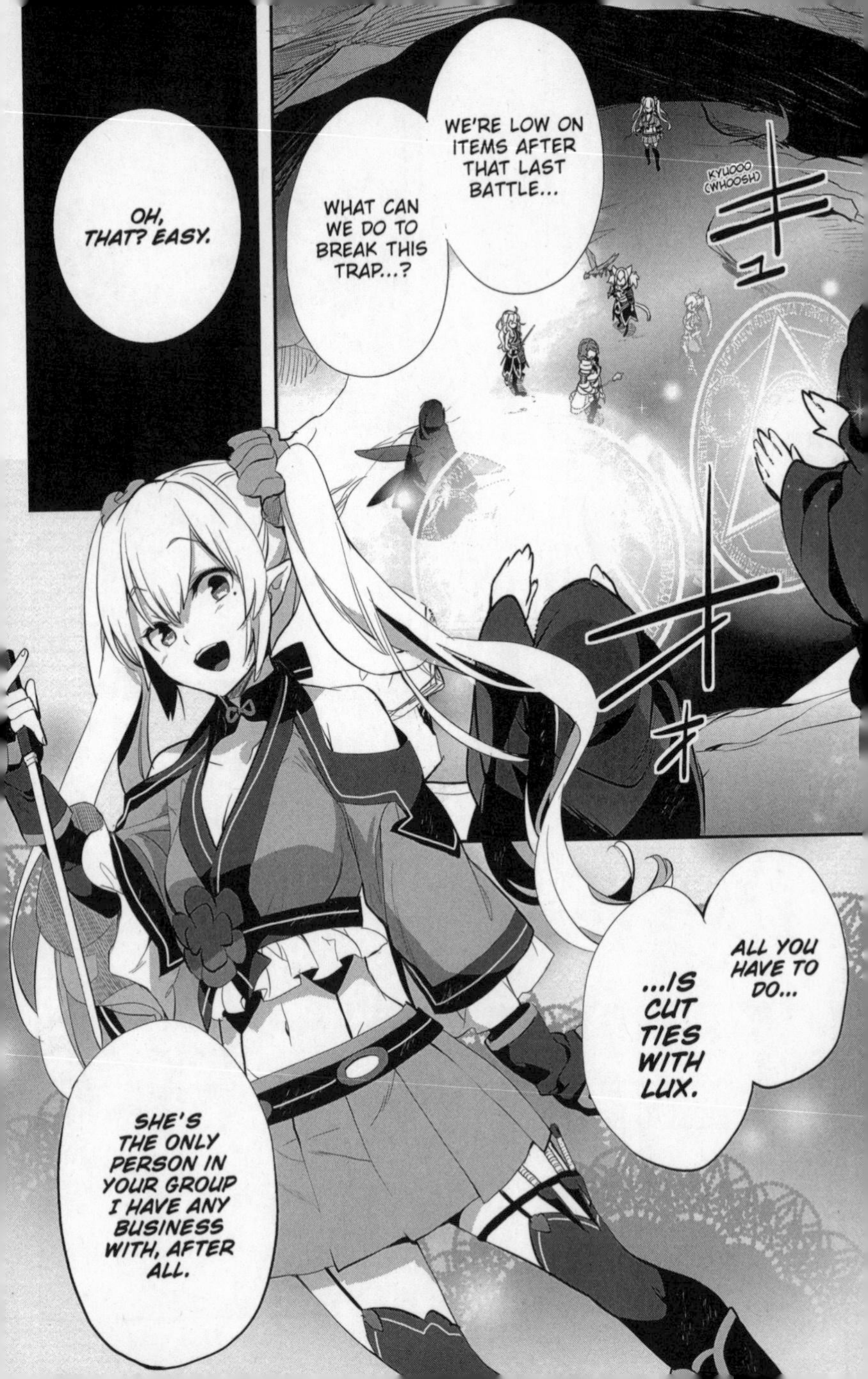

WE'RE LOW ON ITEMS AFTER THAT LAST BATTLE...
WHAT CAN WE DO TO BREAK THIS TRAP...?
OH, THAT? EASY.
KYUOOO (WHOOSH)
キュオォ
ALL YOU HAVE TO DO...
...IS CUT TIES WITH LUX.
SHE'S THE ONLY PERSON IN YOUR GROUP I HAVE ANY BUSINESS WITH, AFTER ALL.

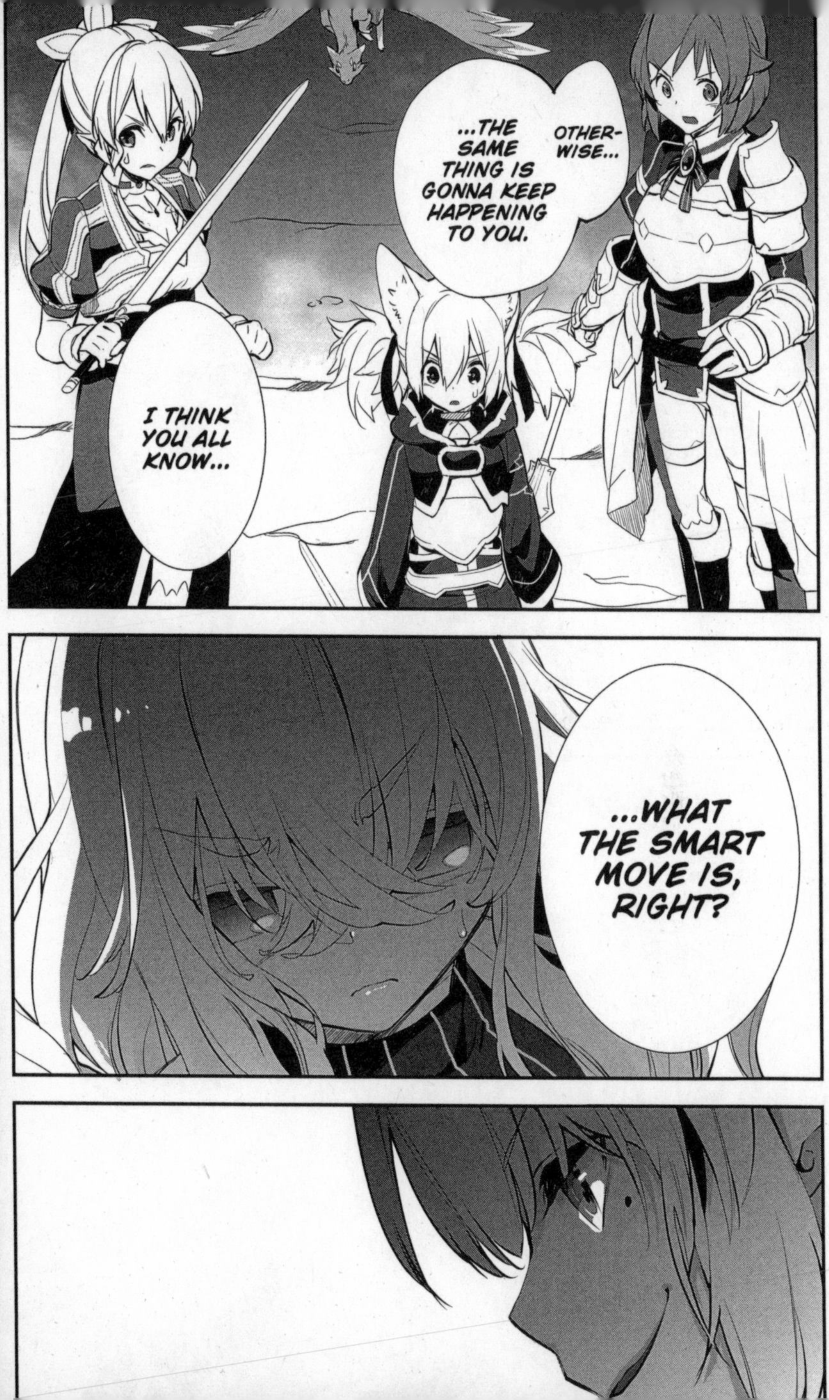
OTHER-WISE...
...THE SAME THING IS GONNA KEEP HAPPENING TO YOU.
I THINK YOU ALL KNOW...
...WHAT THE SMART MOVE IS, RIGHT?

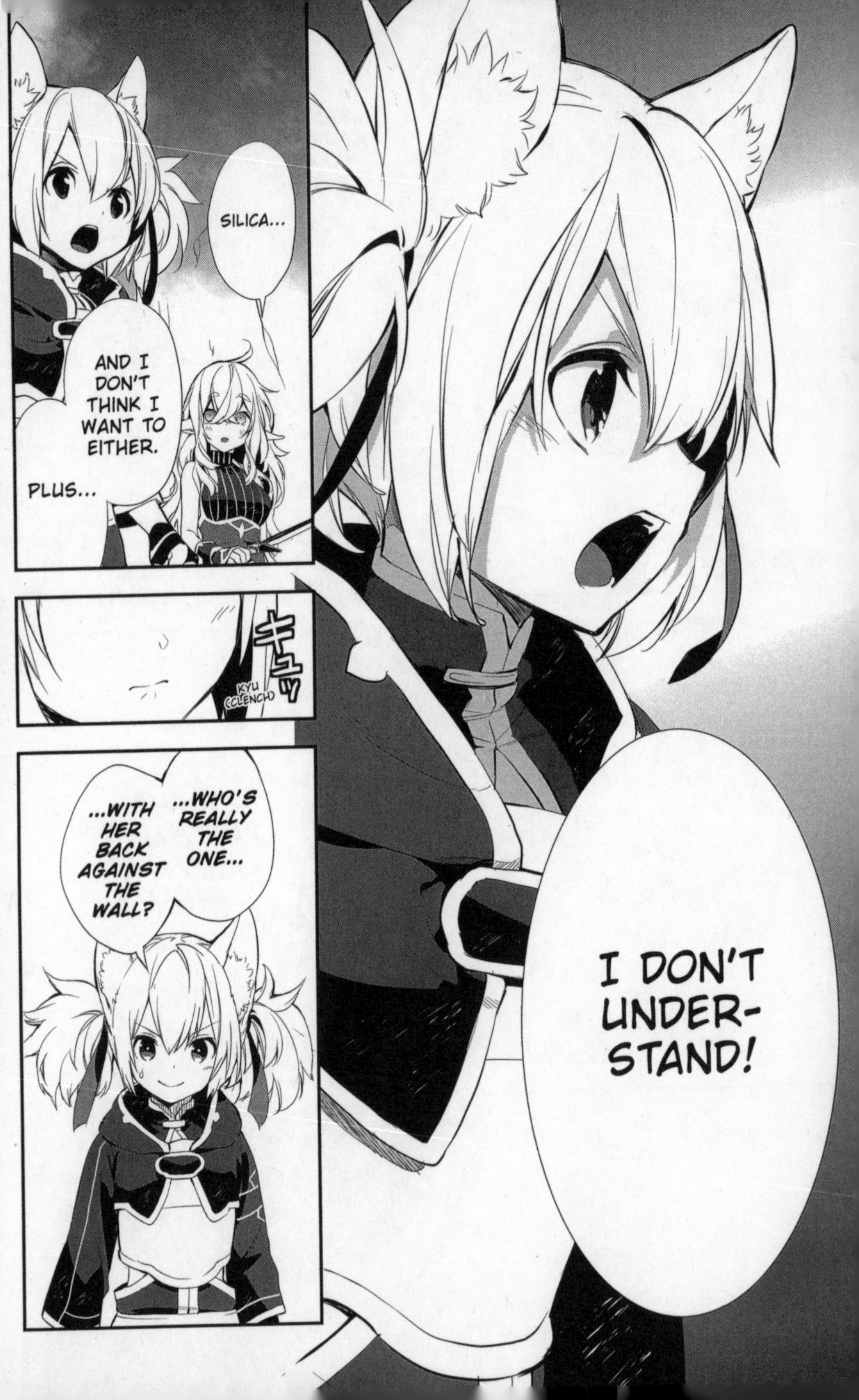
I DON'T UNDER-STAND!
SILICA...
AND I DON'T THINK I WANT TO EITHER.
PLUS...
キュッ
KYU (CLENCH)
...WHO'S REALLY THE ONE...
...WITH HER BACK AGAINST THE WALL?

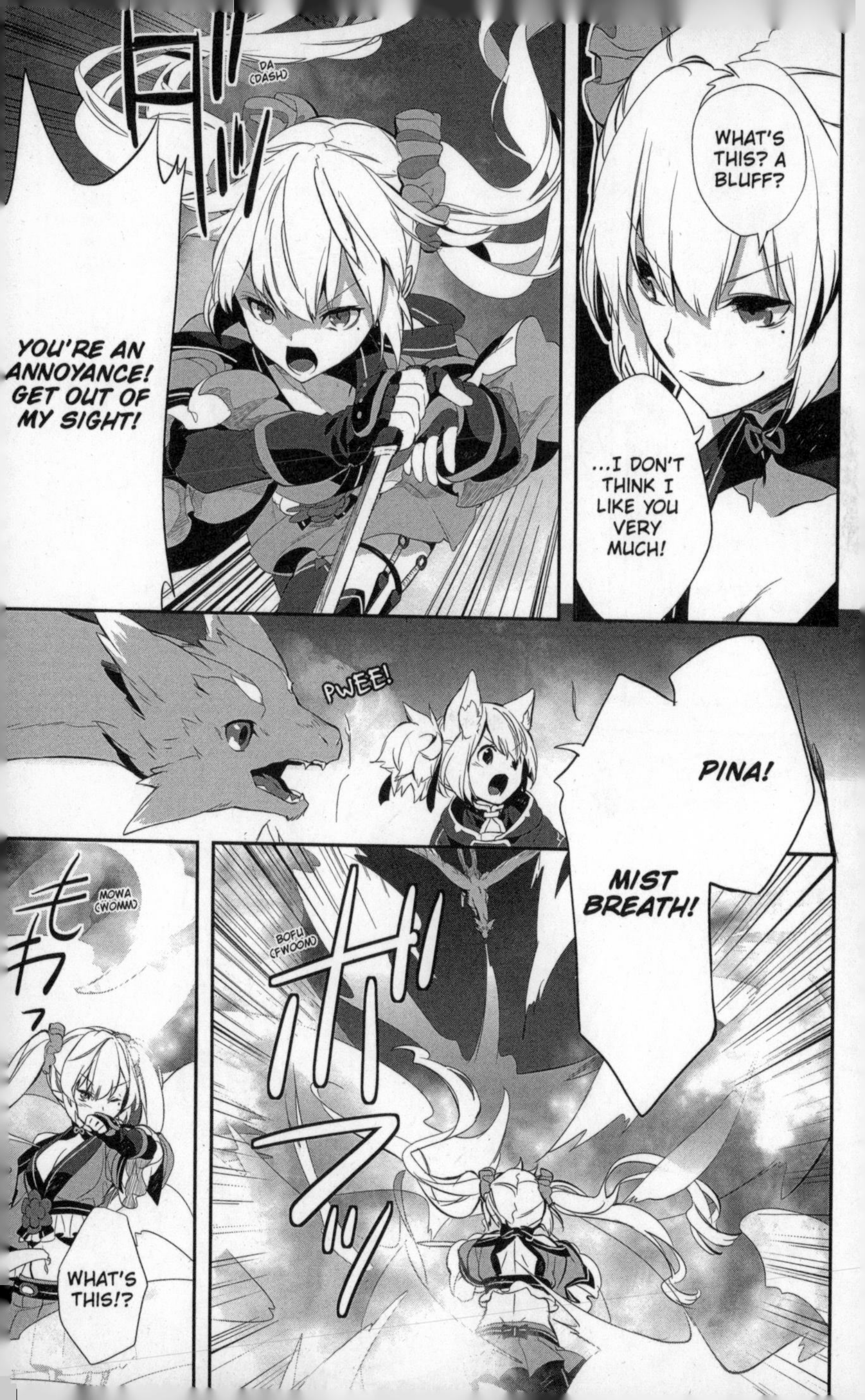
WHAT'S THIS? A BLUFF?
...I DON'T THINK I LIKE YOU VERY MUCH!
DA (DASH)
YOU'RE AN ANNOYANCE! GET OUT OF MY SIGHT!
PINA!
MIST BREATH!
PWEE!
BOFU (FWOOM)
MOWA (WOMM)
WHAT'S THIS!?

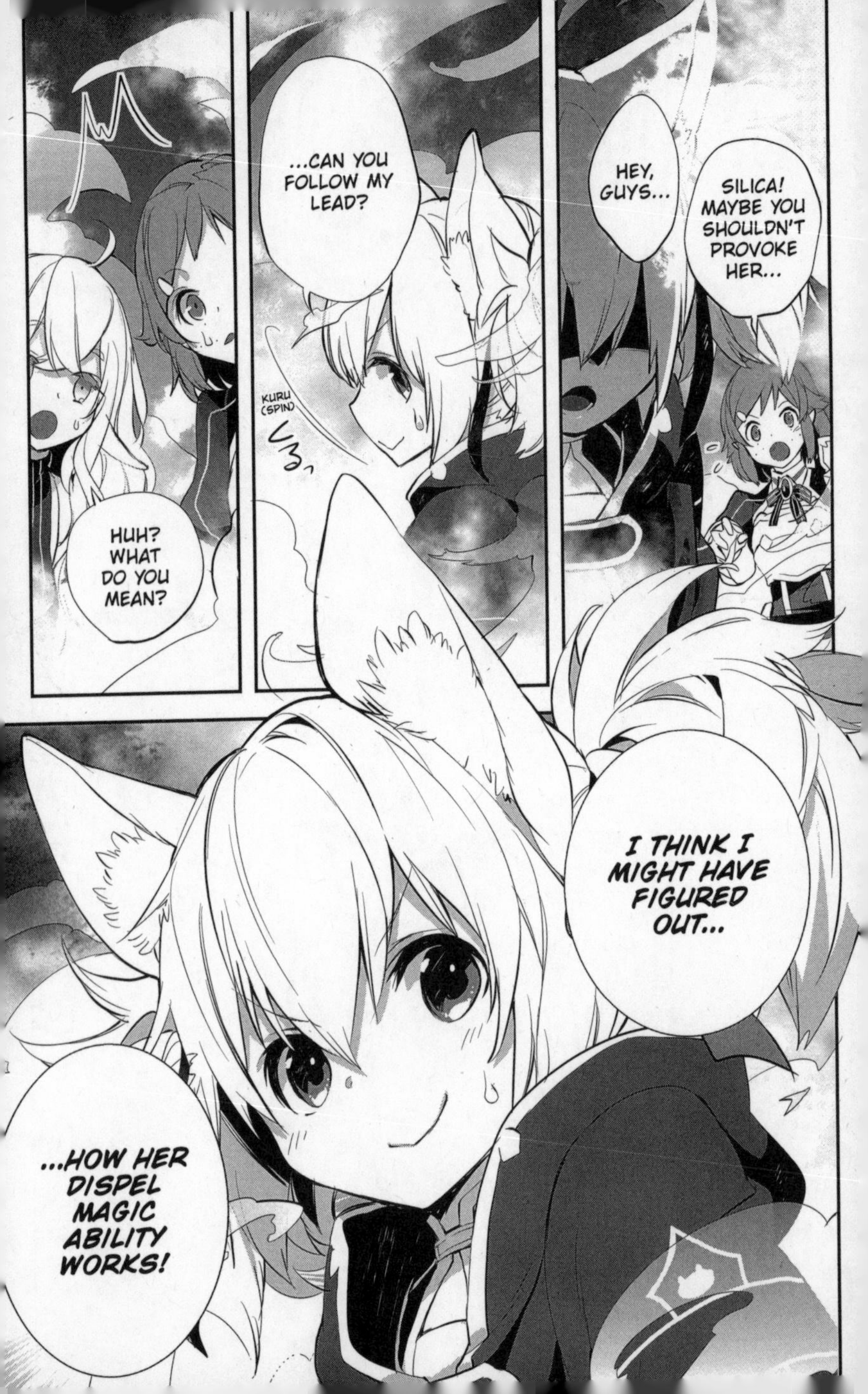
SILICA! MAYBE YOU SHOULDN'T PROVOKE HER...
HEY, GUYS...
...CAN YOU FOLLOW MY LEAD?
KURU (SPIN)
HUH? WHAT DO YOU MEAN?
I THINK I MIGHT HAVE FIGURED OUT...
...HOW HER DISPEL MAGIC ABILITY WORKS!

Sword Art Online
GIRLS' OPS

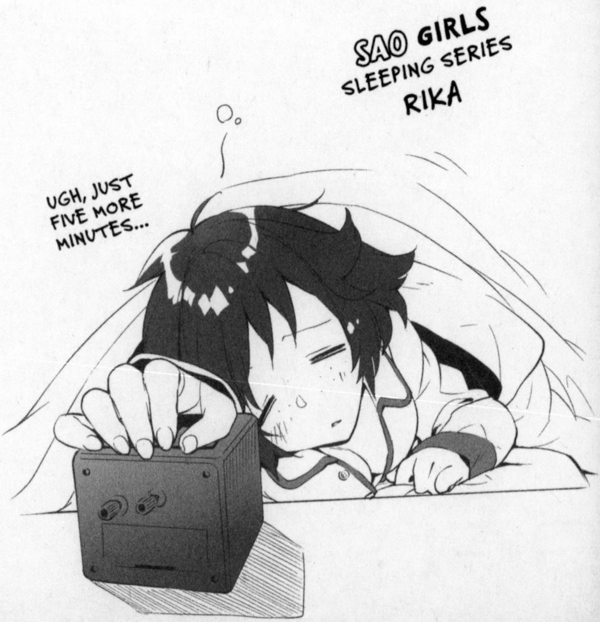
SAO GIRLS
SLEEPING SERIES
RIKA
UGH, JUST
FIVE MORE
MINUTES...

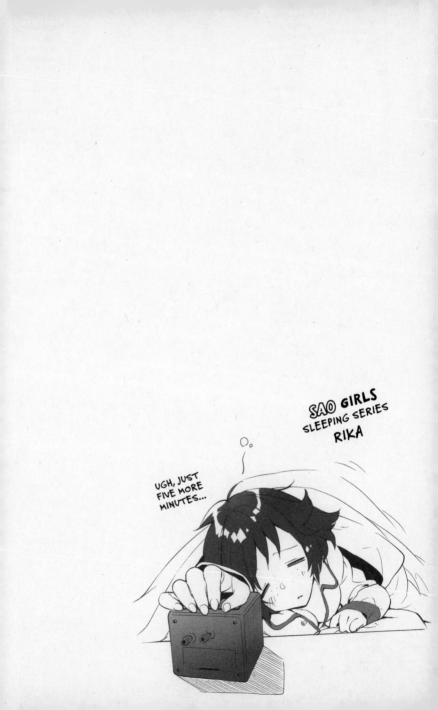

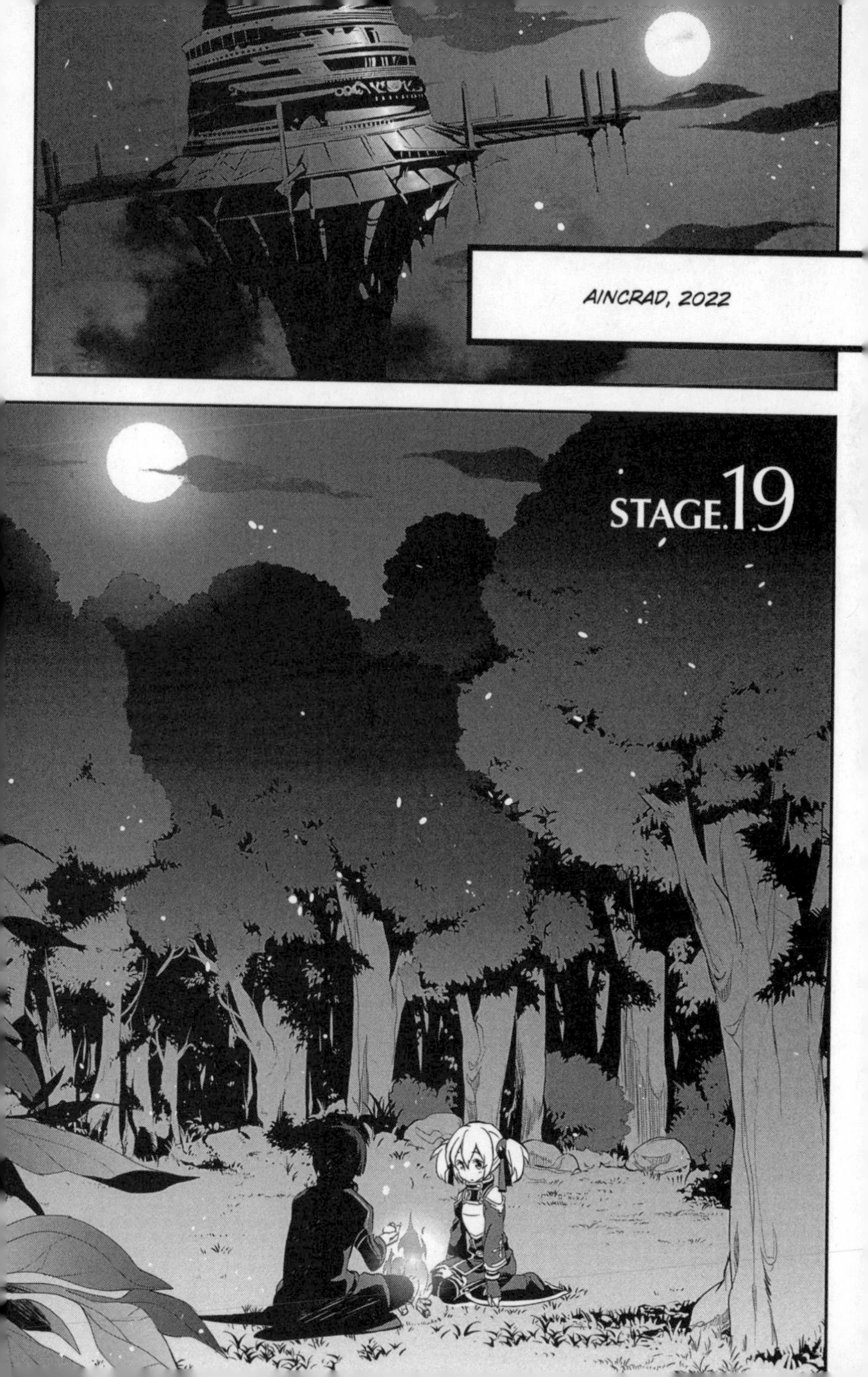
AINCRAD, 2022
STAGE.19

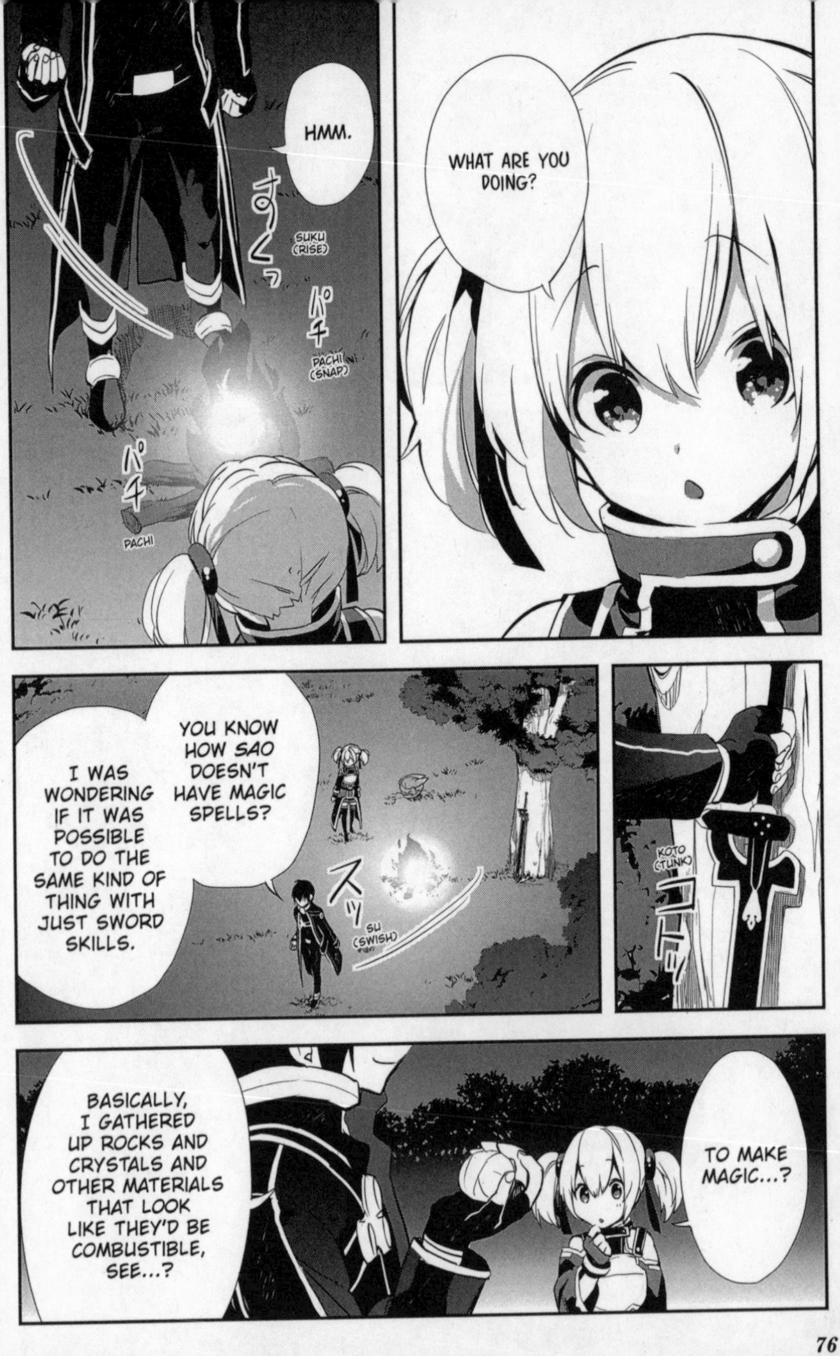
WHAT ARE YOU DOING?
HMM.
すくっ
SUKU (RISE)
パチ
PACHI (SNAP)
パチ
PACHI
コトッ
KOTO (TUNK)
YOU KNOW HOW SAO DOESN'T HAVE MAGIC SPELLS?
I WAS WONDERING IF IT WAS POSSIBLE TO DO THE SAME KIND OF THING WITH JUST SWORD SKILLS.
スッ
SU (SWISH)
TO MAKE MAGIC...?
BASICALLY, I GATHERED UP ROCKS AND CRYSTALS AND OTHER MATERIALS THAT LOOK LIKE THEY'D BE COMBUSTIBLE, SEE...?

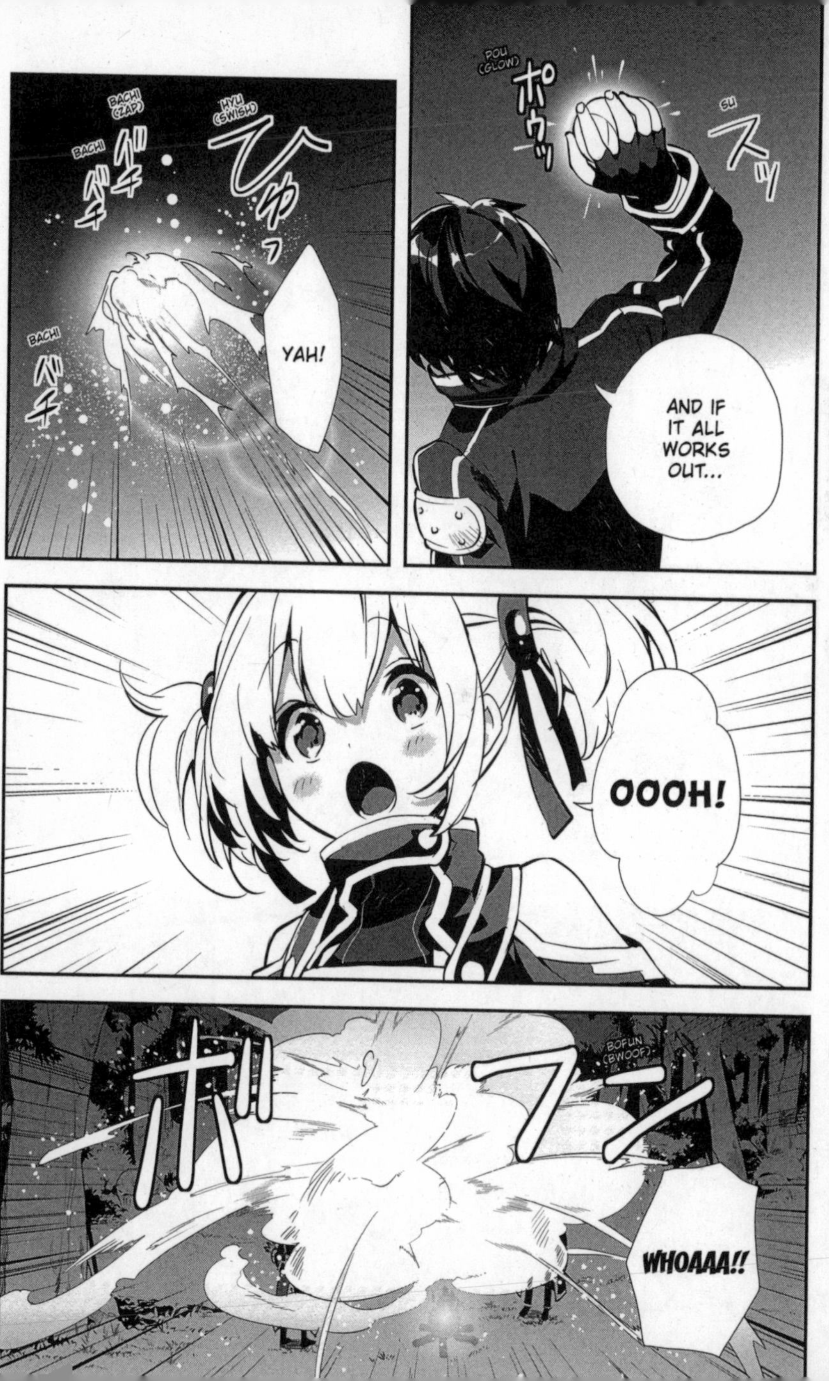
POU (GLOW)
ポウッ
SU
スッ
AND IF IT ALL WORKS OUT...
HYU (SWISH)
ひゅっ
BACHI (ZAP)
バチ
BACHI
バチ
YAH!
BACHI
バチ
OOOH!
BOFUN (BWOOF)
ボフン
WHOAAA!!

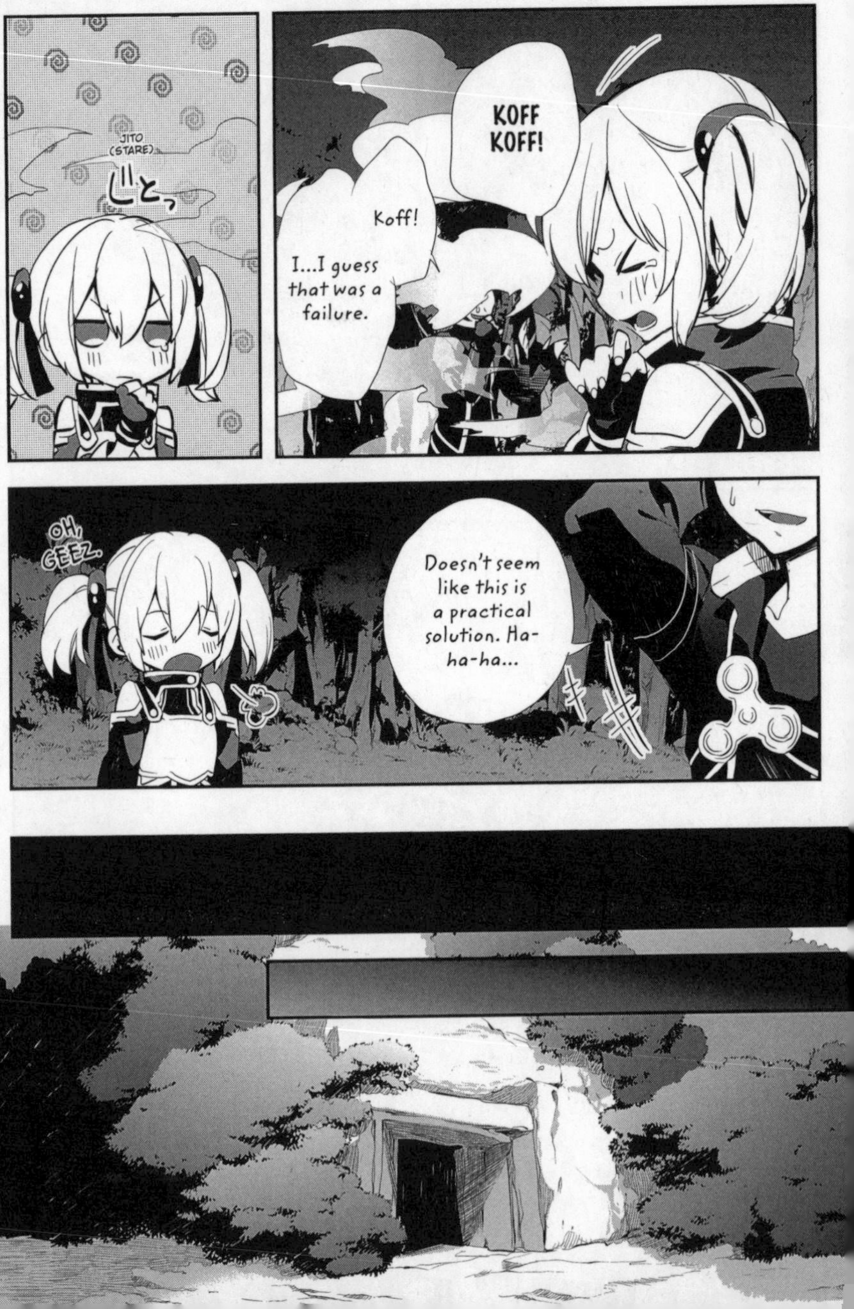
KOFF KOFF!
Koff!
I...I guess that was a failure.
JITO (STARE)
じとっ
Doesn't seem like this is a practical solution. Ha-ha-ha...
OH, GEEZ.

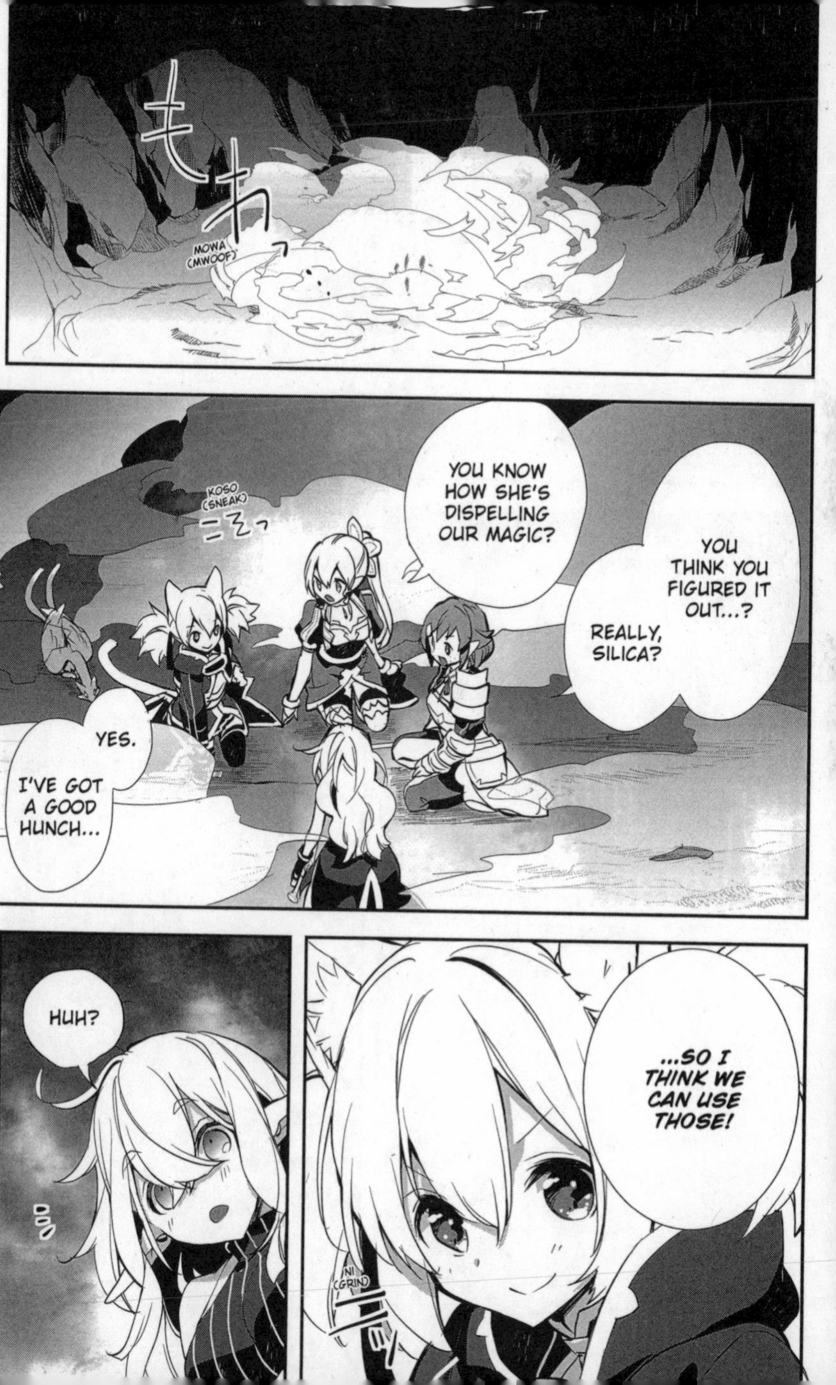

MOWA (MWOOF)
KOSO (SNEAK)
YOU KNOW HOW SHE'S DISPELLING OUR MAGIC?
YOU THINK YOU FIGURED IT OUT...? REALLY, SILICA?
YES. I'VE GOT A GOOD HUNCH...
...SO I THINK WE CAN USE THOSE!
NI (GRIN)
HUH?

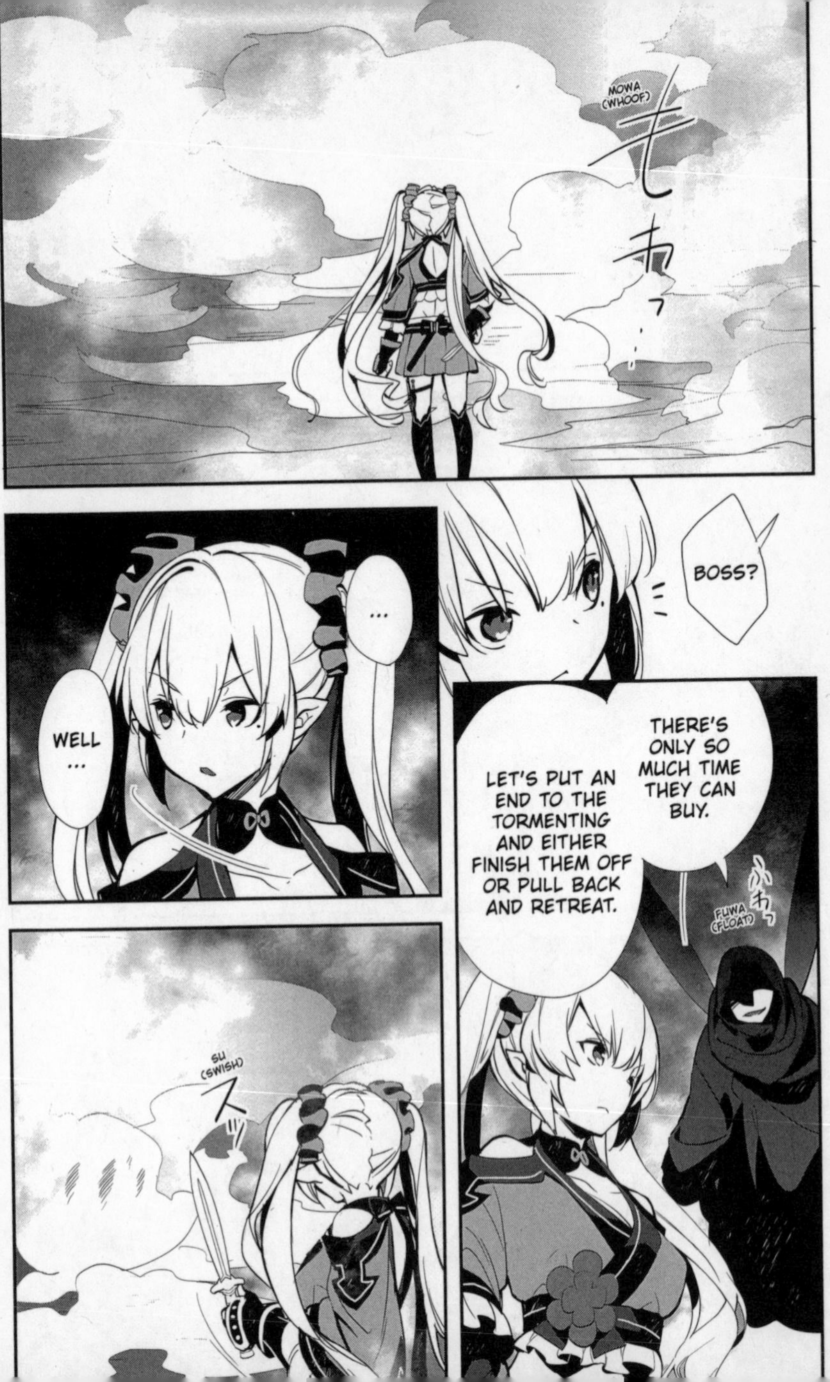
MOWA (WHOOF)
BOSS?
...
WELL ...
THERE'S ONLY SO MUCH TIME THEY CAN BUY.
LET'S PUT AN END TO THE TORMENTING AND EITHER FINISH THEM OFF OR PULL BACK AND RETREAT.
FUWA (FLOAT)
SU (SWISH)

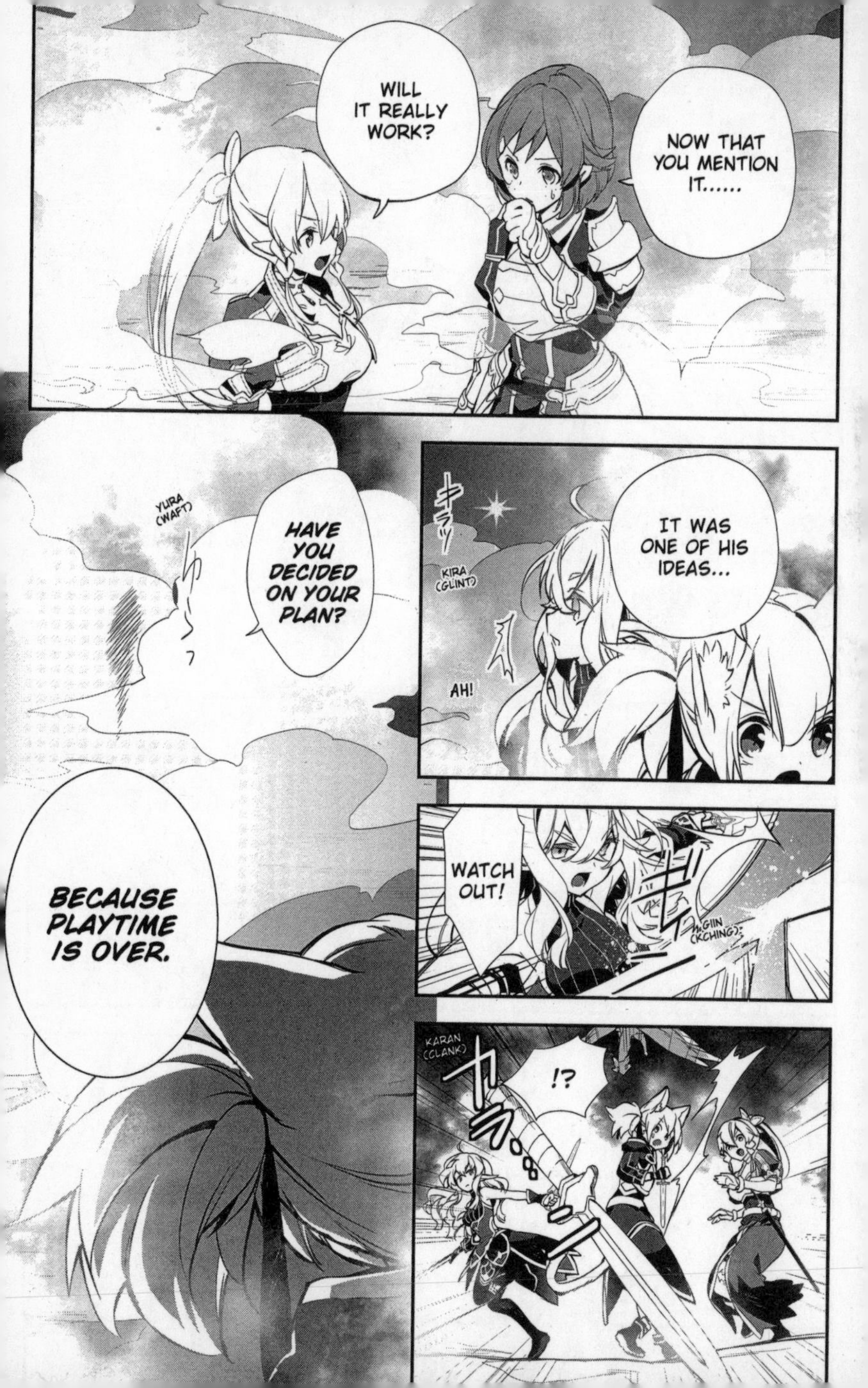
NOW THAT YOU MENTION IT......
WILL IT REALLY WORK?
IT WAS ONE OF HIS IDEAS...
KIRA (GLINT)
AH!
HAVE YOU DECIDED ON YOUR PLAN?
YURA (WAFT)
WATCH OUT!
GIIN (KCHING)
BECAUSE PLAYTIME IS OVER.
KARAN (CLANK)
!?

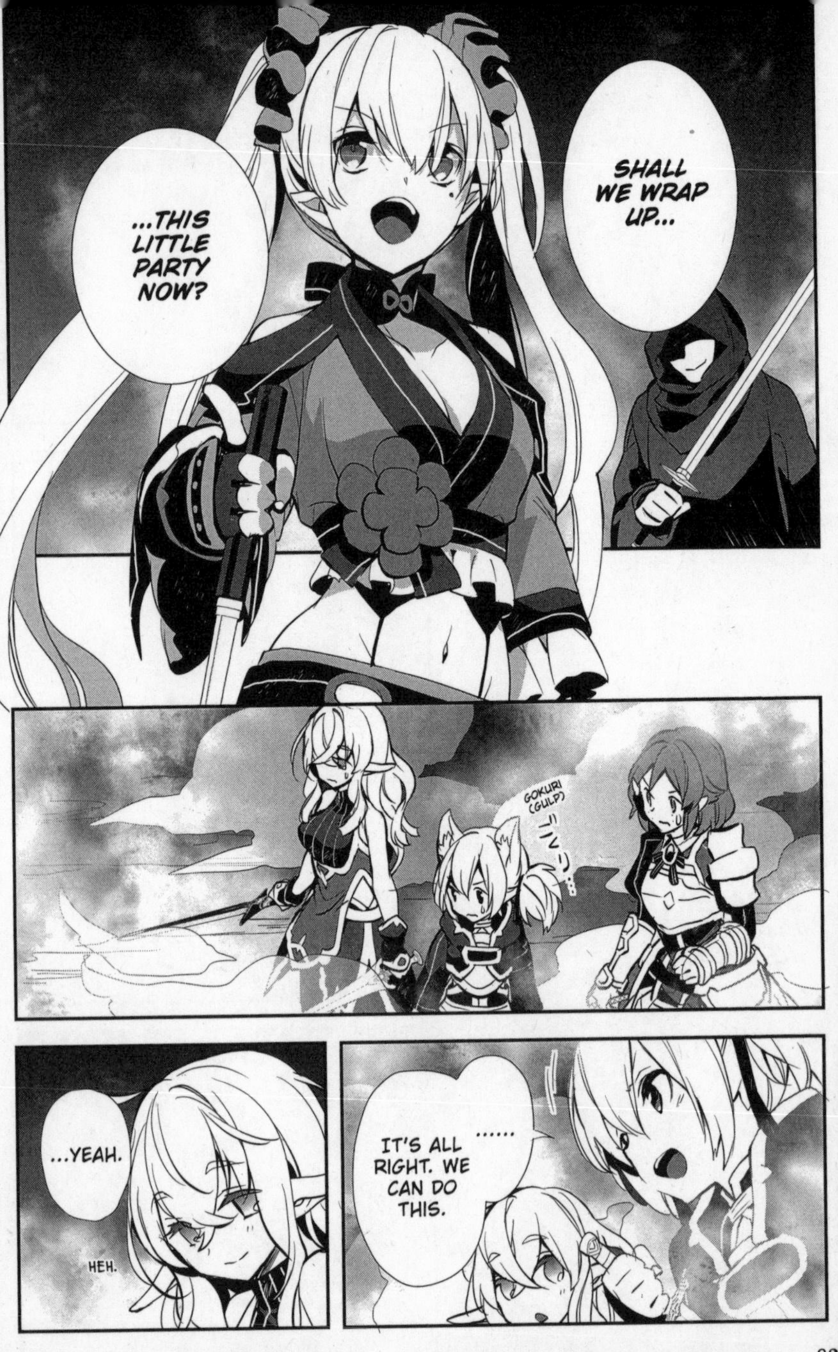
SHALL WE WRAP UP...
...THIS LITTLE PARTY NOW?
GOKURI (GULP)
......
IT'S ALL RIGHT. WE CAN DO THIS.
...YEAH.
HEH.

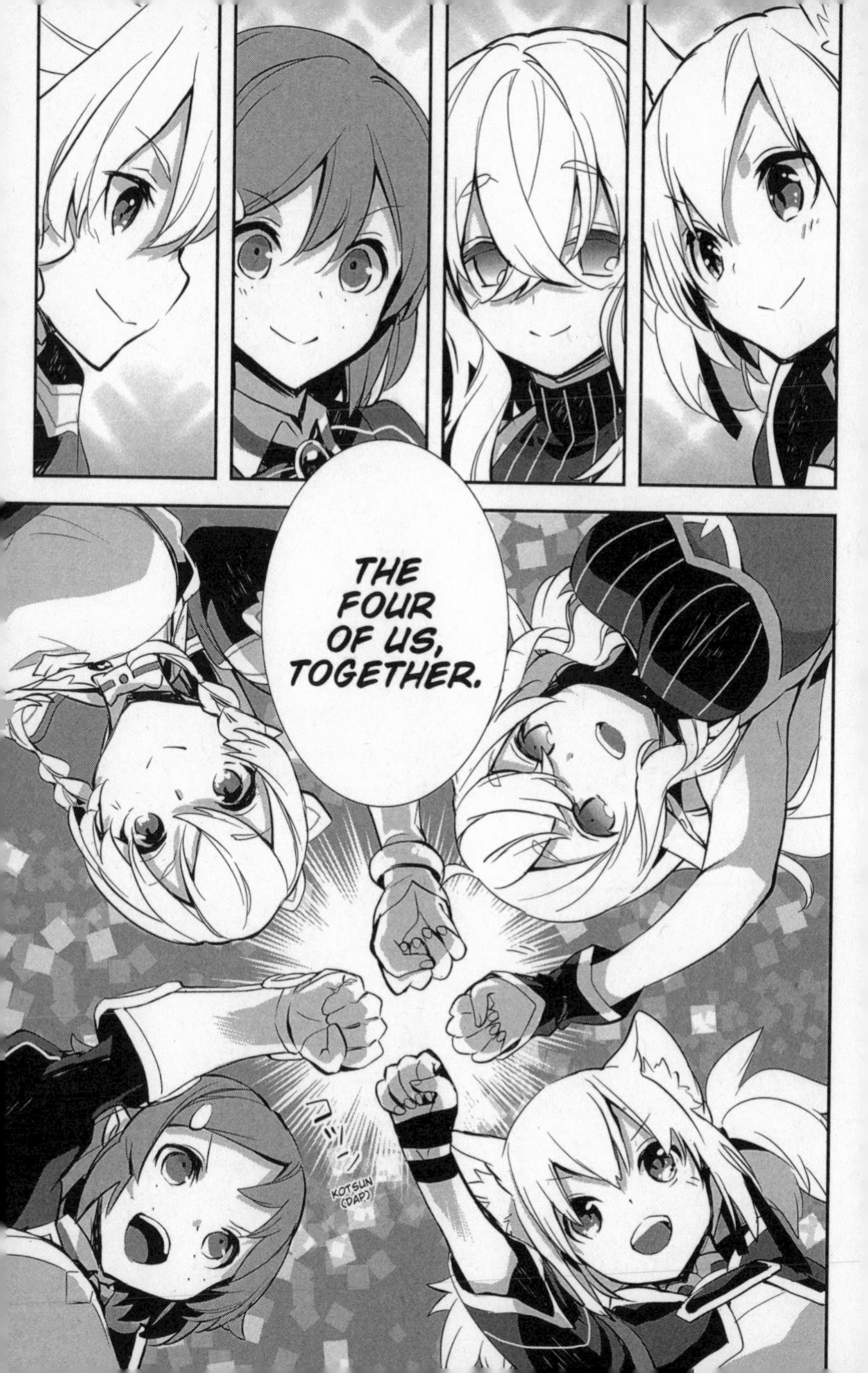
THE FOUR OF US, TOGETHER.
KOTSUN (DAP)

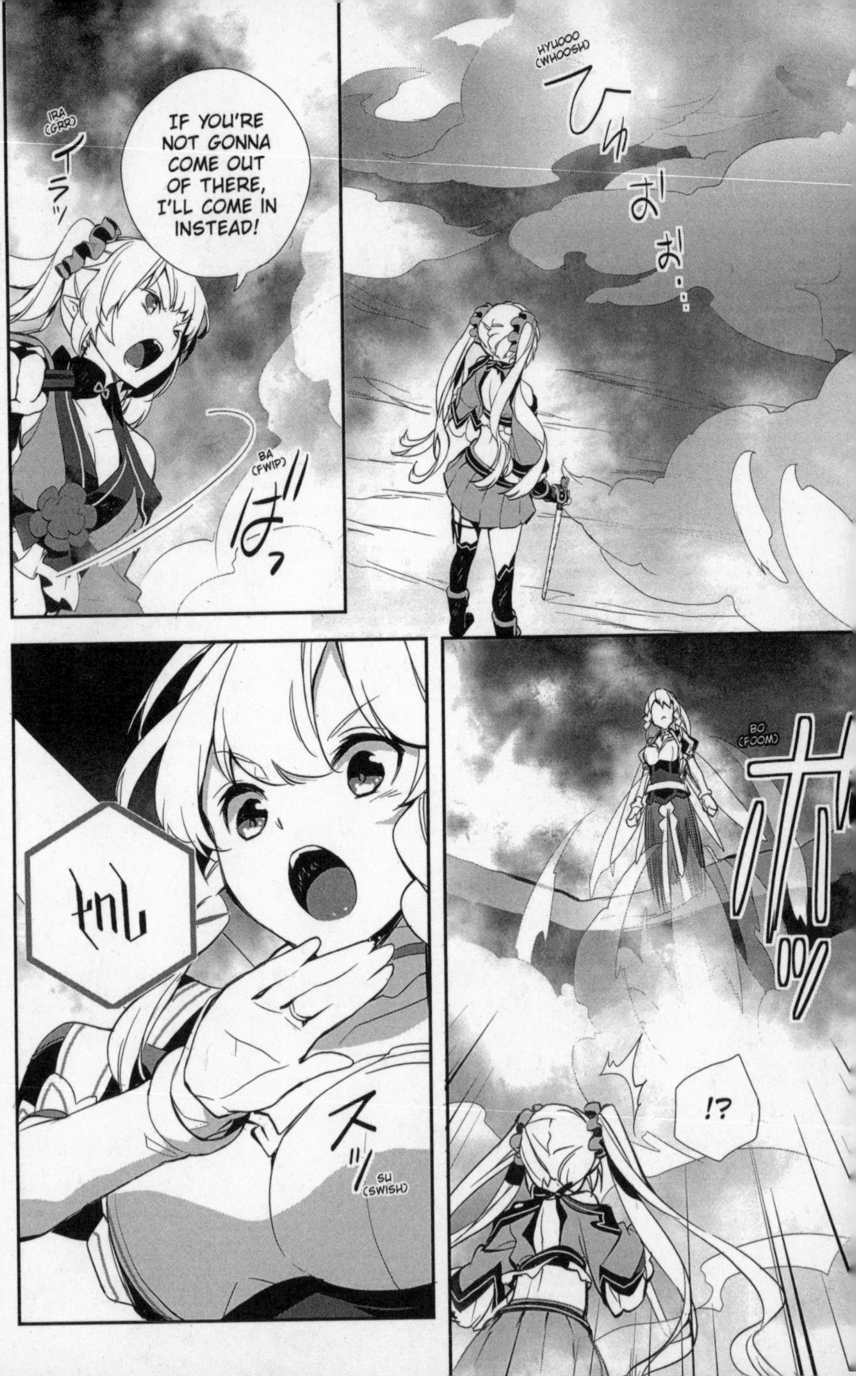

HYUOOO (WHOOSH)
IRA (GRR)
IF YOU'RE NOT GONNA COME OUT OF THERE, I'LL COME IN INSTEAD!
BA (FWIP)
BO (FOOM)
!?
SU (SWISH)

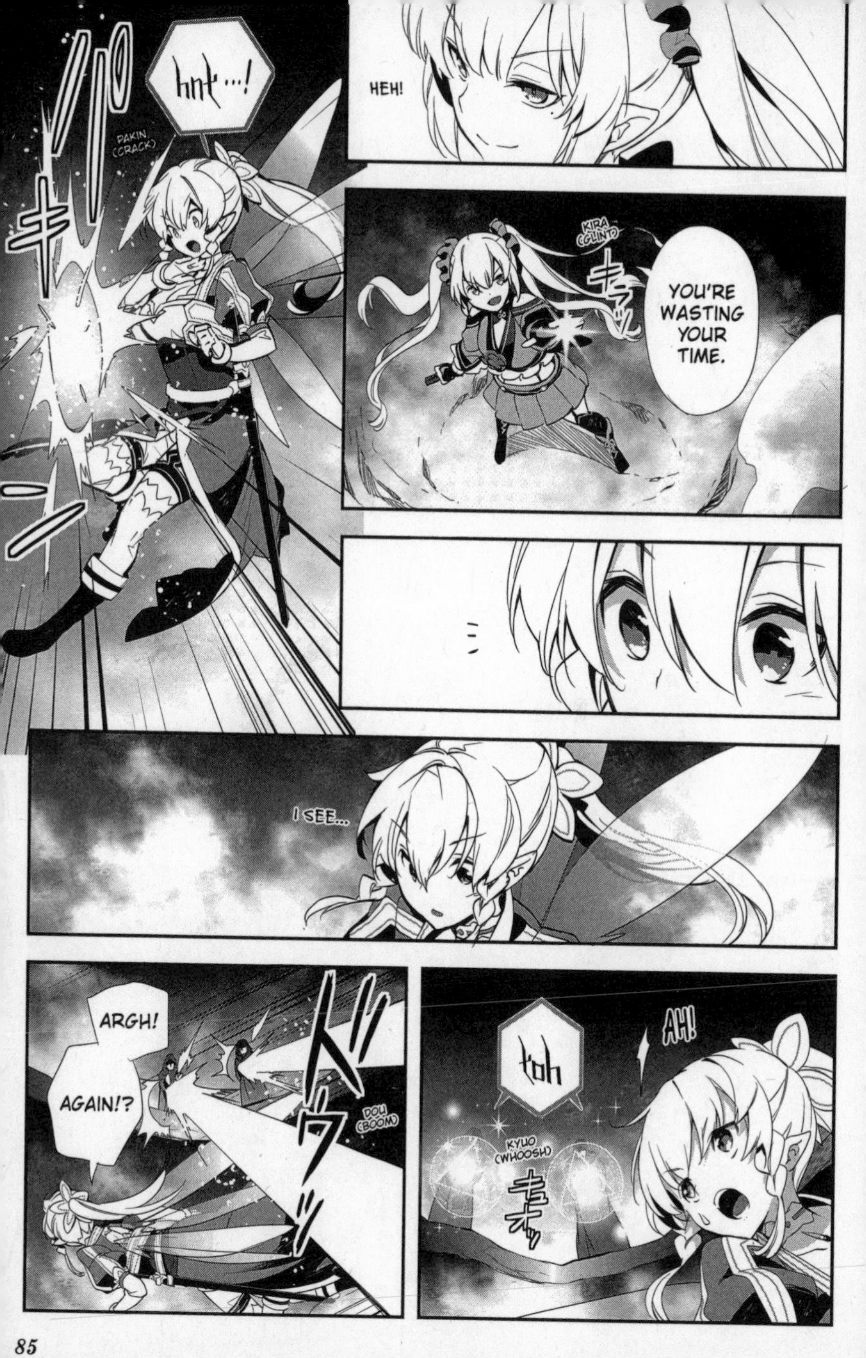
HEH!
hnk...!
PAKIN (CRACK)
KIRA (GLINT)
YOU'RE WASTING YOUR TIME.
I SEE...
AH!
toh
KYUO (WHOOSH)
ARGH!
AGAIN!?
DOU (BOOM)

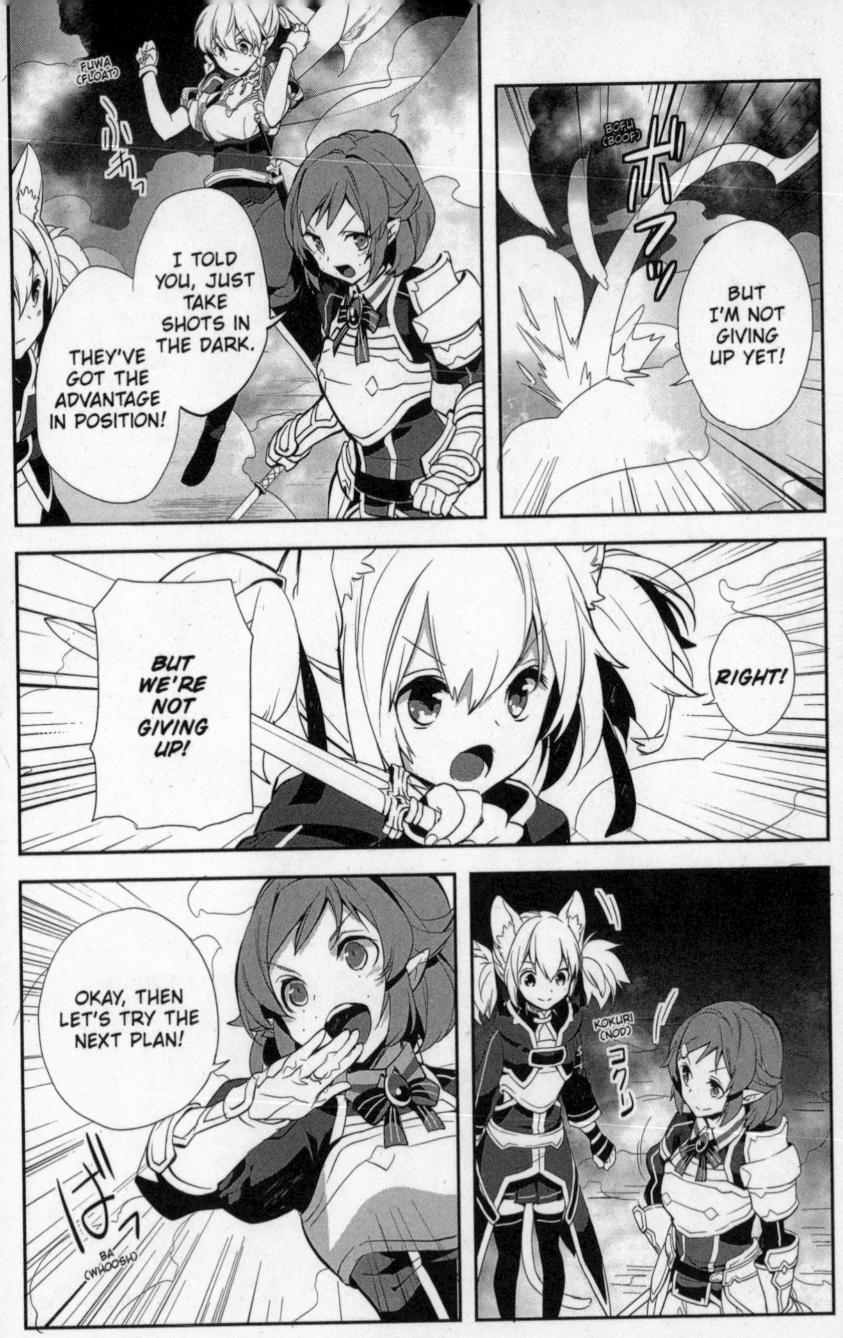
BOFU (BOOF)
BUT I'M NOT GIVING UP YET!
FUWA (FLOAT)
I TOLD YOU, JUST TAKE SHOTS IN THE DARK.
THEY'VE GOT THE ADVANTAGE IN POSITION!
RIGHT!
BUT WE'RE NOT GIVING UP!
KOKURI (NOD)
OKAY, THEN LET'S TRY THE NEXT PLAN!
BA (WHOOSH)

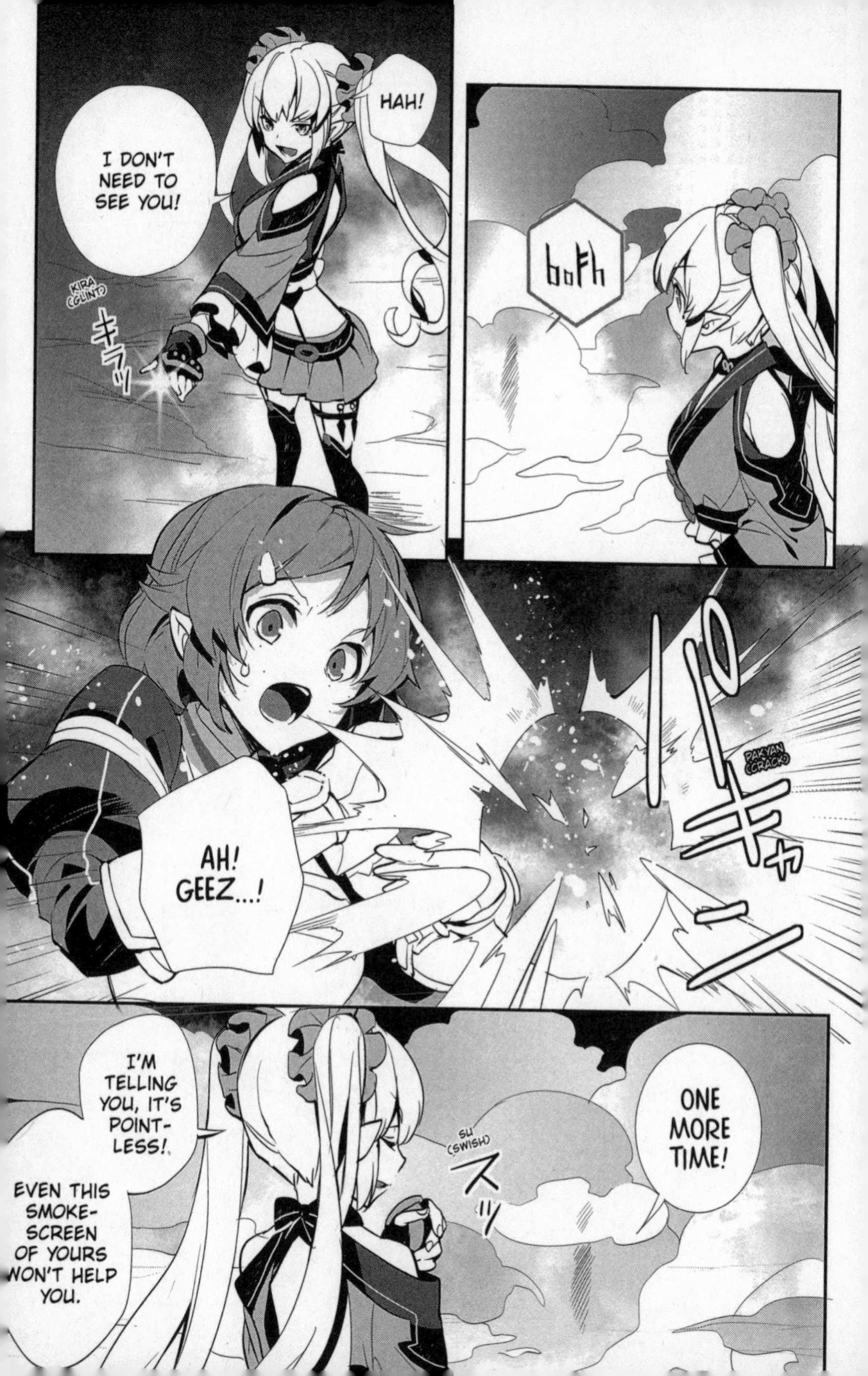
HAH!
I DON'T NEED TO SEE YOU!
KIRA (GLINT)
キラッ
boFh
パキャーン
PAKYAN (CRACK)
AH! GEEZ...!
ONE MORE TIME!
SU (SWISH)
スッ
I'M TELLING YOU, IT'S POINT-LESS!
EVEN THIS SMOKE-SCREEN OF YOURS WON'T HELP YOU.

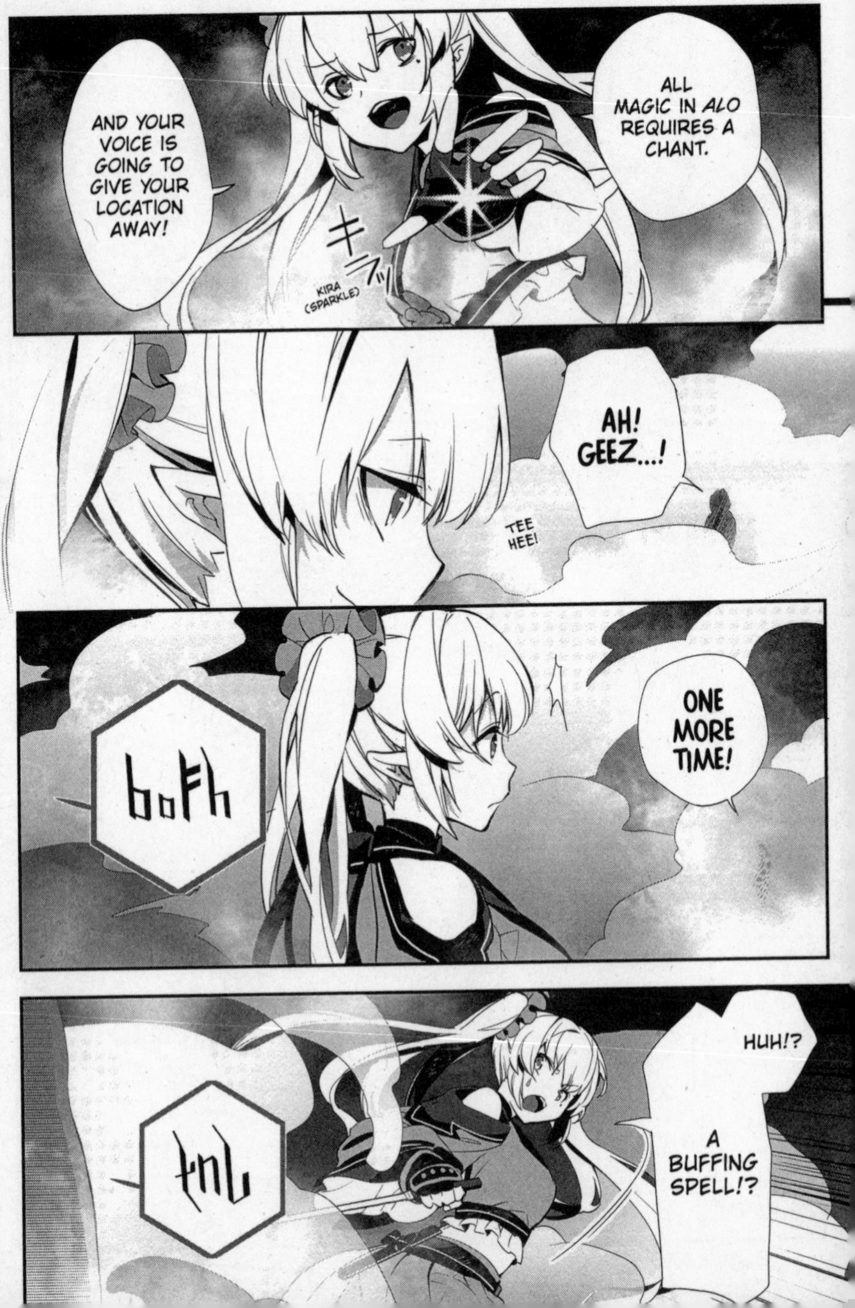
ALL MAGIC IN ALO REQUIRES A CHANT.
AND YOUR VOICE IS GOING TO GIVE YOUR LOCATION AWAY!
KIRA (SPARKLE)
AH! GEEZ...!
TEE HEE!
ONE MORE TIME!
HUH!?
A BUFFING SPELL!?

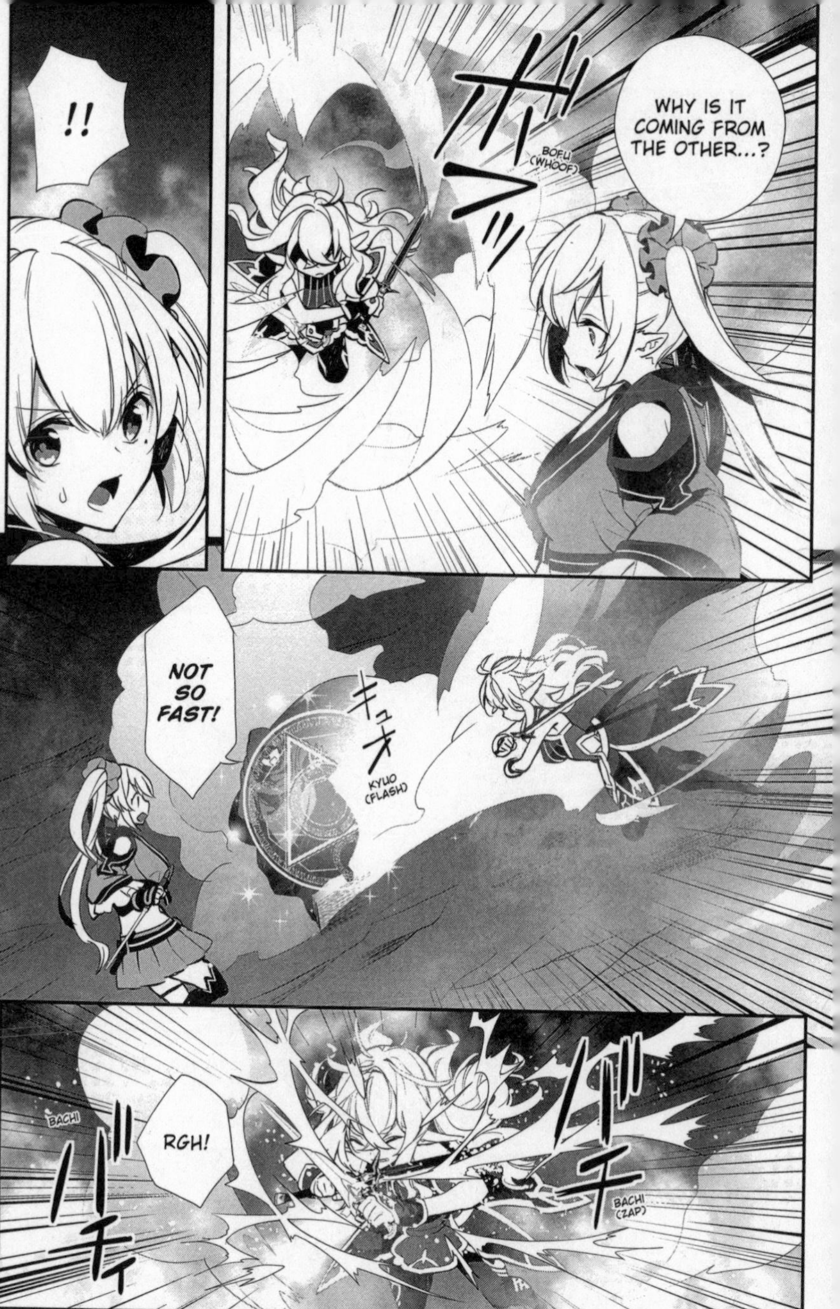
WHY IS IT COMING FROM THE OTHER...?
BOFU (WHOOF)
!!
NOT SO FAST!
KYUO (FLASH)
BACHI (ZAP)
BACHI
RGH!

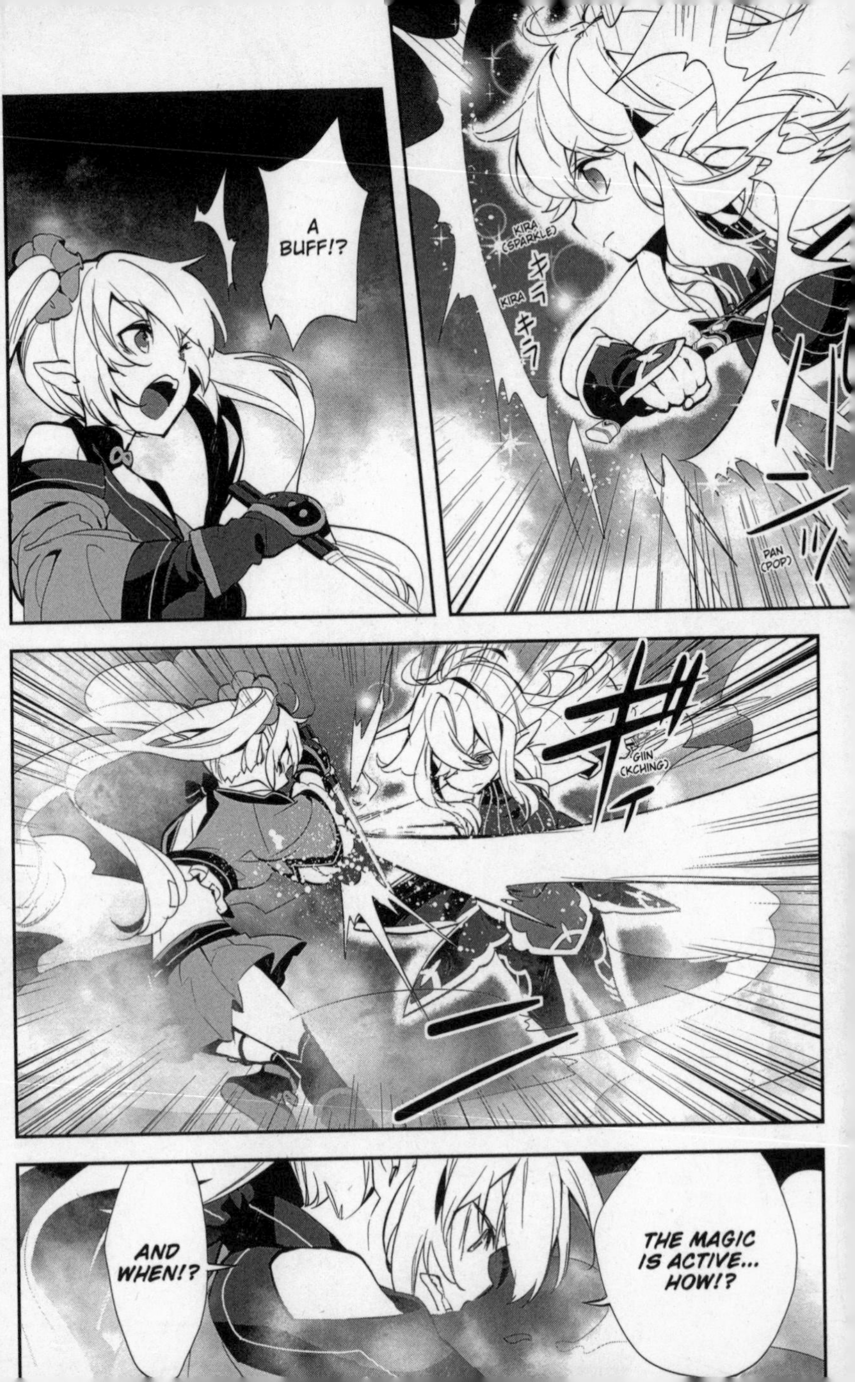
KIRA (SPARKLE)
キラ
KIRA
キラ
PAN (POP)
A BUFF!?
GIIN (KCHING)
THE MAGIC IS ACTIVE... HOW!?
AND WHEN!?

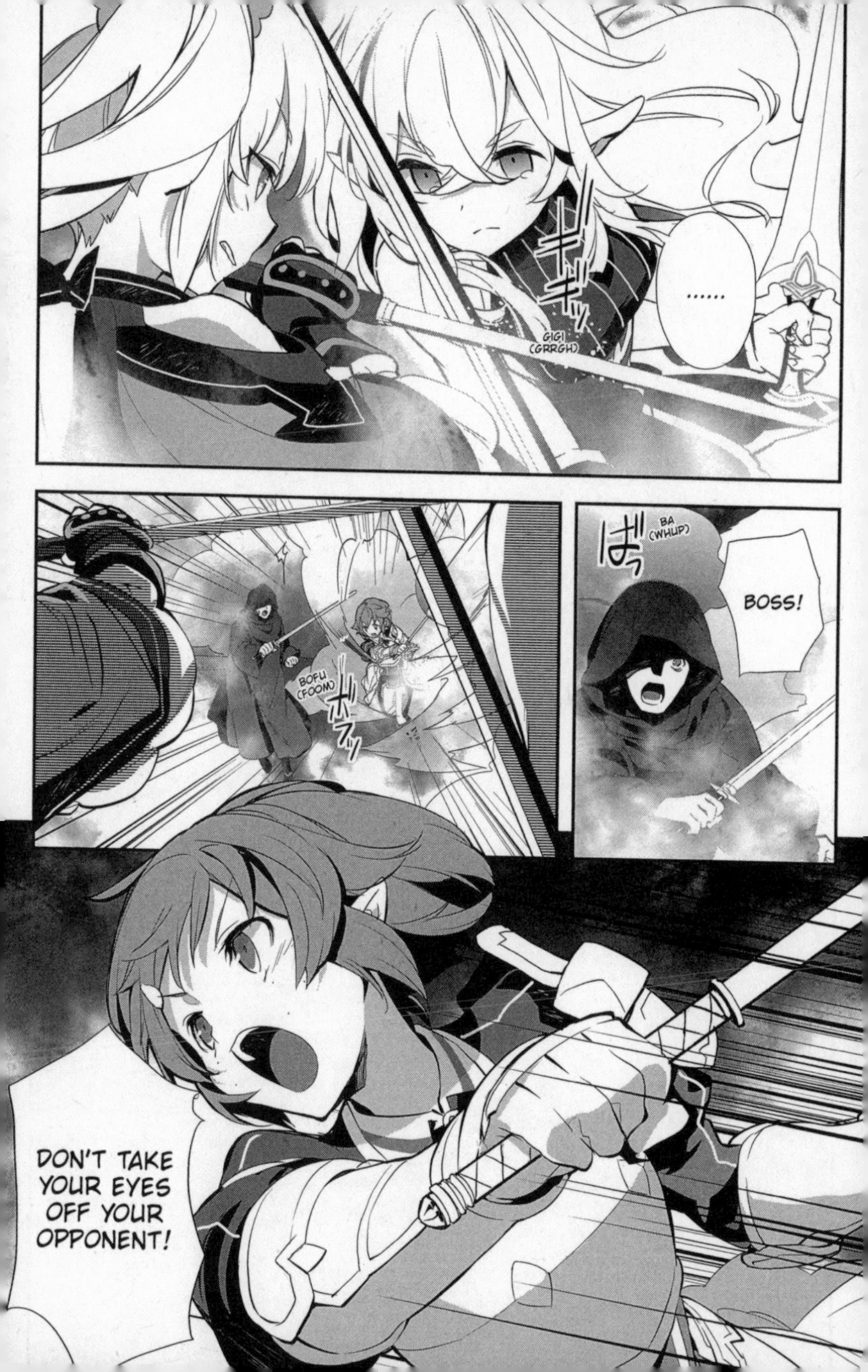
......
GIGI (GRRGH)
BA (WHUP)
BOSS!
BOFU (FOOM)
DON'T TAKE YOUR EYES OFF YOUR OPPONENT!

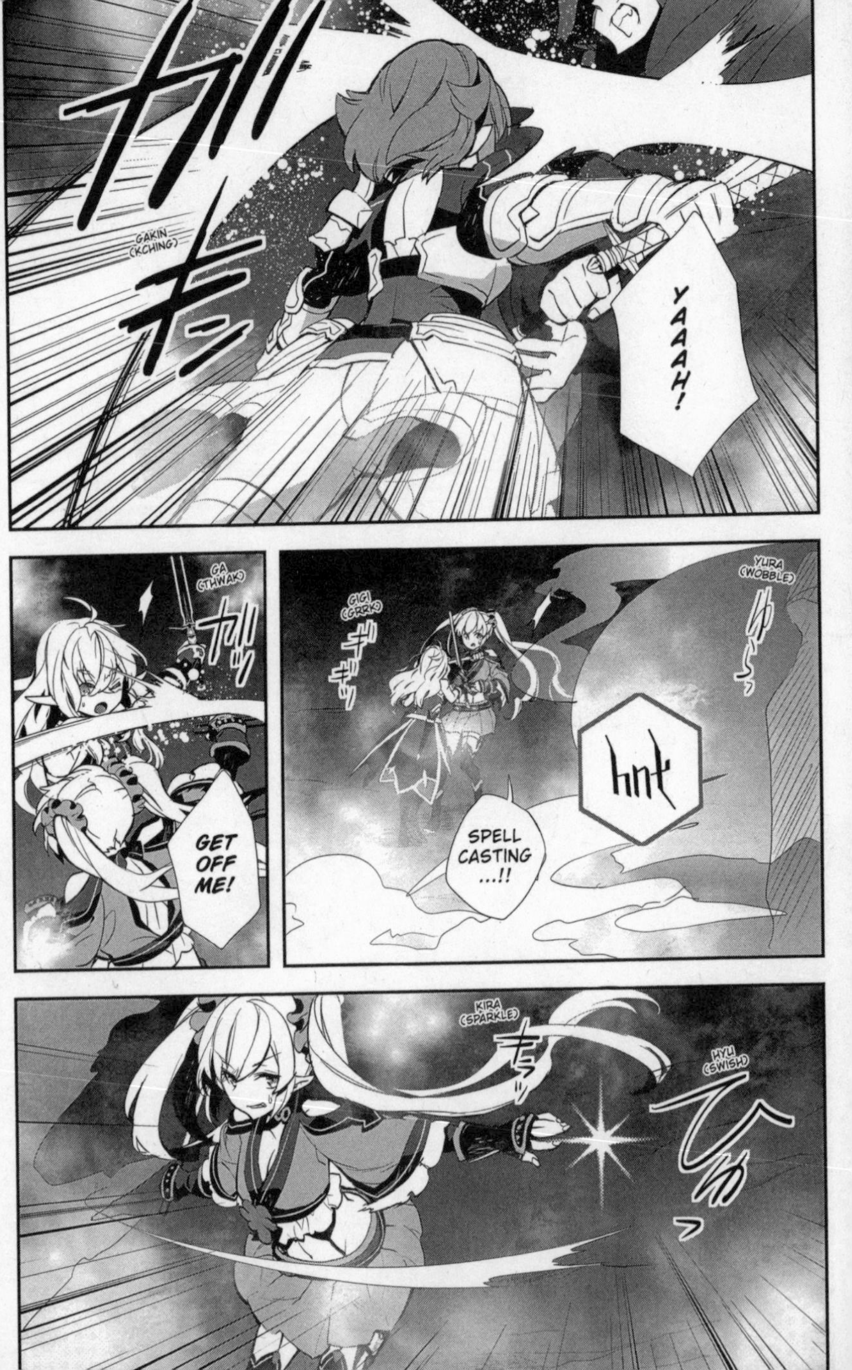

GAKIN (KCHING)
YAAAH!
YURA (WOBBLE)
SPELL CASTING ...!!
GIGI (GRRK)
GA (THWAK)
GET OFF ME!
HYU (SWISH)
KIRA (SPARKLE)

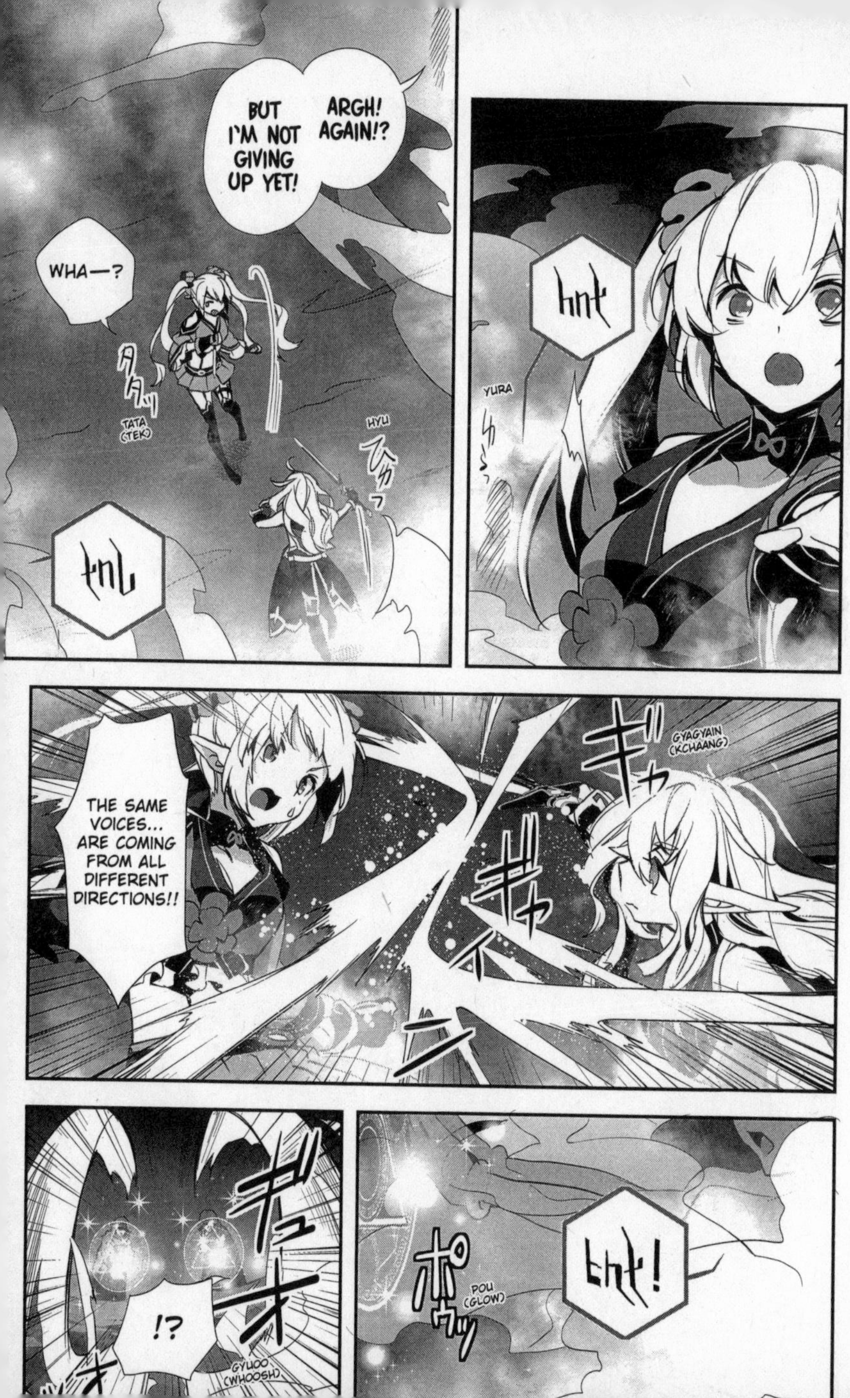

YURA
ARGH! AGAIN!?
BUT I'M NOT GIVING UP YET!
WHA—?
TATA (TEK)
HYU
GYAGYAIN (KCHAANG)
THE SAME VOICES... ARE COMING FROM ALL DIFFERENT DIRECTIONS!!
POU (GLOW)
!?
GYUOO (WHOOSH)

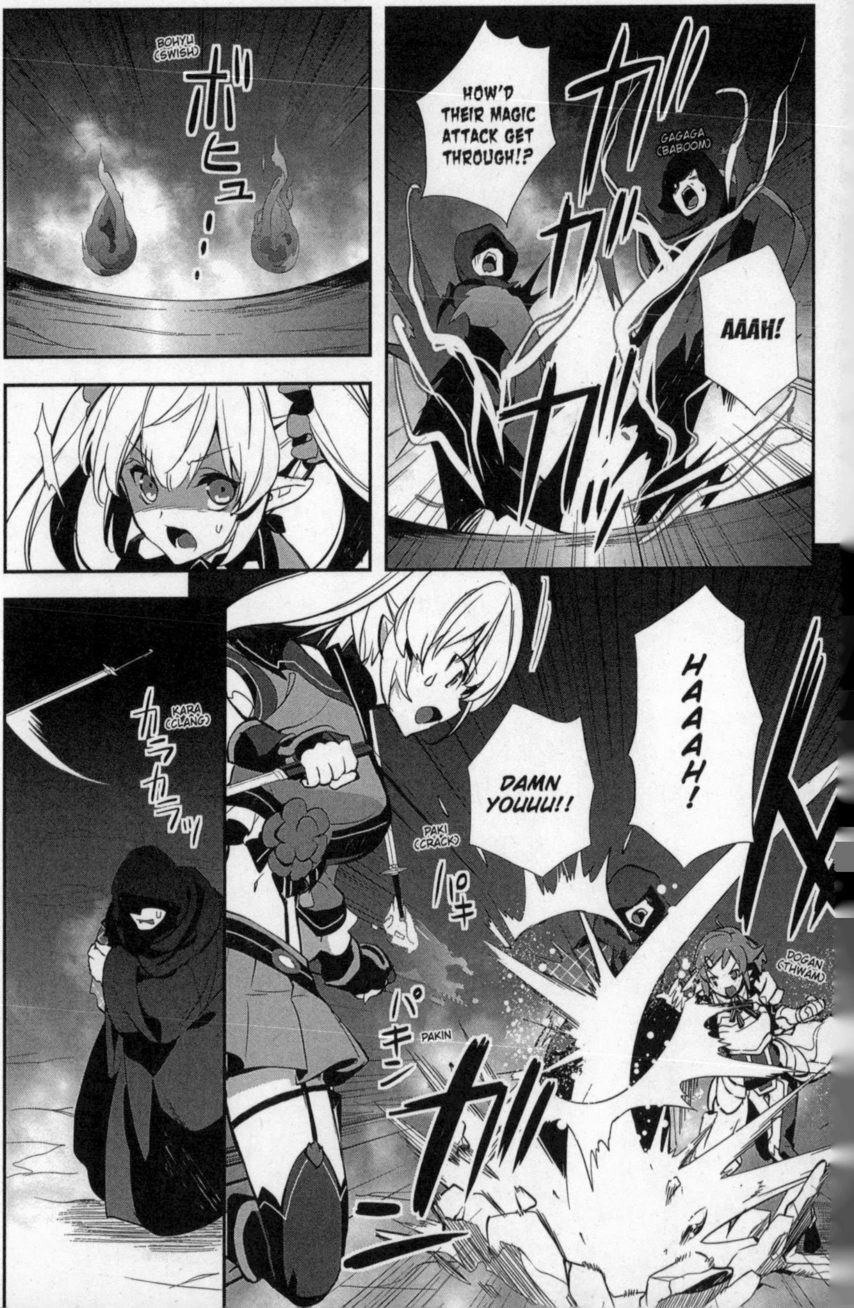
HOW'D THEIR MAGIC ATTACK GET THROUGH!?
GAGAGA (BABOOM)
AAAH!
BOHYU (SWISH)
HAAAAH!
DAMN YOUUUU!!
PAKI (CRACK)
DOGAN (THWAM)
PAKIN
KARA (CLANG)

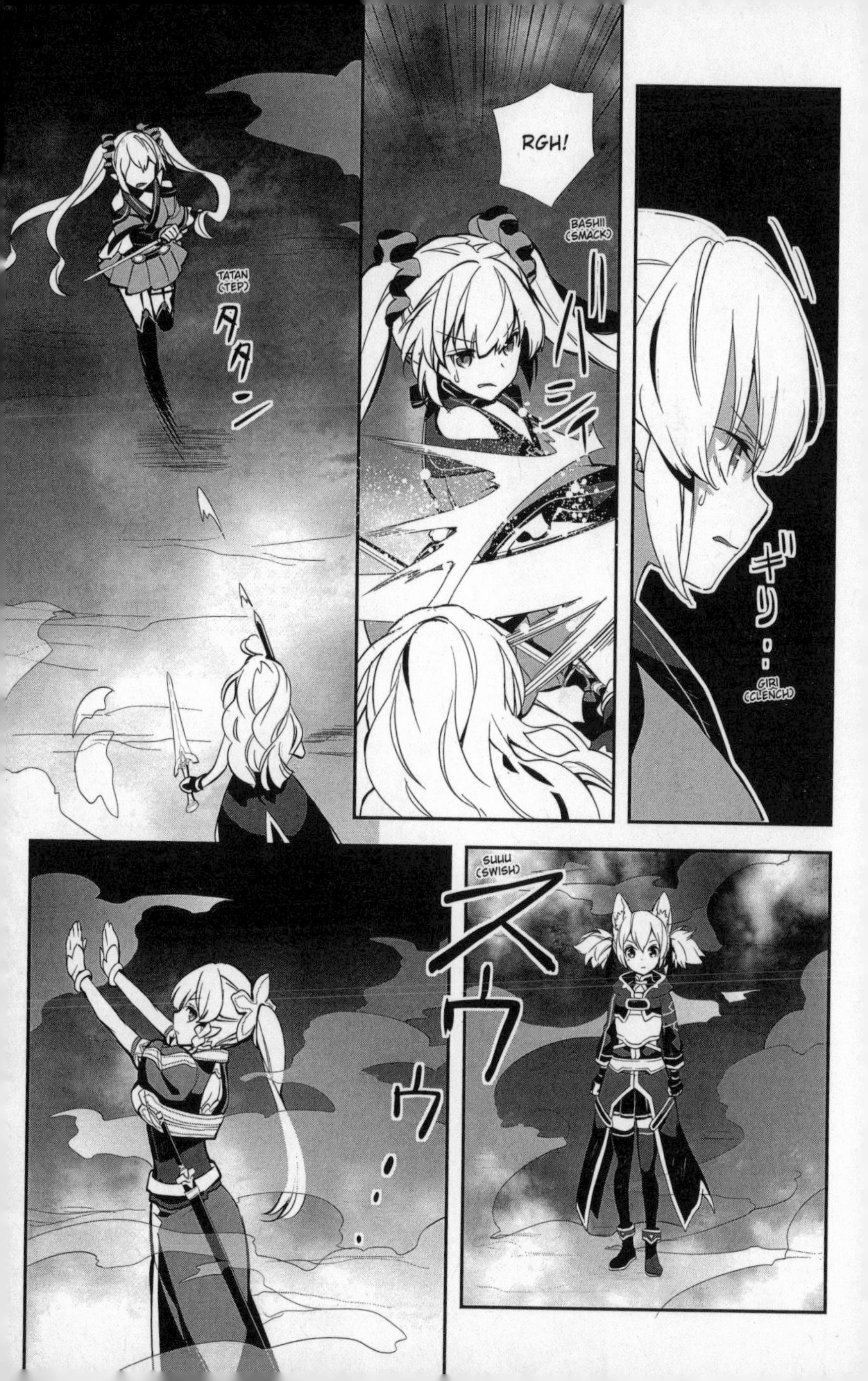
GIRI (CLENCH)
RGH!
BASHII (SMACK)
TATAN (TEP)
SUUU (SWISH)

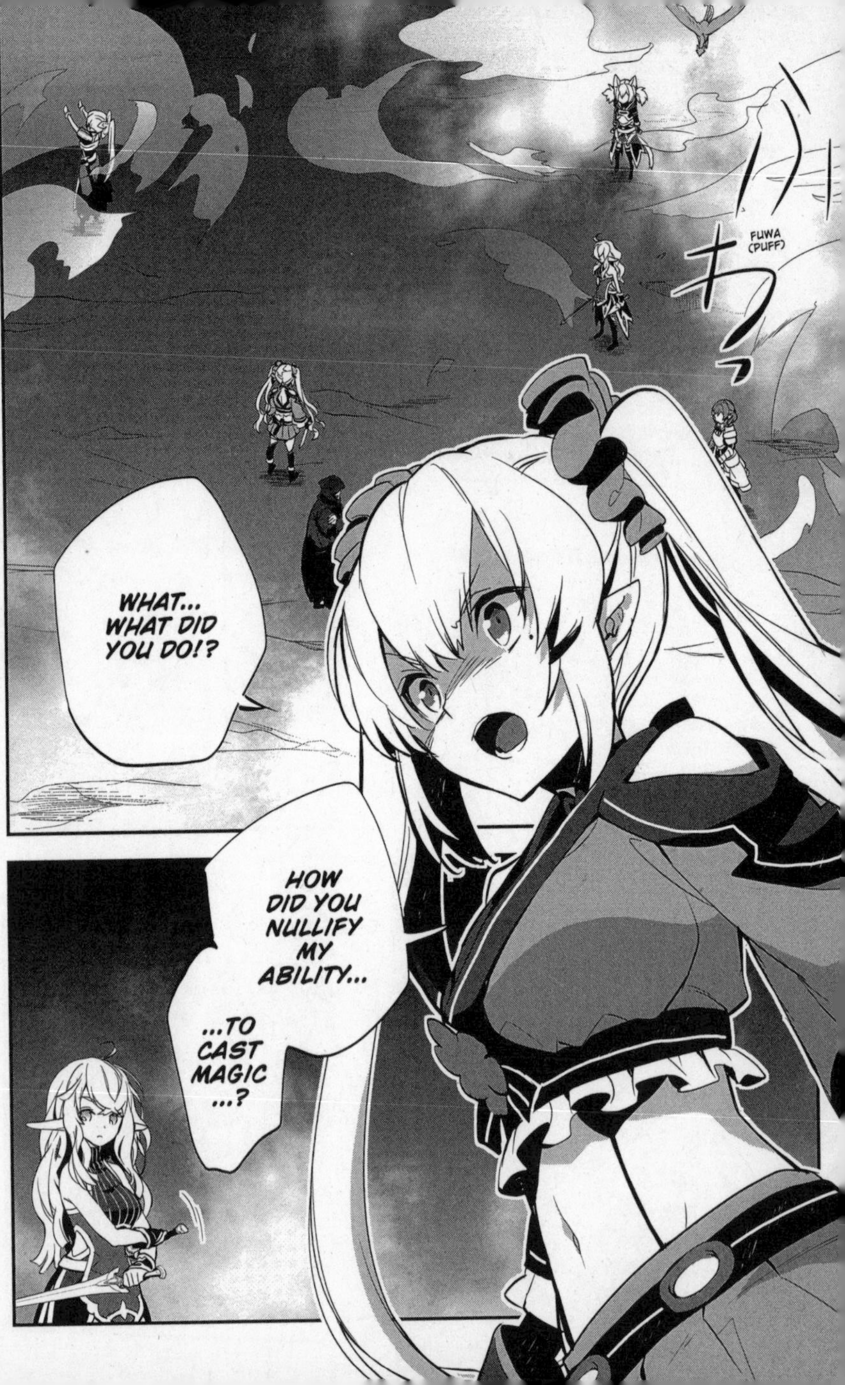
FUWA (PUFF)
WHAT... WHAT DID YOU DO!?
HOW DID YOU NULLIFY MY ABILITY...
...TO CAST MAGIC ...?

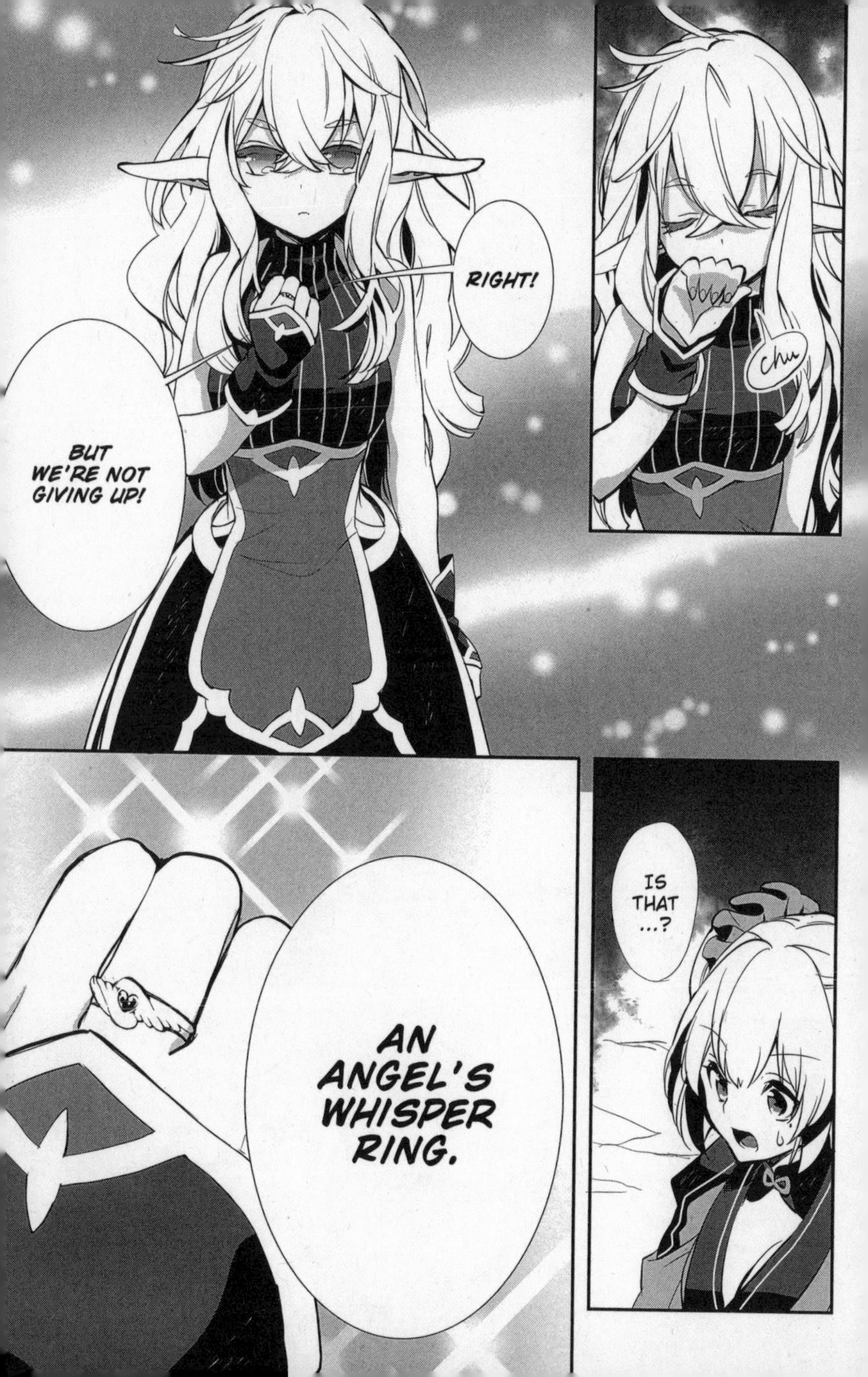
Chu
RIGHT!
BUT WE'RE NOT GIVING UP!
IS THAT ...?
AN ANGEL'S WHISPER RING.

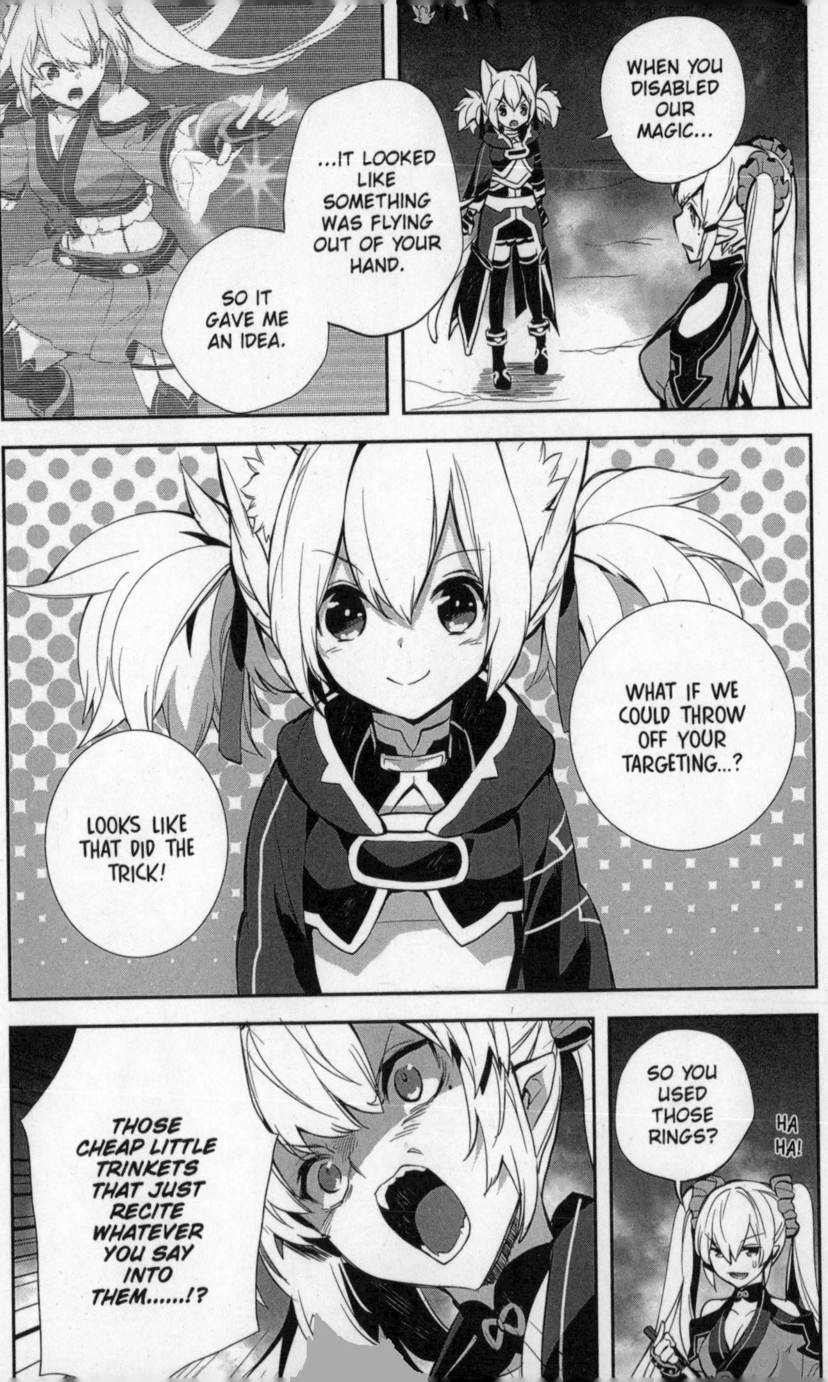
WHEN YOU DISABLED OUR MAGIC...
...IT LOOKED LIKE SOMETHING WAS FLYING OUT OF YOUR HAND.
SO IT GAVE ME AN IDEA.
WHAT IF WE COULD THROW OFF YOUR TARGETING...?
LOOKS LIKE THAT DID THE TRICK!
SO YOU USED THOSE RINGS?
HA HA!
THOSE CHEAP LITTLE TRINKETS THAT JUST RECITE WHATEVER YOU SAY INTO THEM......!?

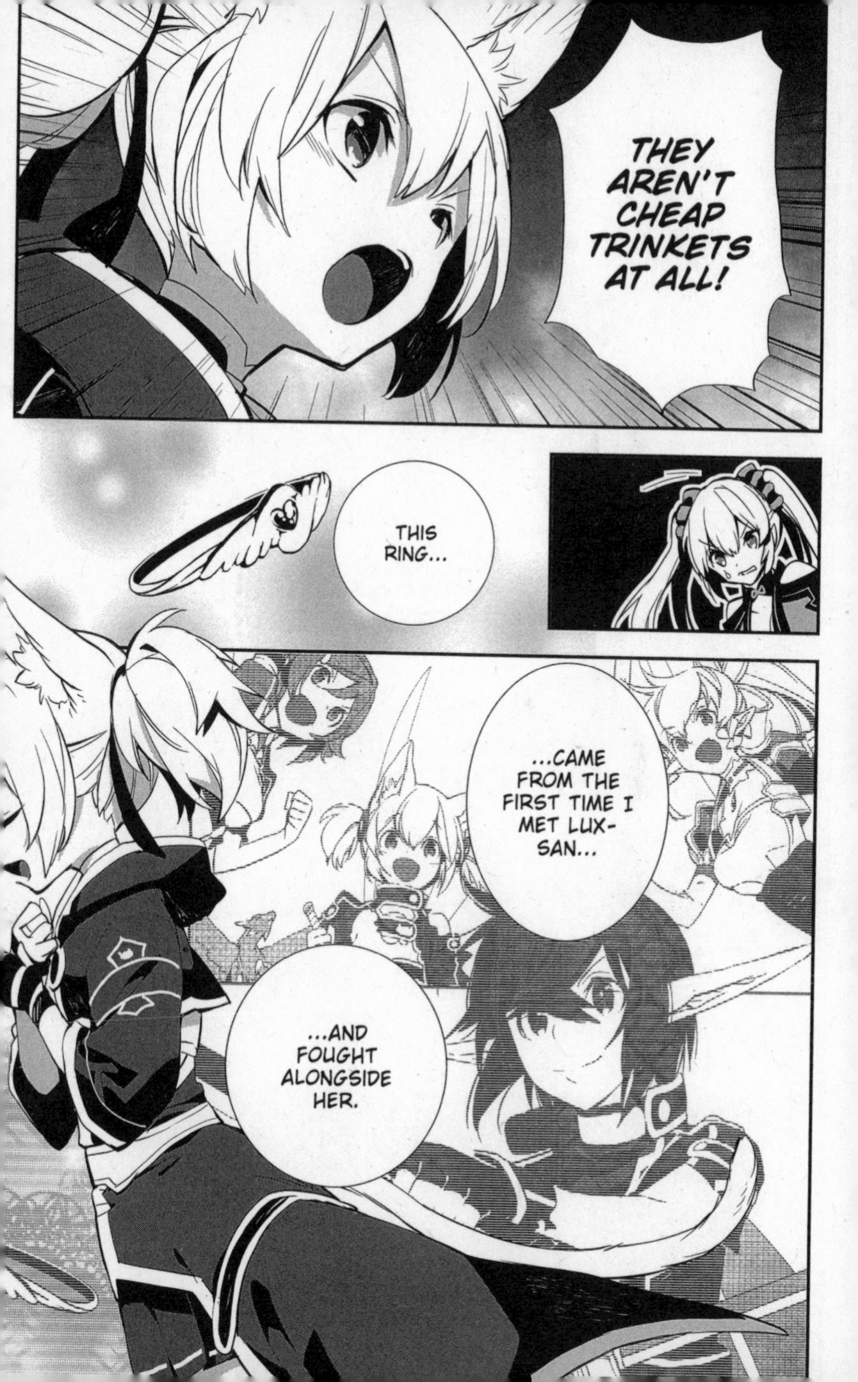
THEY AREN'T CHEAP TRINKETS AT ALL!
THIS RING...
...CAME FROM THE FIRST TIME I MET LUX-SAN...
...AND FOUGHT ALONGSIDE HER.

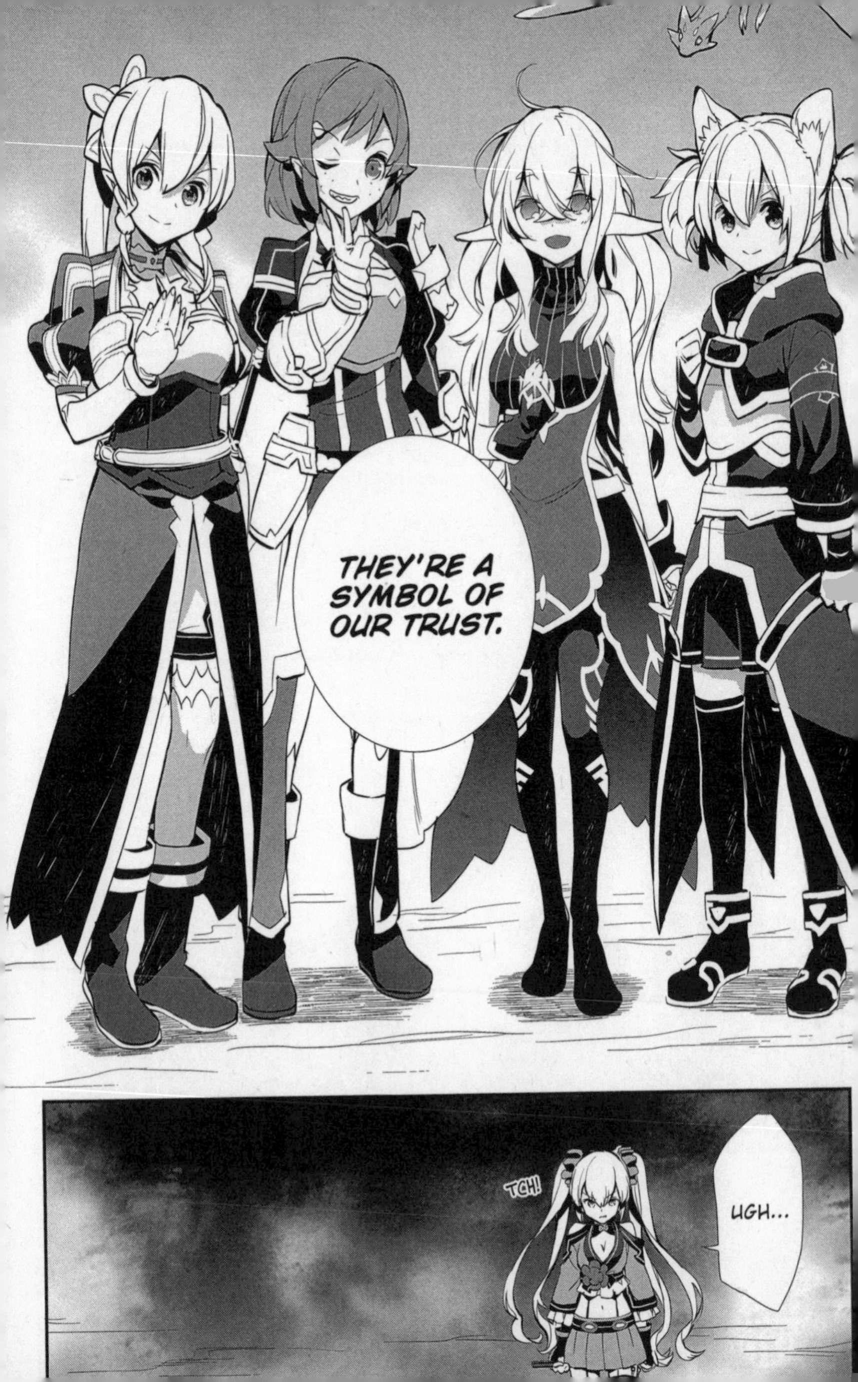
THEY'RE A SYMBOL OF OUR TRUST.
UGH...
TCH!

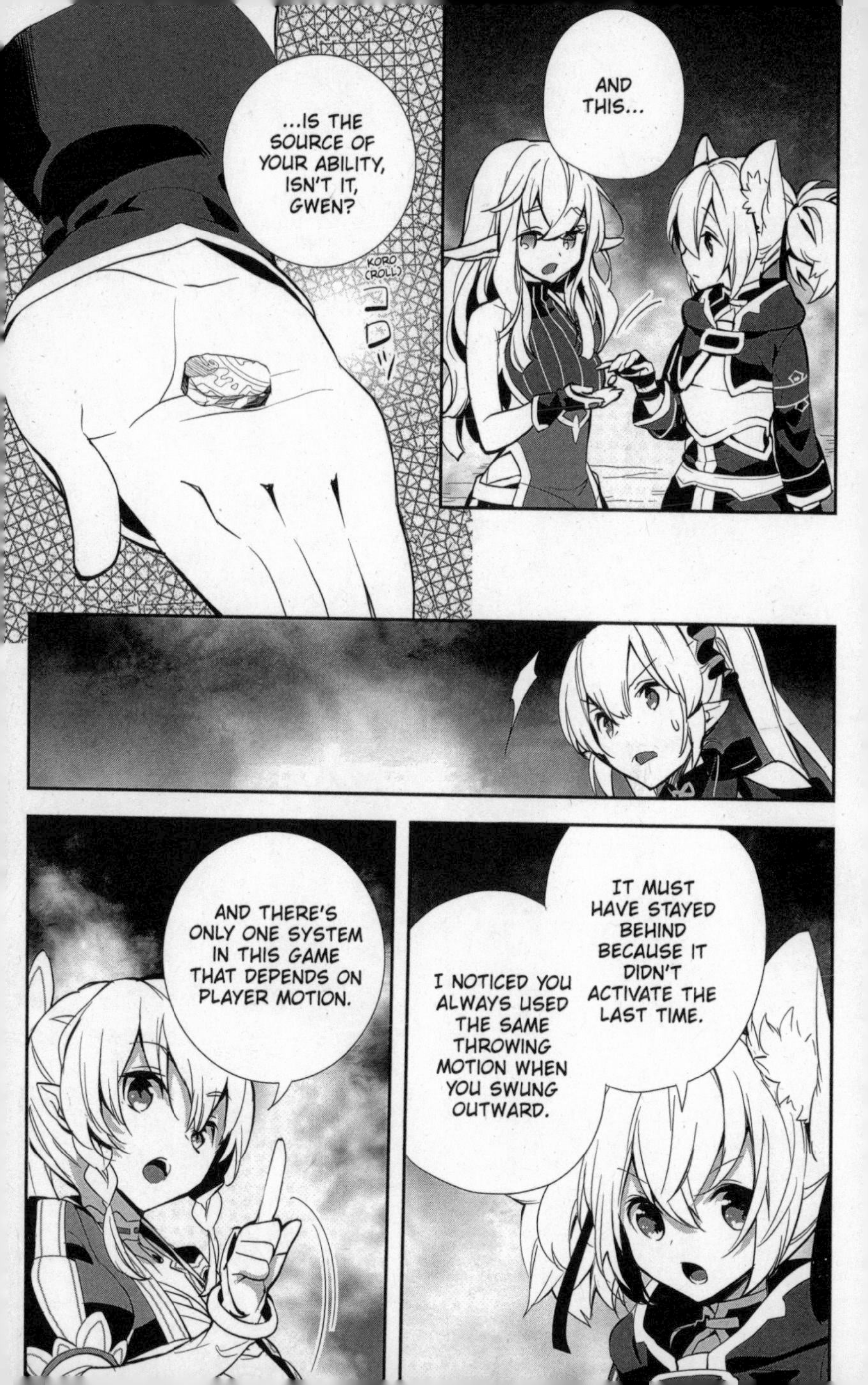
AND THIS...
...IS THE SOURCE OF YOUR ABILITY, ISN'T IT, GWEN?
KORO (ROLL)
IT MUST HAVE STAYED BEHIND BECAUSE IT DIDN'T ACTIVATE THE LAST TIME.
I NOTICED YOU ALWAYS USED THE SAME THROWING MOTION WHEN YOU SWUNG OUTWARD.
AND THERE'S ONLY ONE SYSTEM IN THIS GAME THAT DEPENDS ON PLAYER MOTION.

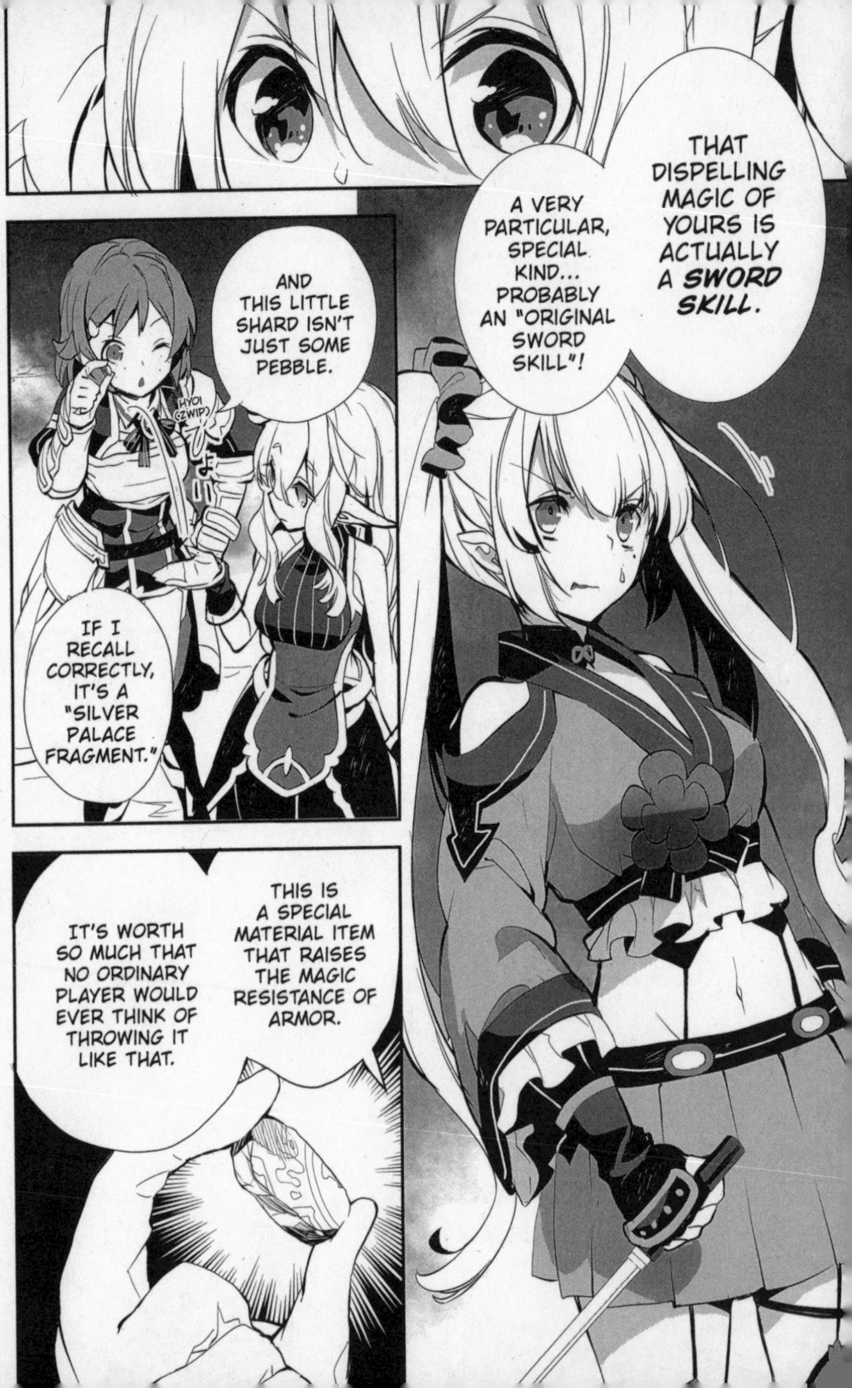
THAT DISPELLING MAGIC OF YOURS IS ACTUALLY A **SWORD SKILL**.
A VERY PARTICULAR, SPECIAL KIND... PROBABLY AN "ORIGINAL SWORD SKILL"!
AND THIS LITTLE SHARD ISN'T JUST SOME PEBBLE.
HYOI (ZWIP)
IF I RECALL CORRECTLY, IT'S A "SILVER PALACE FRAGMENT."
THIS IS A SPECIAL MATERIAL ITEM THAT RAISES THE MAGIC RESISTANCE OF ARMOR.
IT'S WORTH SO MUCH THAT NO ORDINARY PLAYER WOULD EVER THINK OF THROWING IT LIKE THAT.

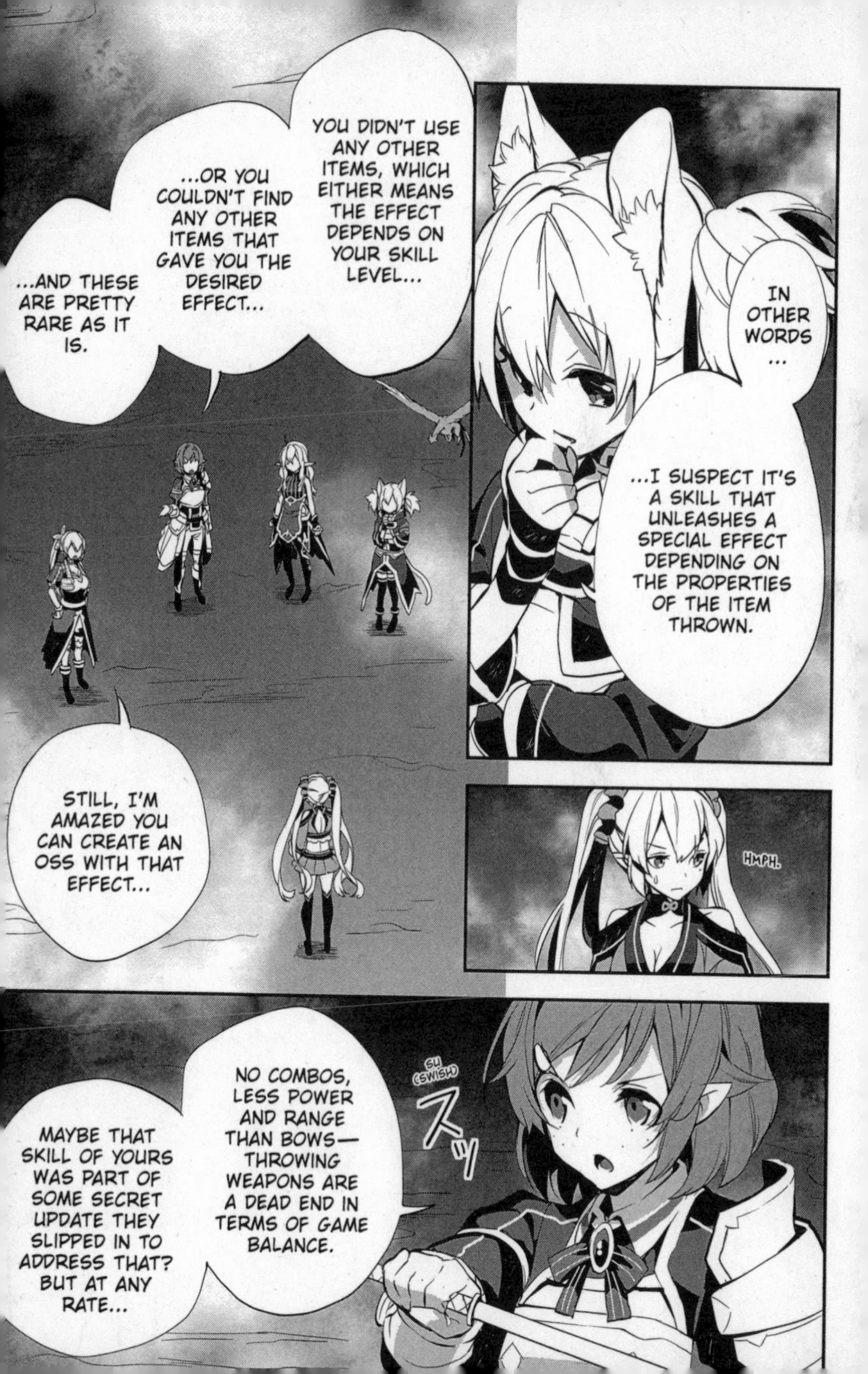
IN OTHER WORDS ...
...I SUSPECT IT'S A SKILL THAT UNLEASHES A SPECIAL EFFECT DEPENDING ON THE PROPERTIES OF THE ITEM THROWN.
YOU DIDN'T USE ANY OTHER ITEMS, WHICH EITHER MEANS THE EFFECT DEPENDS ON YOUR SKILL LEVEL...
...OR YOU COULDN'T FIND ANY OTHER ITEMS THAT GAVE YOU THE DESIRED EFFECT...
...AND THESE ARE PRETTY RARE AS IT IS.
HMPH.
STILL, I'M AMAZED YOU CAN CREATE AN OSS WITH THAT EFFECT...
SU (SWISH)
スッ
NO COMBOS, LESS POWER AND RANGE THAN BOWS—THROWING WEAPONS ARE A DEAD END IN TERMS OF GAME BALANCE.
MAYBE THAT SKILL OF YOURS WAS PART OF SOME SECRET UPDATE THEY SLIPPED IN TO ADDRESS THAT? BUT AT ANY RATE...

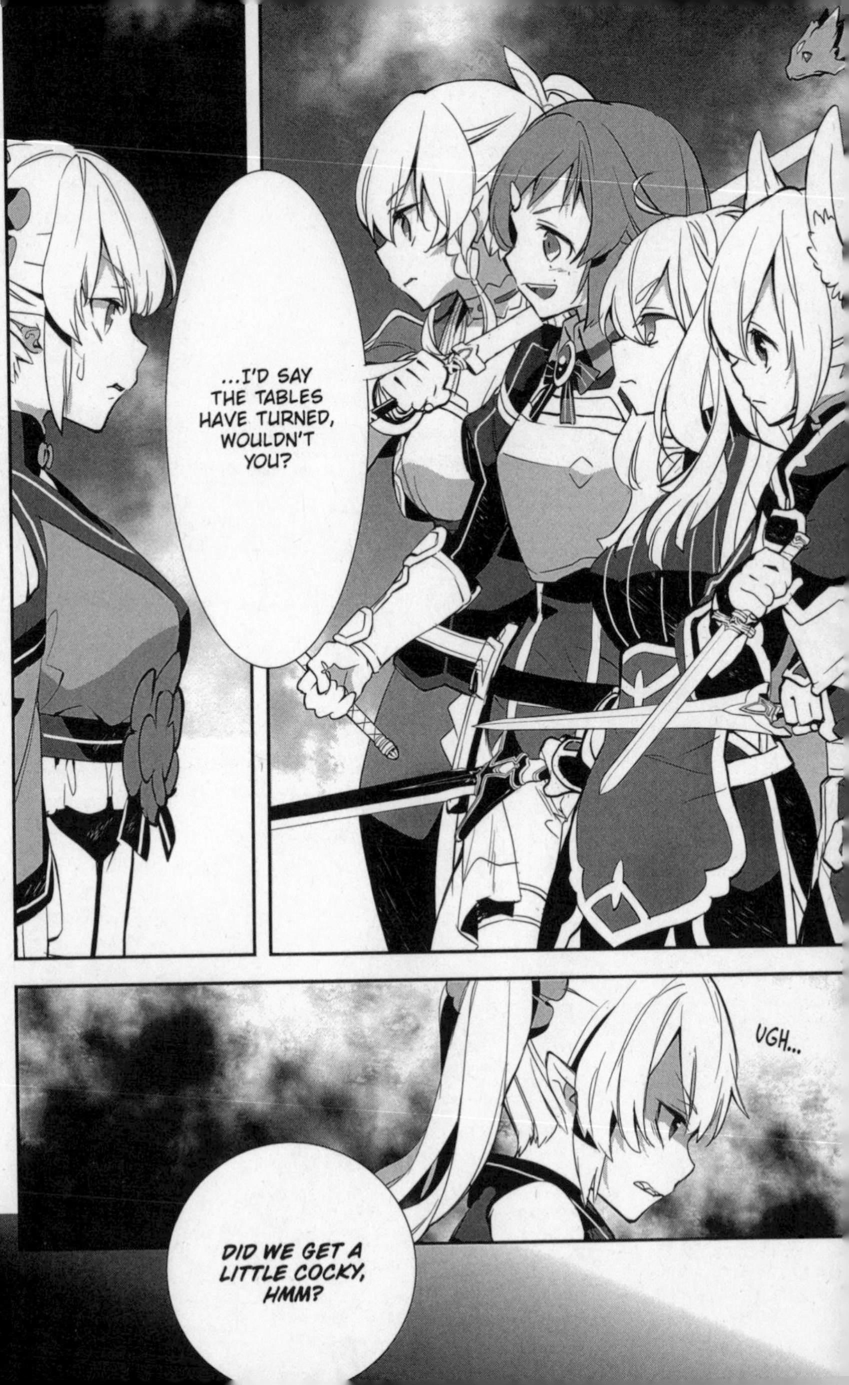
...I'D SAY THE TABLES HAVE TURNED, WOULDN'T YOU?
UGH...
DID WE GET A LITTLE COCKY, HMM?

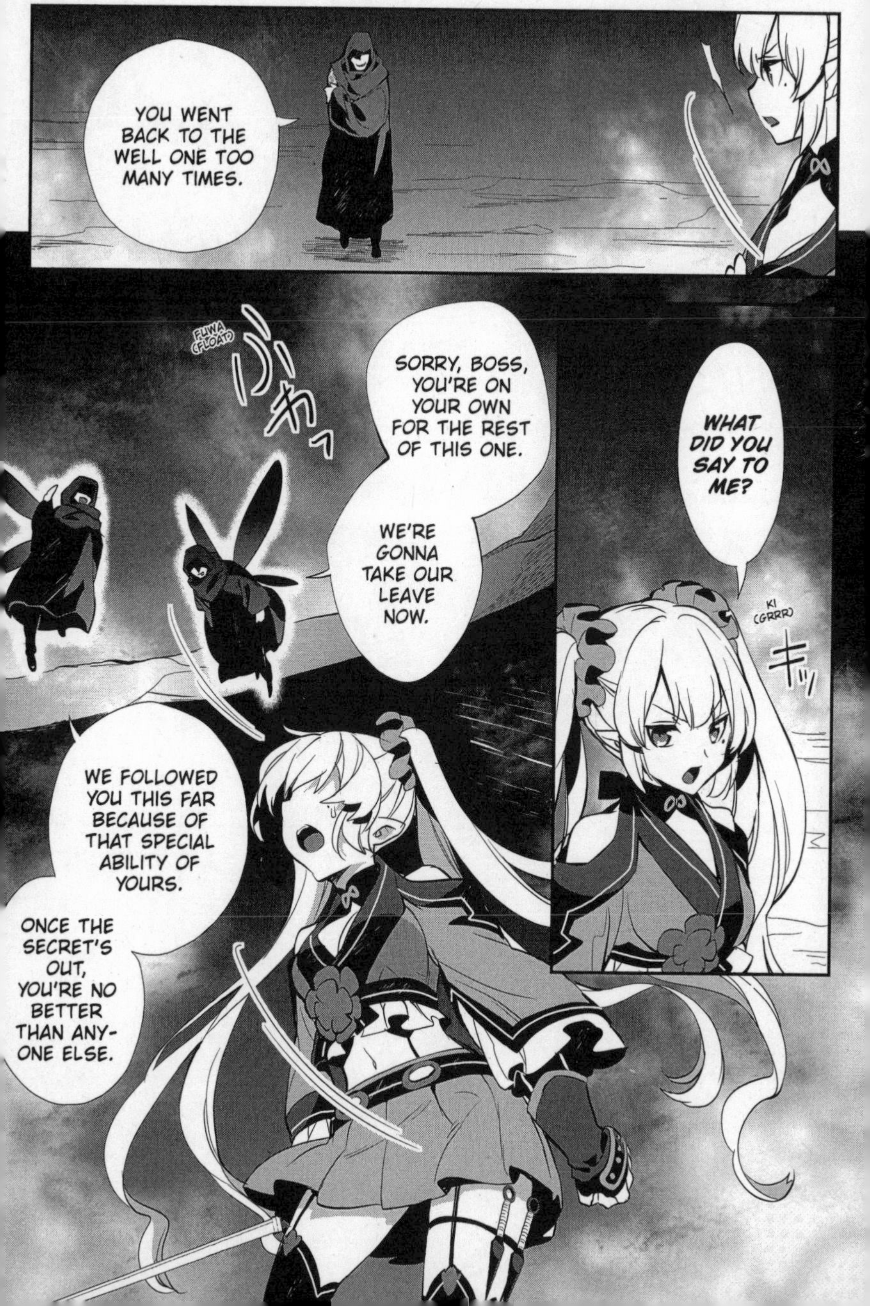
YOU WENT BACK TO THE WELL ONE TOO MANY TIMES.
WHAT DID YOU SAY TO ME?
KI (GRRR)
キッ
FUWA (FLOAT)
ふわっ
SORRY, BOSS, YOU'RE ON YOUR OWN FOR THE REST OF THIS ONE.
WE'RE GONNA TAKE OUR LEAVE NOW.
WE FOLLOWED YOU THIS FAR BECAUSE OF THAT SPECIAL ABILITY OF YOURS.
ONCE THE SECRET'S OUT, YOU'RE NO BETTER THAN ANY-ONE ELSE.

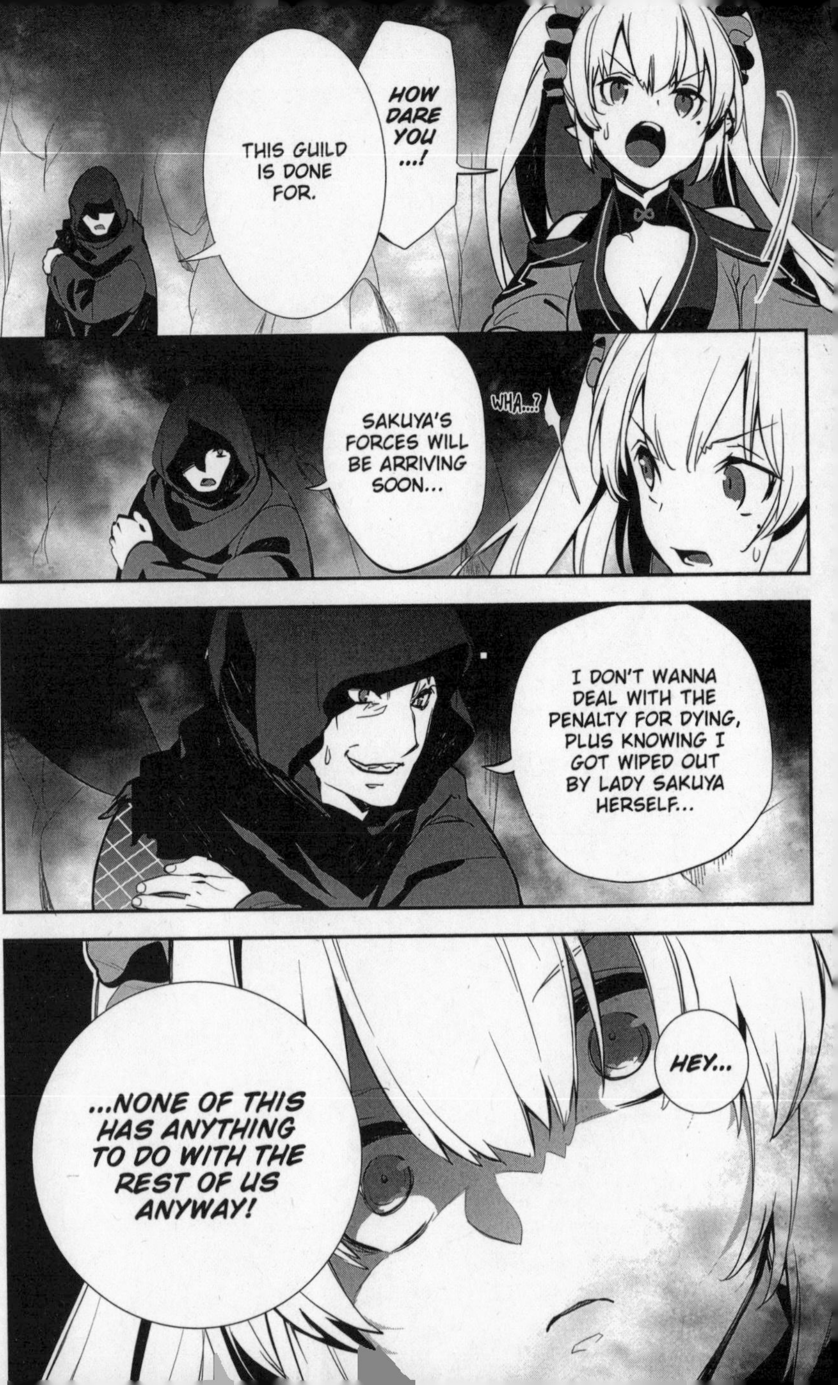
HOW DARE YOU...!
THIS GUILD IS DONE FOR.
WHA...?
SAKUYA'S FORCES WILL BE ARRIVING SOON...
I DON'T WANNA DEAL WITH THE PENALTY FOR DYING, PLUS KNOWING I GOT WIPED OUT BY LADY SAKUYA HERSELF...
HEY...
...NONE OF THIS HAS ANYTHING TO DO WITH THE REST OF US ANYWAY!

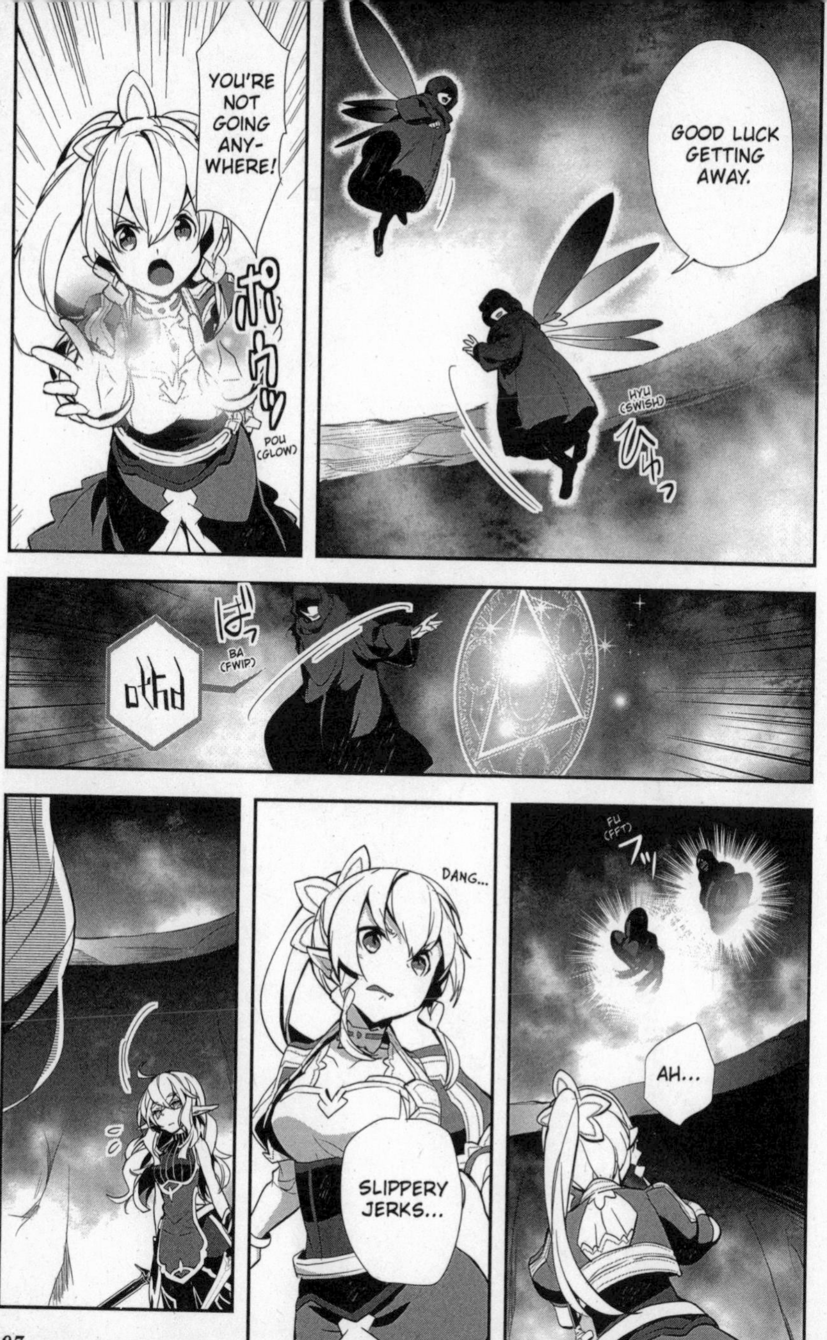
GOOD LUCK GETTING AWAY.
ひゅっ
HYU (SWISH)
YOU'RE NOT GOING ANY-WHERE!
ポゥッ
POU (GLOW)
ばっ
BA (FWIP)
フッ
FU (FFT)
AH...
DANG...
SLIPPERY JERKS...

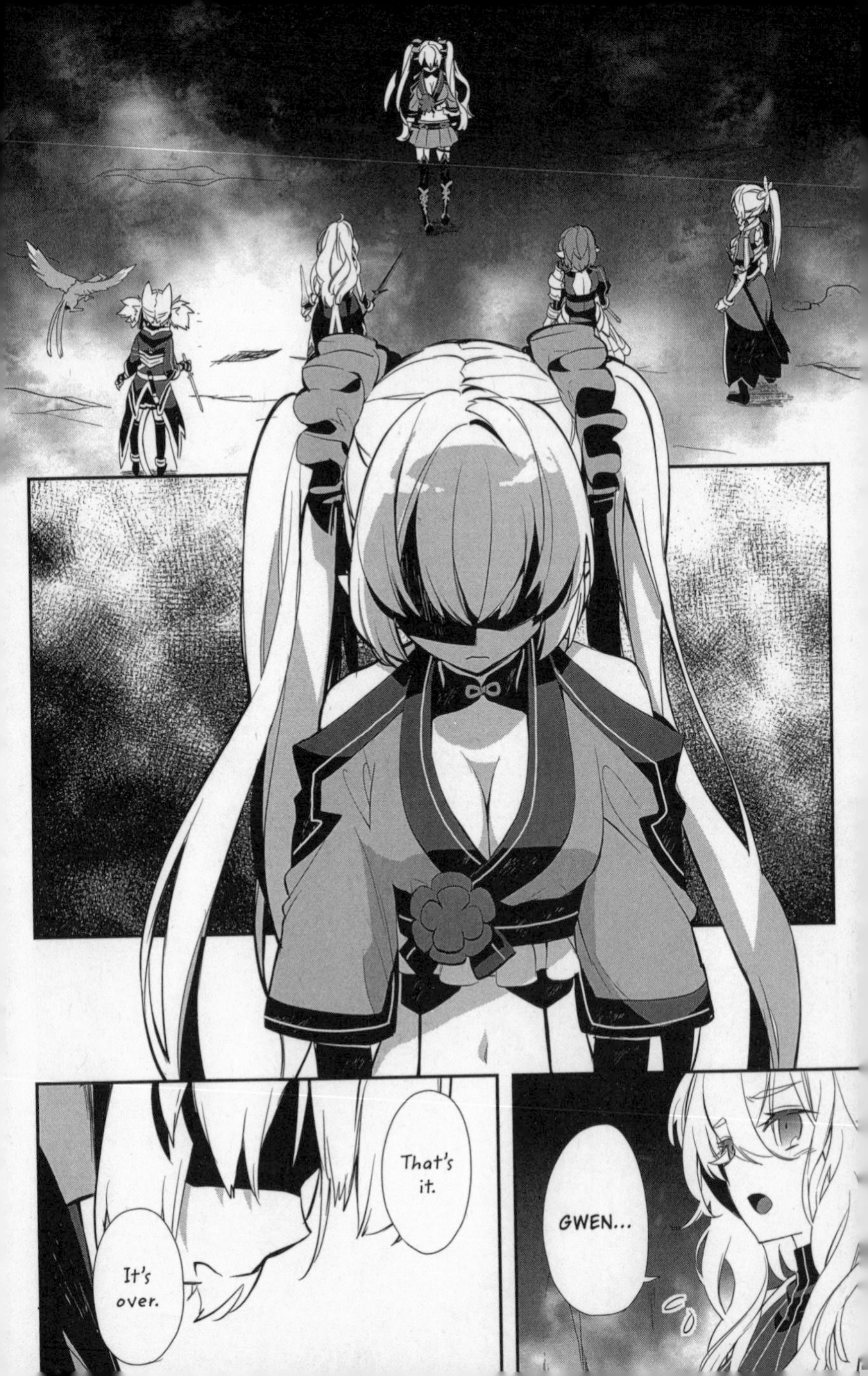
GWEN...
That's it.
It's over.

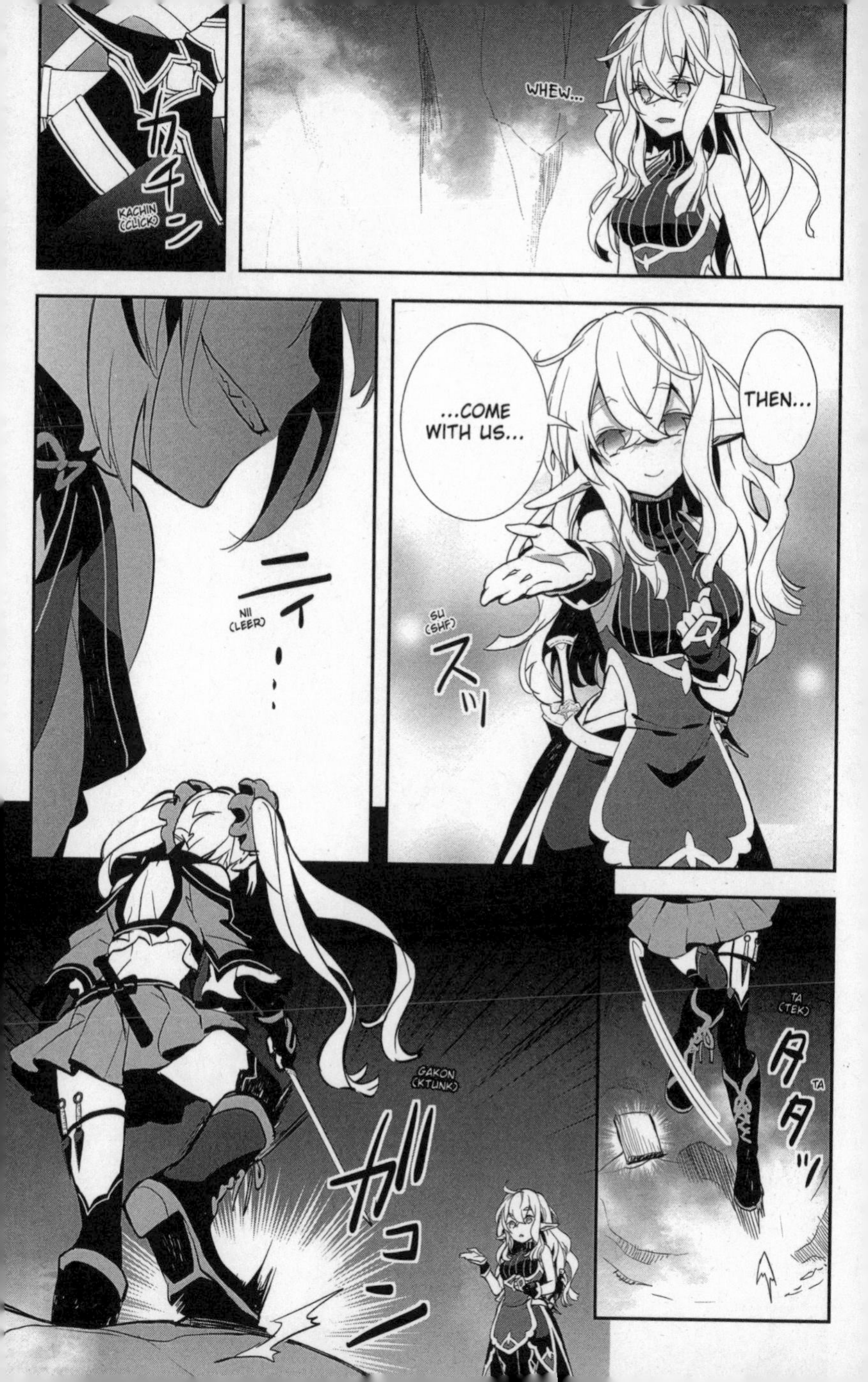
WHEW...
カチーン
KACHIN (CLICK)
THEN...
...COME WITH US...
スッ
SU (SHF)
ニィ・・・
NII (LEER)
タタッ
TA (TEK)
TA
ガッコーン
GAKON (KTUNK)

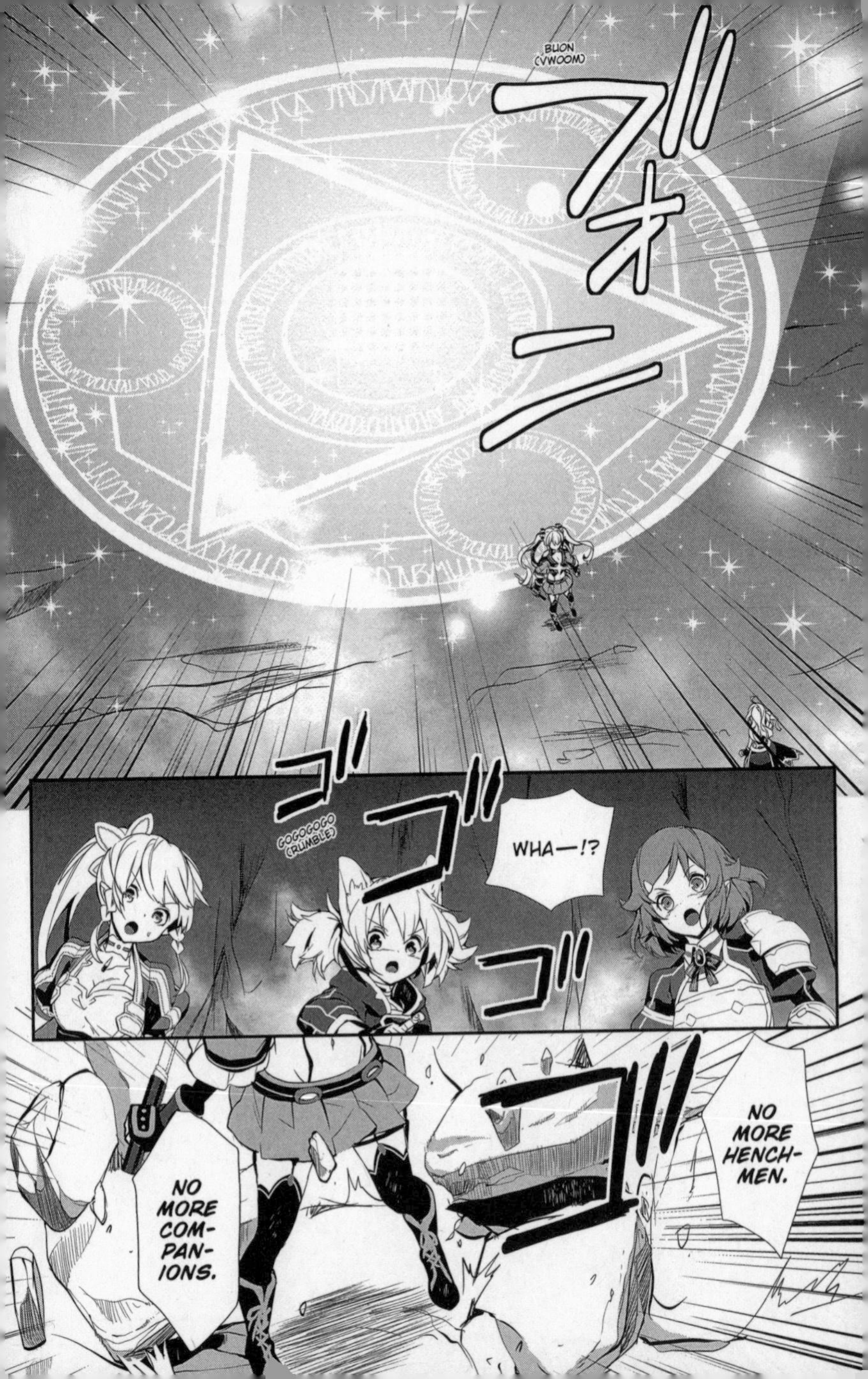
ブォーン
BUON (VWOOM)
ゴゴゴゴ
GOGOGOGO (RUMBLE)
WHA—!?
NO MORE HENCH-MEN.
NO MORE COM-PAN-IONS.

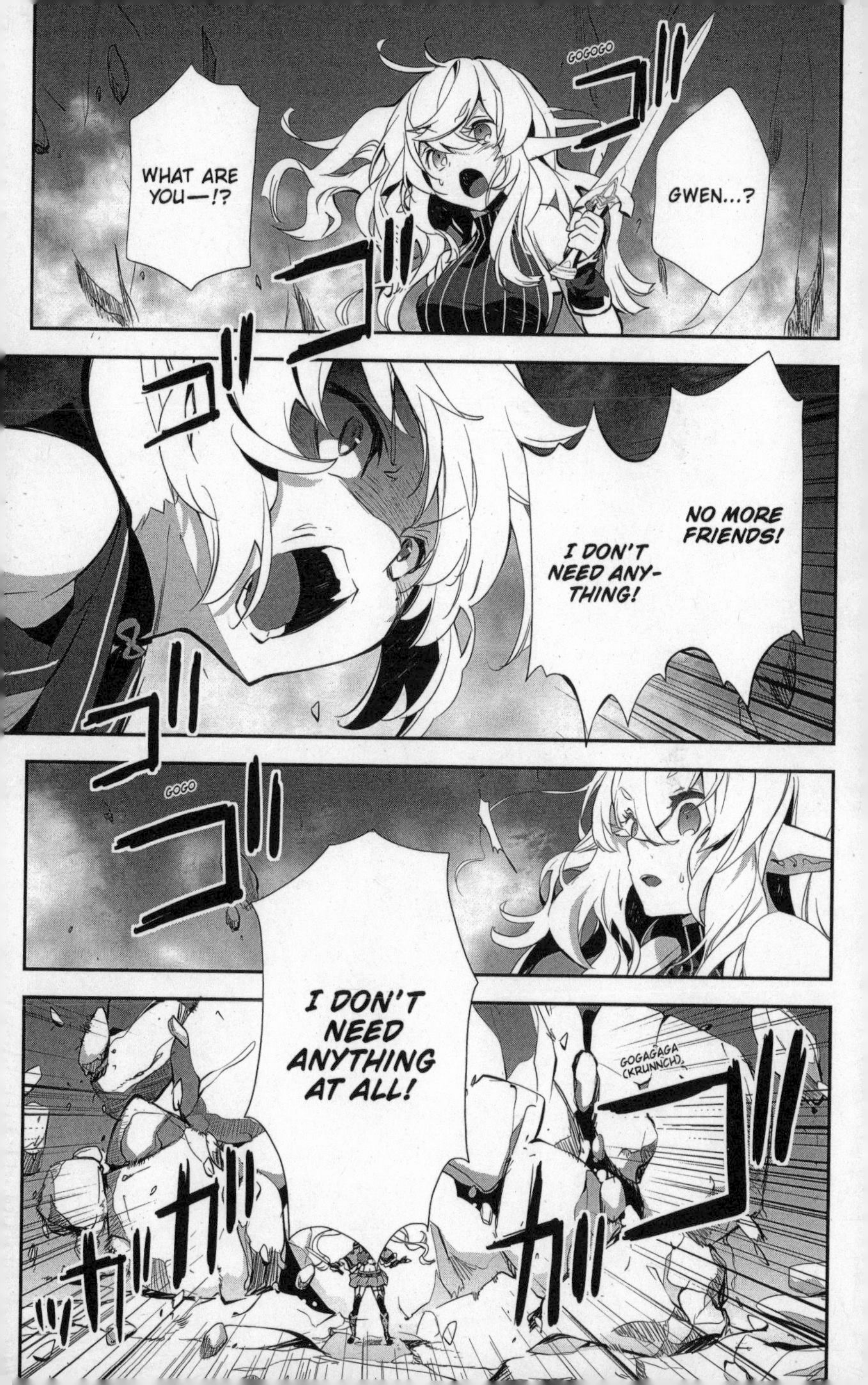
GOGOGO
GWEN...?
WHAT ARE YOU—!?
NO MORE FRIENDS!
I DON'T NEED ANYTHING!
GOGO
I DON'T NEED ANYTHING AT ALL!
GOGAGAGA (KRUNNCH)

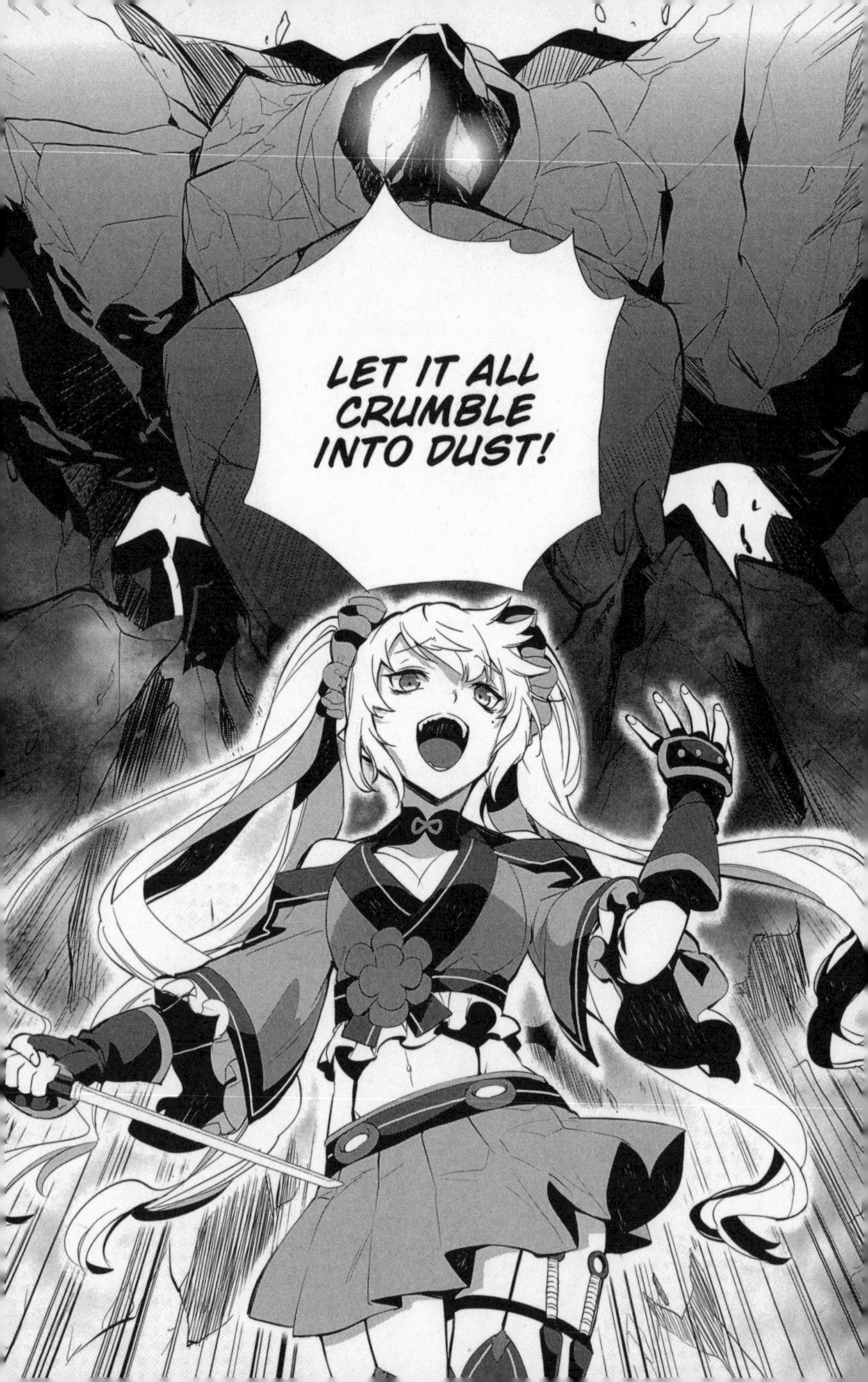
LET IT ALL CRUMBLE INTO DUST!

SWORD ART ONLINE
GIRLS' OPS

SAO GIRLS
SLEEPING SERIES
KEIKO

MMM! ANOTHER BIG DAY TODAY!

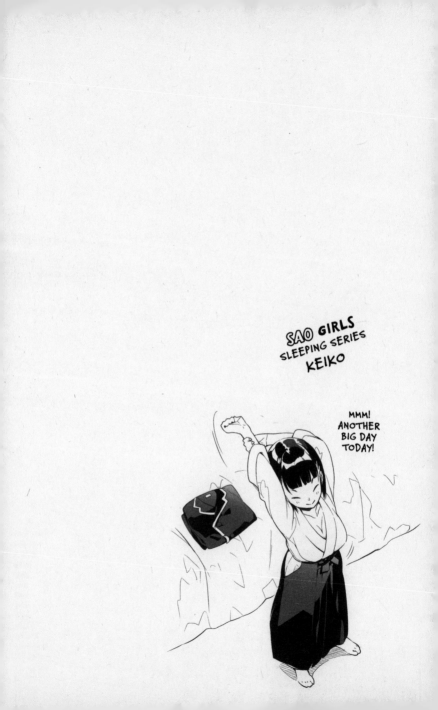

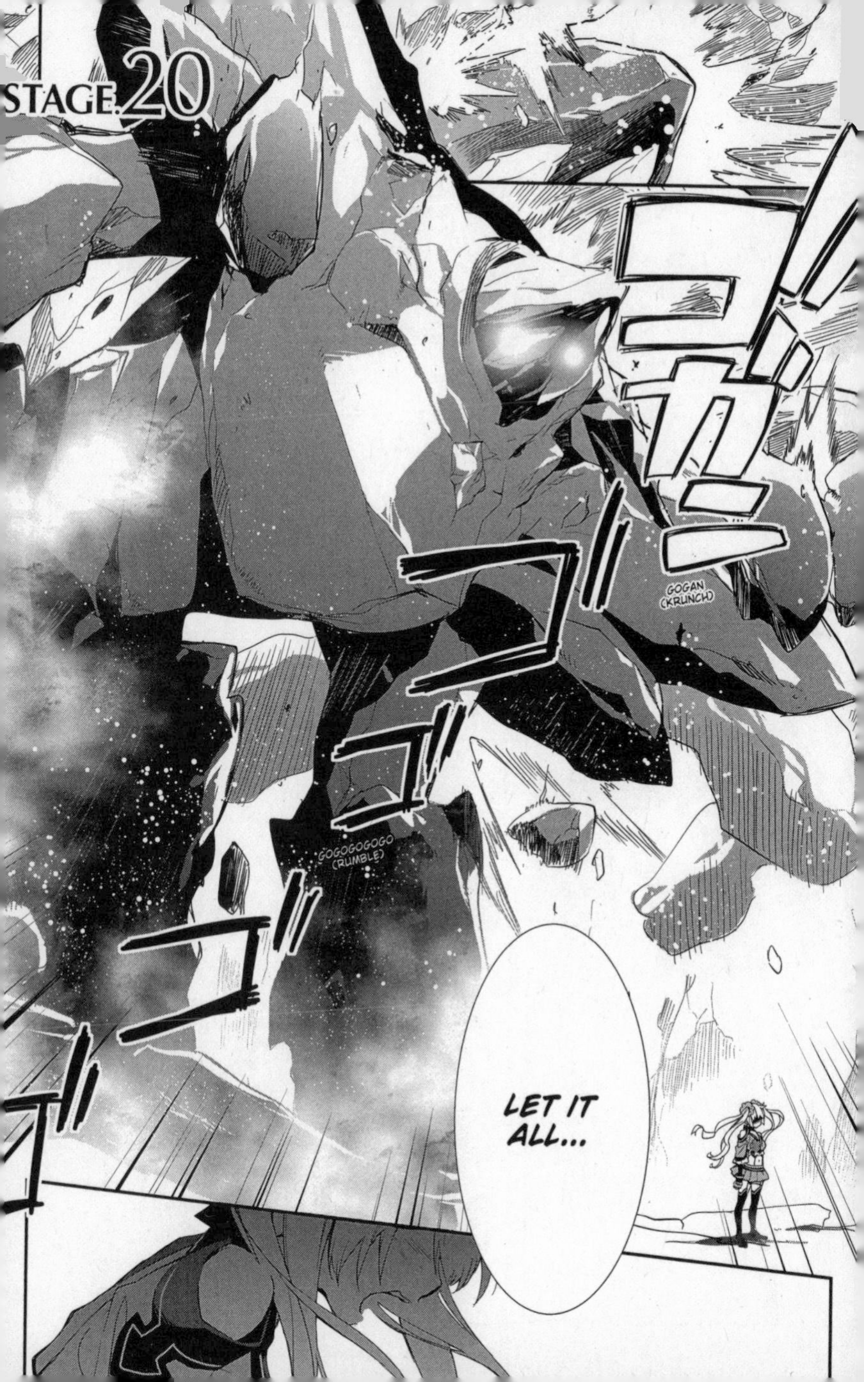
STAGE 20
GOGAN (KRUNCH)
GOGOGOGOGO (RUMBLE)
LET IT ALL...

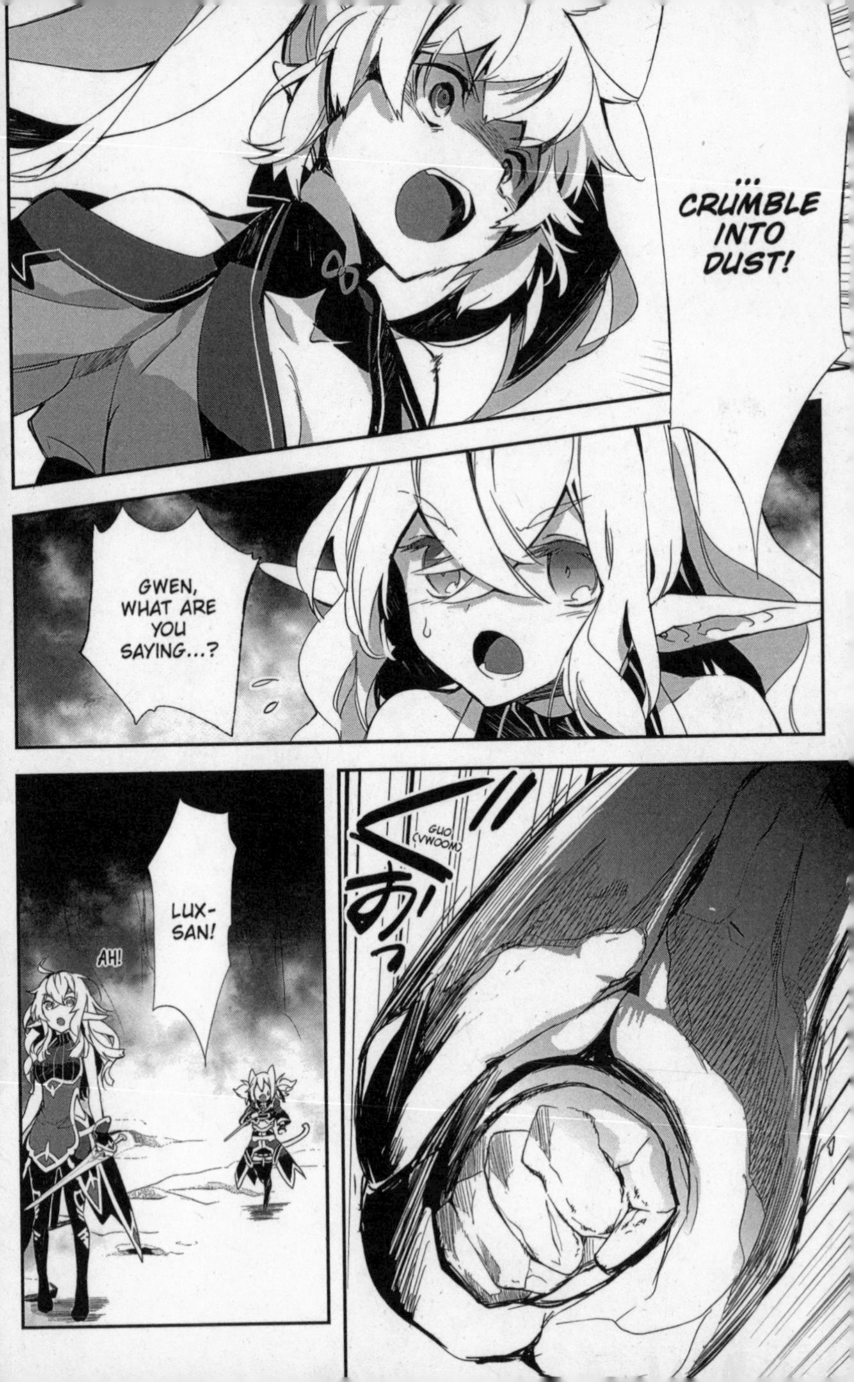

...CRUMBLE INTO DUST!
GWEN, WHAT ARE YOU SAYING...?
ぐおっ
GUO (VWOOM)
LUX-SAN!
AH!

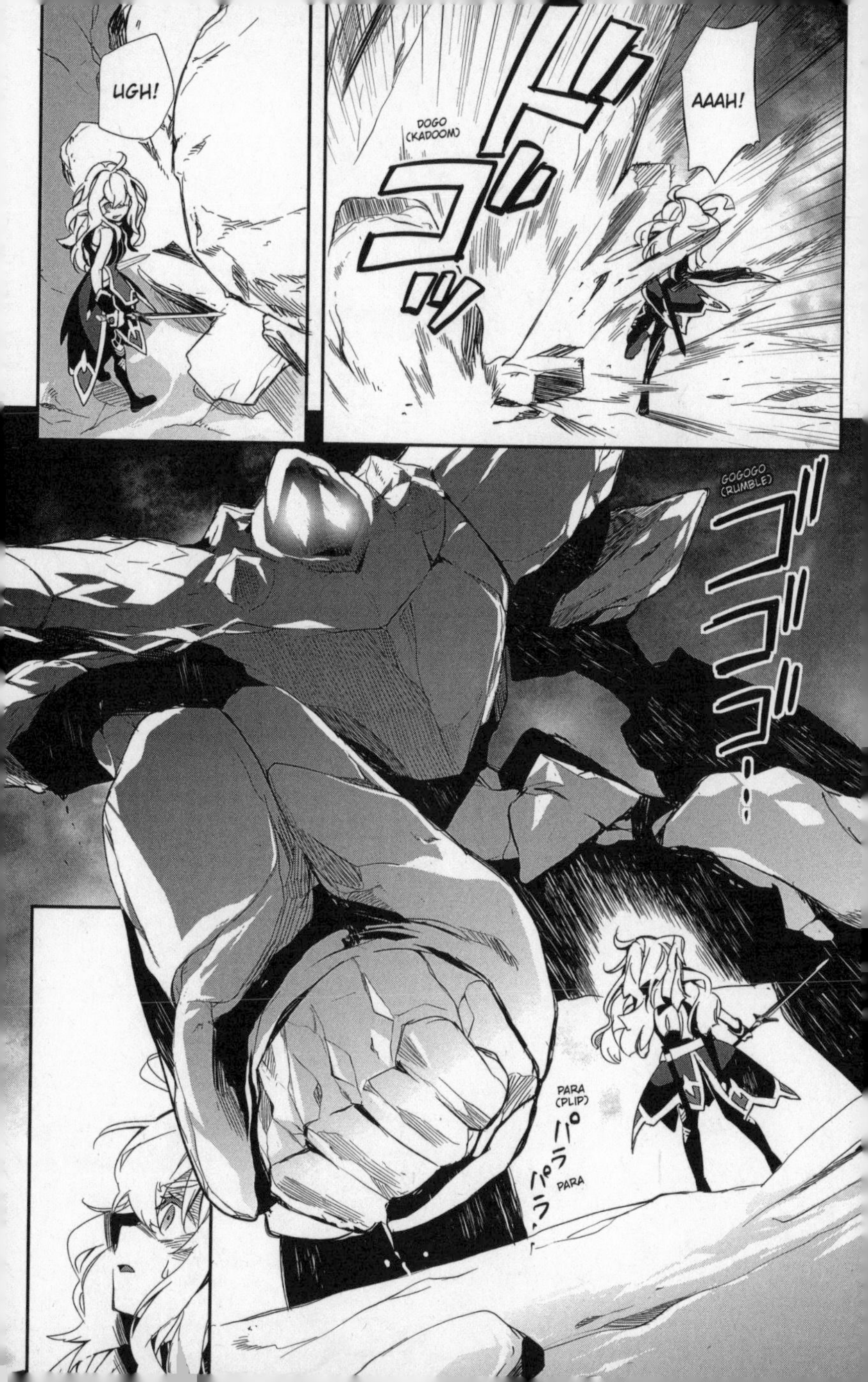

AAAH!
DOGO (KADOOM)
ドゴッ
UGH!
GOGOGO (RUMBLE)
ゴゴゴゴ…
PARA (PLIP)
パラ
PARA
パラ

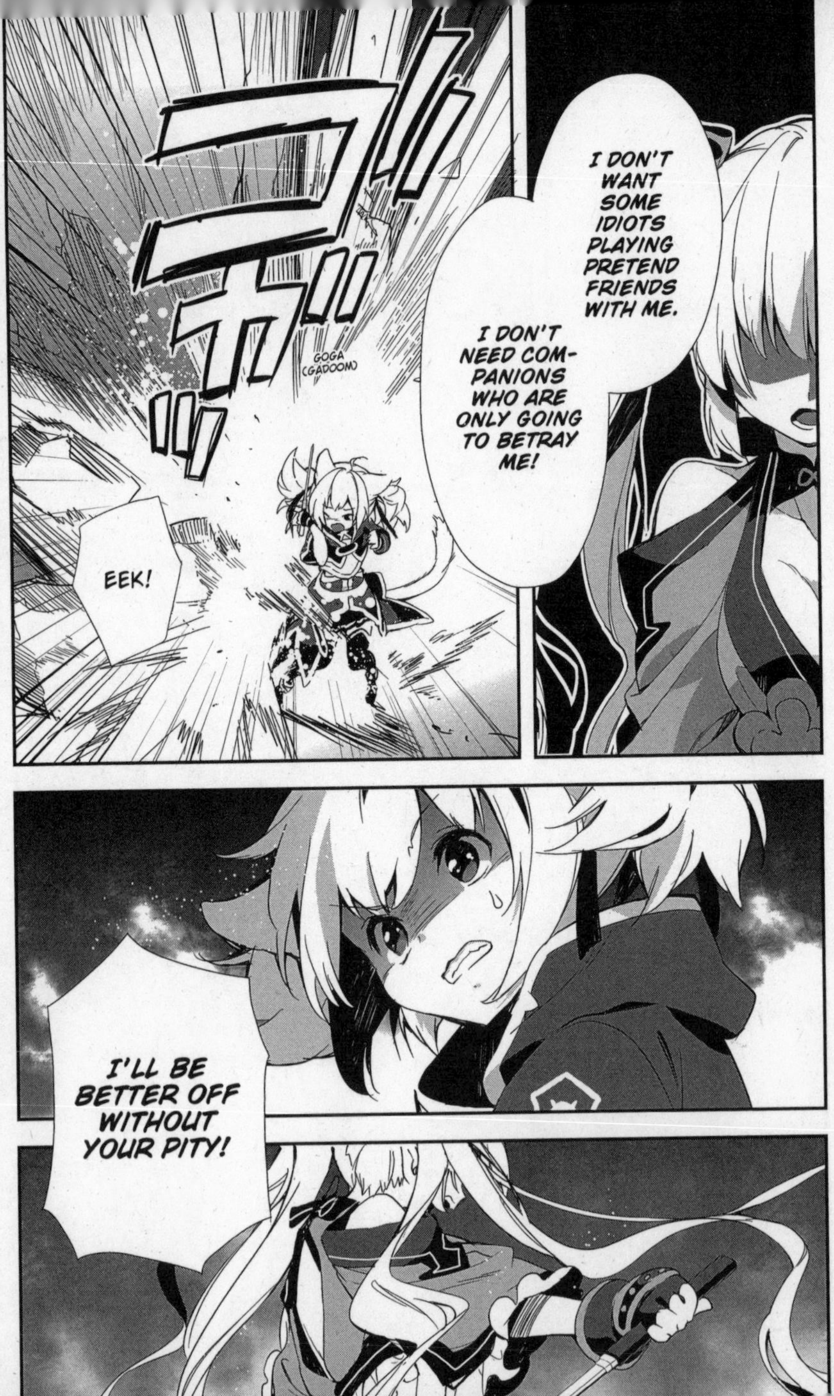
I DON'T WANT SOME IDIOTS PLAYING PRETEND FRIENDS WITH ME.
I DON'T NEED COMPANIONS WHO ARE ONLY GOING TO BETRAY ME!
GOGA (GADOOM)
EEK!
I'LL BE BETTER OFF WITHOUT YOUR PITY!

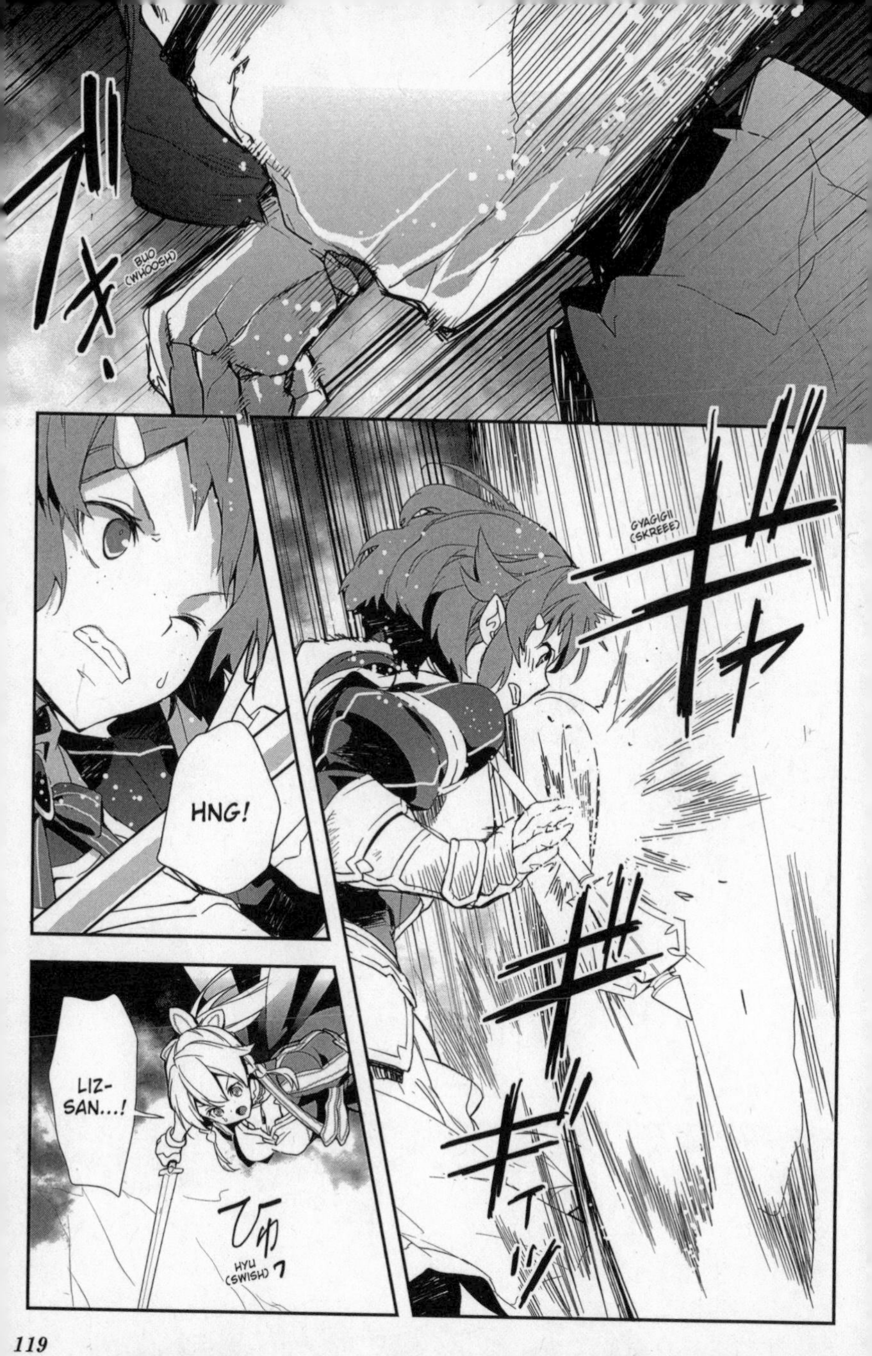
BUO (WHOOSH)
GYAGIGII (SKREEE)
HNG!
LIZ-SAN...!
HYU (SWISH)

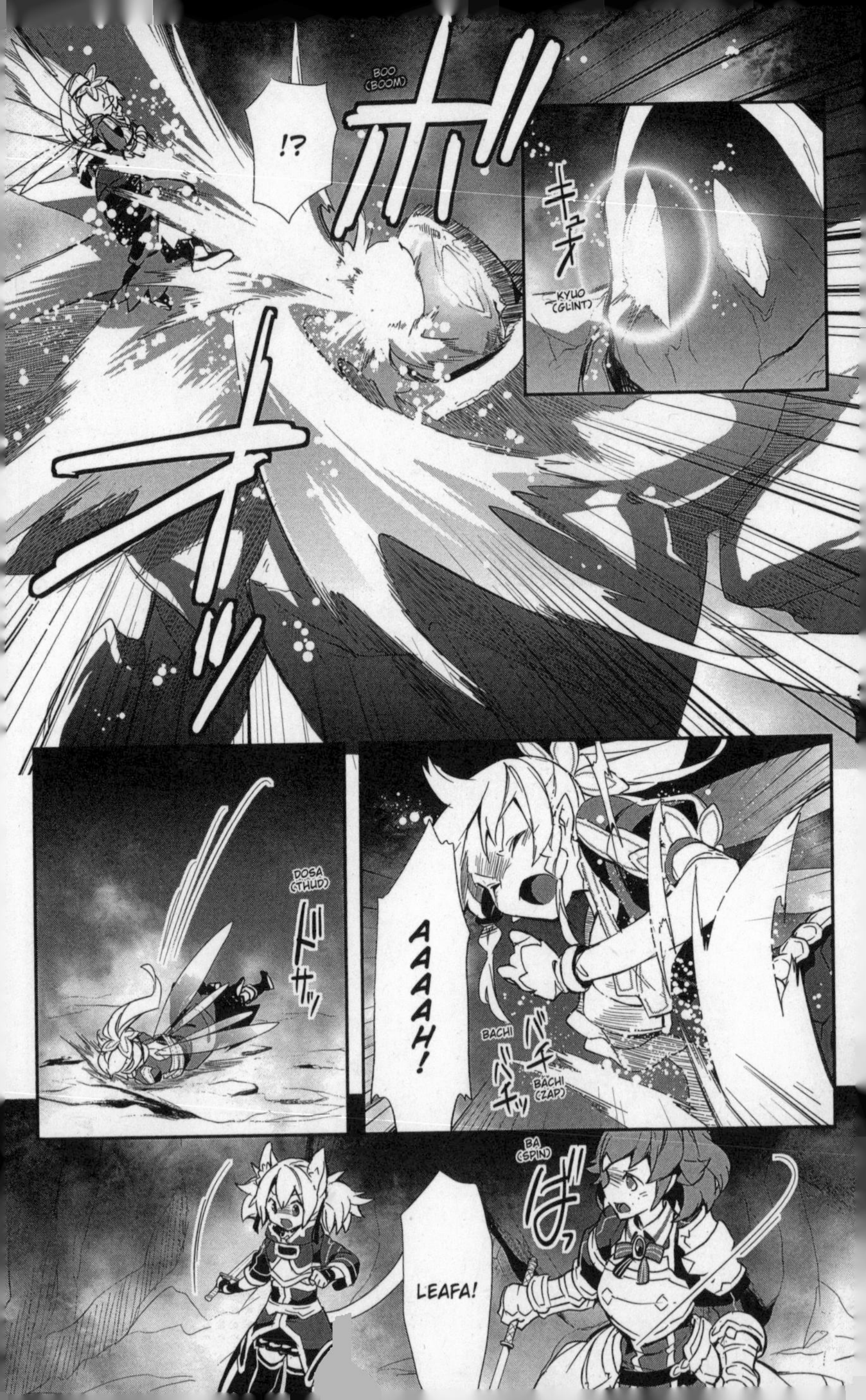
BOO
(BOOM)
!?
キュオ
KYUO
(GLINT)
AAAAH!
バチバチッ
BACHI
BACHI
(ZAP)
ドサッ
DOSA
(THUD)
ばっ
BA
(SPIN)
LEAFA!

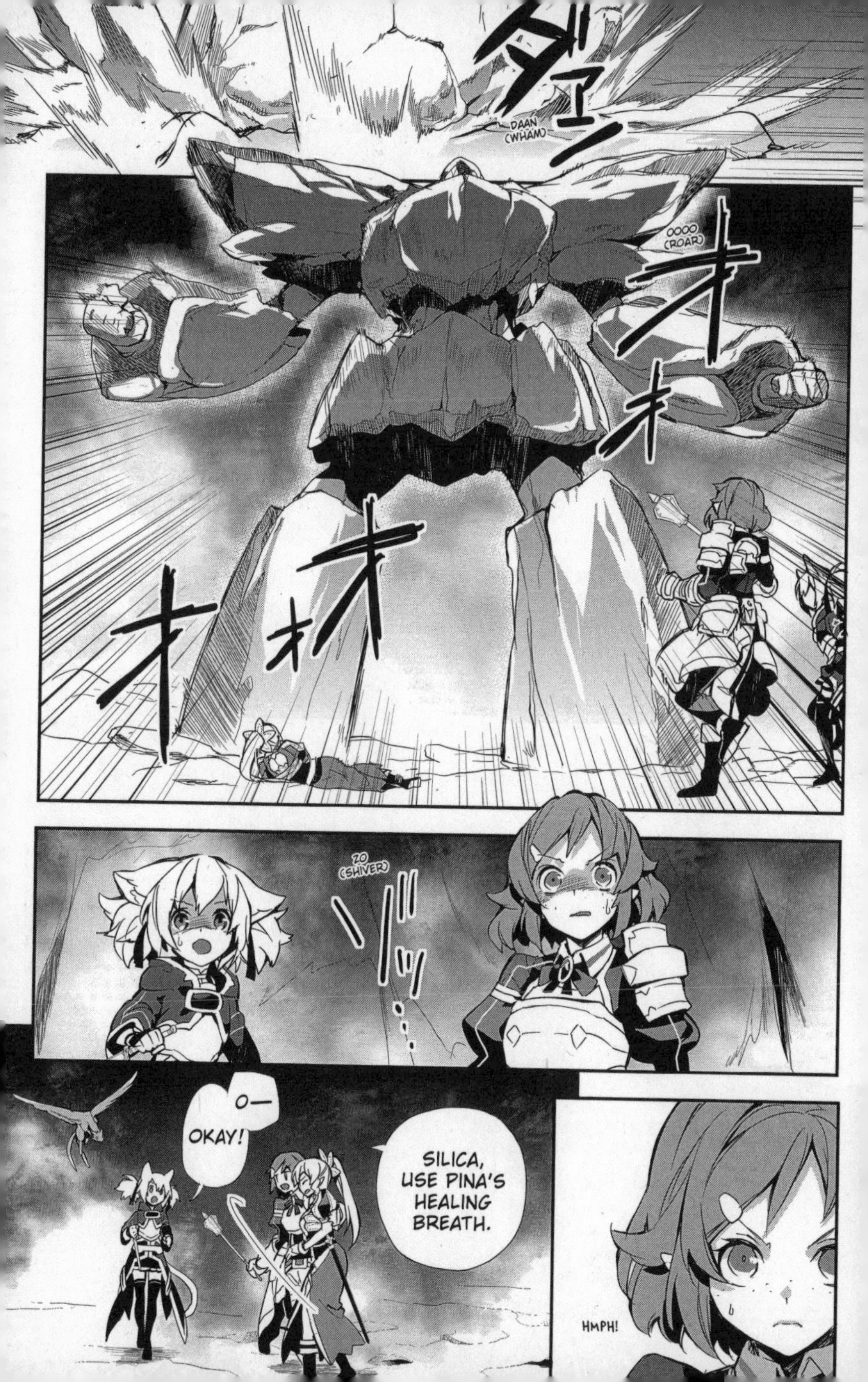
ダァン
DAAN (WHAM)
オオオオオ
OOOO (ROAR)
ゾ…
ZO (SHIVER)
SILICA, USE PINA'S HEALING BREATH.
O— OKAY!
HMPH!

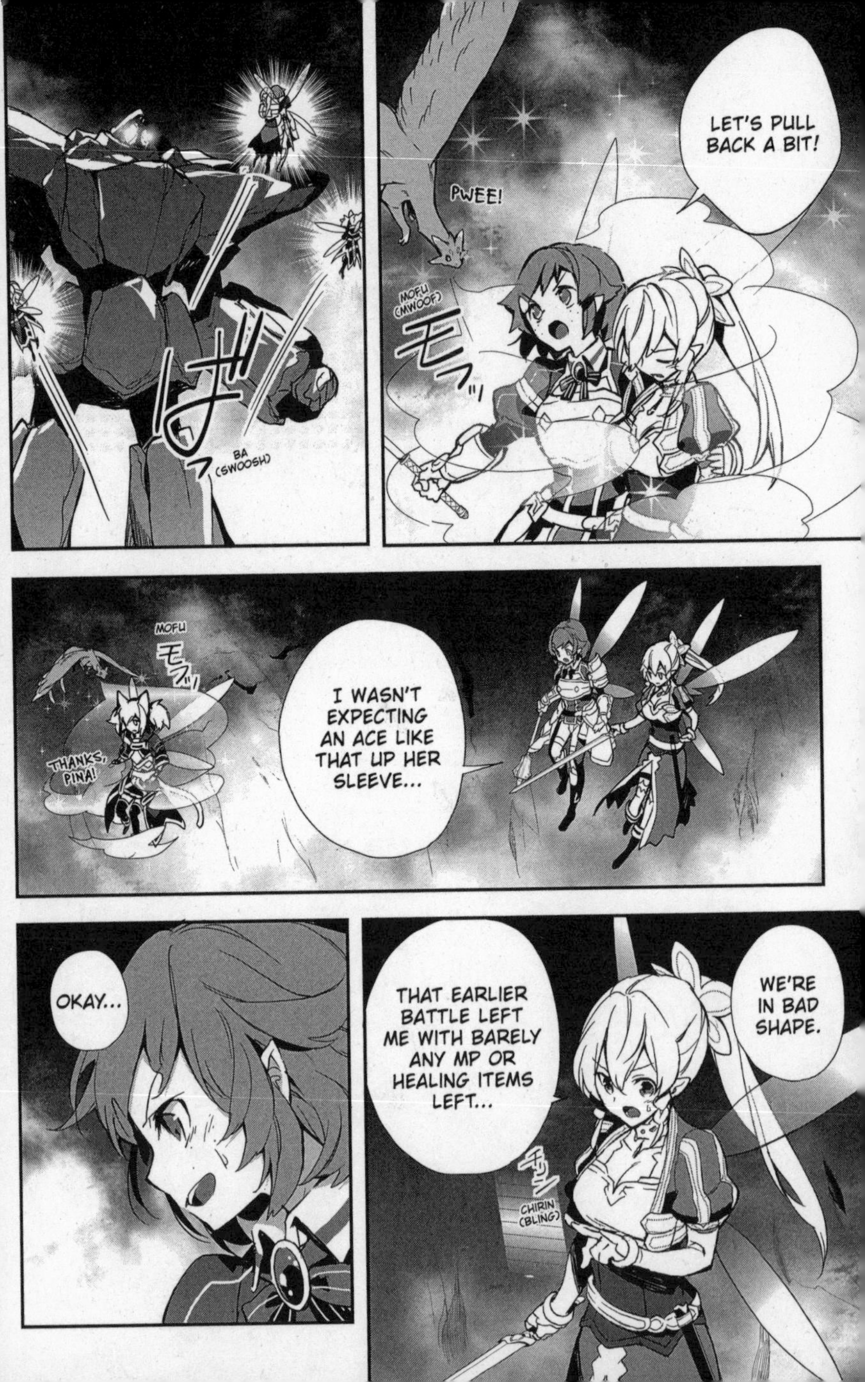
LET'S PULL BACK A BIT!
PWEE!
MOFU (MWOOF)
BA (SWOOSH)
I WASN'T EXPECTING AN ACE LIKE THAT UP HER SLEEVE...
MOFU
THANKS, PINA!
WE'RE IN BAD SHAPE.
THAT EARLIER BATTLE LEFT ME WITH BARELY ANY MP OR HEALING ITEMS LEFT...
CHIRIN (BLING)
OKAY...

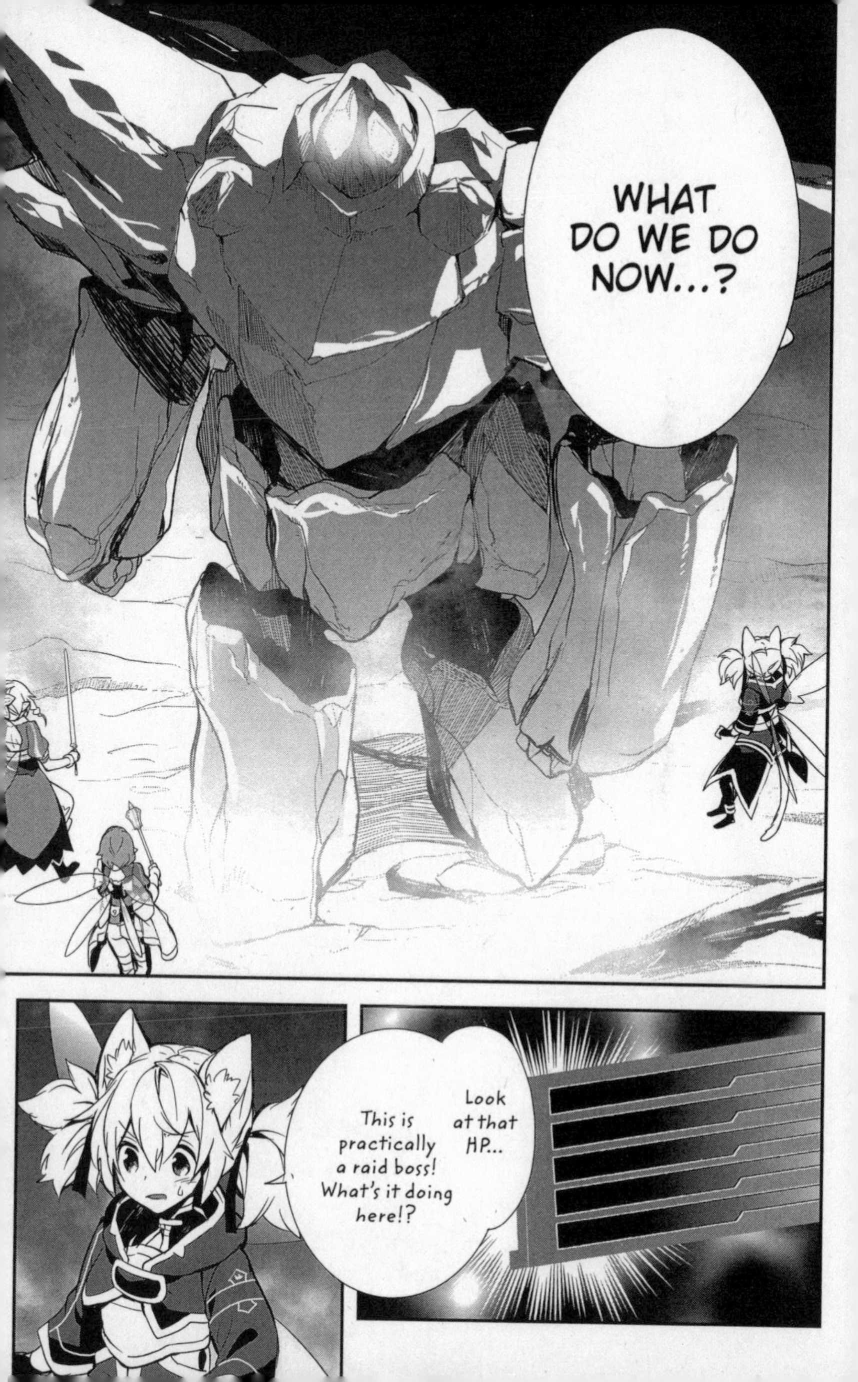
WHAT DO WE DO NOW...?
Look at that HP...
This is practically a raid boss! What's it doing here!?

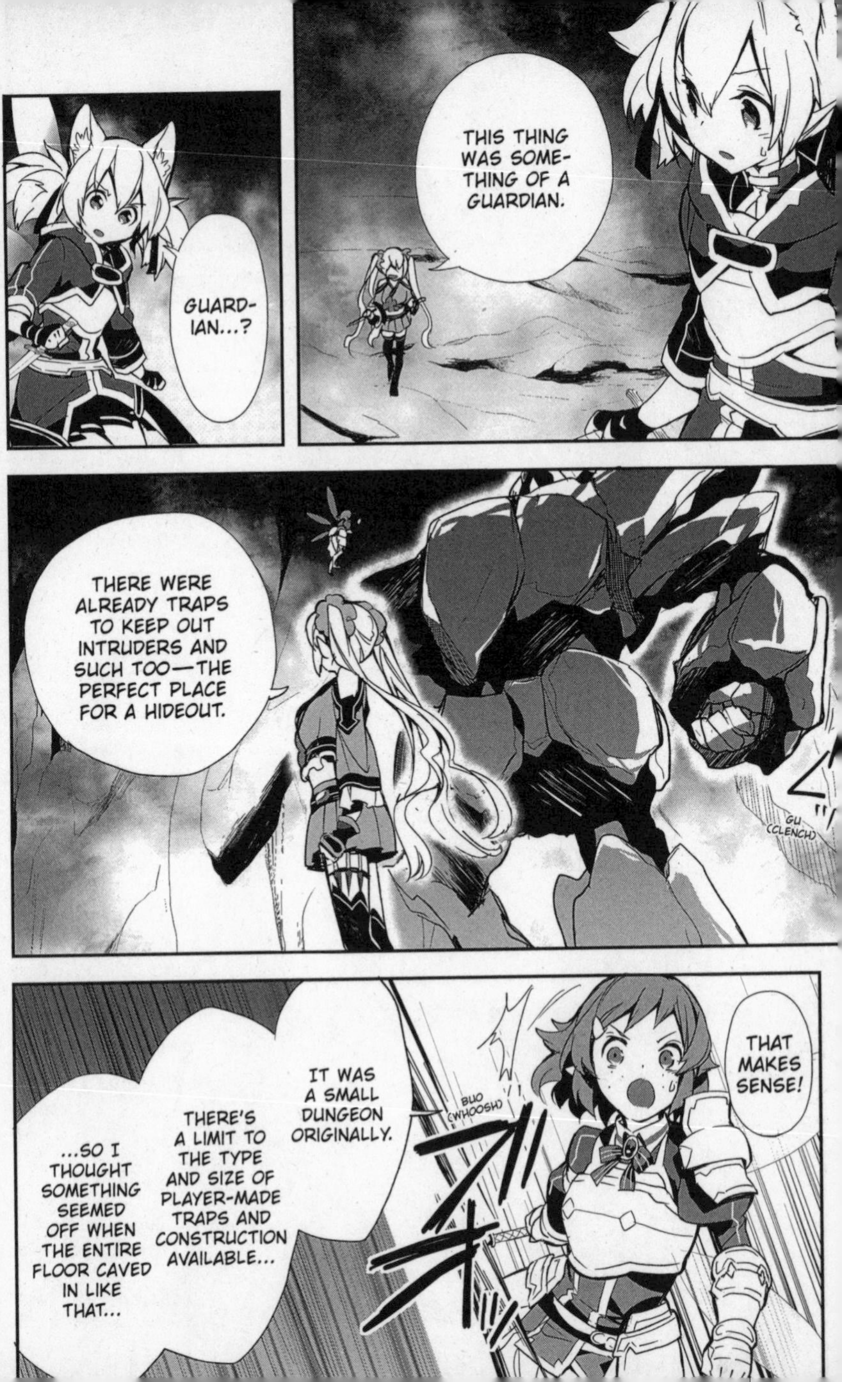
THIS THING WAS SOMETHING OF A GUARDIAN.
GUARDIAN...?
THERE WERE ALREADY TRAPS TO KEEP OUT INTRUDERS AND SUCH TOO—THE PERFECT PLACE FOR A HIDEOUT.
GU (CLENCH)
THAT MAKES SENSE!
BUO (WHOOSH)
IT WAS A SMALL DUNGEON ORIGINALLY.
THERE'S A LIMIT TO THE TYPE AND SIZE OF PLAYER-MADE TRAPS AND CONSTRUCTION AVAILABLE...
...SO I THOUGHT SOMETHING SEEMED OFF WHEN THE ENTIRE FLOOR CAVED IN LIKE THAT...

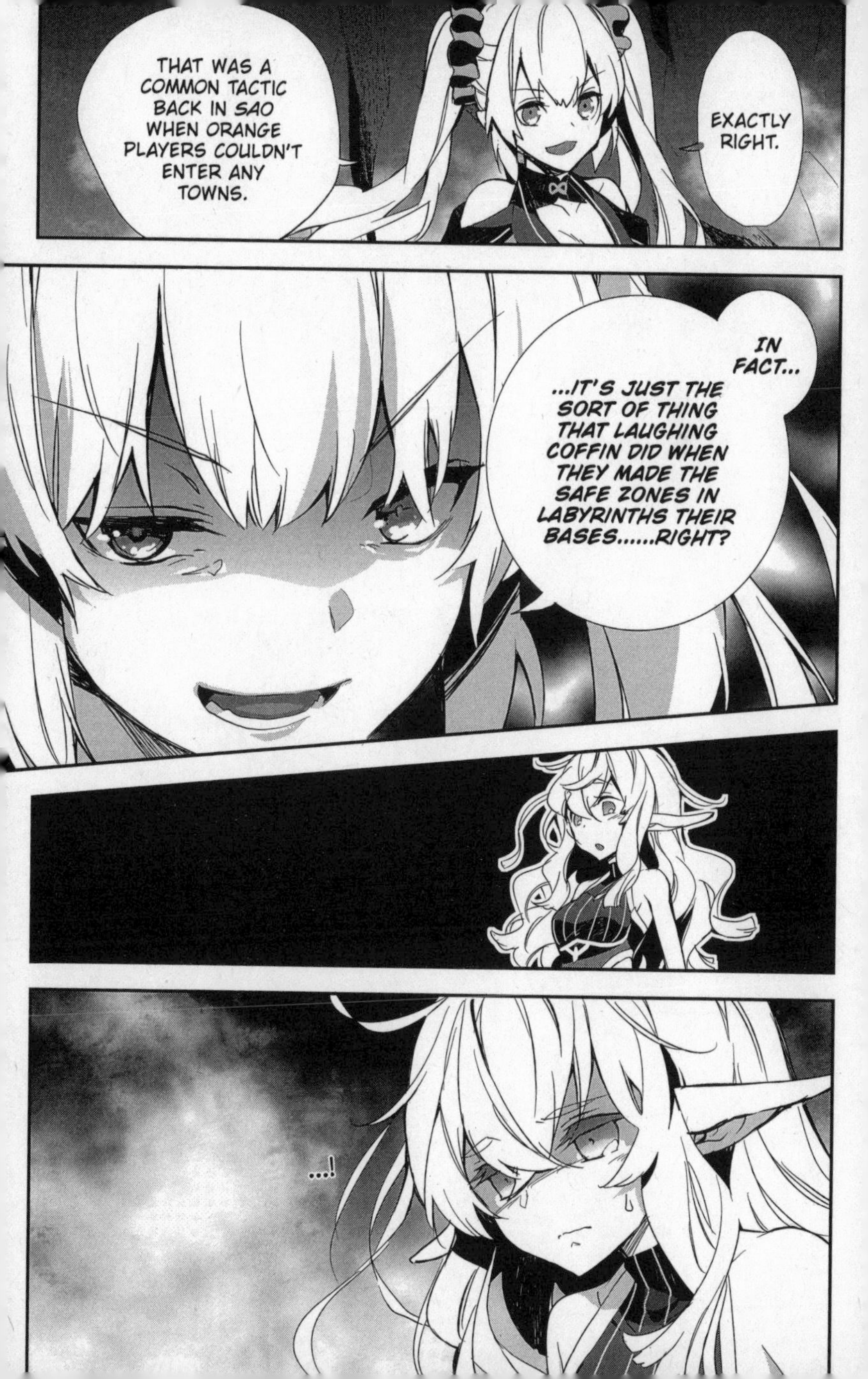
EXACTLY RIGHT.
THAT WAS A COMMON TACTIC BACK IN SAO WHEN ORANGE PLAYERS COULDN'T ENTER ANY TOWNS.
IN FACT...
...IT'S JUST THE SORT OF THING THAT LAUGHING COFFIN DID WHEN THEY MADE THE SAFE ZONES IN LABYRINTHS THEIR BASES......RIGHT?
...!

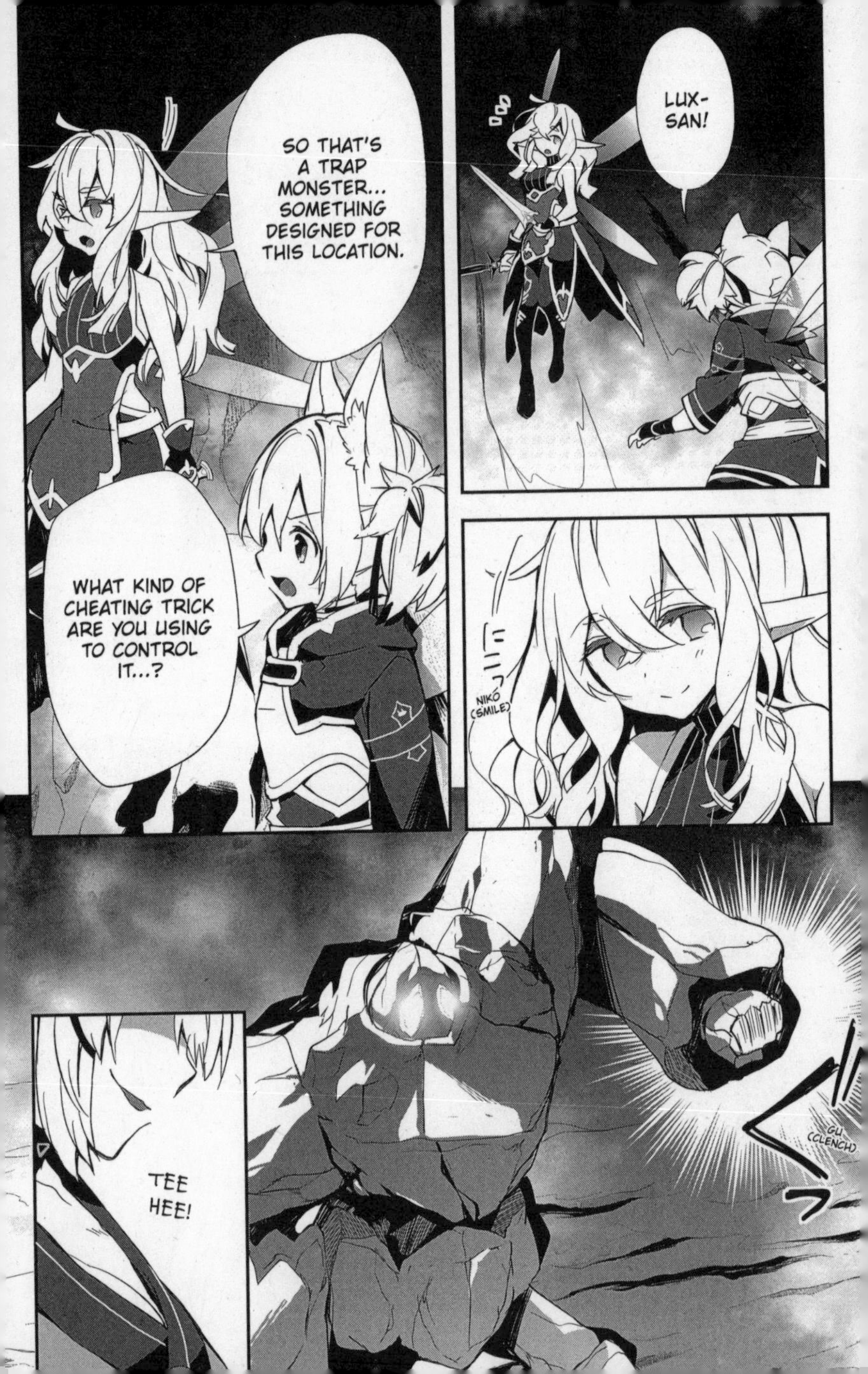
LUX-SAN!
SO THAT'S A TRAP MONSTER... SOMETHING DESIGNED FOR THIS LOCATION.
NIKO (SMILE)
WHAT KIND OF CHEATING TRICK ARE YOU USING TO CONTROL IT...?
GU (CLENCH)
TEE HEE!

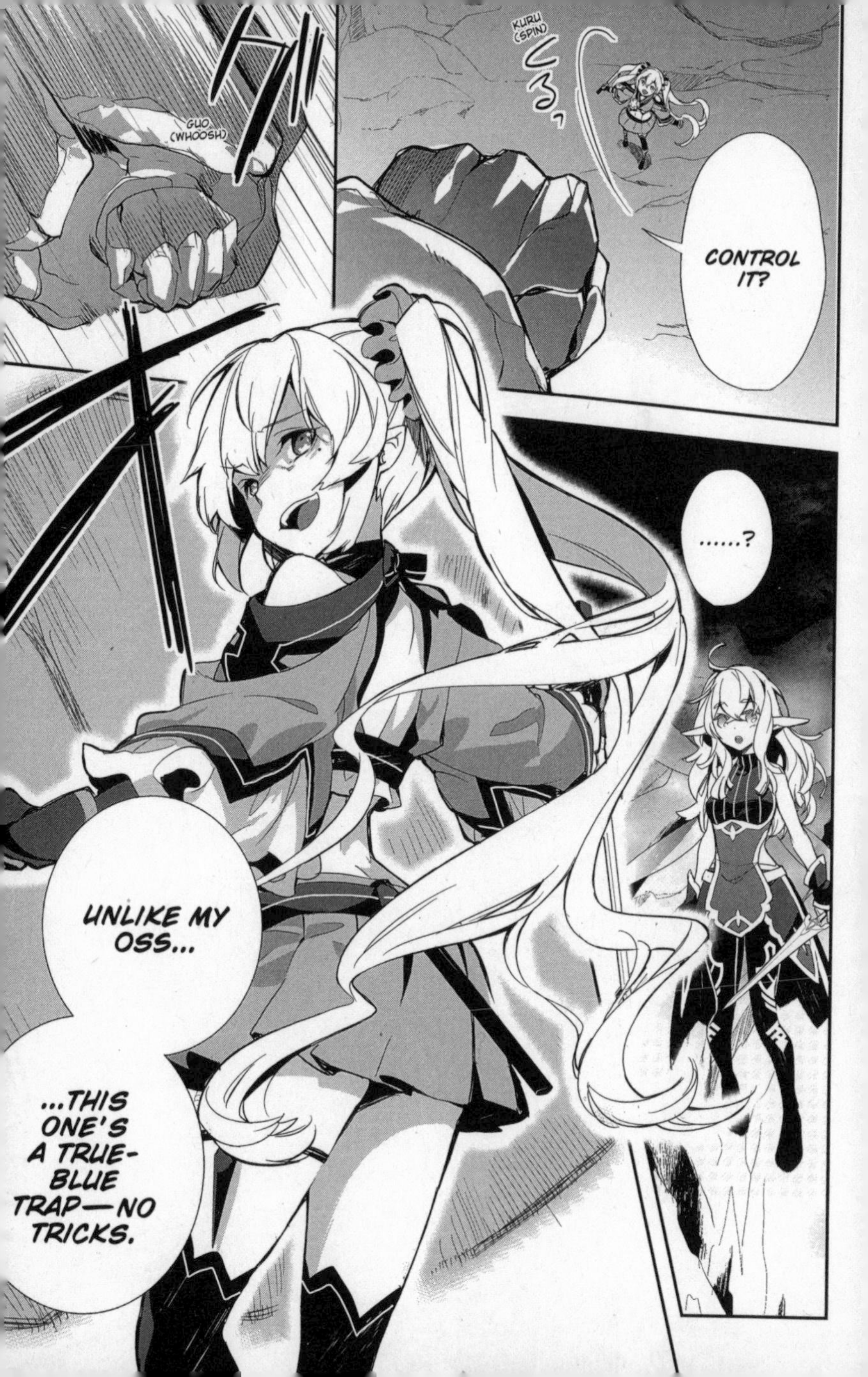
KURU (SPIN)
CONTROL IT?
GUO (WHOOSH)
......?
UNLIKE MY OSS...
...THIS ONE'S A TRUE-BLUE TRAP—NO TRICKS.

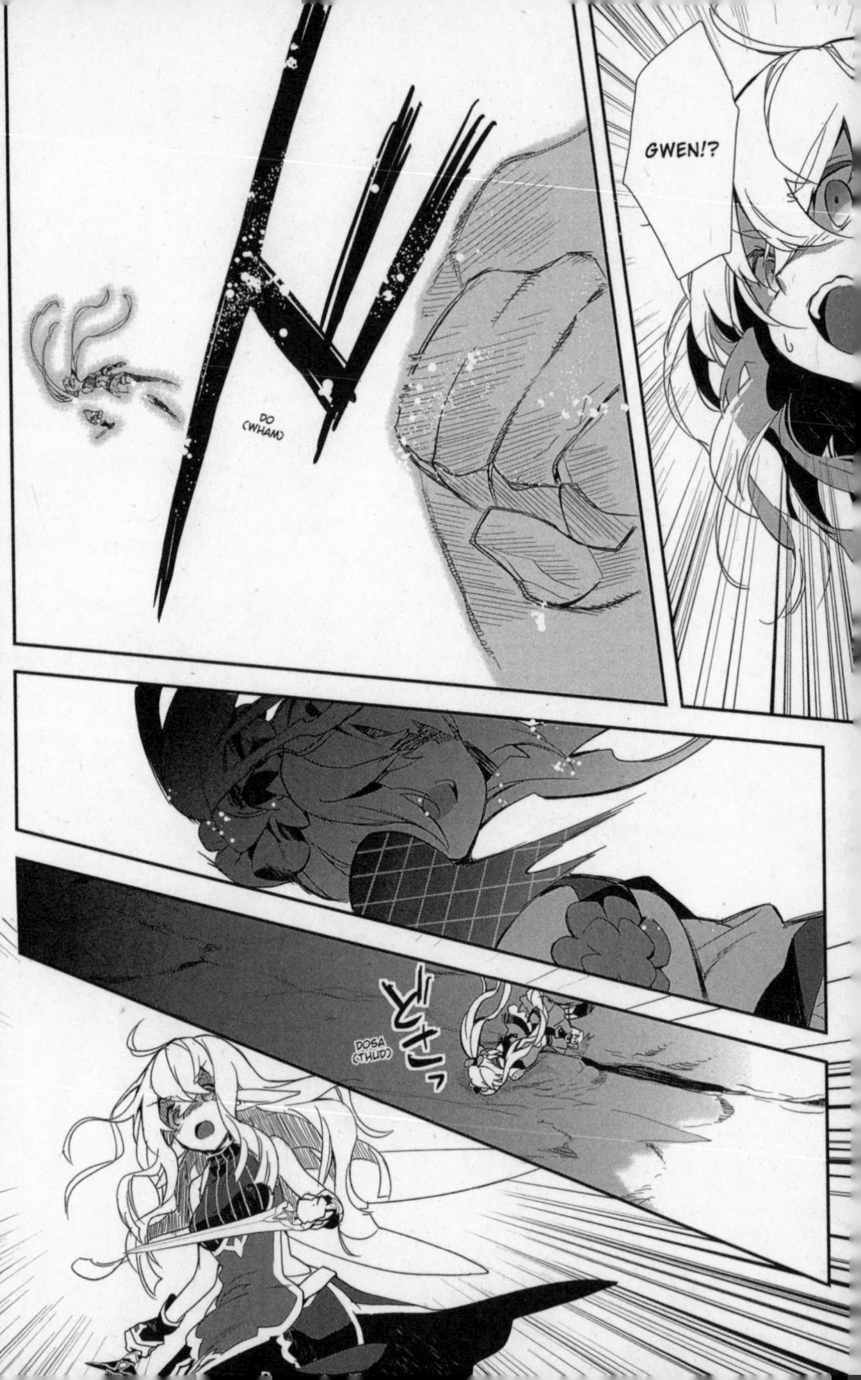
GWEN!?
DO
(WHAM)
DOSA
(THUD)

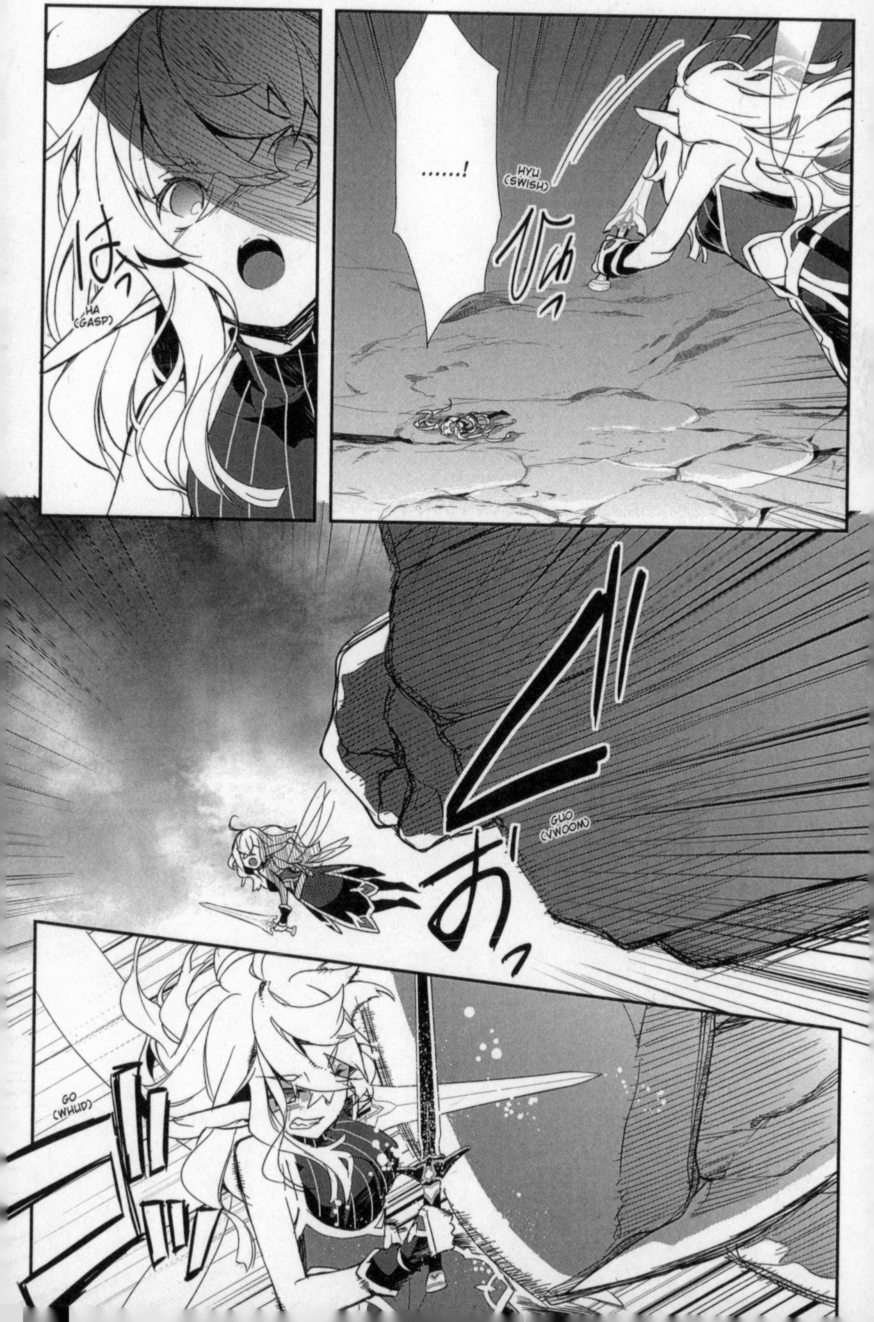

HYU
(SWISH)
......!
HA
(GASP)
GUO
(VWOOM)
GO
(WHUD)

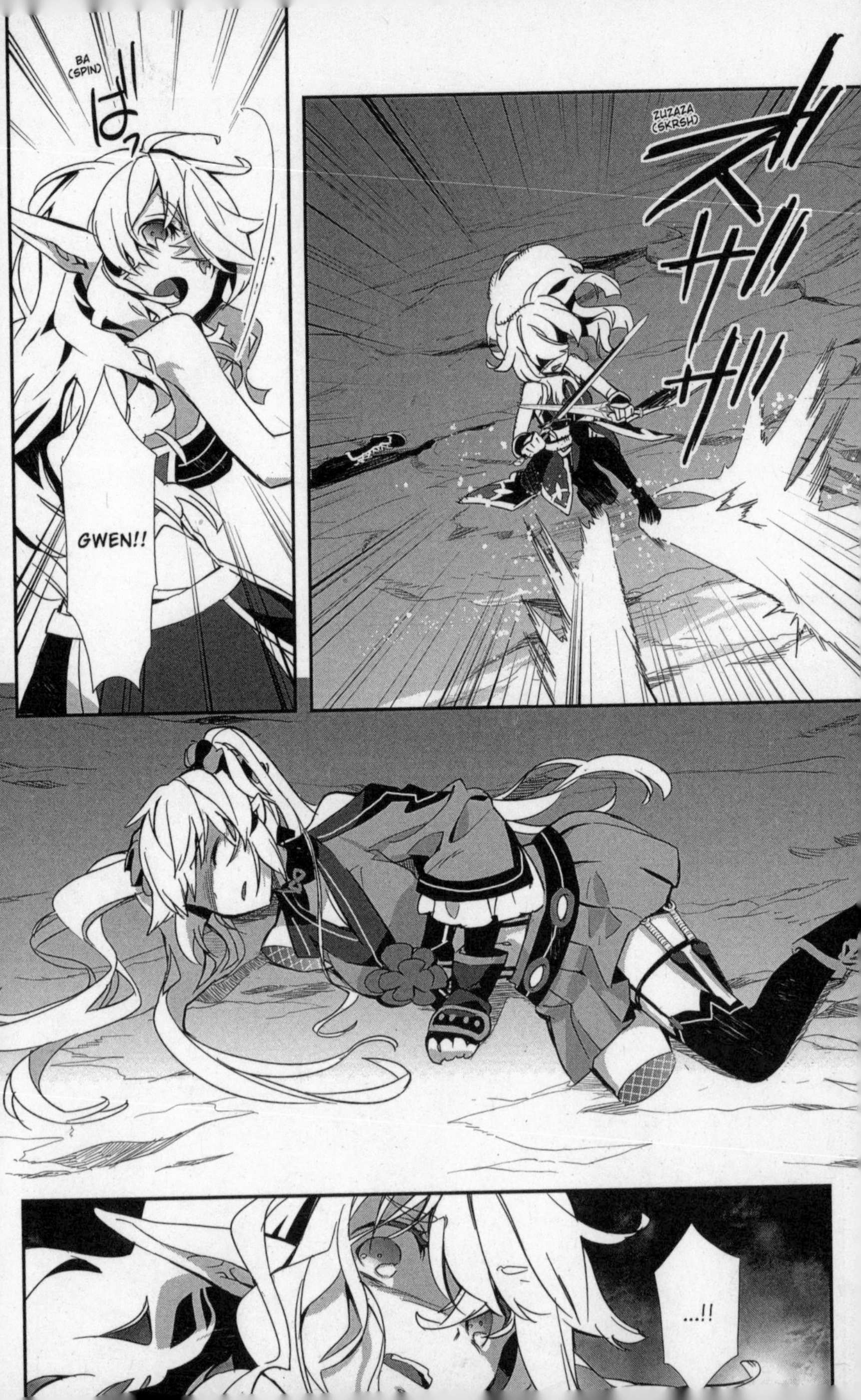
ZUZAZA (SKRSH)
ズザザザ
BA (SPIN)
ばっ
GWEN!!
...!!

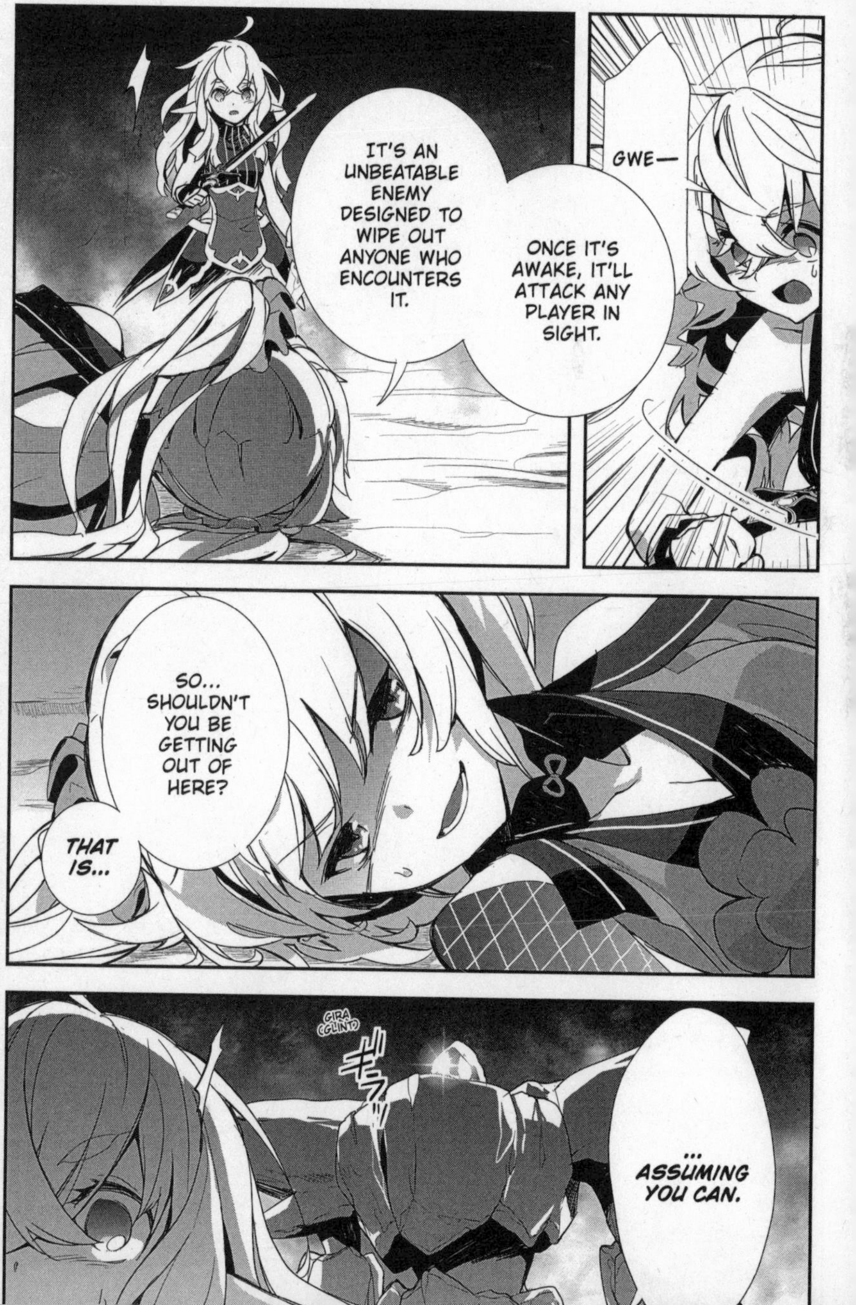
GWE—
IT'S AN UNBEATABLE ENEMY DESIGNED TO WIPE OUT ANYONE WHO ENCOUNTERS IT.
ONCE IT'S AWAKE, IT'LL ATTACK ANY PLAYER IN SIGHT.
SO... SHOULDN'T YOU BE GETTING OUT OF HERE?
THAT IS...
GIRA (GLINT)
...ASSUMING YOU CAN.

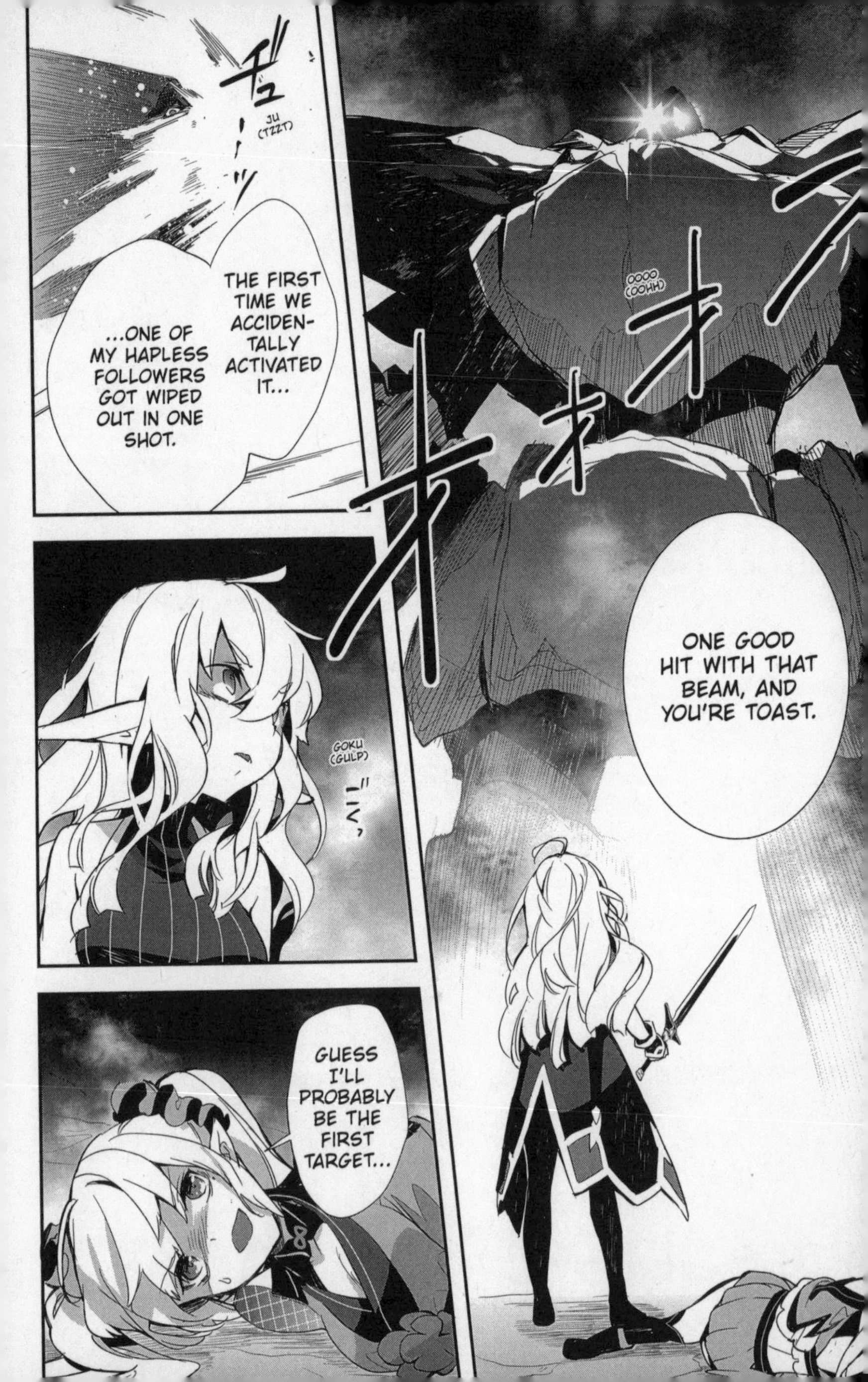
OOOO (OOHH)
ONE GOOD HIT WITH THAT BEAM, AND YOU'RE TOAST.
JU (TZZT)
THE FIRST TIME WE ACCIDENTALLY ACTIVATED IT...
...ONE OF MY HAPLESS FOLLOWERS GOT WIPED OUT IN ONE SHOT.
GOKU (GULP)
GUESS I'LL PROBABLY BE THE FIRST TARGET...

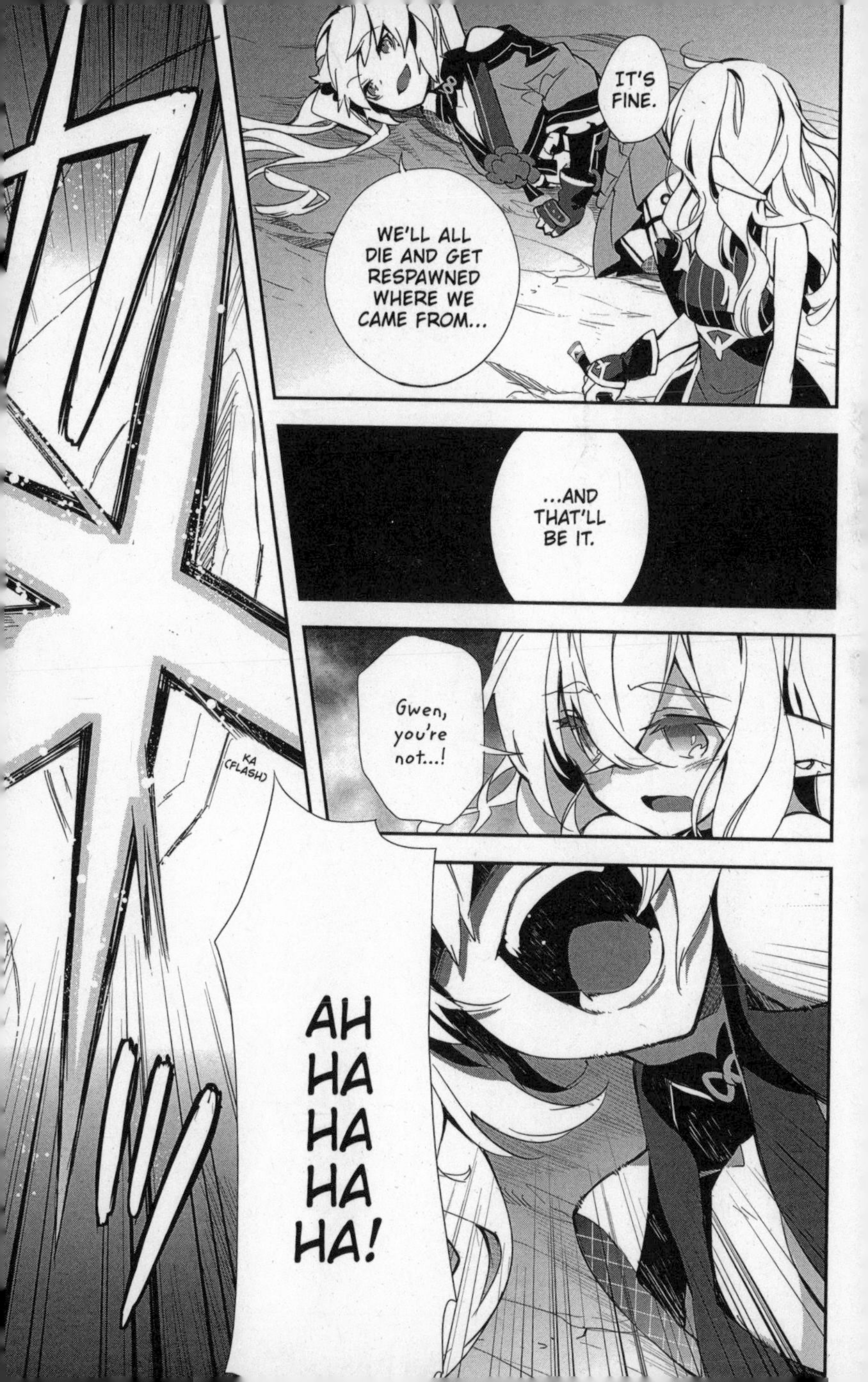
IT'S FINE.
WE'LL ALL DIE AND GET RESPAWNED WHERE WE CAME FROM...
...AND THAT'LL BE IT.
Gwen, you're not...!
KA (FLASH)
AH HA HA HA HA!

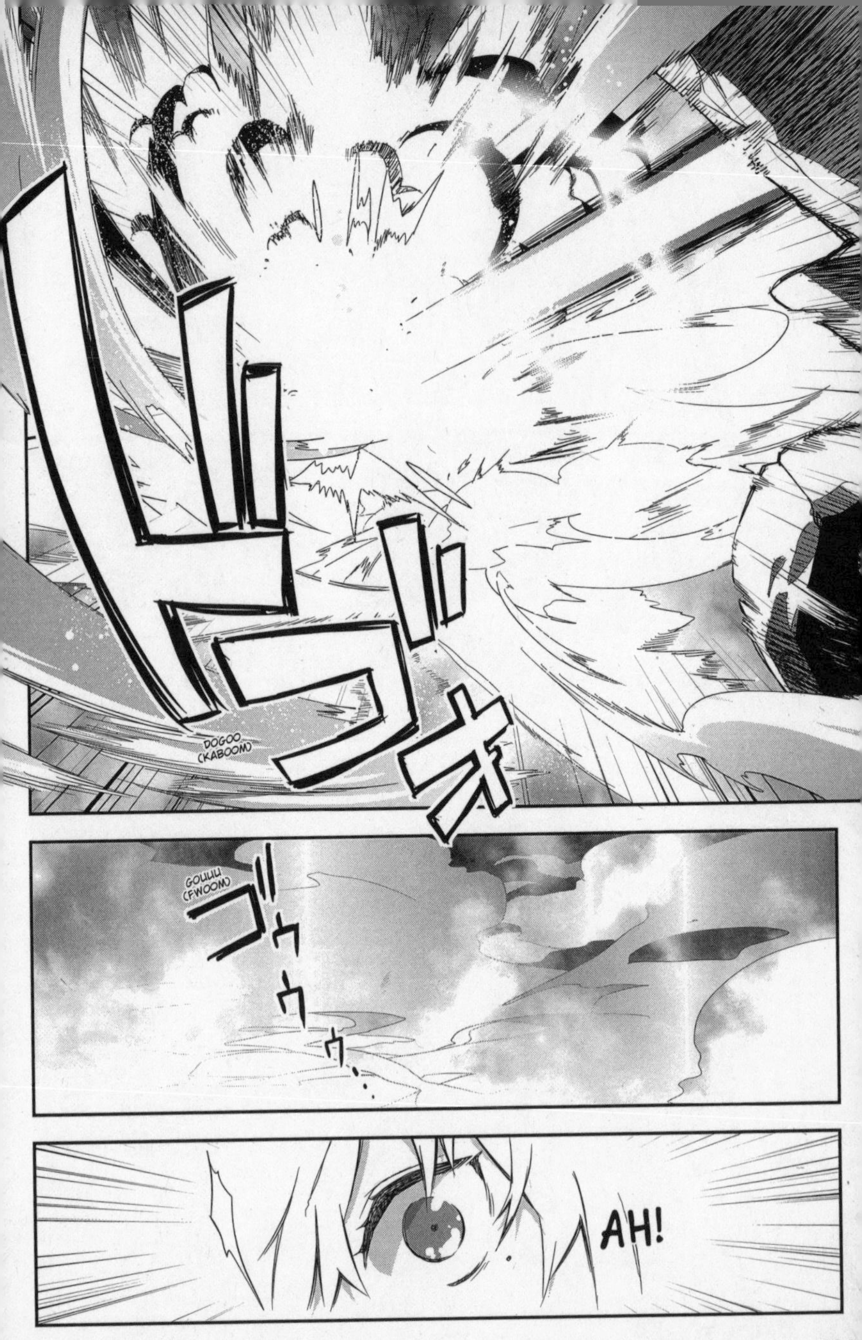
DOGOO
(KABOOM)
GOUUU
(FWOOM)
AH!

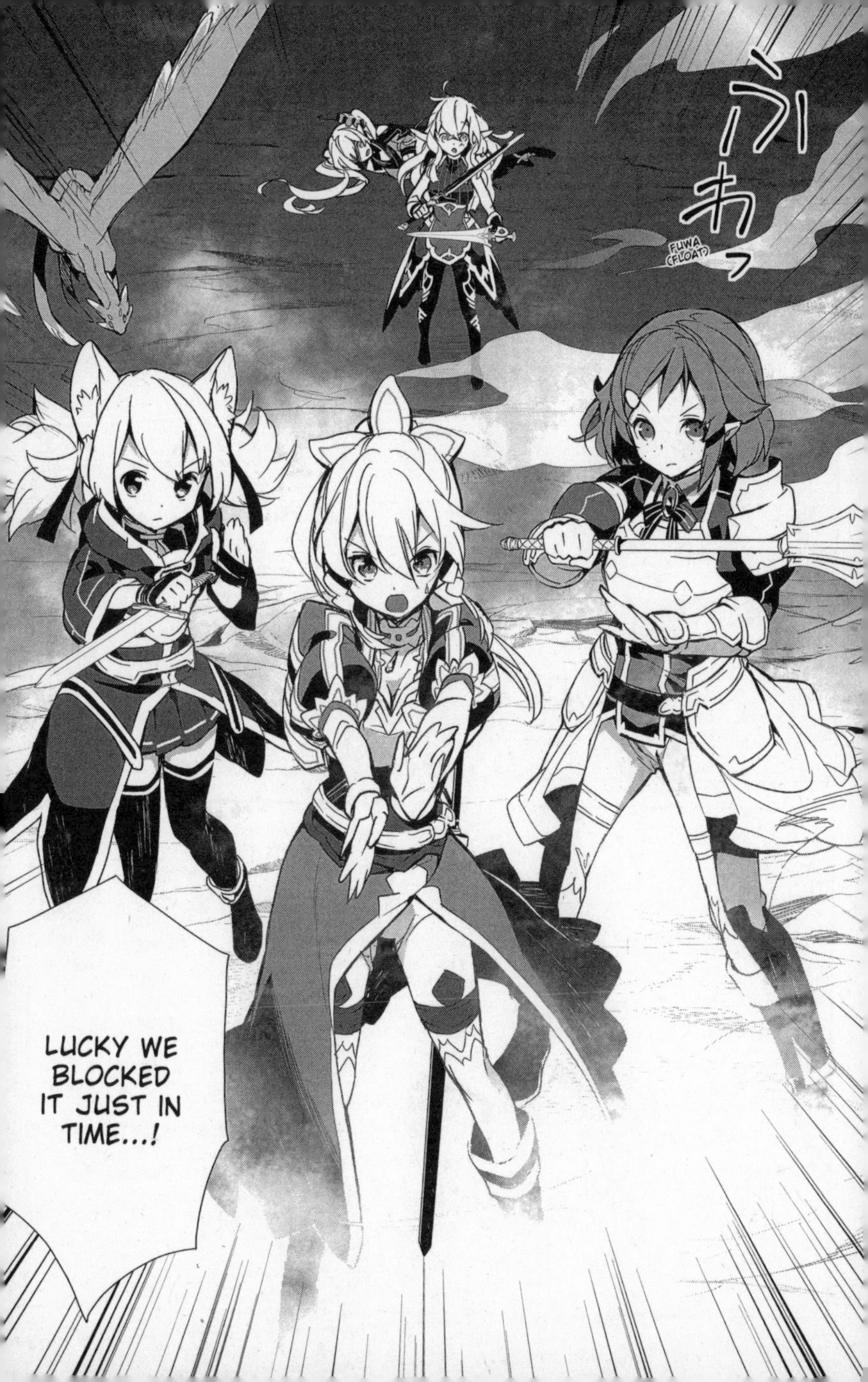
ふわっ
FUWA (FLOAT)
LUCKY WE BLOCKED IT JUST IN TIME...!

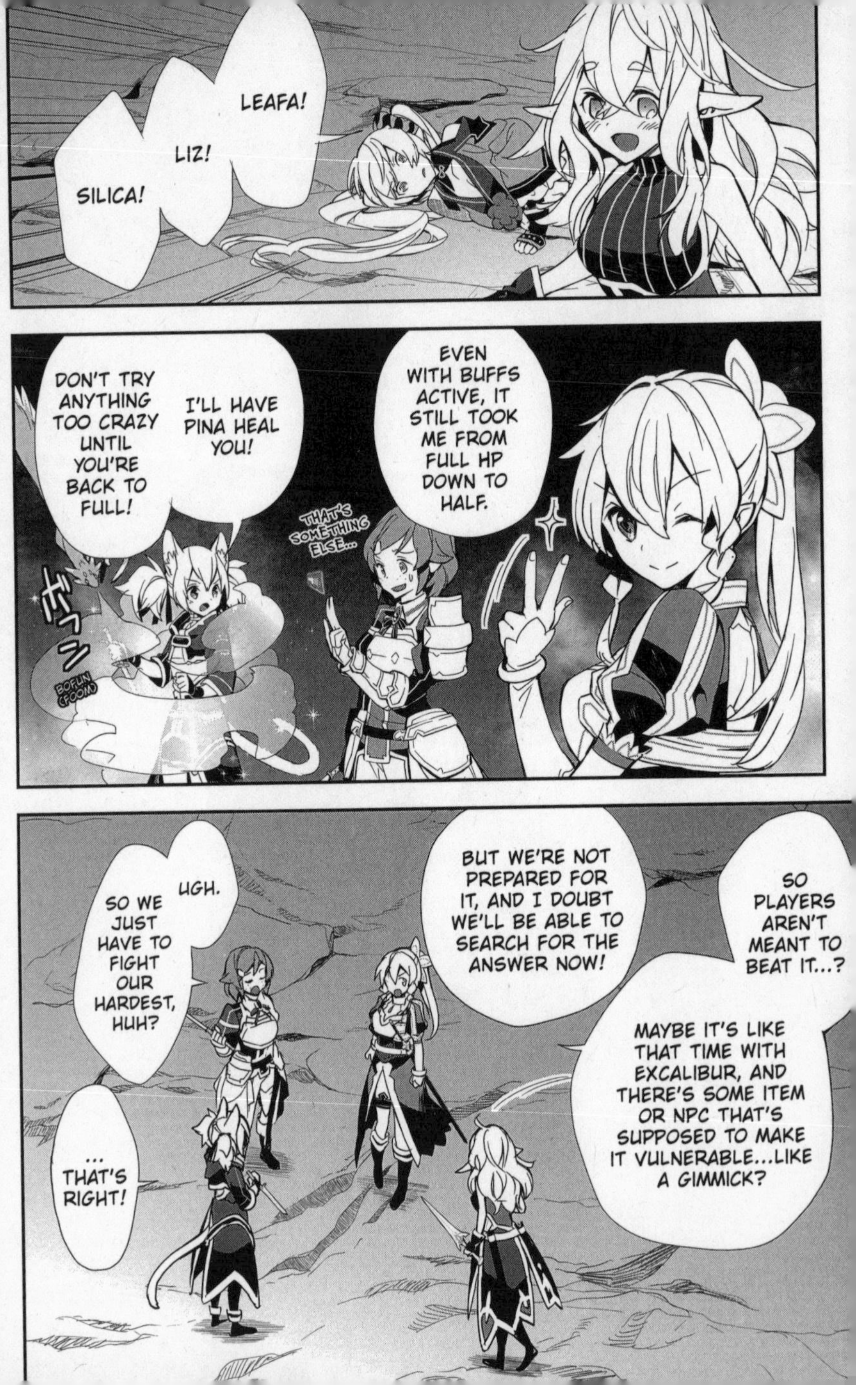
LEAFA!
LIZ!
SILICA!
EVEN WITH BUFFS ACTIVE, IT STILL TOOK ME FROM FULL HP DOWN TO HALF.
THAT'S SOMETHING ELSE...
I'LL HAVE PINA HEAL YOU!
DON'T TRY ANYTHING TOO CRAZY UNTIL YOU'RE BACK TO FULL!
BOFUN (FOOM)
SO PLAYERS AREN'T MEANT TO BEAT IT...?
MAYBE IT'S LIKE THAT TIME WITH EXCALIBUR, AND THERE'S SOME ITEM OR NPC THAT'S SUPPOSED TO MAKE IT VULNERABLE...LIKE A GIMMICK?
BUT WE'RE NOT PREPARED FOR IT, AND I DOUBT WE'LL BE ABLE TO SEARCH FOR THE ANSWER NOW!
UGH.
SO WE JUST HAVE TO FIGHT OUR HARDEST, HUH?
... THAT'S RIGHT!

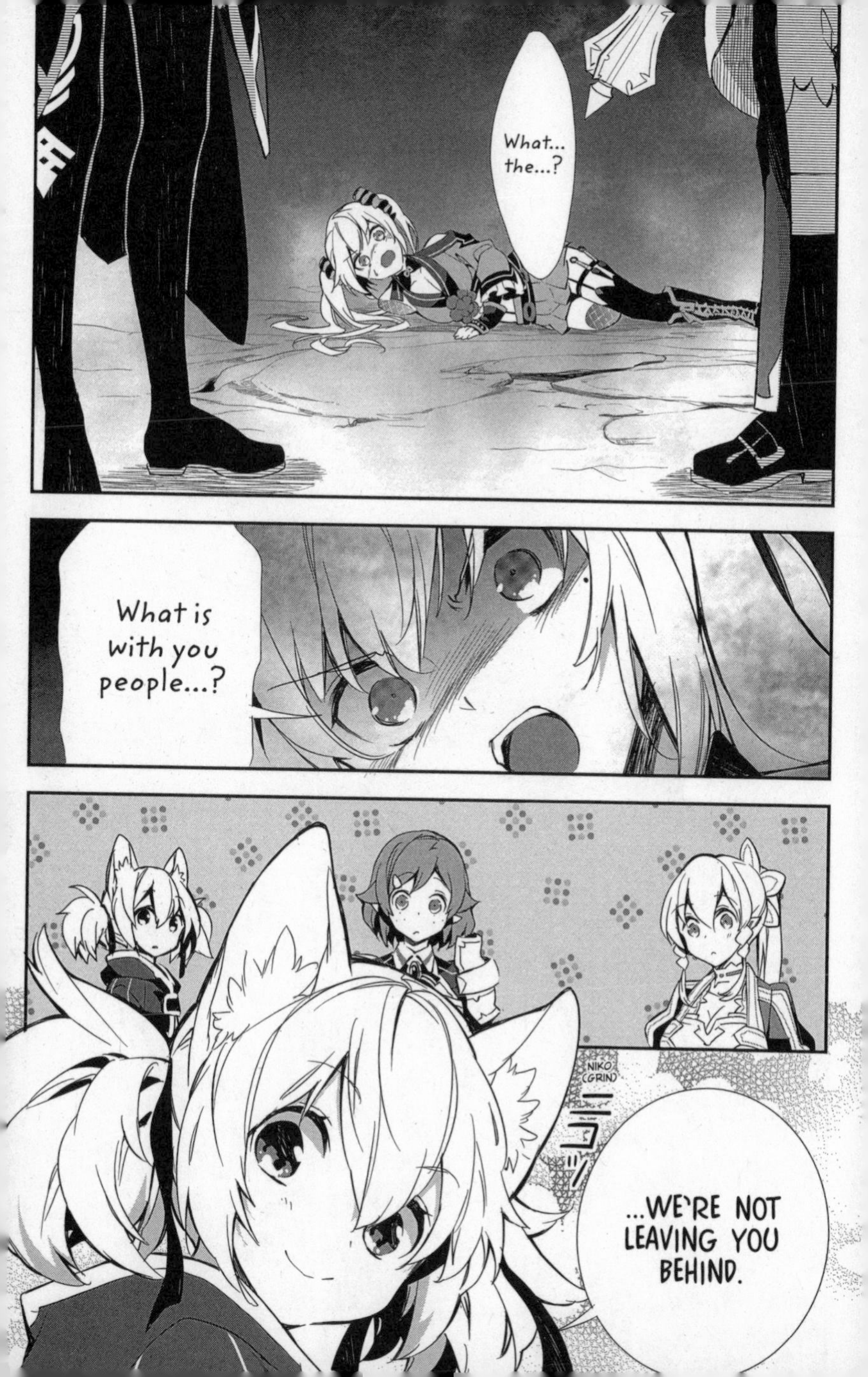
What... the...?
What is with you people...?
NIKO (GRIN)
...WE'RE NOT LEAVING YOU BEHIND.

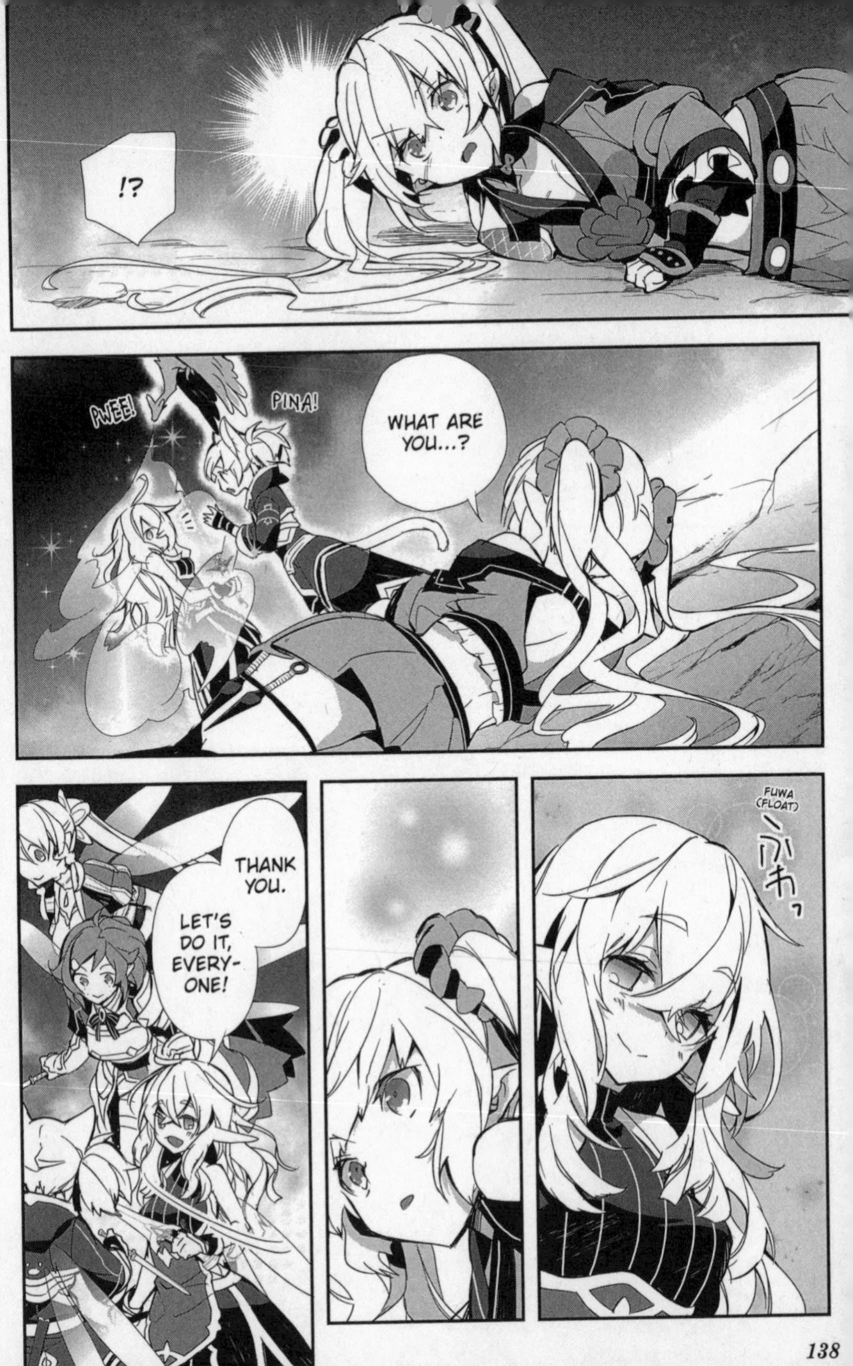
!?
PINA!
PWEE!
WHAT ARE YOU...?
FUWA (FLOAT)
ふわっ
THANK YOU.
LET'S DO IT, EVERYONE!

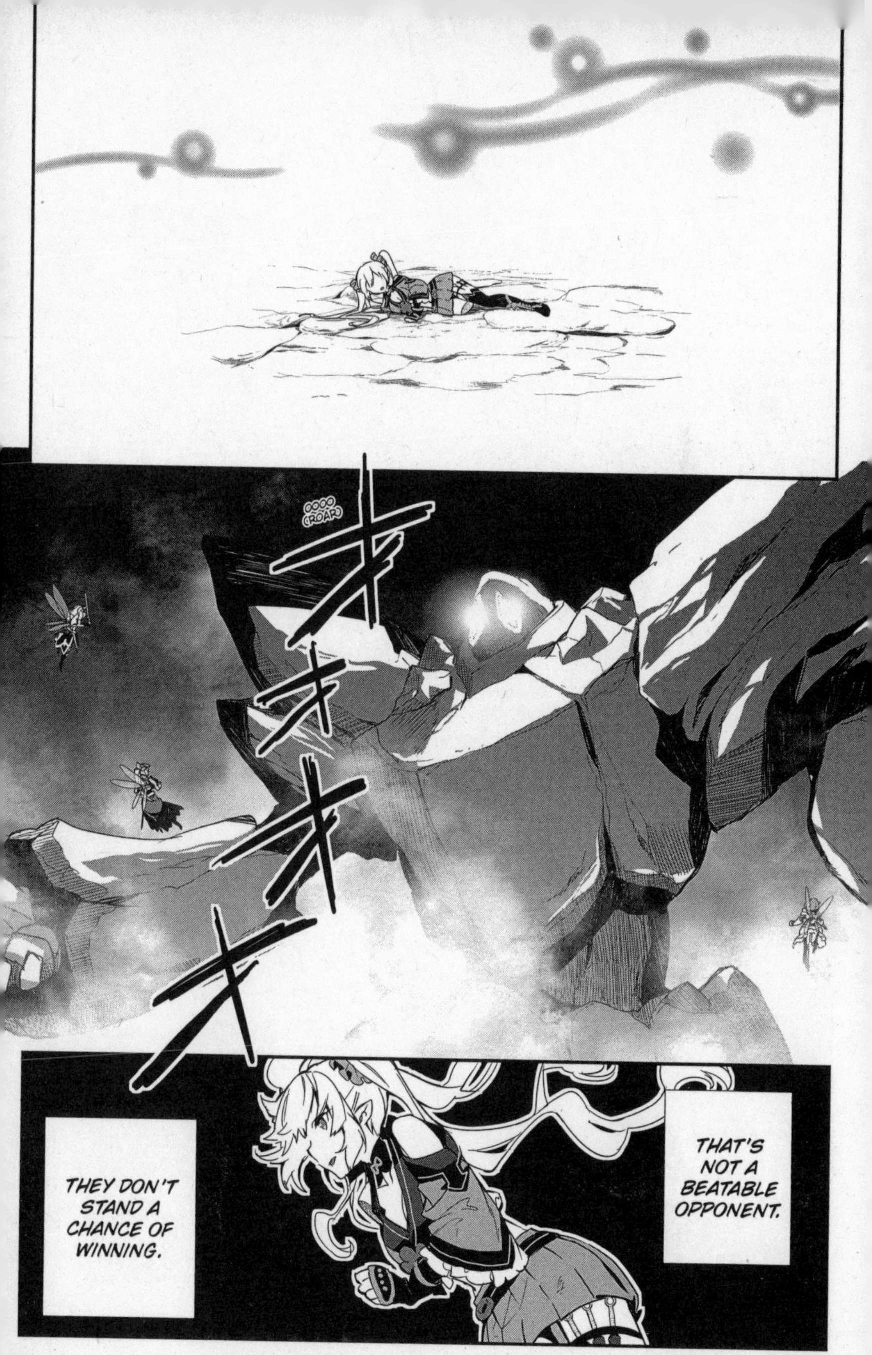
OOOO
(ROAR)
THAT'S NOT A BEATABLE OPPONENT.
THEY DON'T STAND A CHANCE OF WINNING.

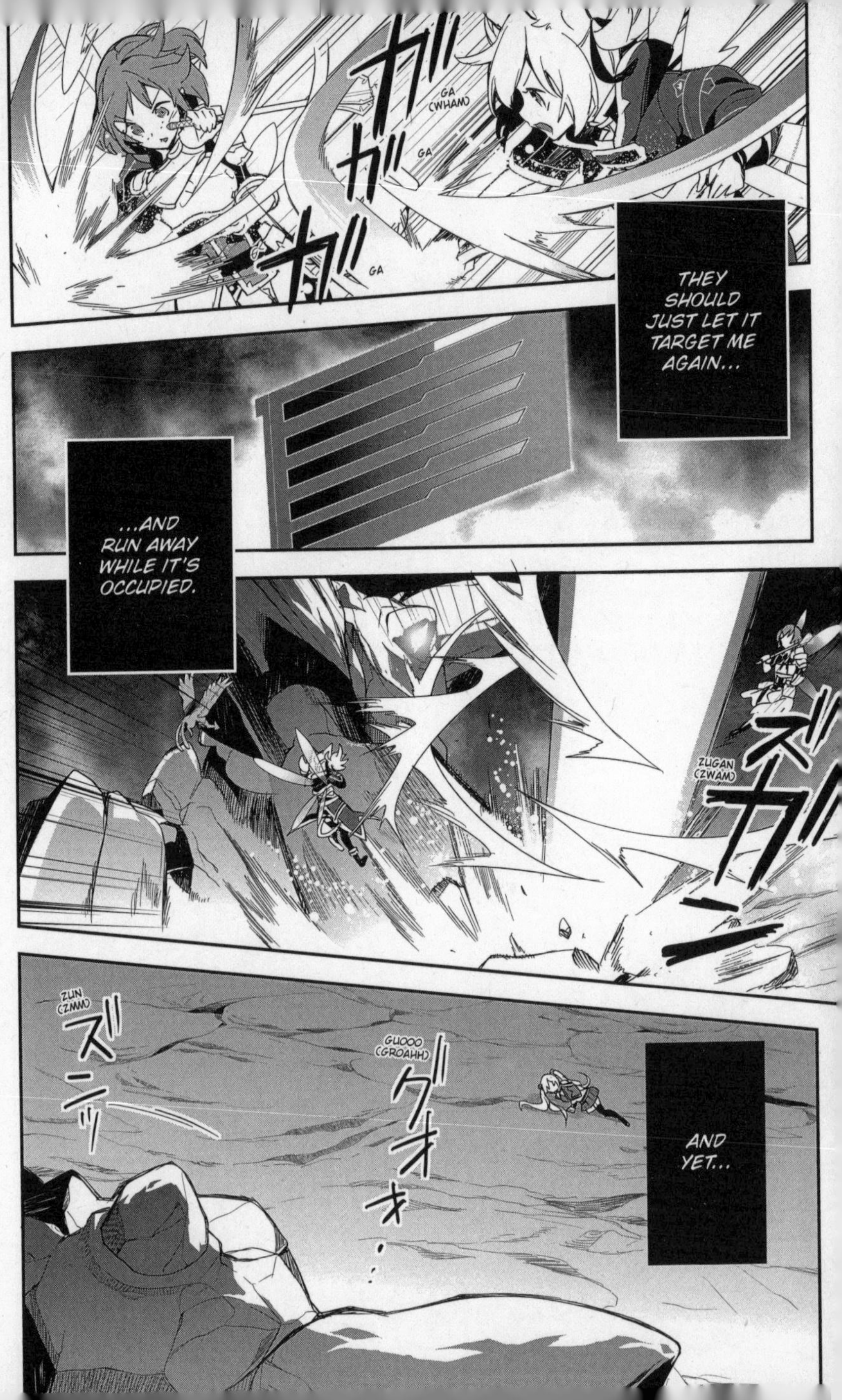

ガ
GA (WHAM)
ガ
GA
ガ
GA
THEY SHOULD JUST LET IT TARGET ME AGAIN...
...AND RUN AWAY WHILE IT'S OCCUPIED.
ズガ
ZUGAN (ZWAM)
ズーッ
ZUN (ZMM)
グオォ…
GUOOO (GROAHH)
AND YET...

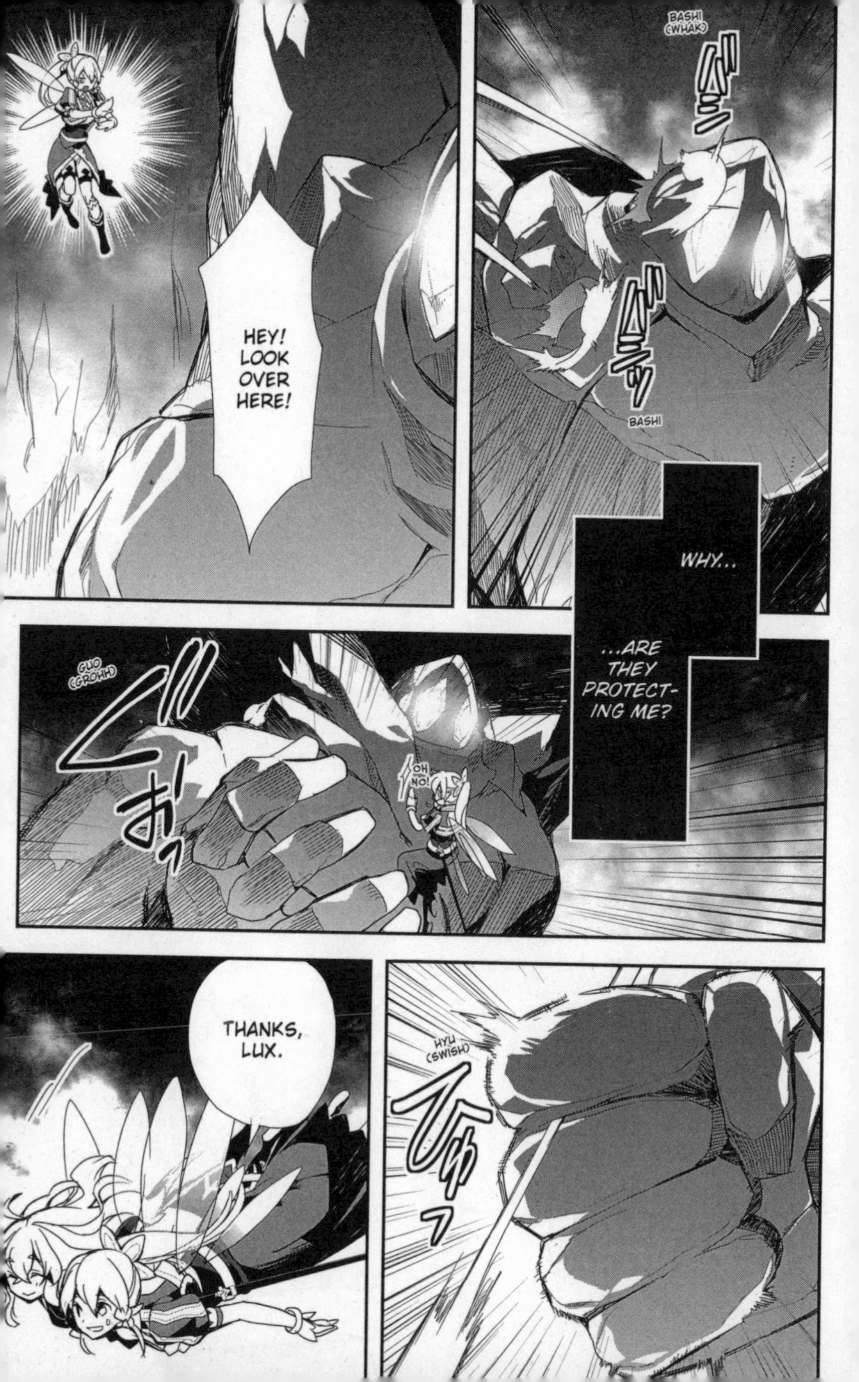
BASHI (WHAK)
BASHI
HEY! LOOK OVER HERE!
WHY...
...ARE THEY PROTECTING ME?
GUO (GROHH)
OH NO!
HYU (SWISH)
THANKS, LUX.

AREN'T I...
...YOUR ENEMY?
GU (CLENCH)
I'M NOT YOUR FRIEND OR YOUR COMPANION OR YOUR ANYTHING!
GUGU (RUMBLE)
DOBAAN (DWOOSH)

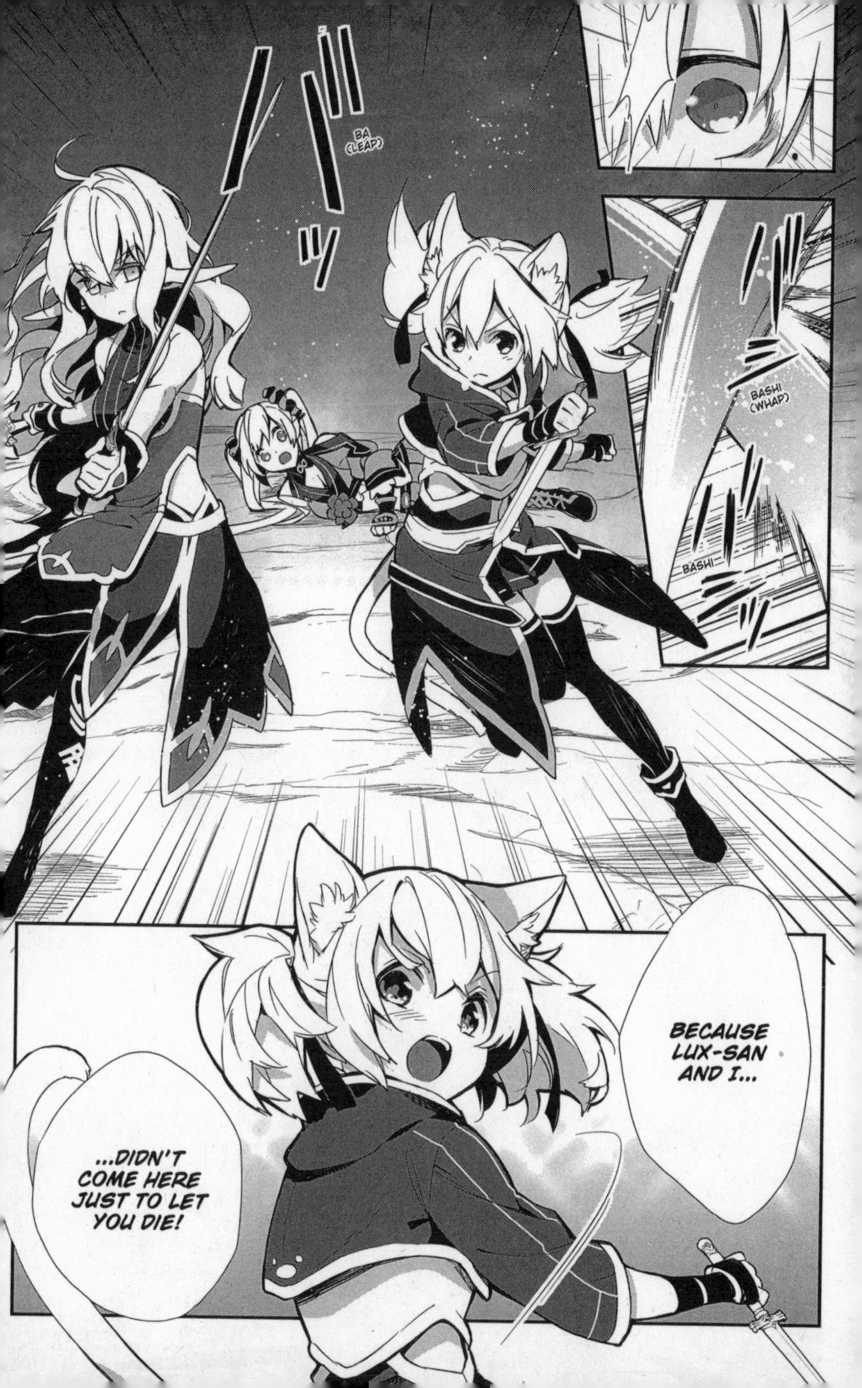

BA (LEAP)
BASHI (WHAP)
BASHI
BECAUSE LUX-SAN AND I...
...DIDN'T COME HERE JUST TO LET YOU DIE!

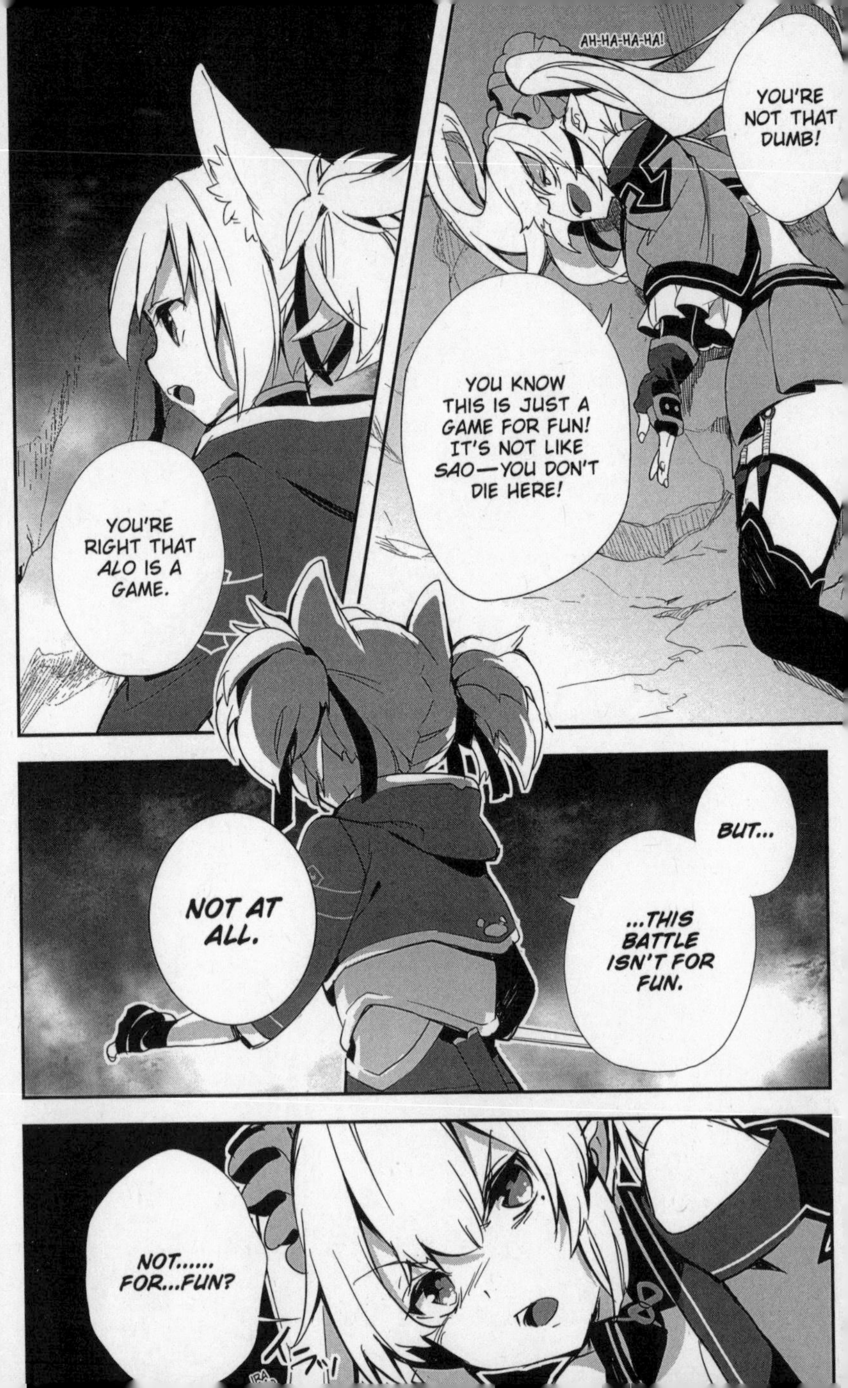
AH-HA-HA-HA!
YOU'RE NOT THAT DUMB!
YOU KNOW THIS IS JUST A GAME FOR FUN! IT'S NOT LIKE SAO—YOU DON'T DIE HERE!
YOU'RE RIGHT THAT ALO IS A GAME.
BUT...
...THIS BATTLE ISN'T FOR FUN.
NOT AT ALL.
NOT...... FOR...FUN?

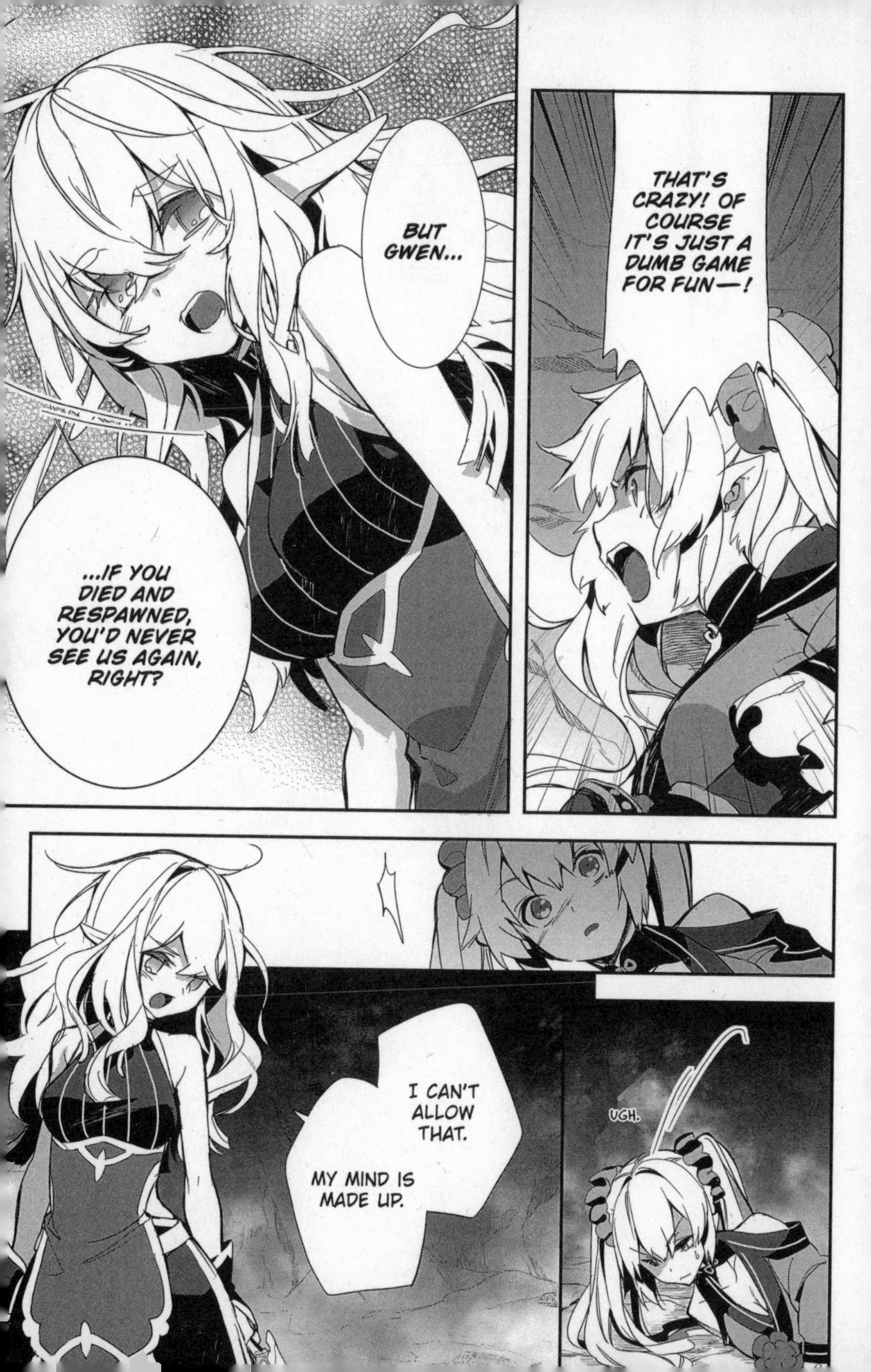
THAT'S CRAZY! OF COURSE IT'S JUST A DUMB GAME FOR FUN—!
BUT GWEN...
...IF YOU DIED AND RESPAWNED, YOU'D NEVER SEE US AGAIN, RIGHT?
UGH.
I CAN'T ALLOW THAT.
MY MIND IS MADE UP.

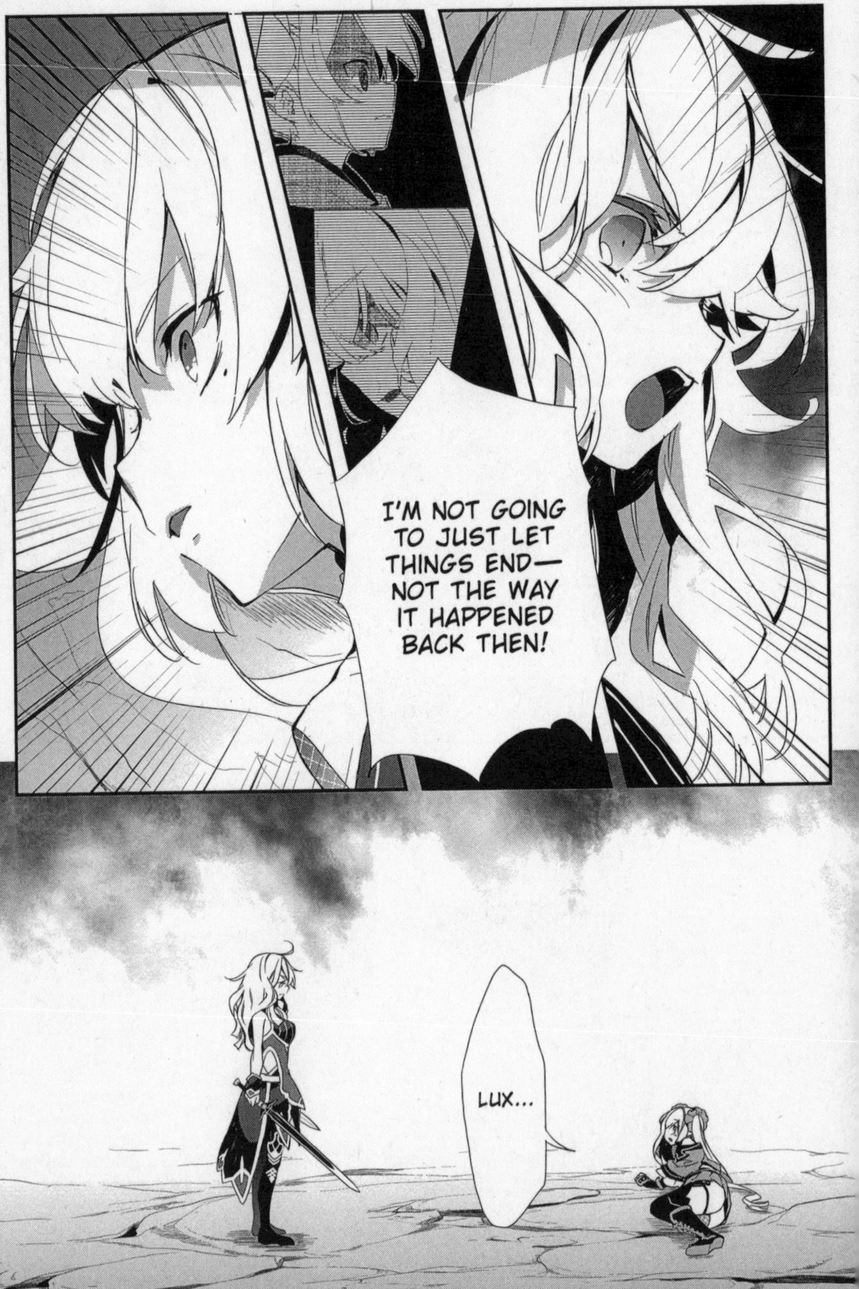
I'M NOT GOING TO JUST LET THINGS END—NOT THE WAY IT HAPPENED BACK THEN!
LUX...

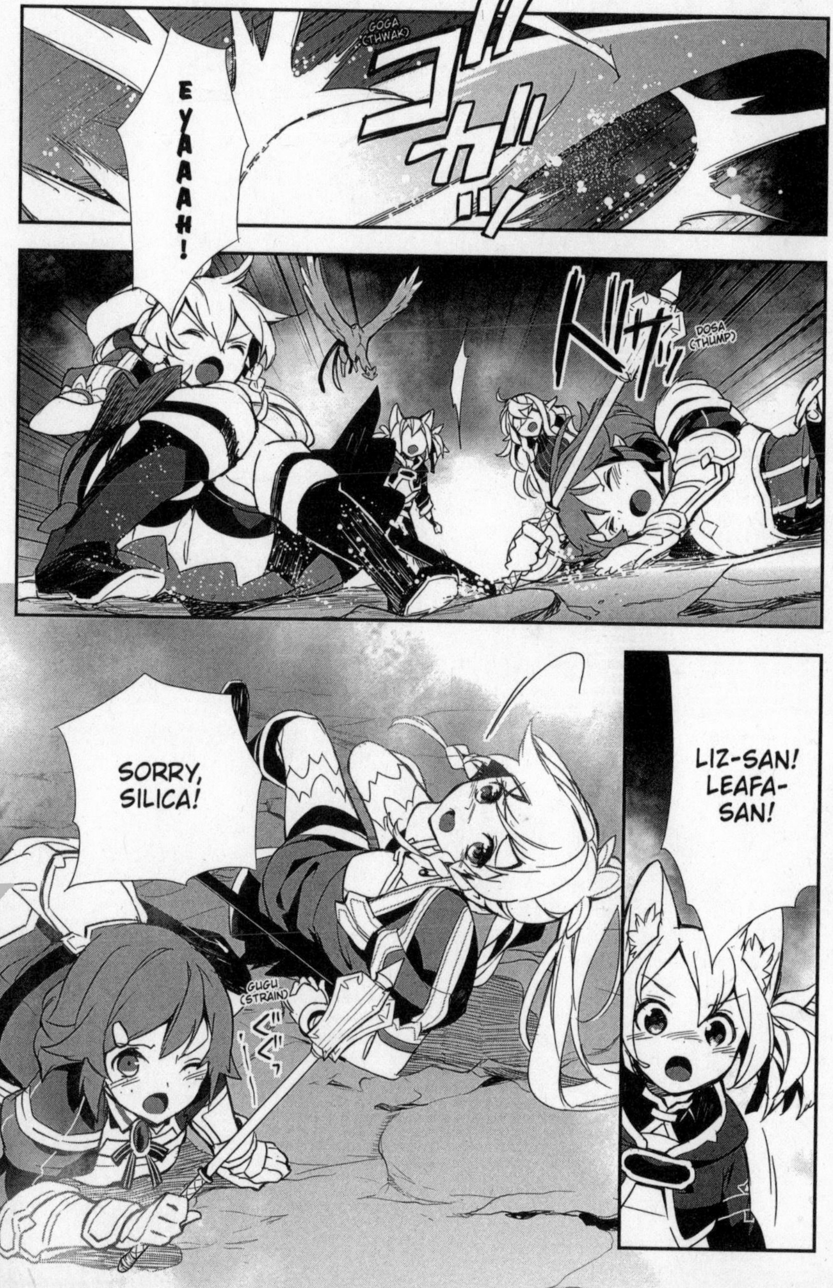
GOGA (THWAK)
ゴガッ
EYAAAH!
DOSA (THUMP)
ドサッ
LIZ-SAN! LEAFA-SAN!
SORRY, SILICA!
GUGU (STRAIN)

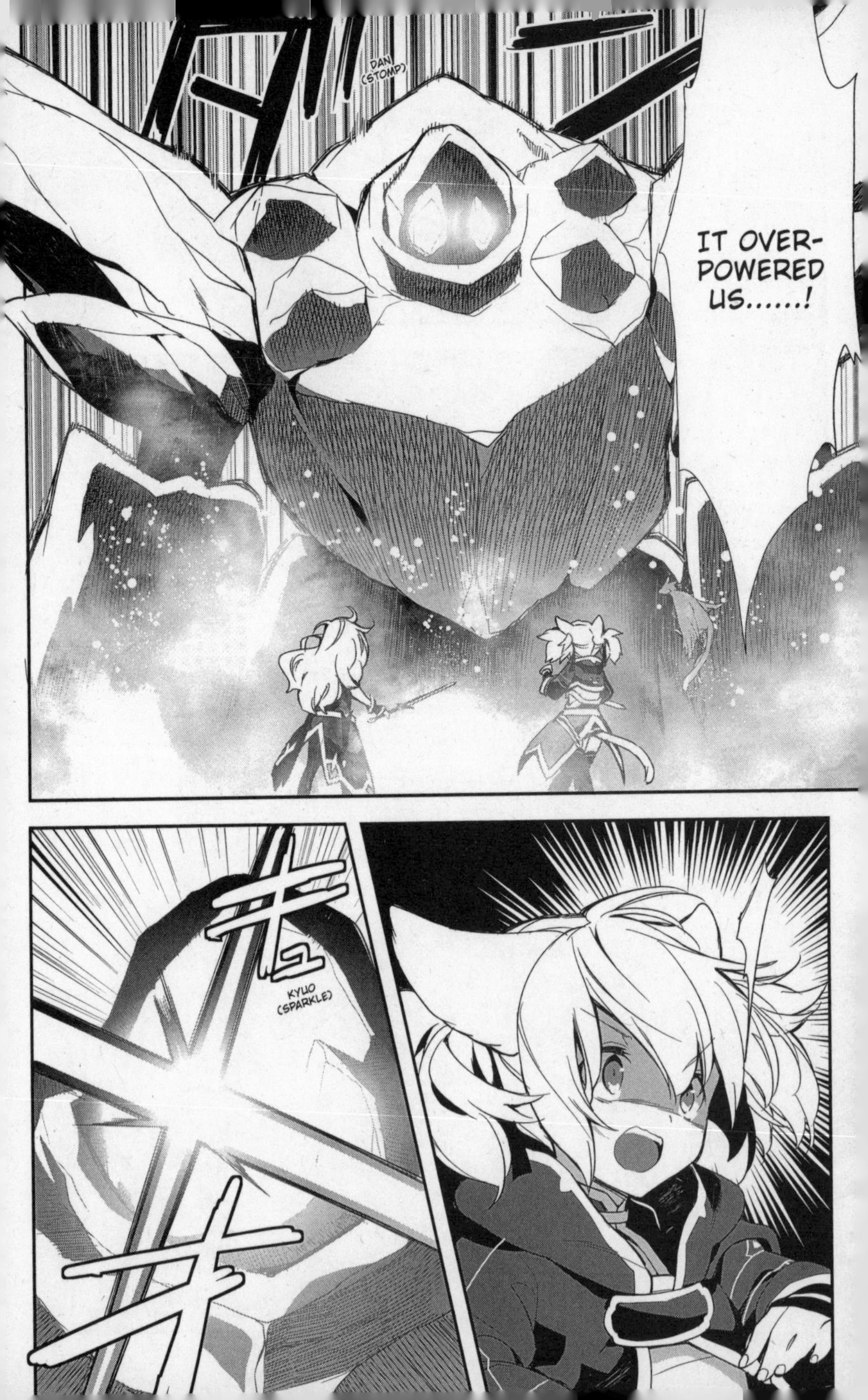
DAN
(STOMP)
IT OVER-
POWERED
US......!
KYUO
(SPARKLE)

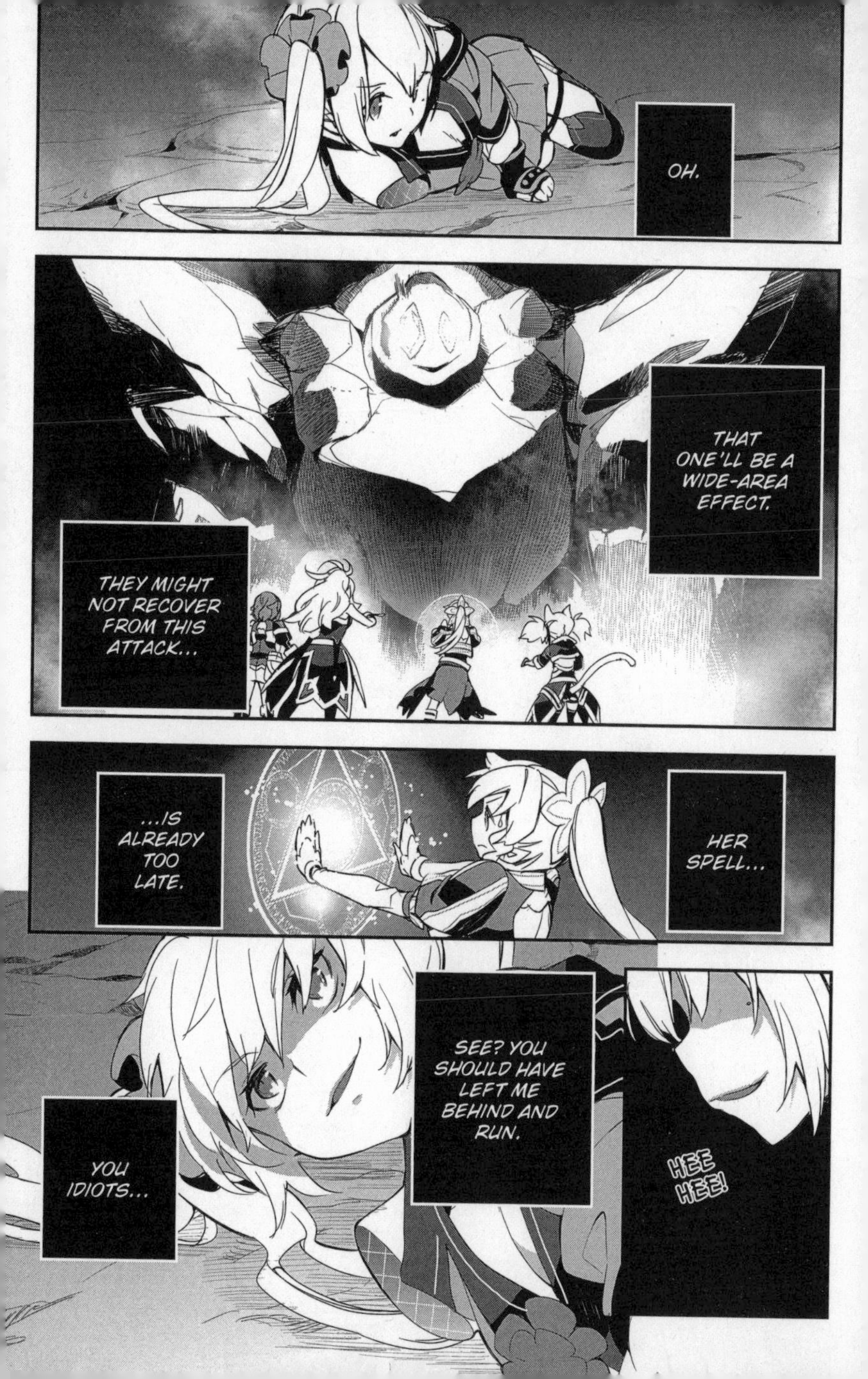
OH.
THAT ONE'LL BE A WIDE-AREA EFFECT.
THEY MIGHT NOT RECOVER FROM THIS ATTACK...
HER SPELL...
...IS ALREADY TOO LATE.
HEE HEE!
SEE? YOU SHOULD HAVE LEFT ME BEHIND AND RUN.
YOU IDIOTS...

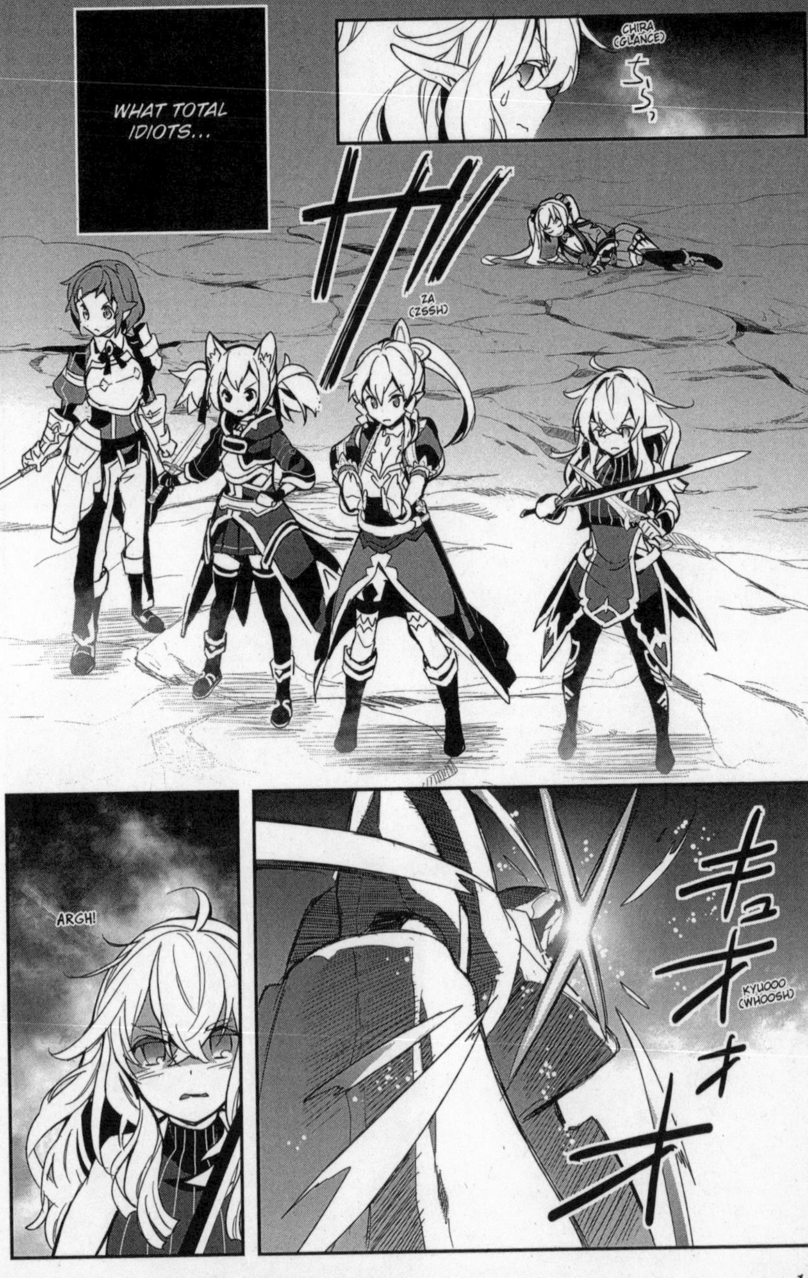
CHIRA
(GLANCE)
ちら
WHAT TOTAL
IDIOTS...
ザ
ZA
(ZSSH)
キュオォォ
KYUOOO
(WHOOSH)
ARGH!

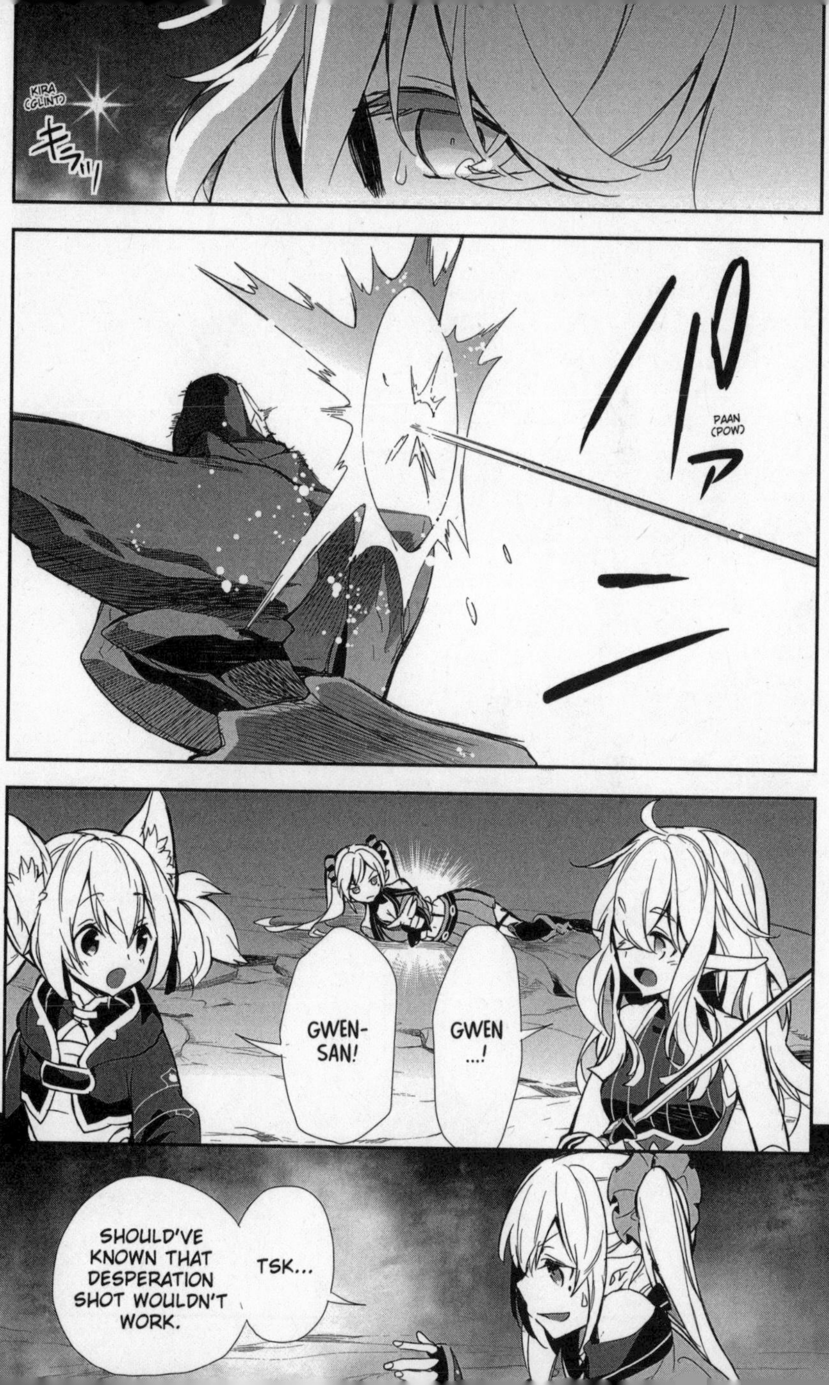
KIRA (GLINT)
PAAN (POW)
GWEN ...!
GWEN-SAN!
TSK...
SHOULD'VE KNOWN THAT DESPERATION SHOT WOULDN'T WORK.

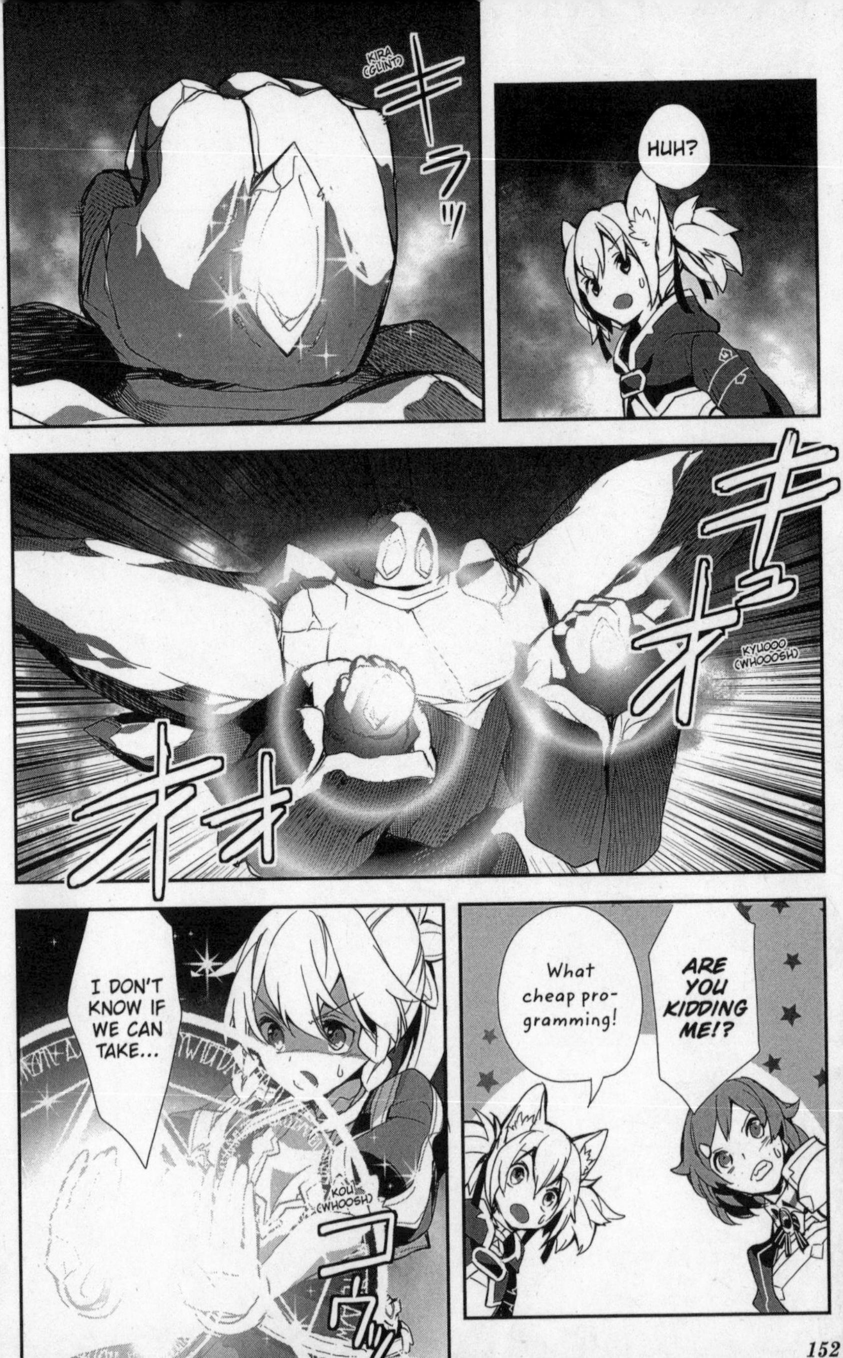
キラッ
KIRA (GLINT)
HUH?
キュオオォ
KYUOOO (WHOOOSH)
ARE YOU KIDDING ME!?
What cheap pro-gramming!
I DON'T KNOW IF WE CAN TAKE...
コウッ
KOU (WHOOSH)

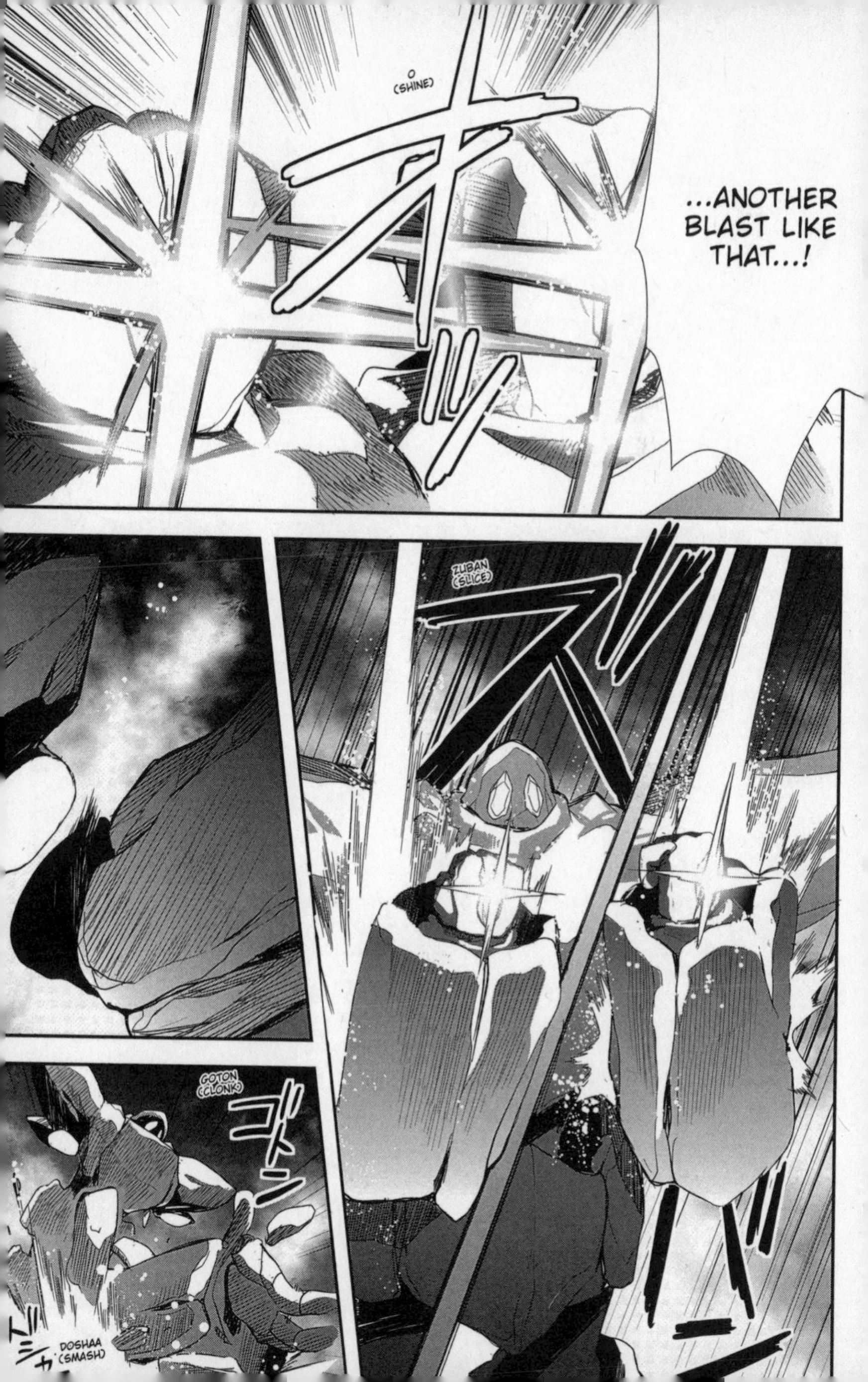
O
(SHINE)
...ANOTHER BLAST LIKE THAT...!
ZUBAN
(SLICE)
GOTON
(CLONK)
DOSHAA
(SMASH)

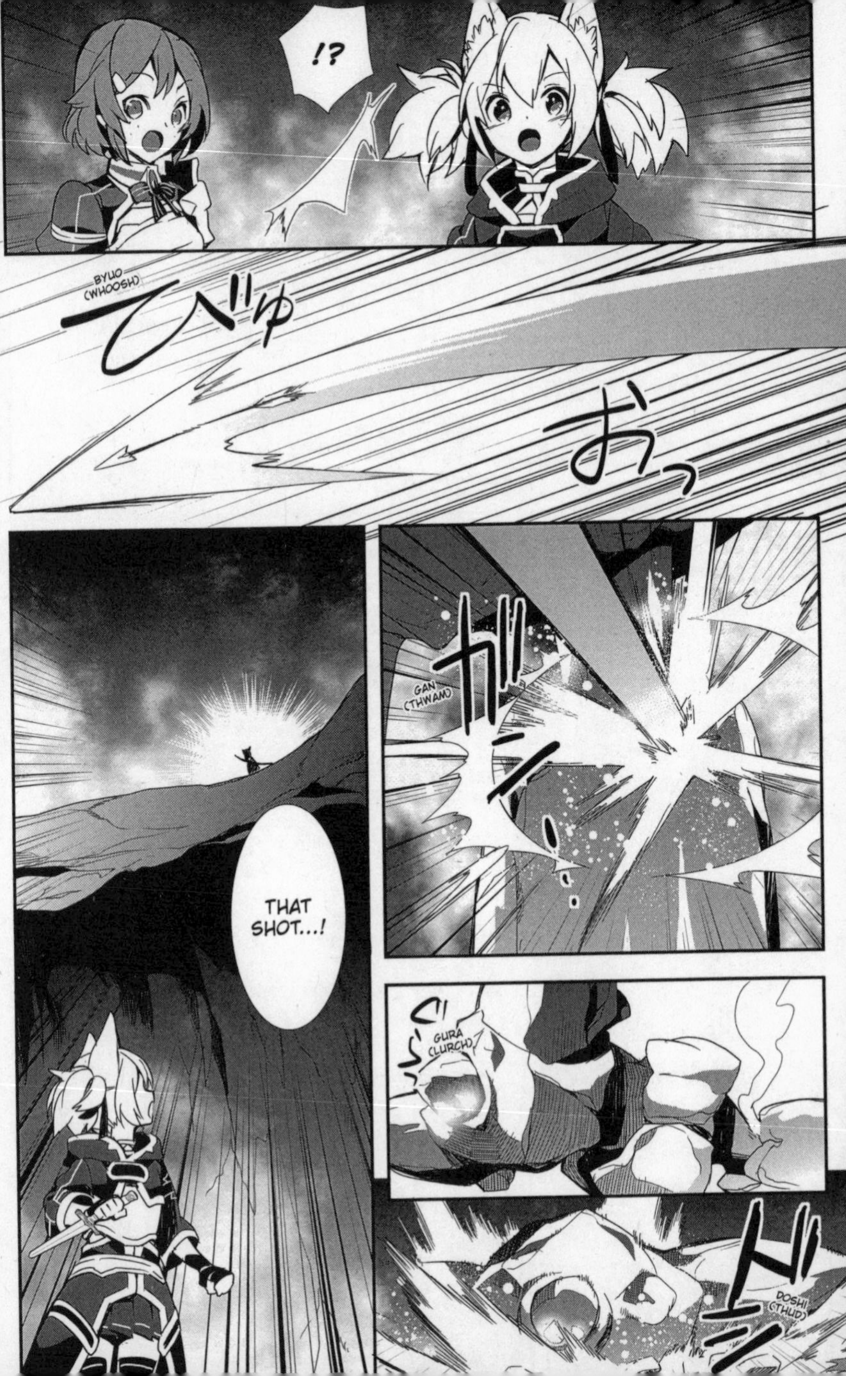

!?
BYUO (WHOOSH)
びゅ
おっ
GAN (THWAN)
ガン
THAT SHOT...!
GURA (LURCH)
ぐら
DOSHI (THUD)
ドシン

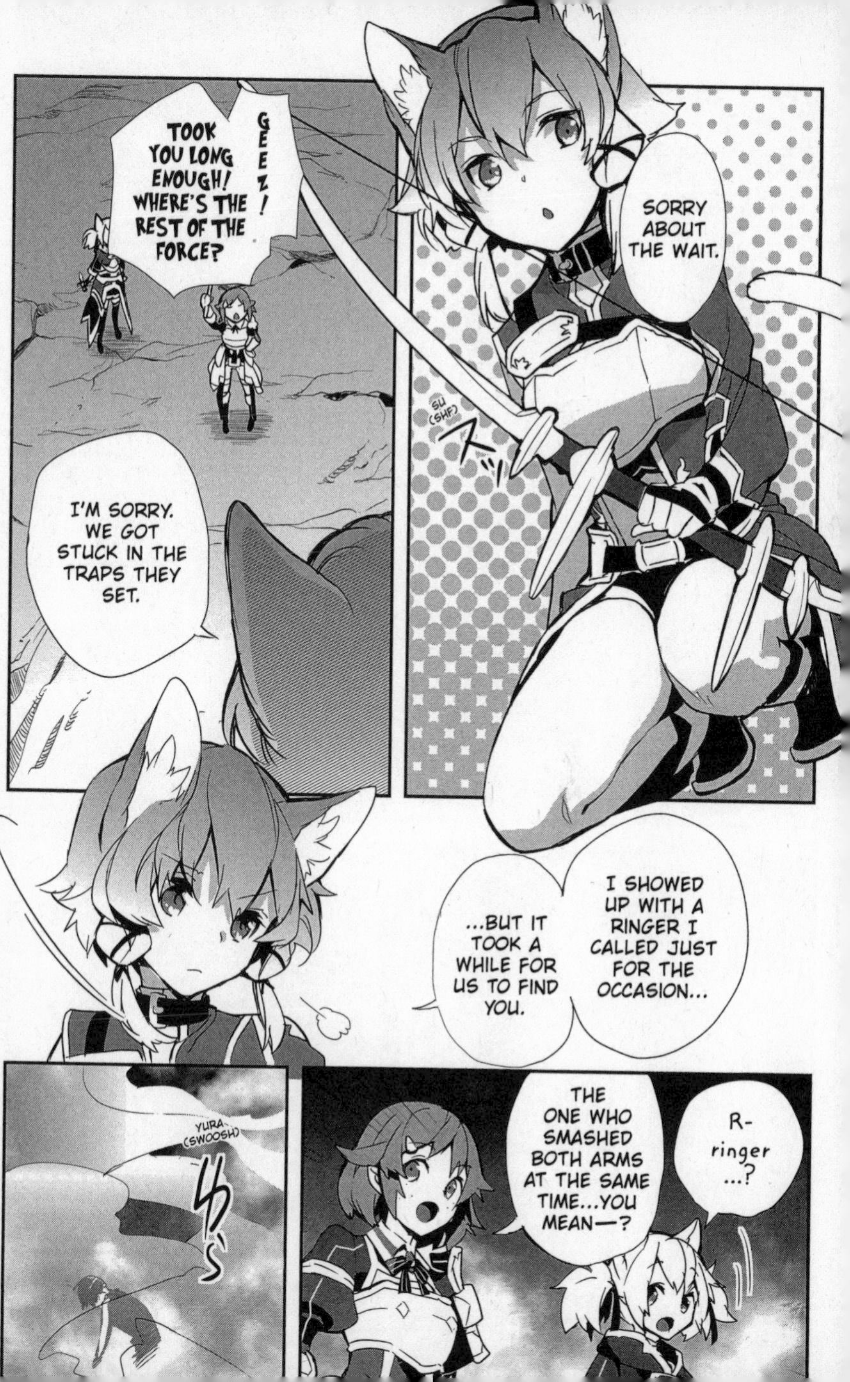
SORRY ABOUT THE WAIT.
GEEZ!
TOOK YOU LONG ENOUGH! WHERE'S THE REST OF THE FORCE?
SU (SHF)
I'M SORRY. WE GOT STUCK IN THE TRAPS THEY SET.
I SHOWED UP WITH A RINGER I CALLED JUST FOR THE OCCASION...
...BUT IT TOOK A WHILE FOR US TO FIND YOU.
R-ringer ...?
THE ONE WHO SMASHED BOTH ARMS AT THE SAME TIME...YOU MEAN—?
YURA (SWOOSH)

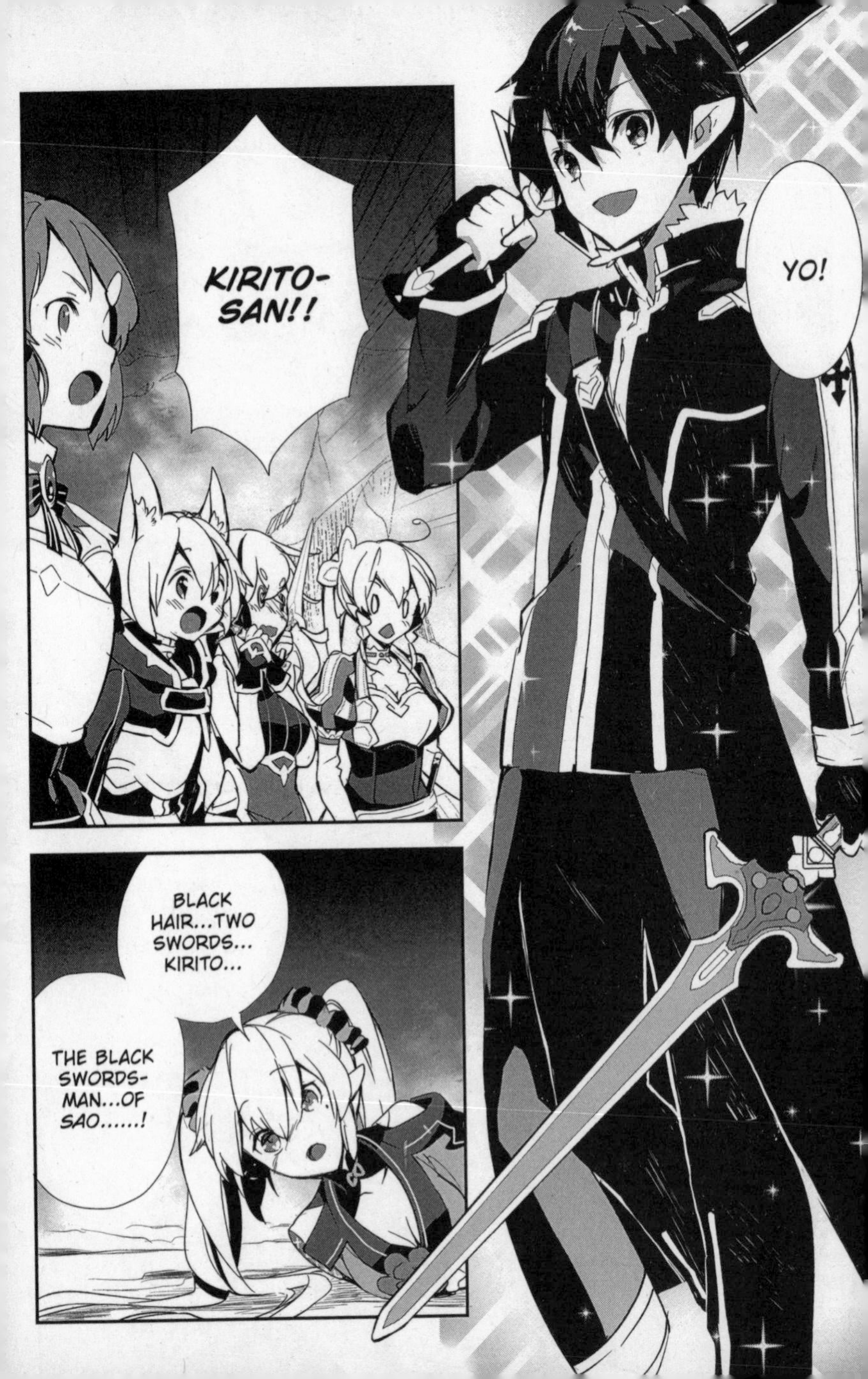
YO!
KIRITO-SAN!!
BLACK HAIR...TWO SWORDS... KIRITO...
THE BLACK SWORDS-MAN...OF SAO......!

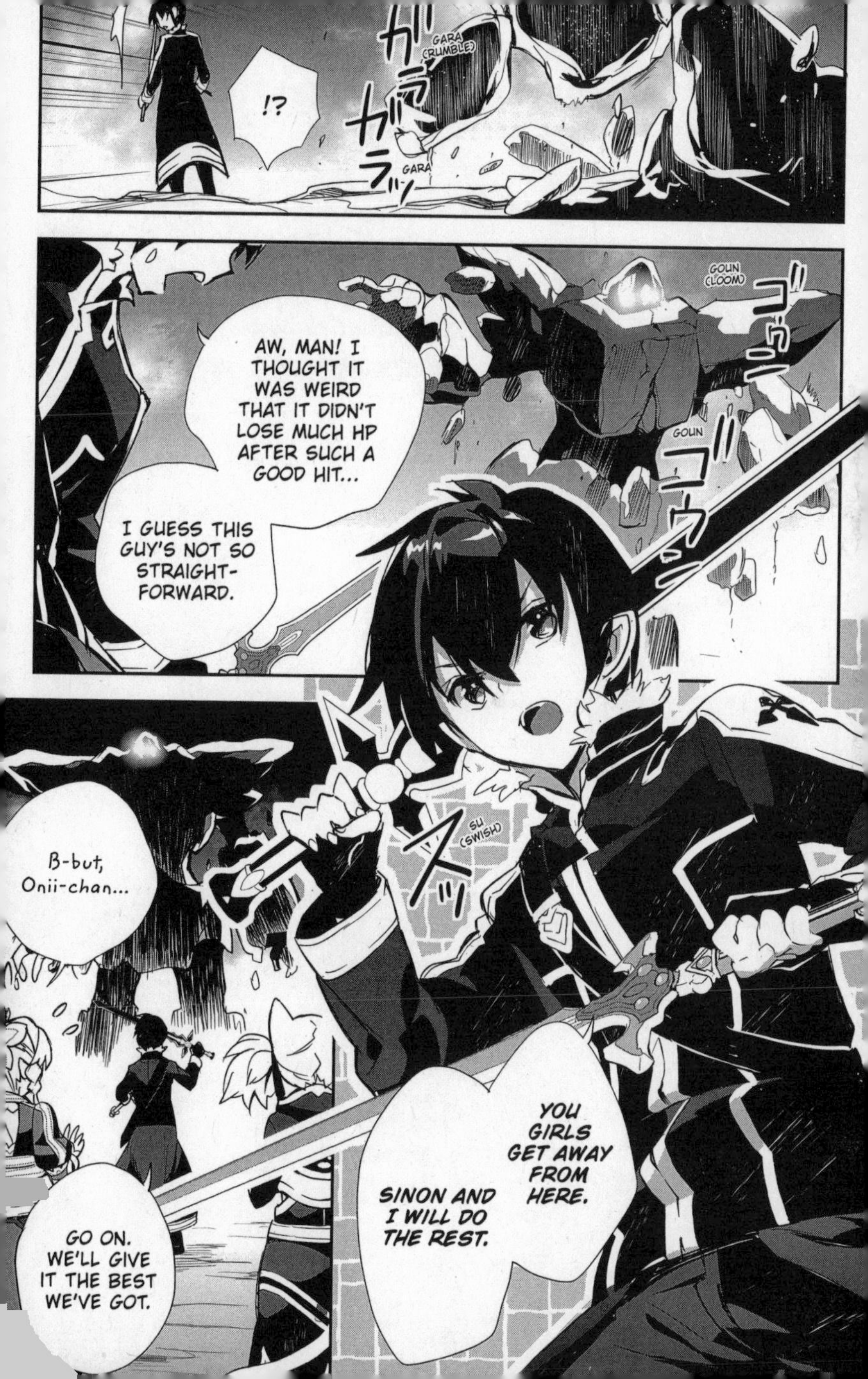
GARA (RUMBLE)
GARA
!?
GOUN (LOOM)
GOUN
AW, MAN! I THOUGHT IT WAS WEIRD THAT IT DIDN'T LOSE MUCH HP AFTER SUCH A GOOD HIT...
I GUESS THIS GUY'S NOT SO STRAIGHT-FORWARD.
SU (SWISH)
B-but, Onii-chan...
YOU GIRLS GET AWAY FROM HERE.
SINON AND I WILL DO THE REST.
GO ON. WE'LL GIVE IT THE BEST WE'VE GOT.

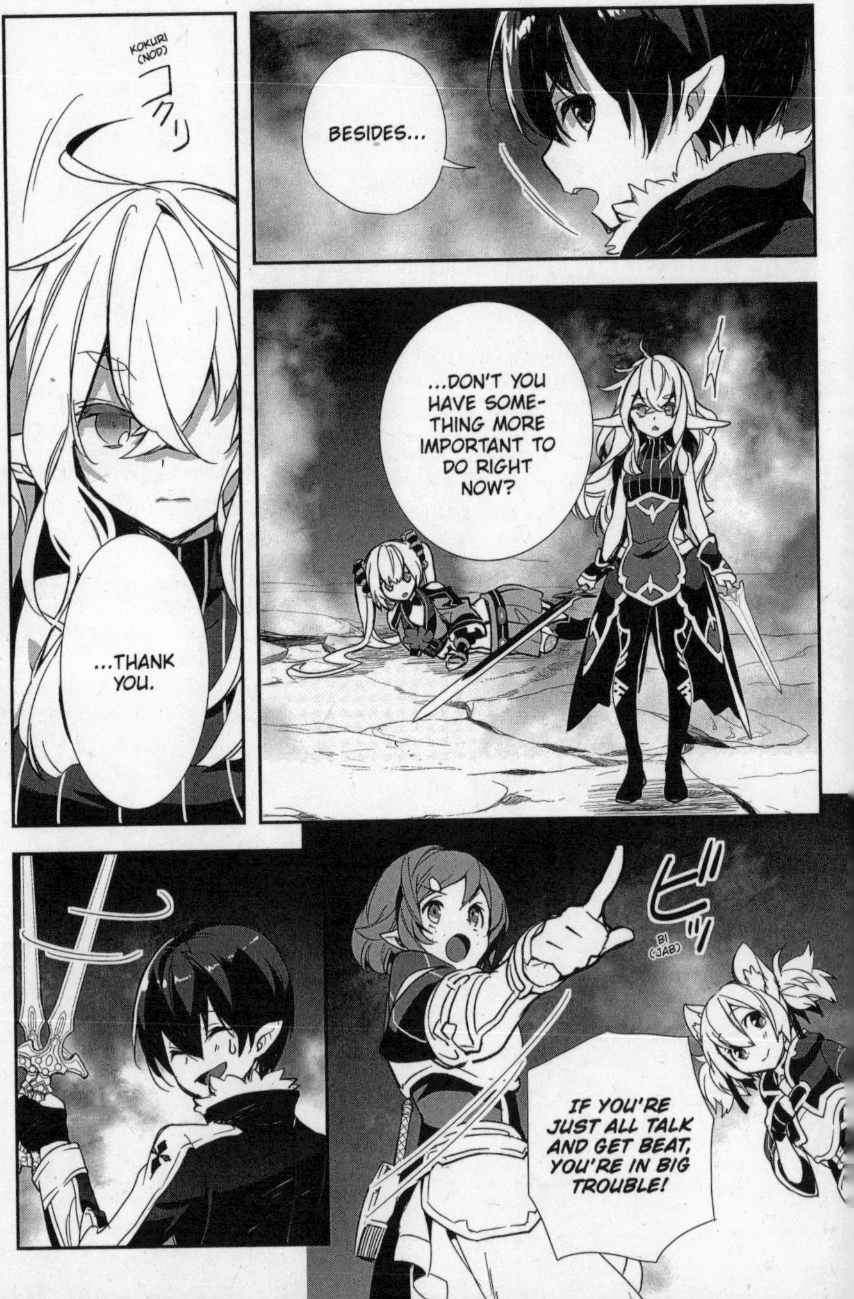
BESIDES...
...DON'T YOU HAVE SOME-THING MORE IMPORTANT TO DO RIGHT NOW?
コクリ
KOKURI (NOD)
...THANK YOU.
ビッ
BI (JAB)
IF YOU'RE JUST ALL TALK AND GET BEAT, YOU'RE IN BIG TROUBLE!

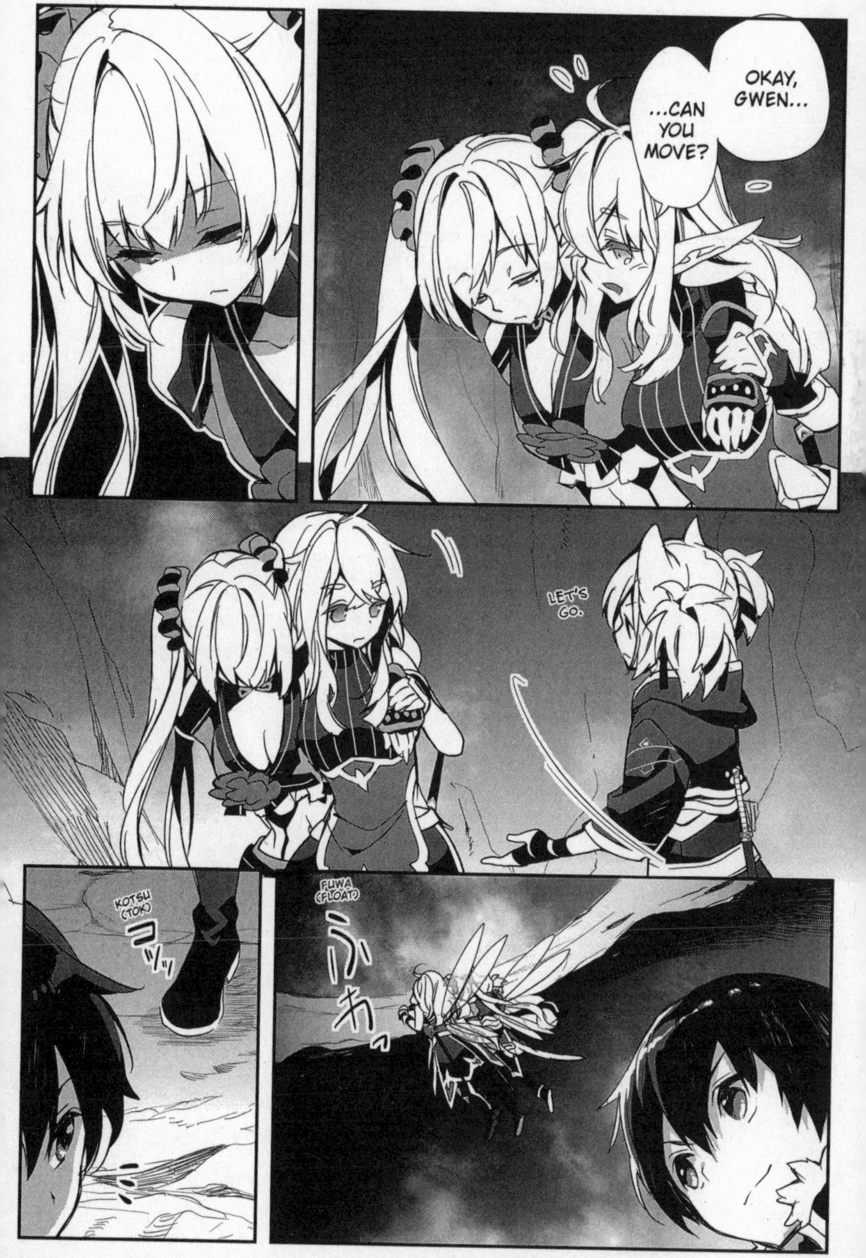
OKAY, GWEN...
...CAN YOU MOVE?
LET'S GO.
KOTSU (TOK)
コツッ
FUWA (FLOAT)
ふわっ

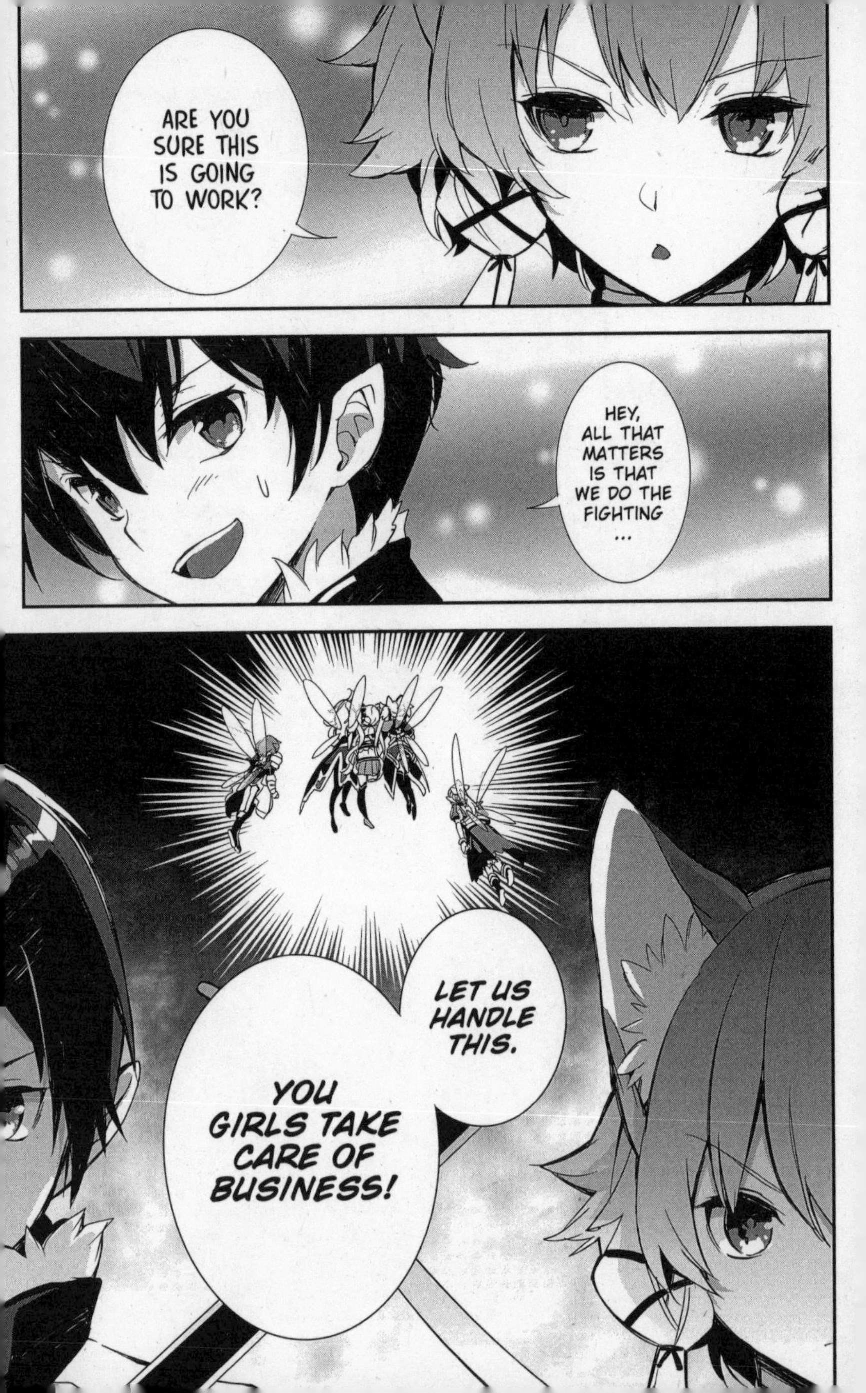
ARE YOU SURE THIS IS GOING TO WORK?
HEY, ALL THAT MATTERS IS THAT WE DO THE FIGHTING ...
LET US HANDLE THIS.
YOU GIRLS TAKE CARE OF BUSINESS!

SWORD ART ONLINE
GIRLS' OPS

SAO GIRLS
SLEEPING SERIES
HIYORI

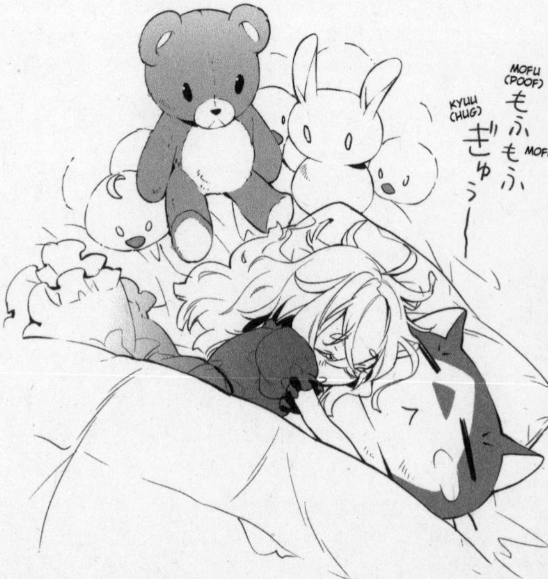
MOFU (POOF) もふもふ MOFU
KYUU (HUG) ぎゅうー

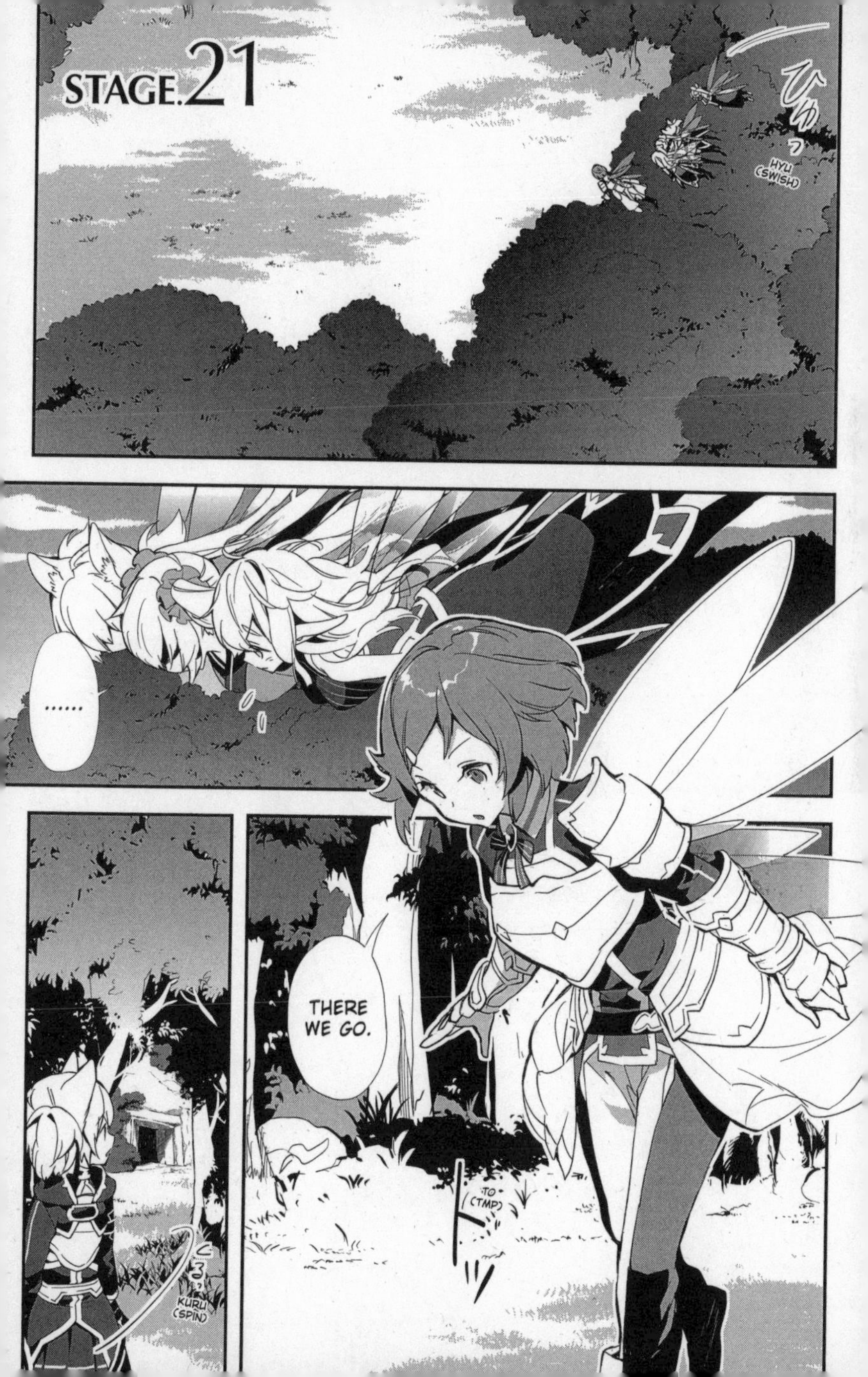
STAGE.21
ひゅっ
HYU (SWISH)
......
THERE WE GO.
TO (TMP)
くるっ
KURU (SPIN)

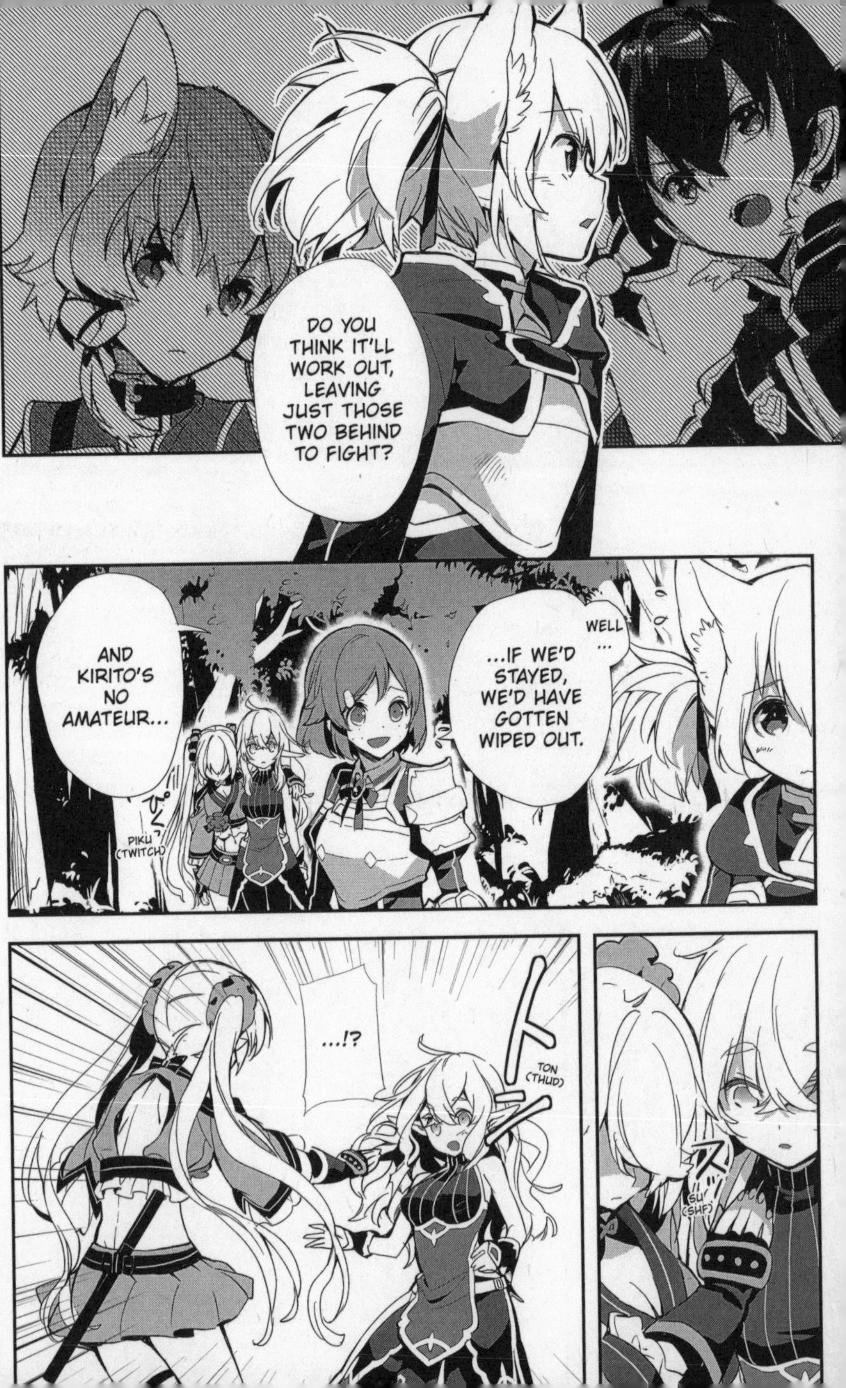

DO YOU THINK IT'LL WORK OUT, LEAVING JUST THOSE TWO BEHIND TO FIGHT?
WELL...
...IF WE'D STAYED, WE'D HAVE GOTTEN WIPED OUT.
AND KIRITO'S NO AMATEUR...
PIKU (TWITCH)
SU (SHF)
TON (THUD)
...!?

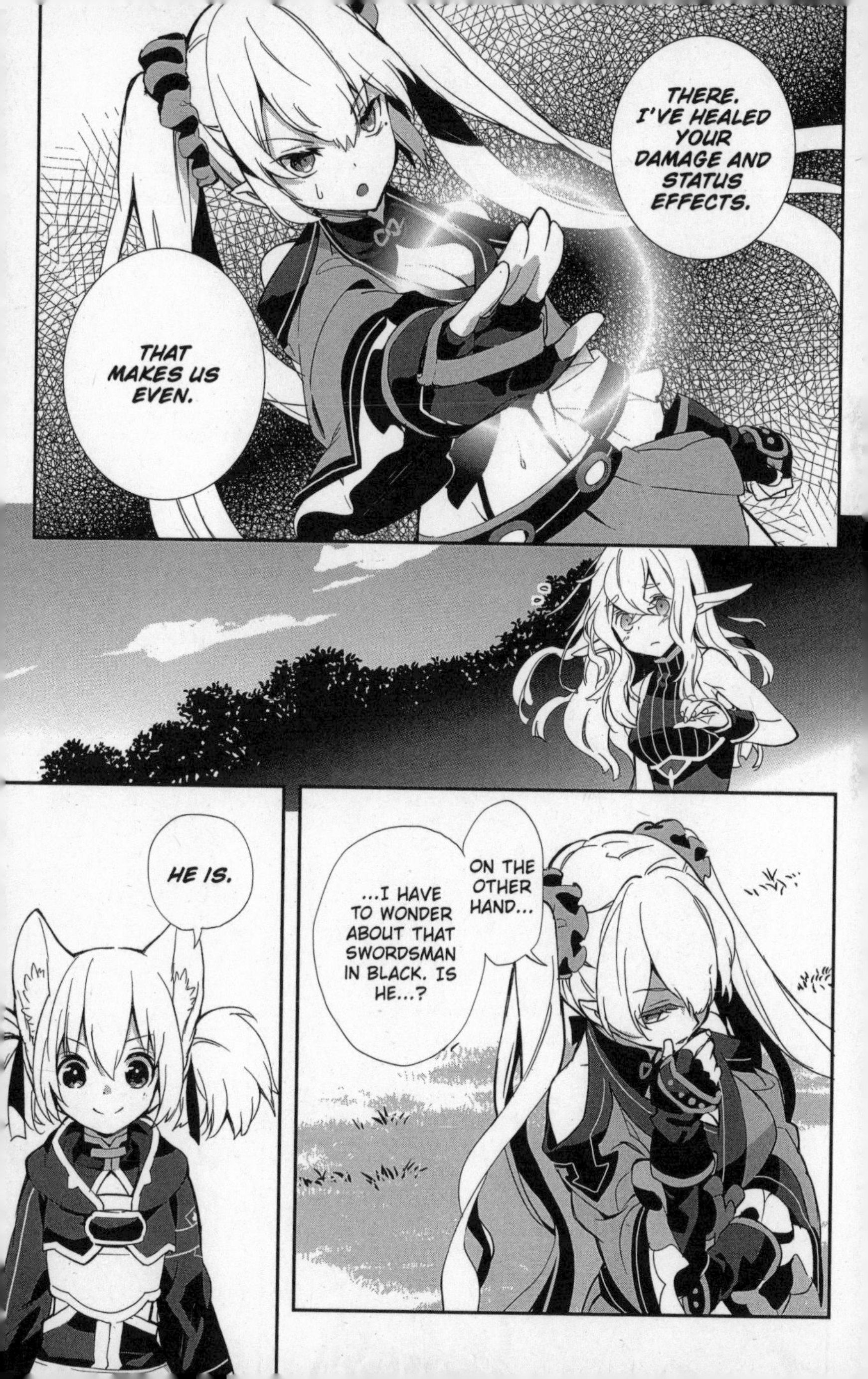
THERE. I'VE HEALED YOUR DAMAGE AND STATUS EFFECTS.
THAT MAKES US EVEN.
ON THE OTHER HAND...
...I HAVE TO WONDER ABOUT THAT SWORDSMAN IN BLACK. IS HE...?
HE IS.

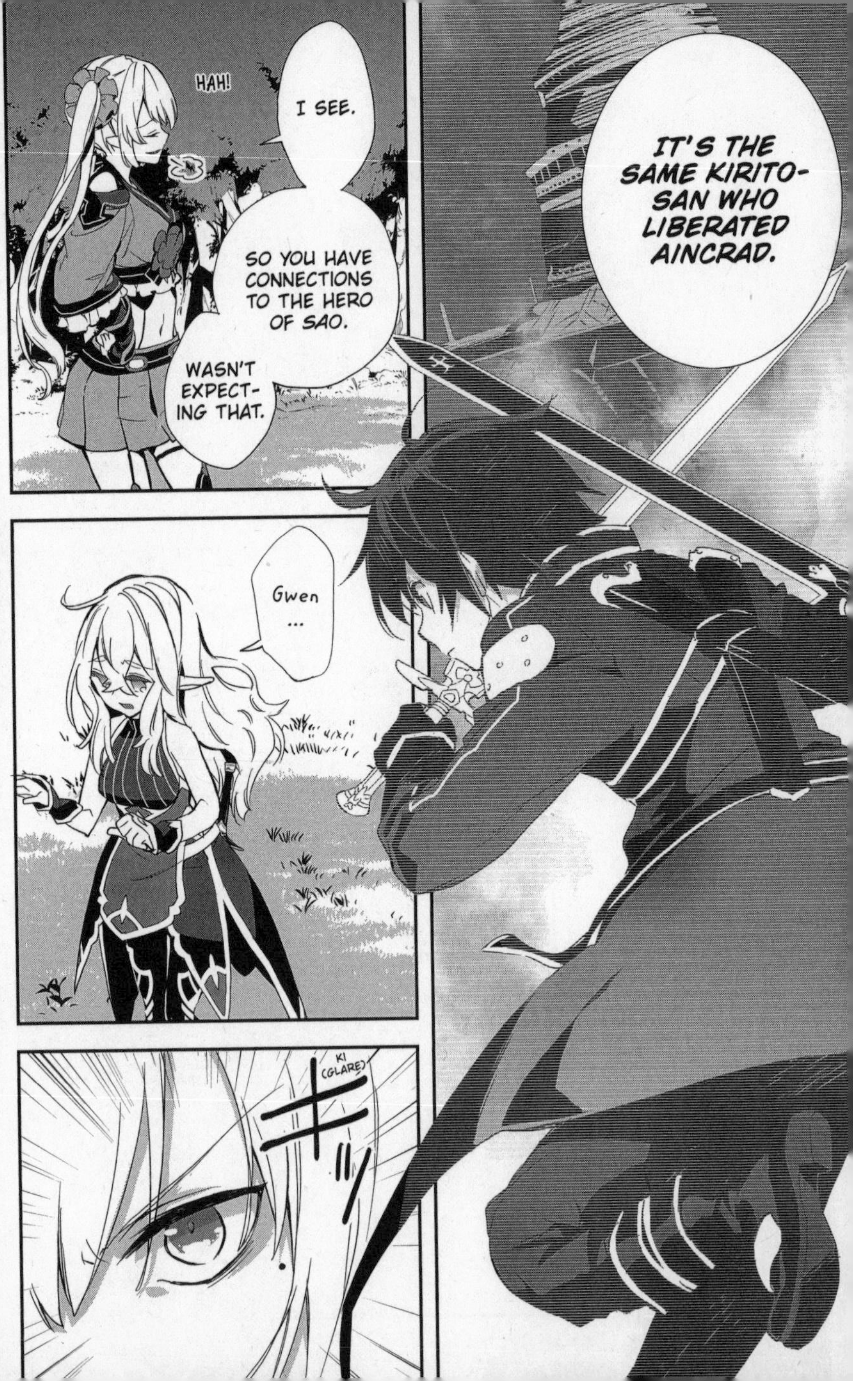
IT'S THE SAME KIRITO-SAN WHO LIBERATED AINCRAD.
HAH!
I SEE.
SO YOU HAVE CONNECTIONS TO THE HERO OF SAO.
WASN'T EXPECTING THAT.
Gwen ...
KI (GLARE)

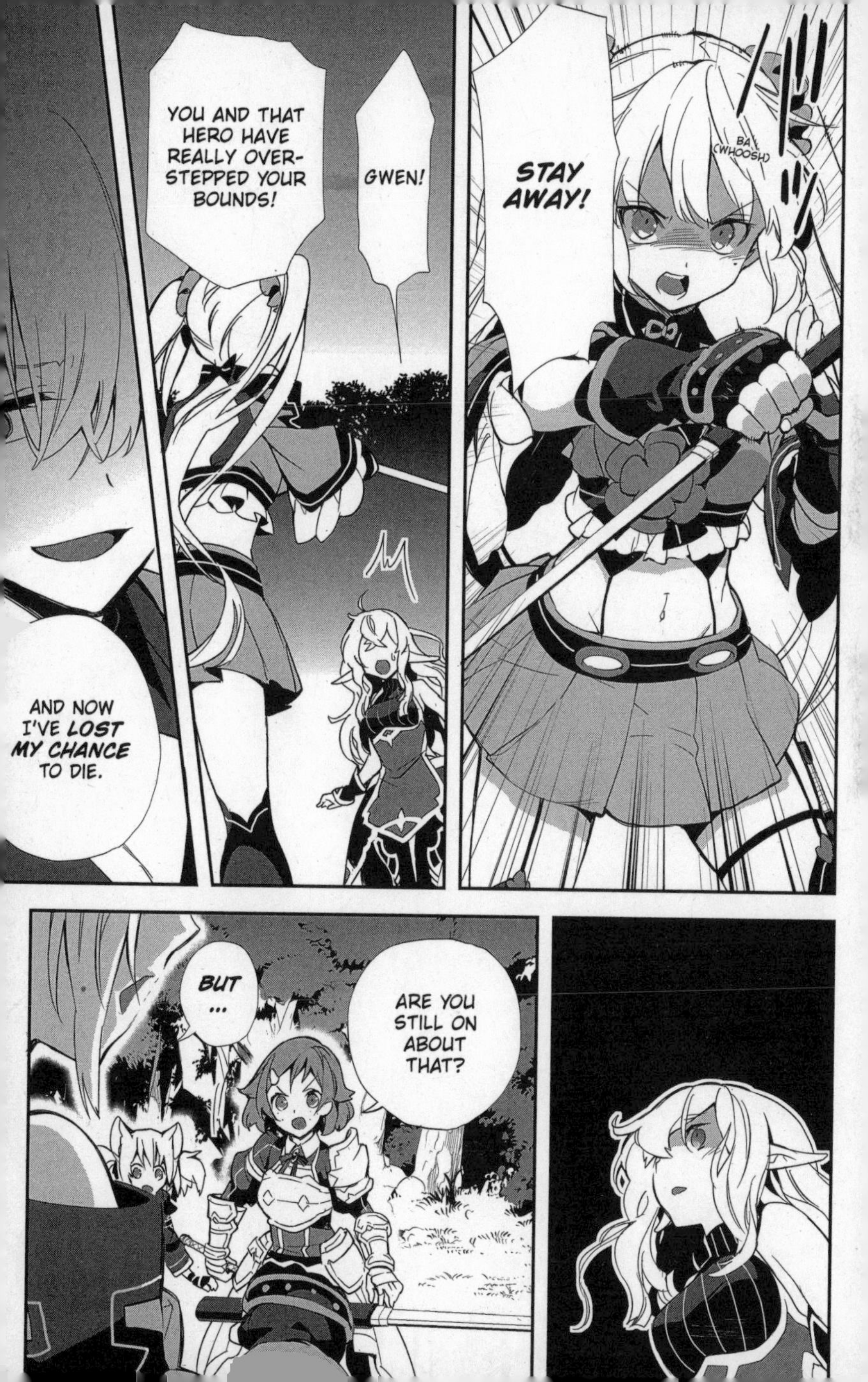
BA (WHOOSH)
STAY AWAY!
GWEN!
YOU AND THAT HERO HAVE REALLY OVER-STEPPED YOUR BOUNDS!
AND NOW I'VE LOST MY CHANCE TO DIE.
ARE YOU STILL ON ABOUT THAT?
BUT ...

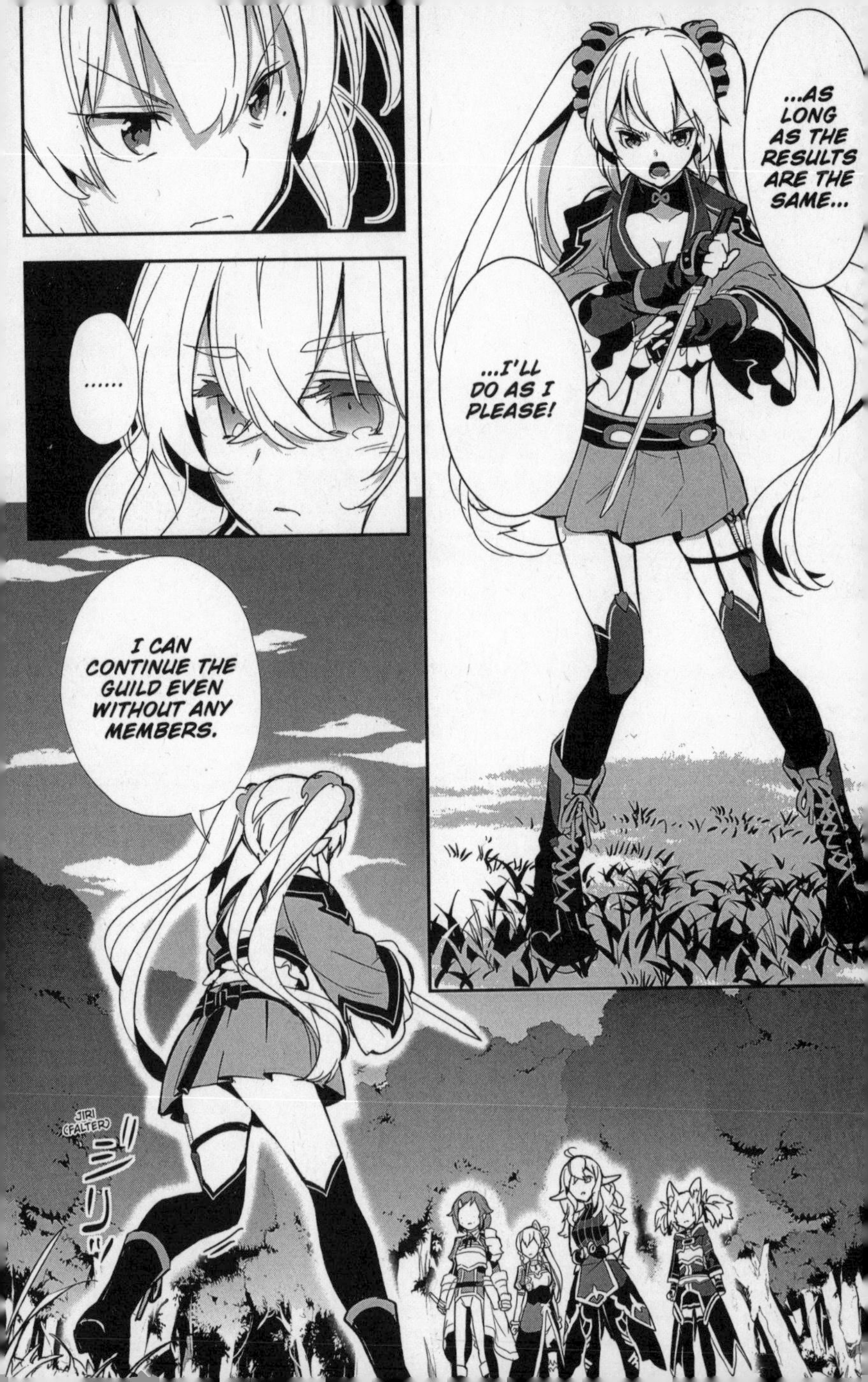

...AS LONG AS THE RESULTS ARE THE SAME...
...I'LL DO AS I PLEASE!
......
I CAN CONTINUE THE GUILD EVEN WITHOUT ANY MEMBERS.
JIRI (FALTER)

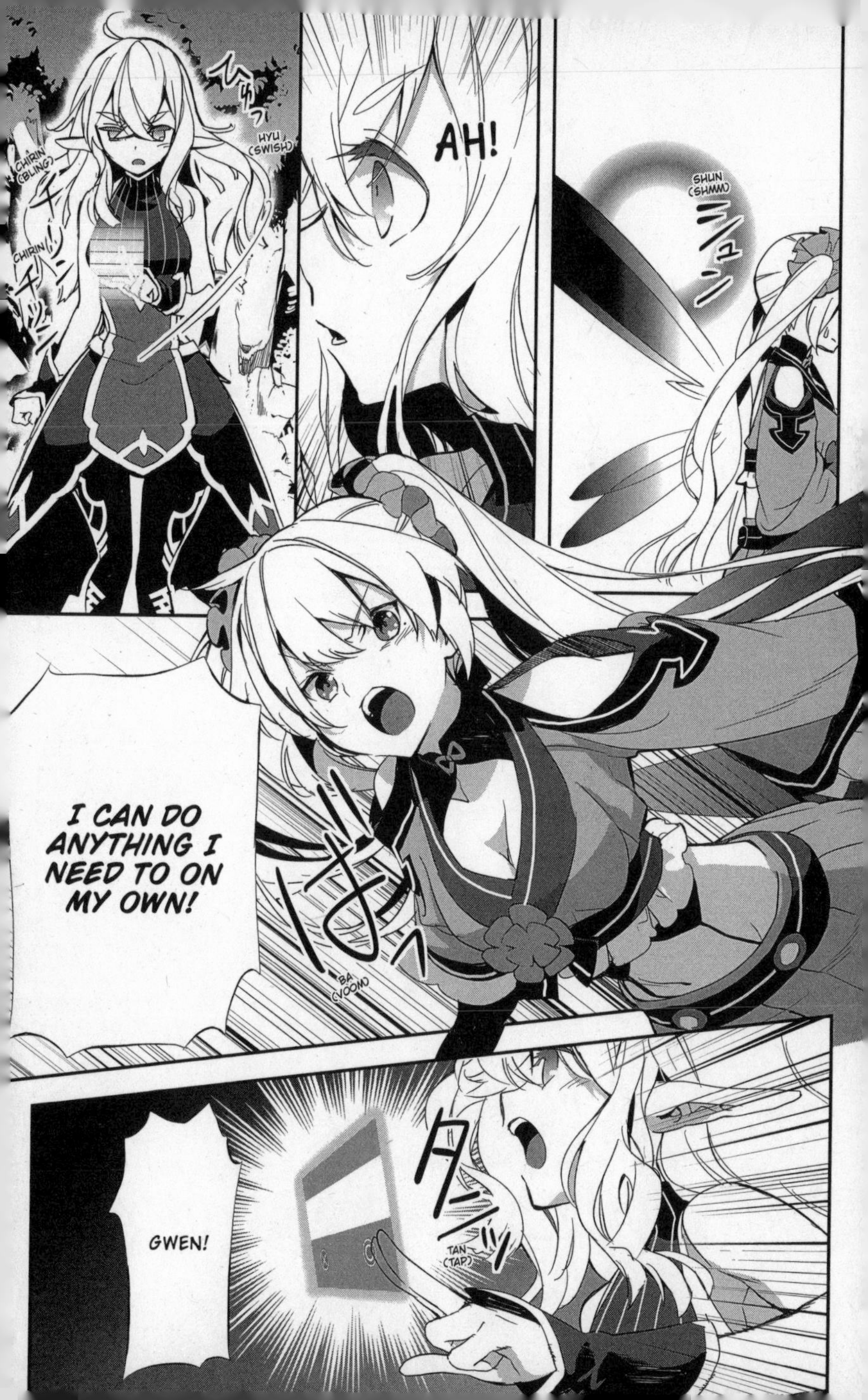
SHUN (SHMM)
AH!
HYU (SWISH)
CHIRIN (BLING)
CHIRIN
I CAN DO ANYTHING I NEED TO ON MY OWN!
BA (VOOM)
TAN (TAP)
GWEN!

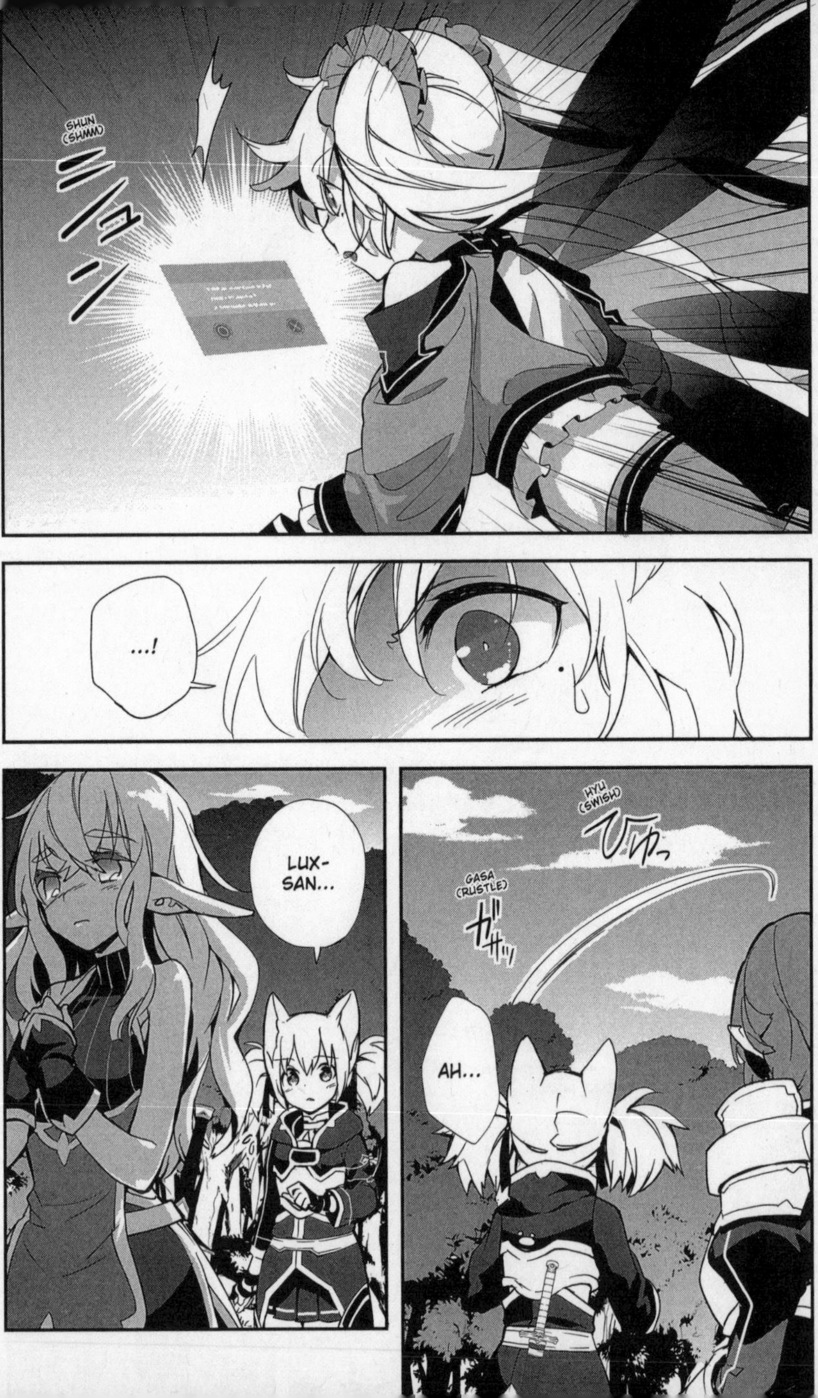
SHUN (SHMM)
ミュン
...!
HYU (SWISH)
ひゅっ
GASA (RUSTLE)
ガサッ
AH...
LUX-SAN...

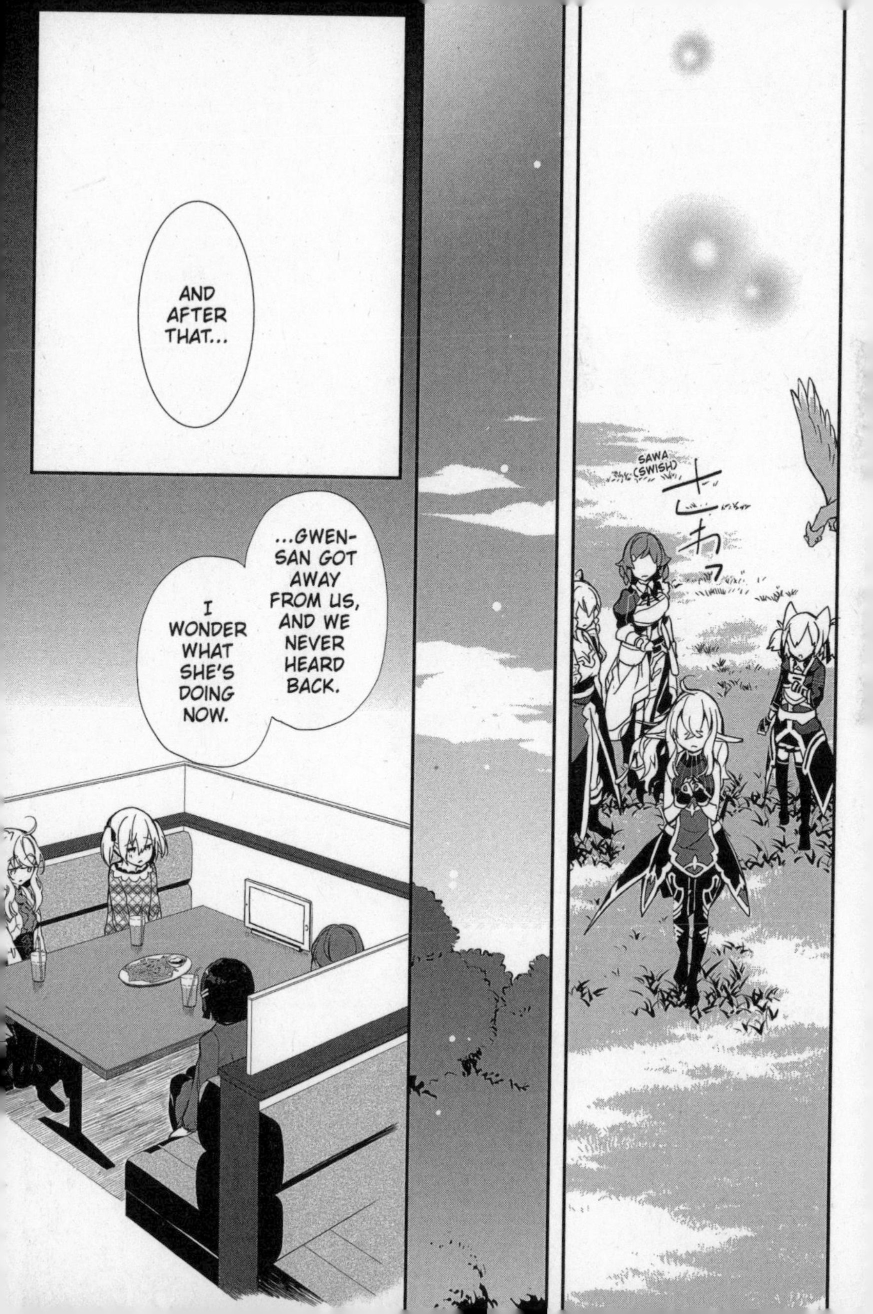
SAWA (SWISH)
さわっ
AND AFTER THAT...
...GWEN-SAN GOT AWAY FROM US, AND WE NEVER HEARD BACK.
I WONDER WHAT SHE'S DOING NOW.

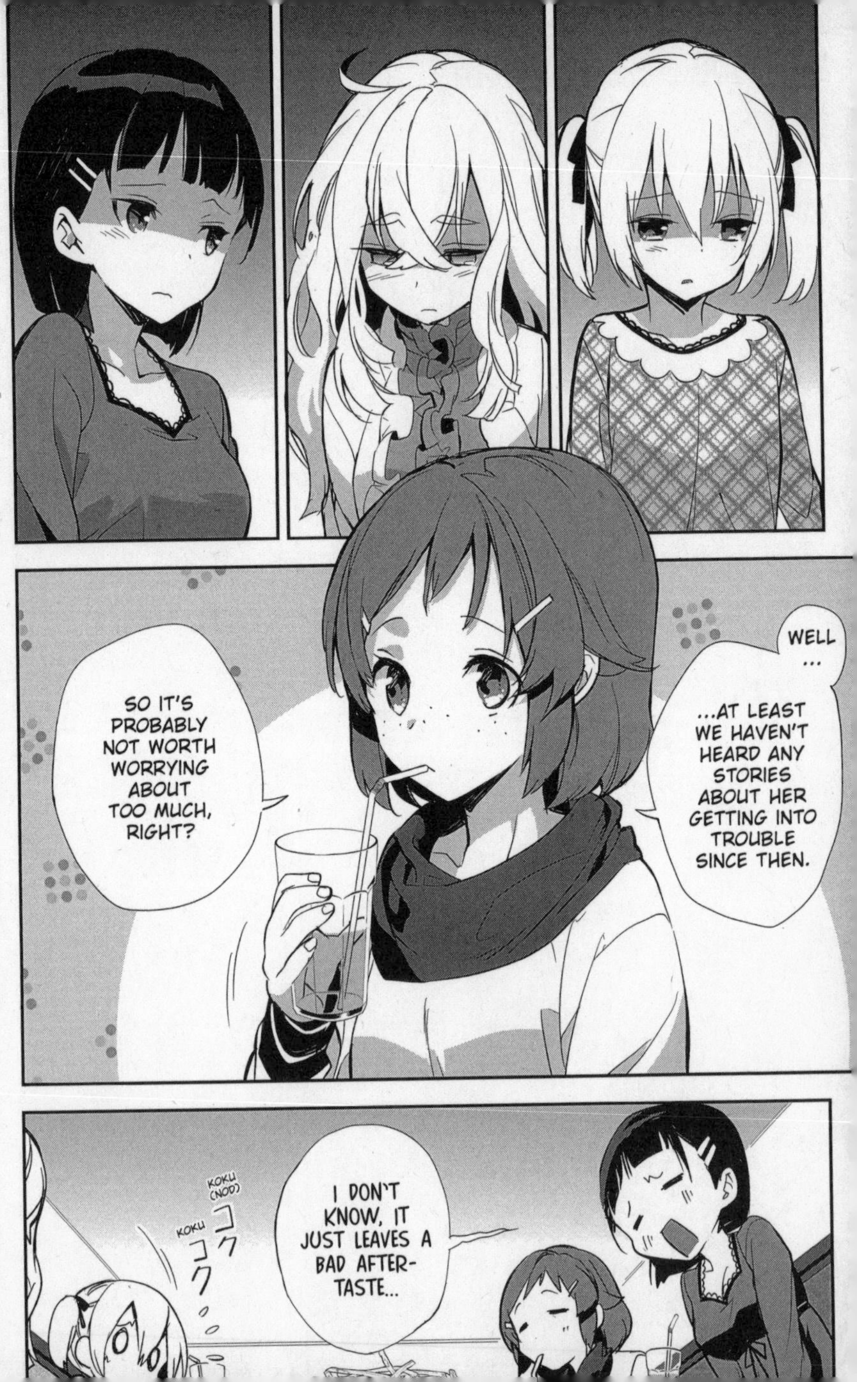
WELL ...
...AT LEAST WE HAVEN'T HEARD ANY STORIES ABOUT HER GETTING INTO TROUBLE SINCE THEN.
SO IT'S PROBABLY NOT WORTH WORRYING ABOUT TOO MUCH, RIGHT?
I DON'T KNOW, IT JUST LEAVES A BAD AFTER-TASTE...
KOKU (NOD)
KOKU
コク
コク

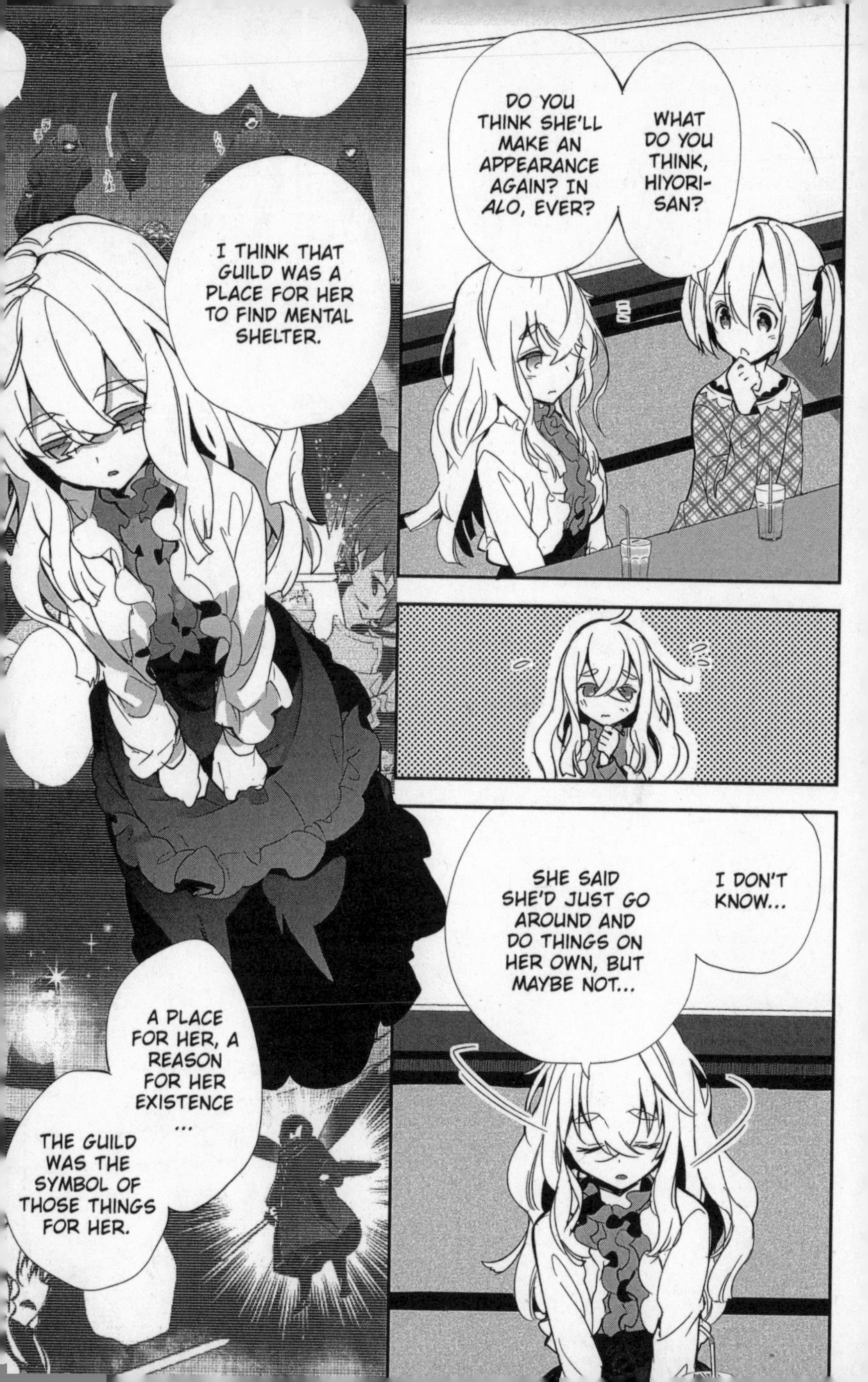
WHAT DO YOU THINK, HIYORI-SAN?
DO YOU THINK SHE'LL MAKE AN APPEARANCE AGAIN? IN ALO, EVER?
I DON'T KNOW...
SHE SAID SHE'D JUST GO AROUND AND DO THINGS ON HER OWN, BUT MAYBE NOT...
I THINK THAT GUILD WAS A PLACE FOR HER TO FIND MENTAL SHELTER.
A PLACE FOR HER, A REASON FOR HER EXISTENCE...
THE GUILD WAS THE SYMBOL OF THOSE THINGS FOR HER.

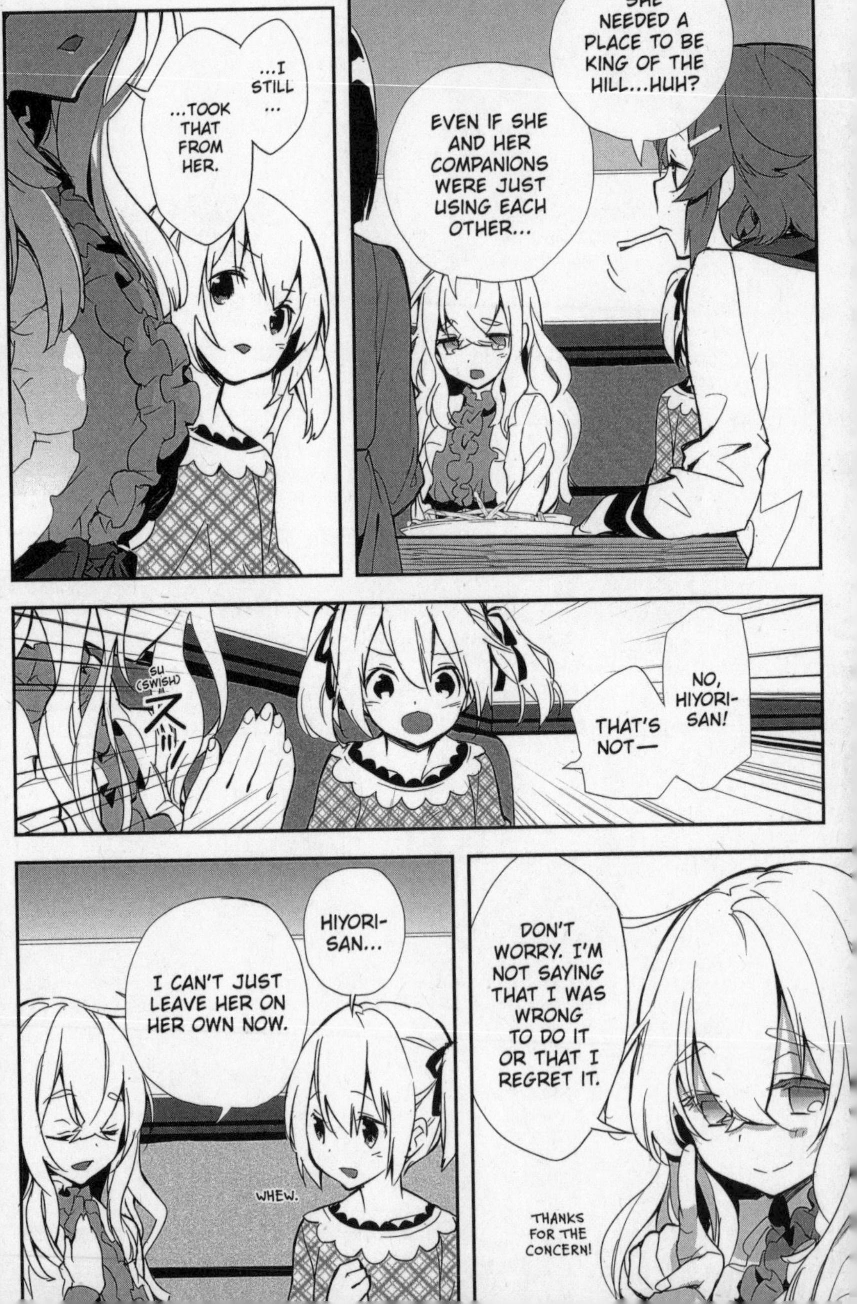

SHE NEEDED A PLACE TO BE KING OF THE HILL...HUH?
EVEN IF SHE AND HER COMPANIONS WERE JUST USING EACH OTHER...
...I STILL ...
...TOOK THAT FROM HER.
NO, HIYORI-SAN!
THAT'S NOT—
SU (SWISH)
ス
DON'T WORRY. I'M NOT SAYING THAT I WAS WRONG TO DO IT OR THAT I REGRET IT.
THANKS FOR THE CONCERN!
HIYORI-SAN...
I CAN'T JUST LEAVE HER ON HER OWN NOW.
WHEW.

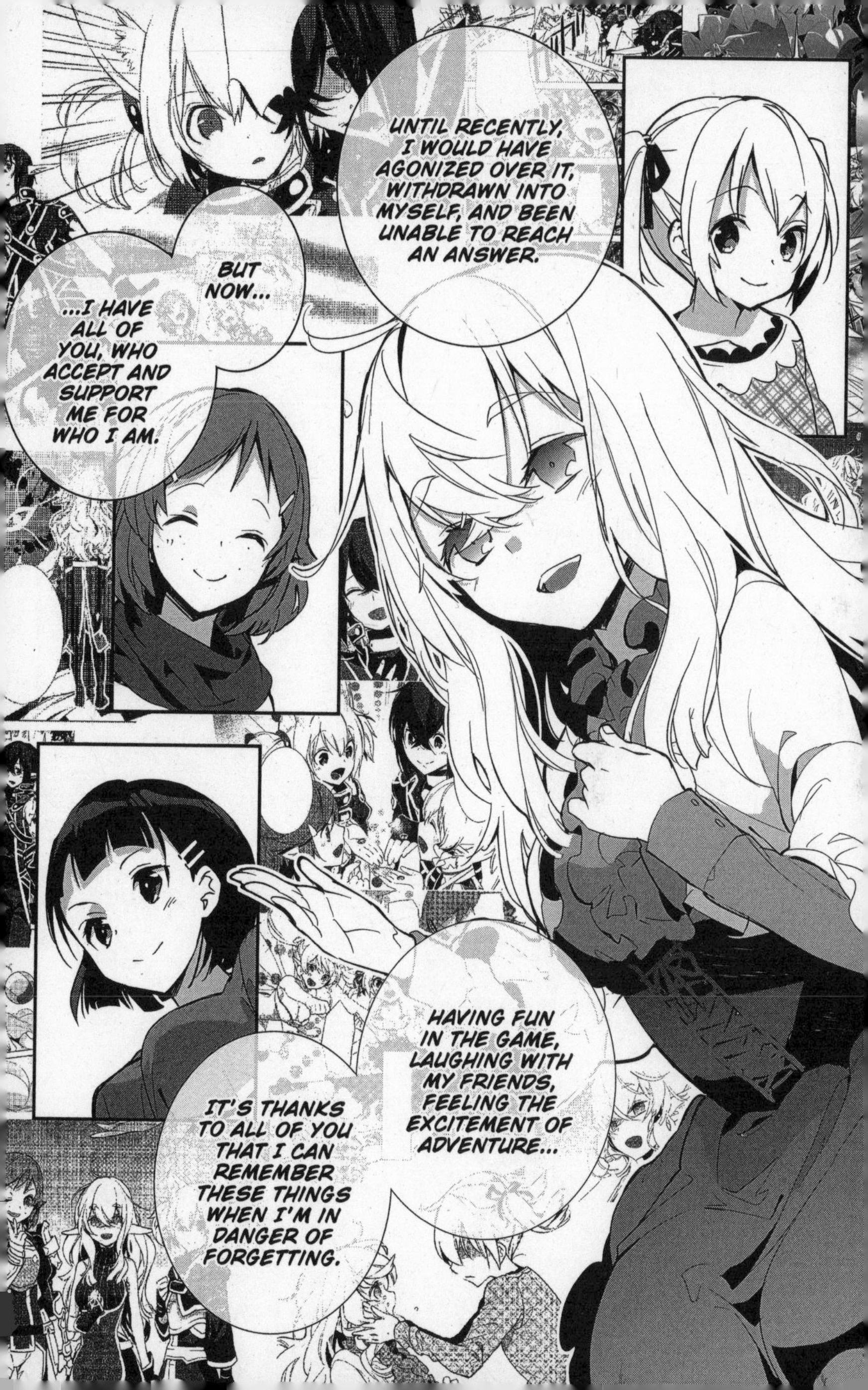
UNTIL RECENTLY, I WOULD HAVE AGONIZED OVER IT, WITHDRAWN INTO MYSELF, AND BEEN UNABLE TO REACH AN ANSWER.
BUT NOW...
...I HAVE ALL OF YOU, WHO ACCEPT AND SUPPORT ME FOR WHO I AM.
HAVING FUN IN THE GAME, LAUGHING WITH MY FRIENDS, FEELING THE EXCITEMENT OF ADVENTURE...
IT'S THANKS TO ALL OF YOU THAT I CAN REMEMBER THESE THINGS WHEN I'M IN DANGER OF FORGETTING.

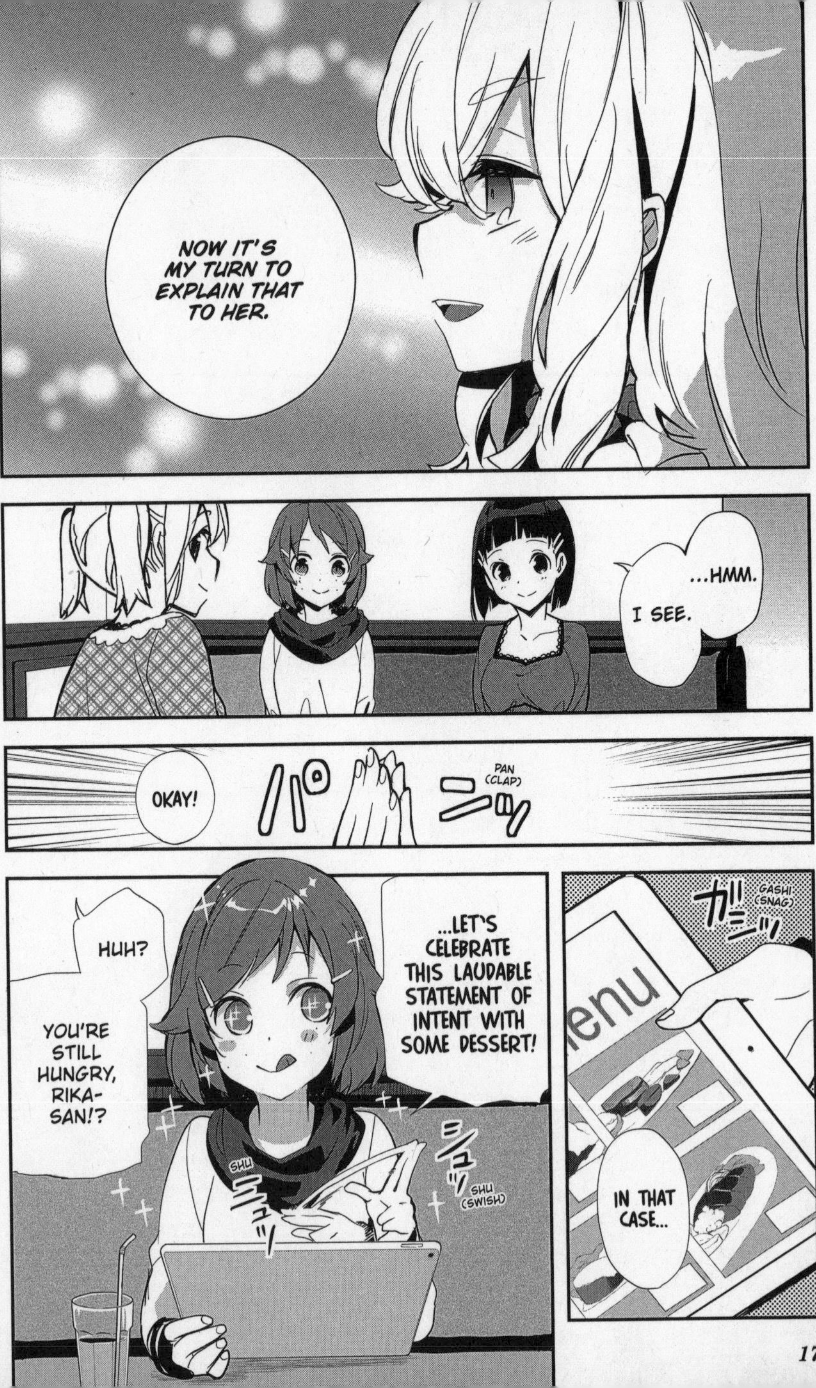
NOW IT'S MY TURN TO EXPLAIN THAT TO HER.
...HMM.
I SEE.
OKAY!
PAN (CLAP)
GASHI (SNAG)
IN THAT CASE...
...LET'S CELEBRATE THIS LAUDABLE STATEMENT OF INTENT WITH SOME DESSERT!
SHU SHU (SWISH)
HUH?
YOU'RE STILL HUNGRY, RIKA-SAN!?

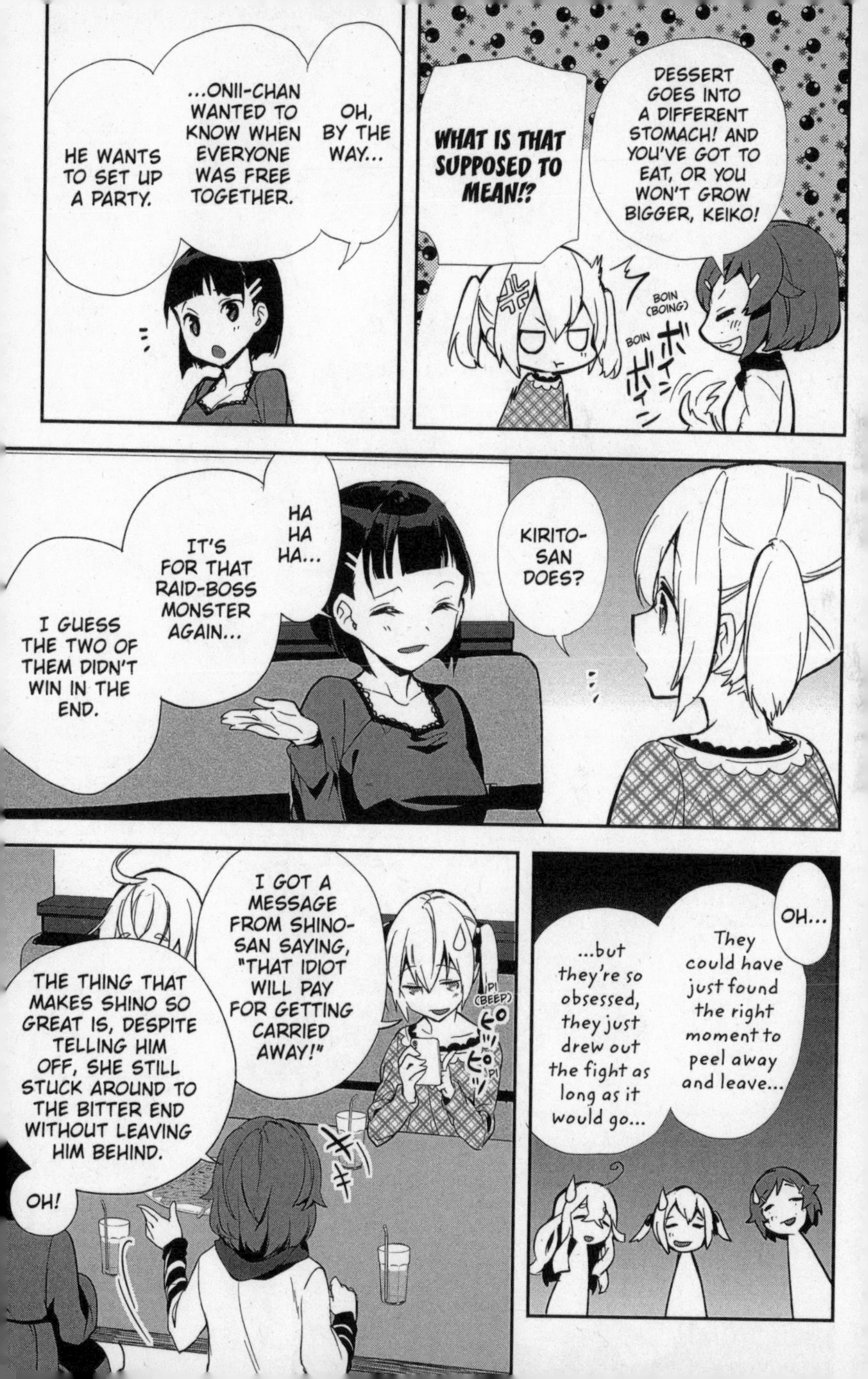
DESSERT GOES INTO A DIFFERENT STOMACH! AND YOU'VE GOT TO EAT, OR YOU WON'T GROW BIGGER, KEIKO!
WHAT IS THAT SUPPOSED TO MEAN!?
BOIN (BOING)
BOIN
ボイン ボイン
OH, BY THE WAY...
...ONII-CHAN WANTED TO KNOW WHEN EVERYONE WAS FREE TOGETHER.
HE WANTS TO SET UP A PARTY.
KIRITO-SAN DOES?
HA HA HA...
IT'S FOR THAT RAID-BOSS MONSTER AGAIN...
I GUESS THE TWO OF THEM DIDN'T WIN IN THE END.
OH...
They could have just found the right moment to peel away and leave...
...but they're so obsessed, they just drew out the fight as long as it would go...
I GOT A MESSAGE FROM SHINO-SAN SAYING, "THAT IDIOT WILL PAY FOR GETTING CARRIED AWAY!"
PI (BEEP)
PI
THE THING THAT MAKES SHINO SO GREAT IS, DESPITE TELLING HIM OFF, SHE STILL STUCK AROUND TO THE BITTER END WITHOUT LEAVING HIM BEHIND.
OH!

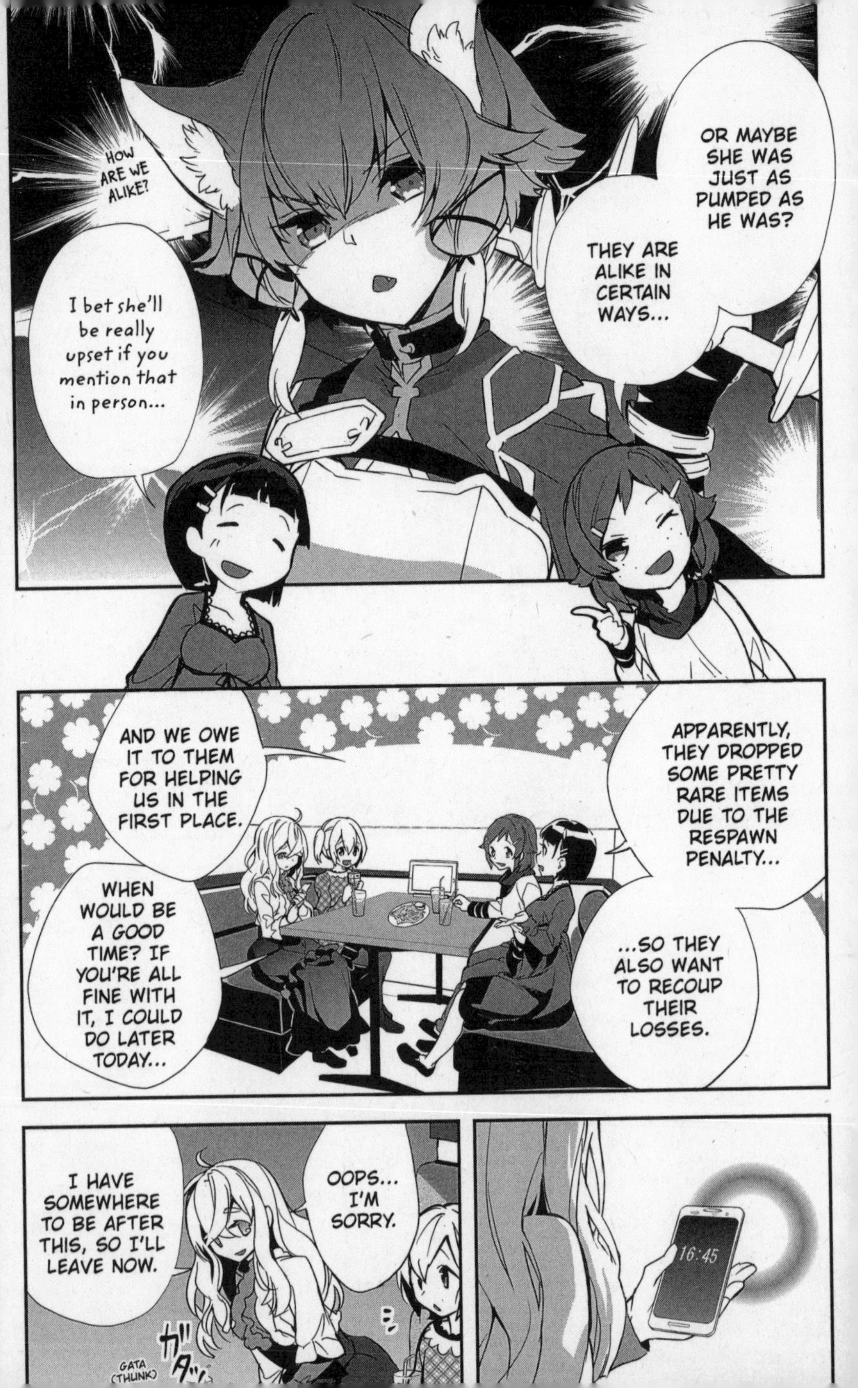
OR MAYBE SHE WAS JUST AS PUMPED AS HE WAS?
THEY ARE ALIKE IN CERTAIN WAYS...
HOW ARE WE ALIKE?
I bet she'll be really upset if you mention that in person...
APPARENTLY, THEY DROPPED SOME PRETTY RARE ITEMS DUE TO THE RESPAWN PENALTY...
...SO THEY ALSO WANT TO RECOUP THEIR LOSSES.
AND WE OWE IT TO THEM FOR HELPING US IN THE FIRST PLACE.
WHEN WOULD BE A GOOD TIME? IF YOU'RE ALL FINE WITH IT, I COULD DO LATER TODAY...
16:45
OOPS... I'M SORRY.
I HAVE SOMEWHERE TO BE AFTER THIS, SO I'LL LEAVE NOW.
GATA (THUNK)

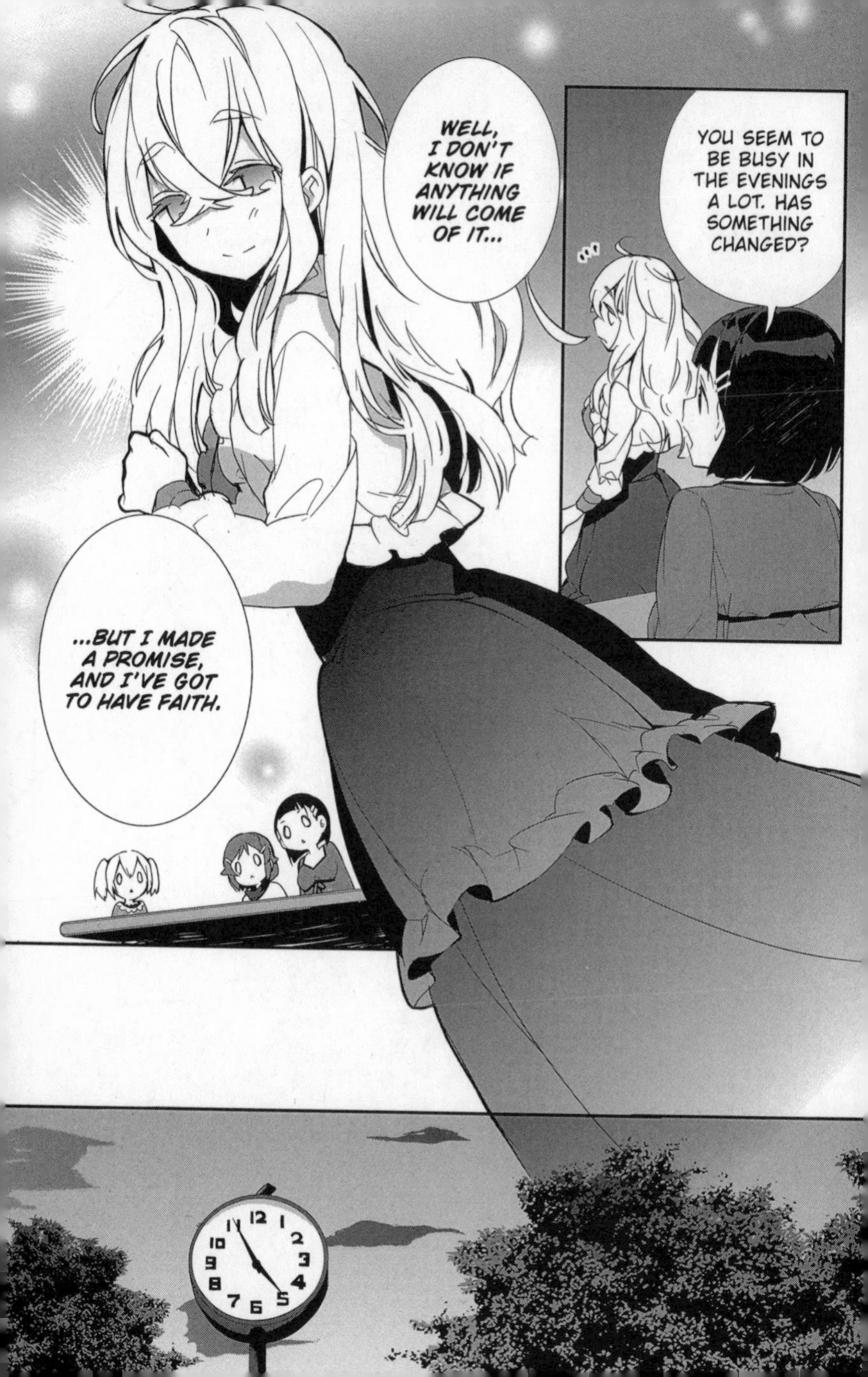
YOU SEEM TO BE BUSY IN THE EVENINGS A LOT. HAS SOMETHING CHANGED?
WELL, I DON'T KNOW IF ANYTHING WILL COME OF IT...
...BUT I MADE A PROMISE, AND I'VE GOT TO HAVE FAITH.

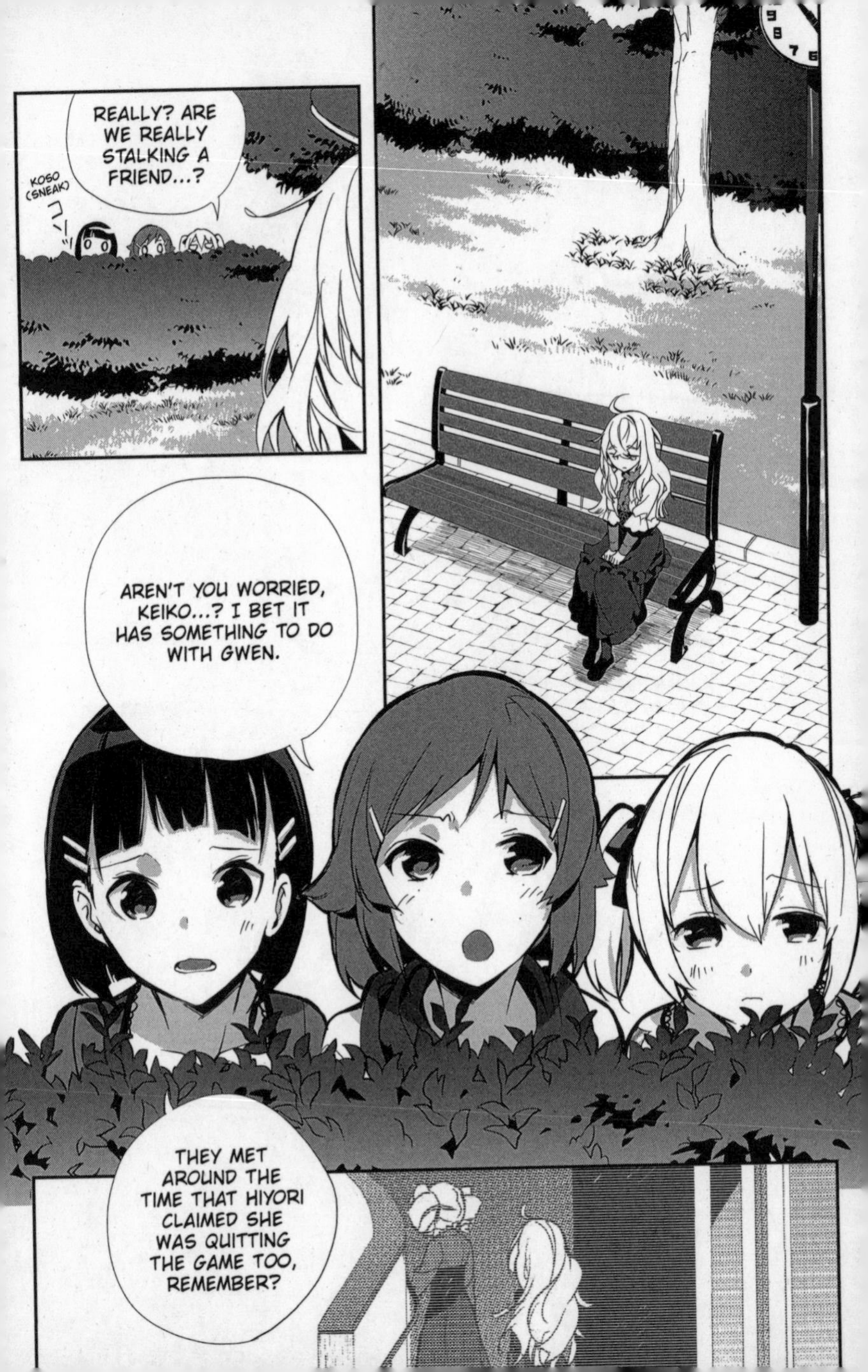
REALLY? ARE WE REALLY STALKING A FRIEND...?
KOSO (SNEAK)
AREN'T YOU WORRIED, KEIKO...? I BET IT HAS SOMETHING TO DO WITH GWEN.
THEY MET AROUND THE TIME THAT HIYORI CLAIMED SHE WAS QUITTING THE GAME TOO, REMEMBER?

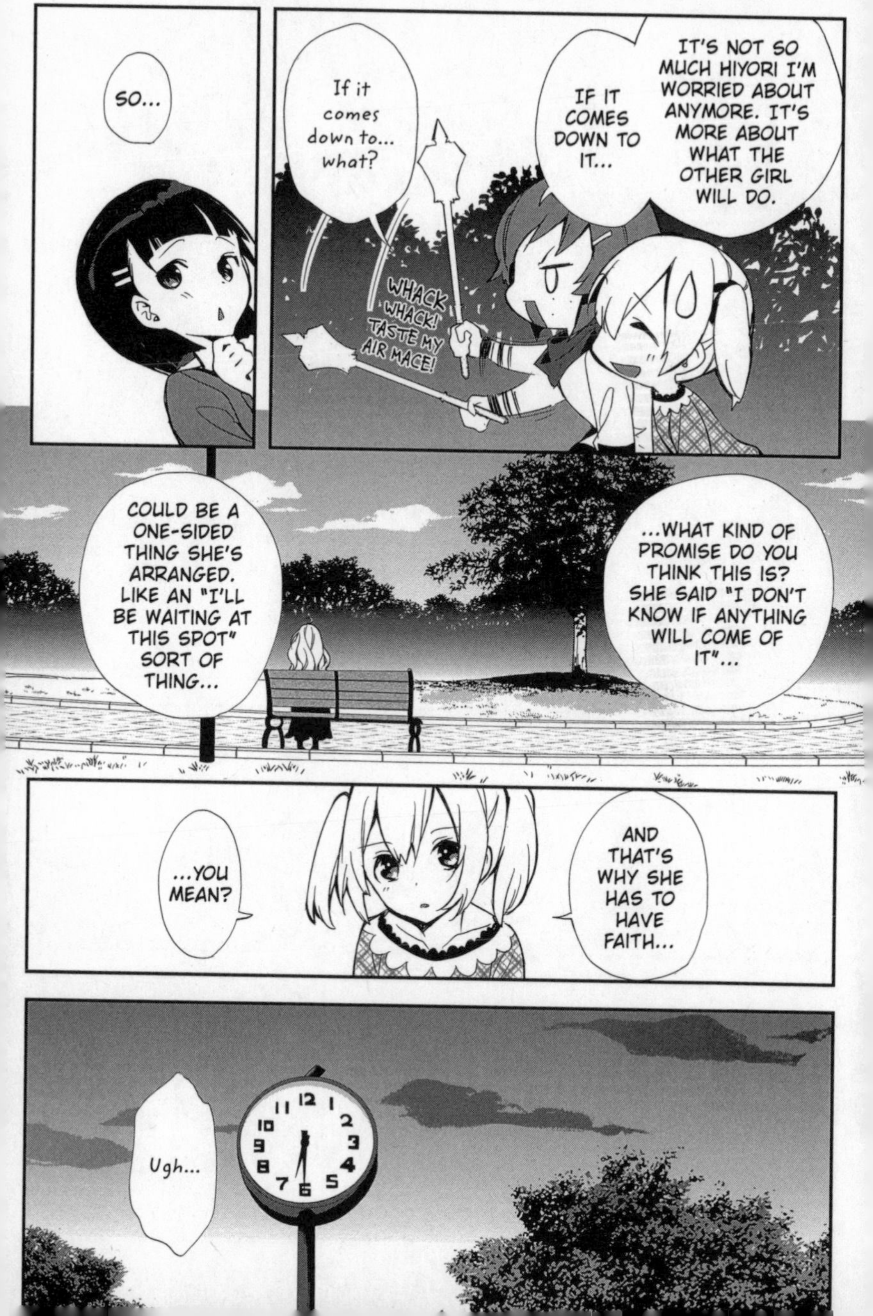
IT'S NOT SO MUCH HIYORI I'M WORRIED ABOUT ANYMORE. IT'S MORE ABOUT WHAT THE OTHER GIRL WILL DO.
IF IT COMES DOWN TO IT...
If it comes down to... what?
WHACK WHACK! TASTE MY AIR MACE!
SO...
...WHAT KIND OF PROMISE DO YOU THINK THIS IS? SHE SAID "I DON'T KNOW IF ANYTHING WILL COME OF IT"...
COULD BE A ONE-SIDED THING SHE'S ARRANGED. LIKE AN "I'LL BE WAITING AT THIS SPOT" SORT OF THING...
AND THAT'S WHY SHE HAS TO HAVE FAITH...
...YOU MEAN?
Ugh...

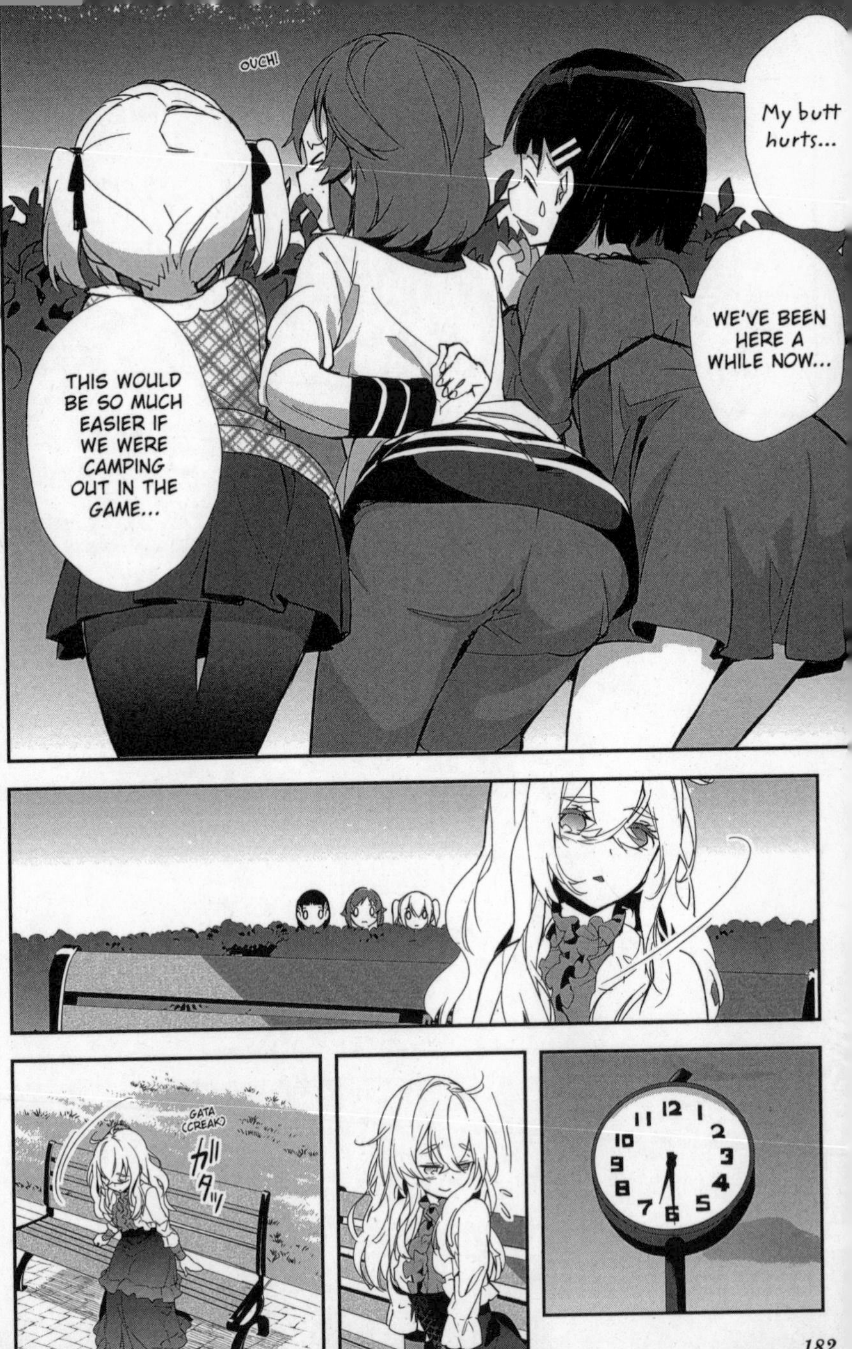
My butt hurts...
WE'VE BEEN HERE A WHILE NOW...
OUCH!
THIS WOULD BE SO MUCH EASIER IF WE WERE CAMPING OUT IN THE GAME...
GATA (CREAK)

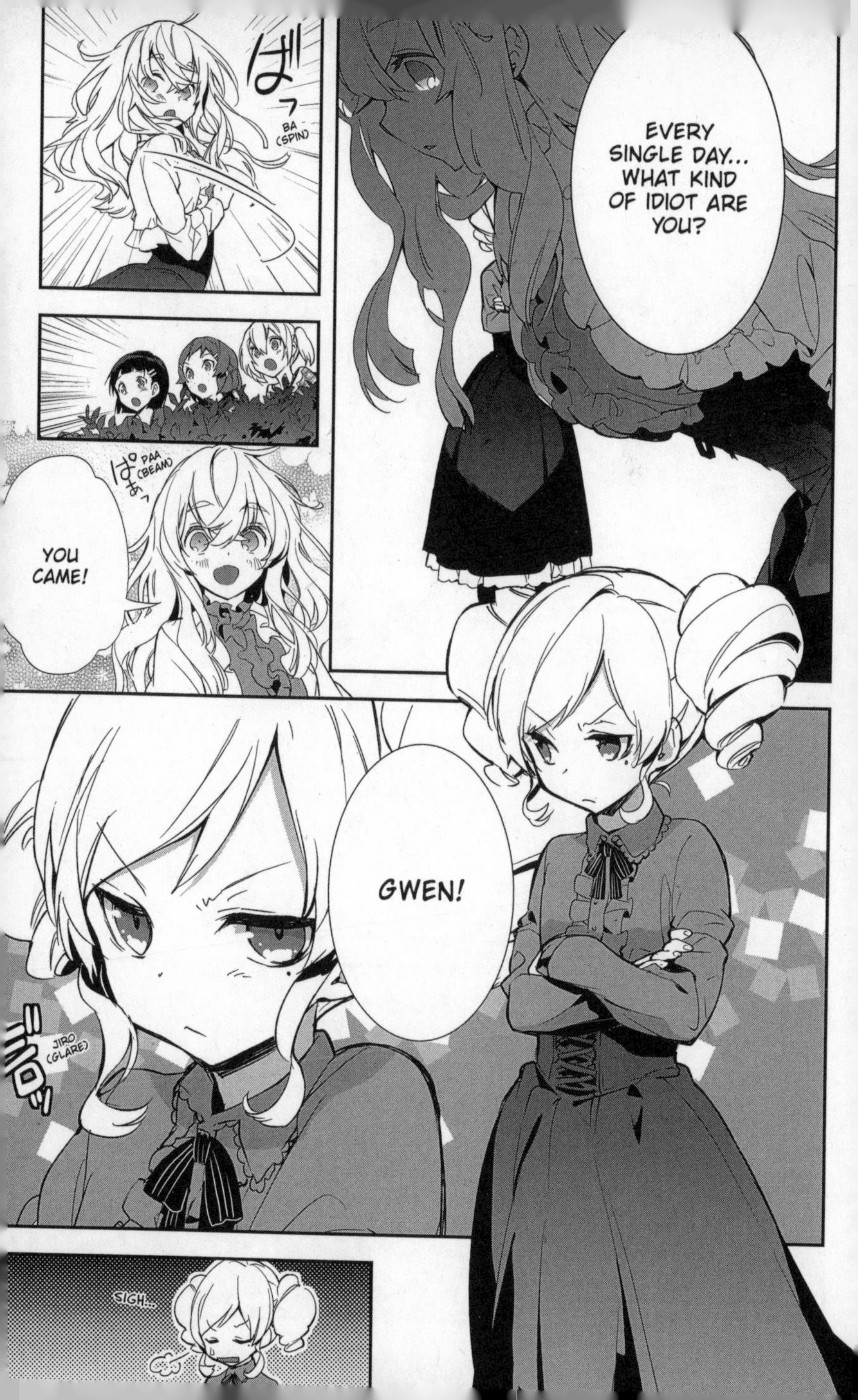
EVERY SINGLE DAY... WHAT KIND OF IDIOT ARE YOU?
BA (SPIN)
PAA (BEAM)
YOU CAME!
GWEN!
JIRO (GLARE)
SIGH...

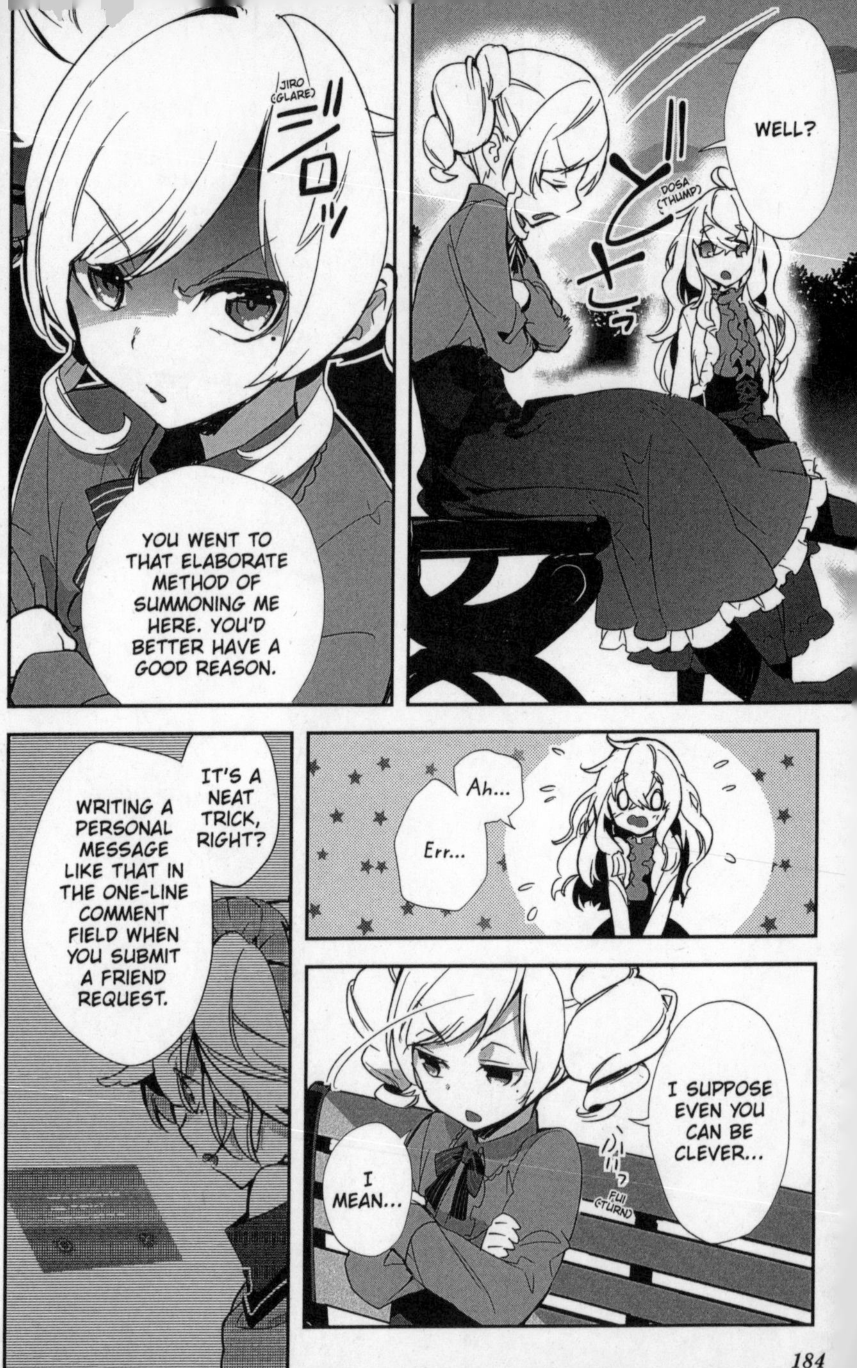
WELL?
DOSA (THUMP)
JIRO (GLARE)
YOU WENT TO THAT ELABORATE METHOD OF SUMMONING ME HERE. YOU'D BETTER HAVE A GOOD REASON.
Ah...
Err...
I SUPPOSE EVEN YOU CAN BE CLEVER...
FUI (TURN)
I MEAN...
IT'S A NEAT TRICK, RIGHT?
WRITING A PERSONAL MESSAGE LIKE THAT IN THE ONE-LINE COMMENT FIELD WHEN YOU SUBMIT A FRIEND REQUEST.

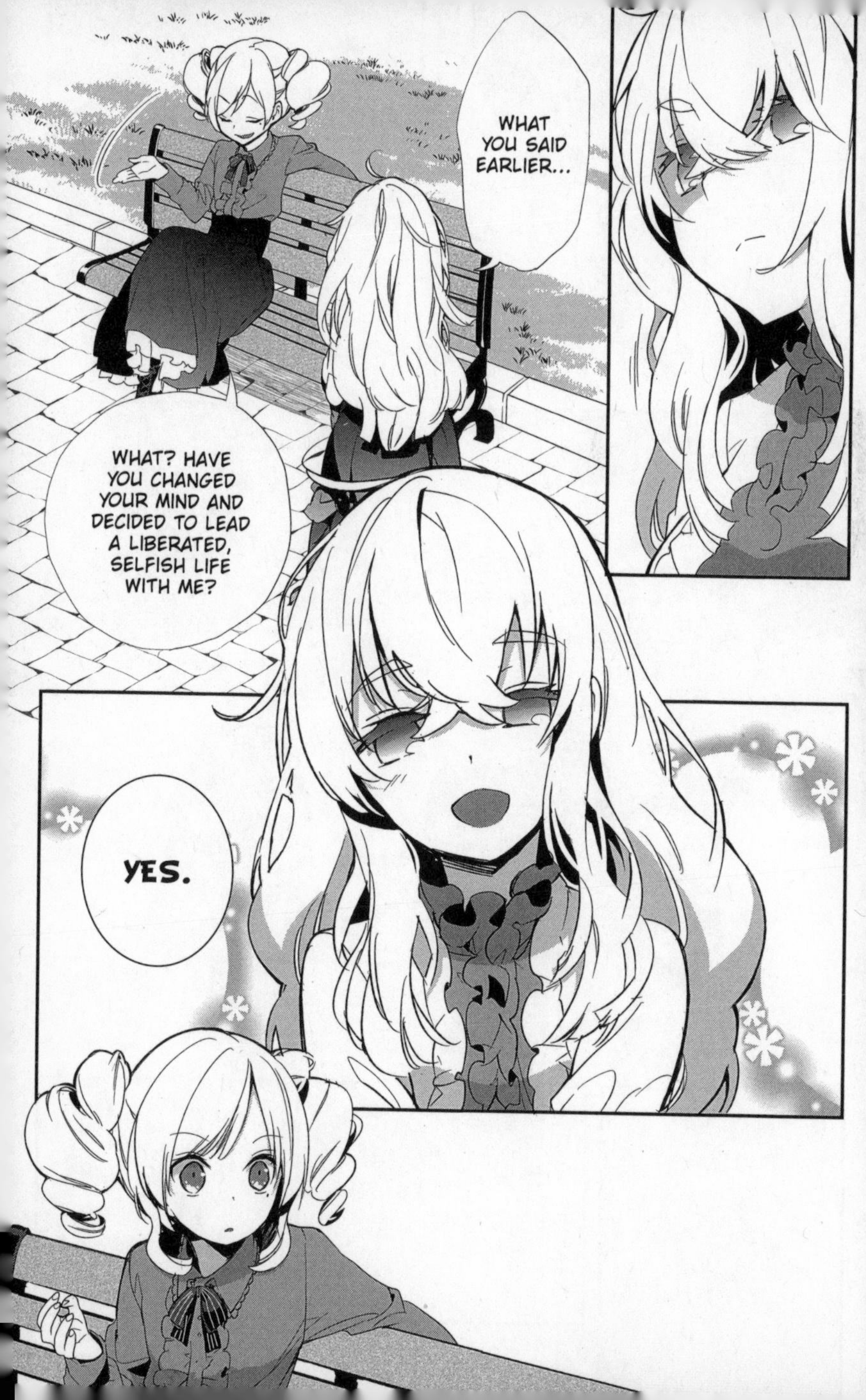
WHAT YOU SAID EARLIER...
WHAT? HAVE YOU CHANGED YOUR MIND AND DECIDED TO LEAD A LIBERATED, SELFISH LIFE WITH ME?
YES.

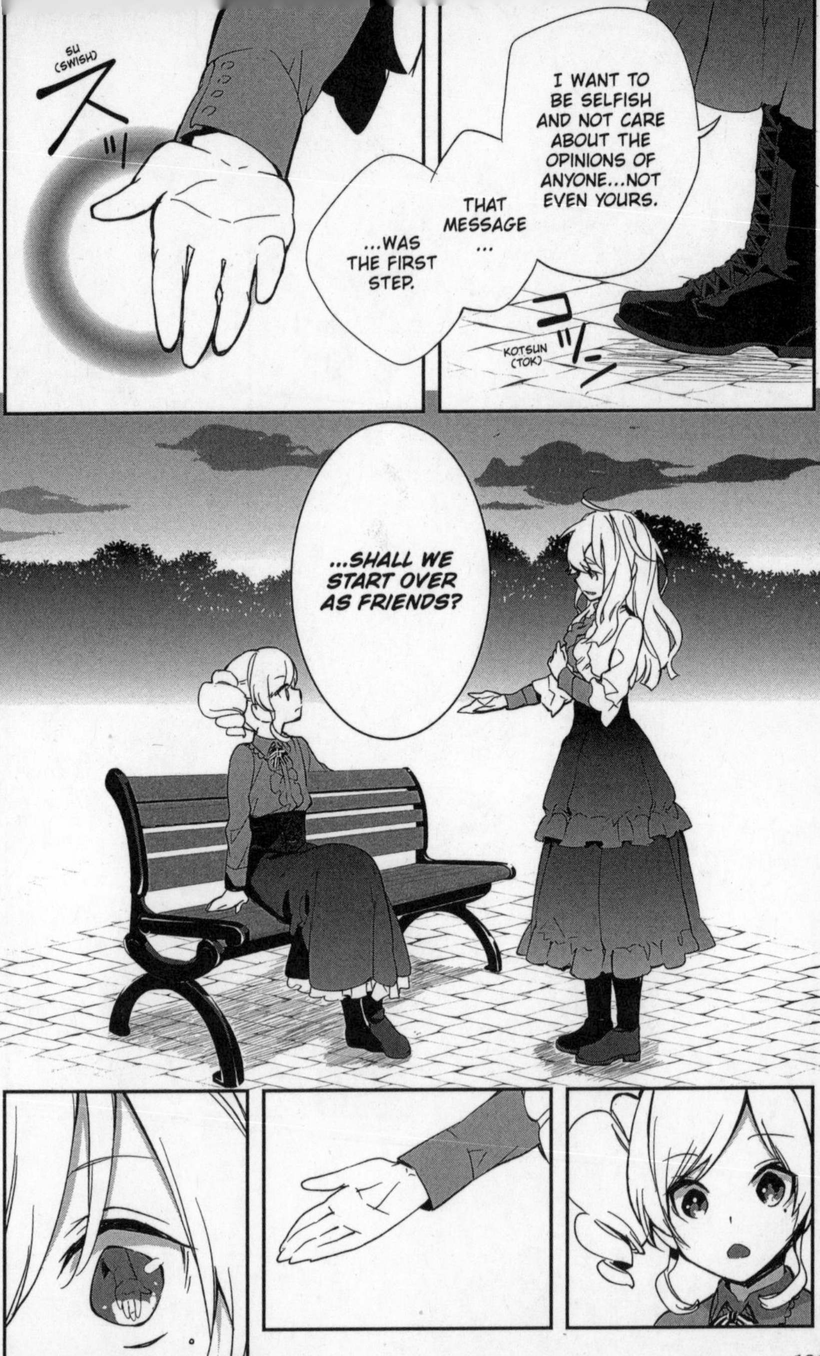
I WANT TO BE SELFISH AND NOT CARE ABOUT THE OPINIONS OF ANYONE...NOT EVEN YOURS.
THAT MESSAGE...
...WAS THE FIRST STEP.
KOTSUN (TOK)
SU (SWISH)
...SHALL WE START OVER AS FRIENDS?

...HAH!
AH HA HA HA HA HA!
WHAT'S THAT!? SOME KIND OF JOKE?
OH MY GOD, YOU'RE SO HILARIOUS!
HONESTLY, THE LAUGHS NEVER STOP...
KI (GLANCE)

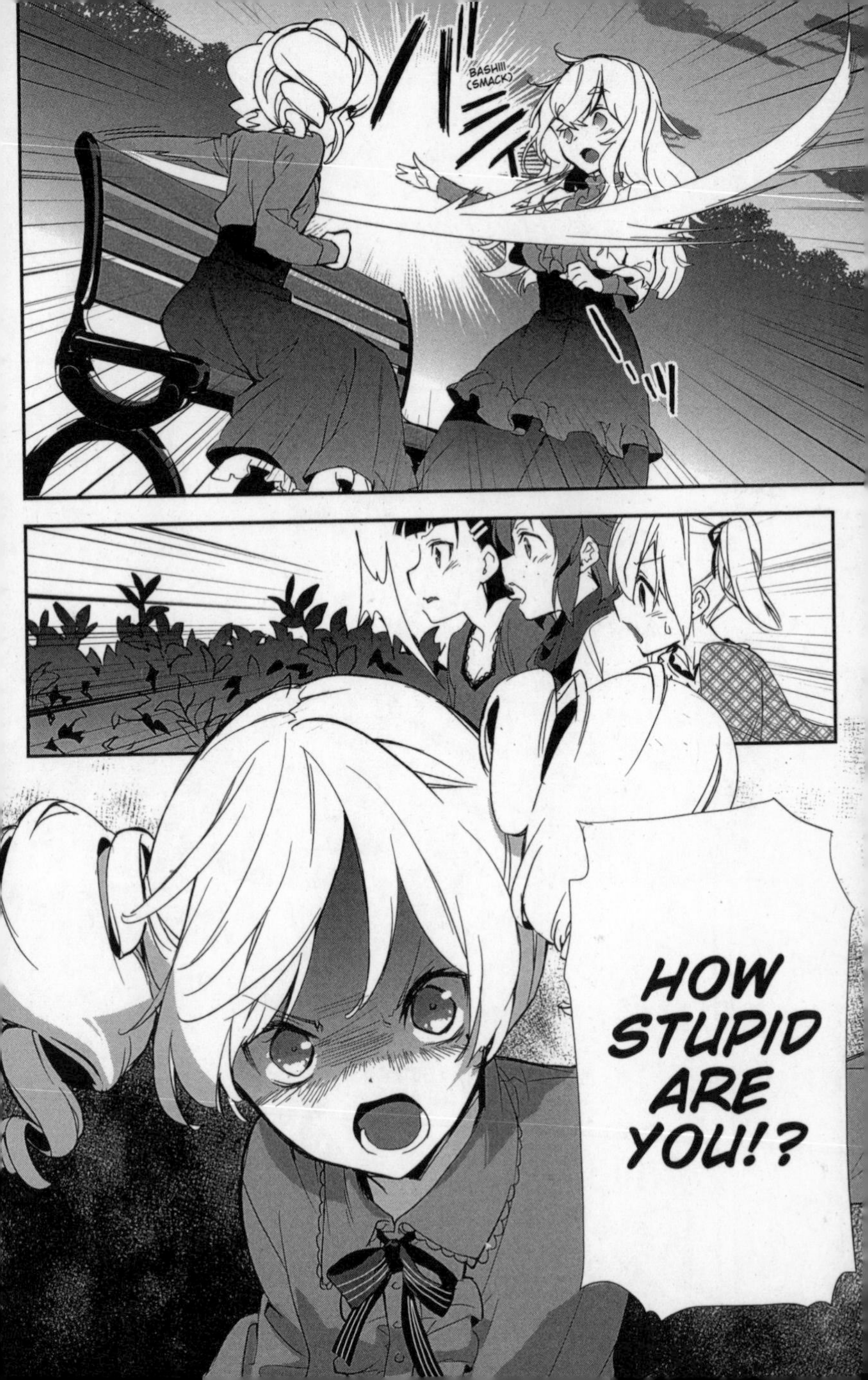
BASHIII (SMACK)
HOW STUPID ARE YOU!?

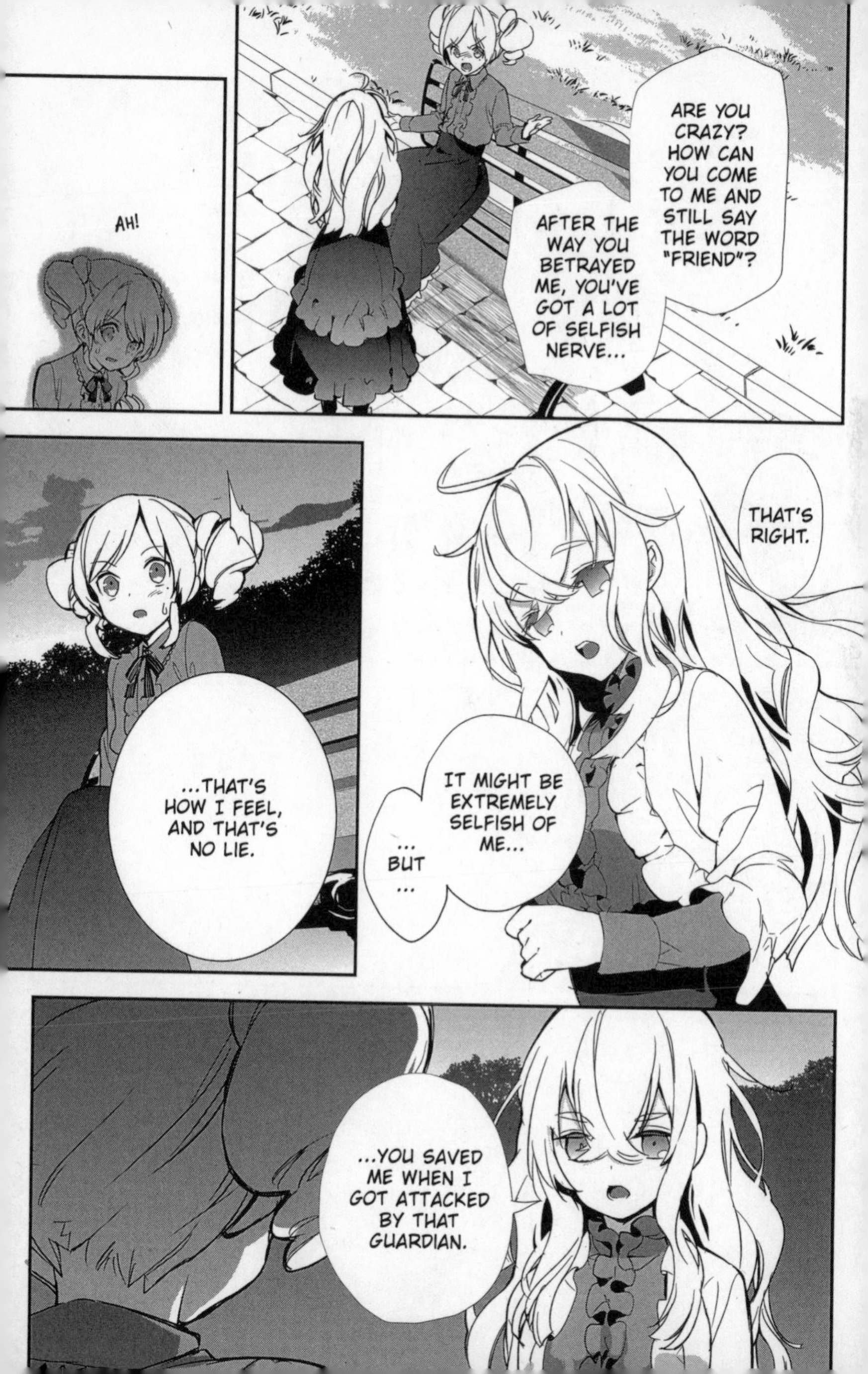

ARE YOU CRAZY? HOW CAN YOU COME TO ME AND STILL SAY THE WORD "FRIEND"?
AFTER THE WAY YOU BETRAYED ME, YOU'VE GOT A LOT OF SELFISH NERVE...
AH!
THAT'S RIGHT.
IT MIGHT BE EXTREMELY SELFISH OF ME...
...BUT...
...THAT'S HOW I FEEL, AND THAT'S NO LIE.
...YOU SAVED ME WHEN I GOT ATTACKED BY THAT GUARDIAN.

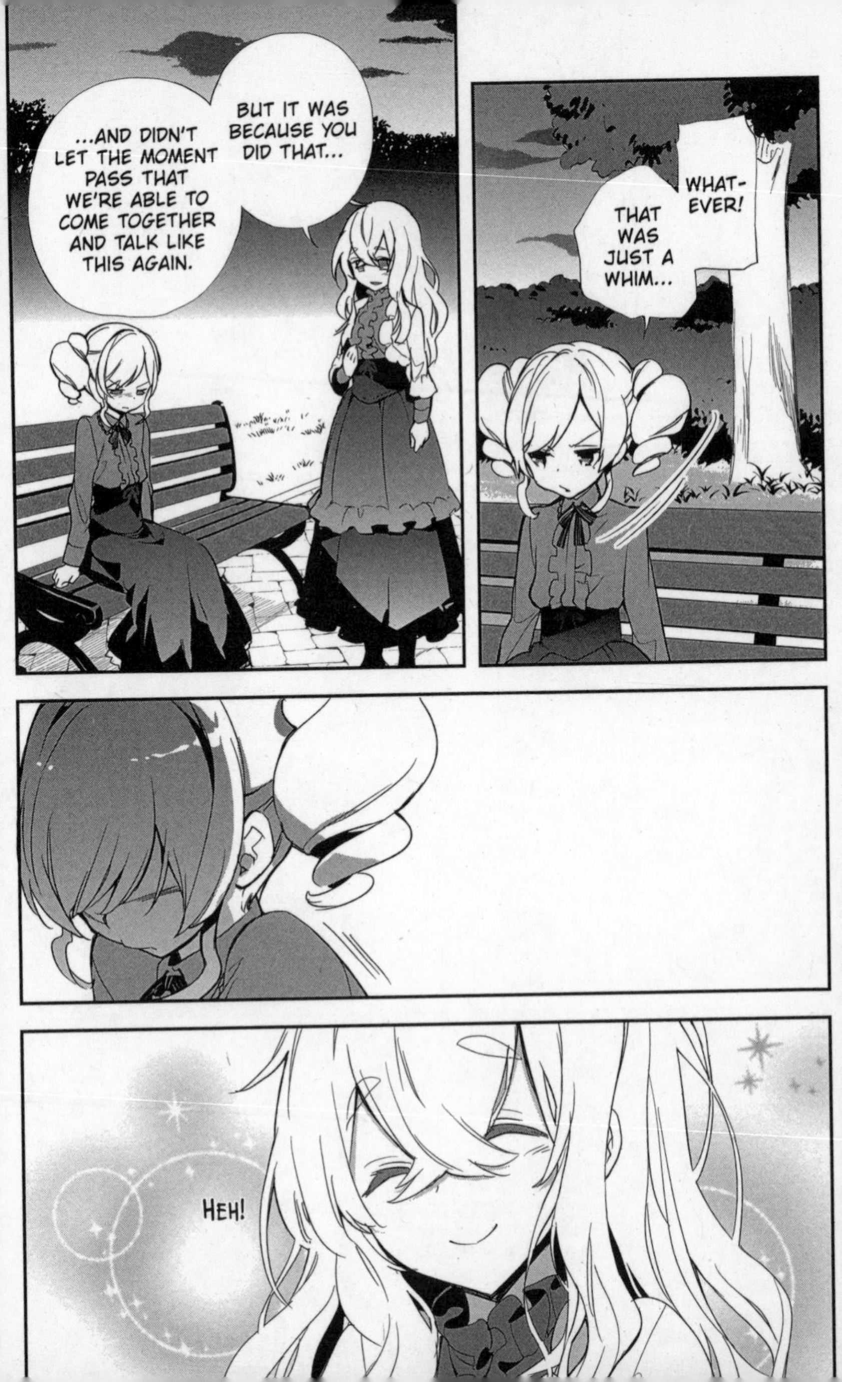
BUT IT WAS BECAUSE YOU DID THAT...
...AND DIDN'T LET THE MOMENT PASS THAT WE'RE ABLE TO COME TOGETHER AND TALK LIKE THIS AGAIN.
WHAT-EVER!
THAT WAS JUST A WHIM...
HEH!

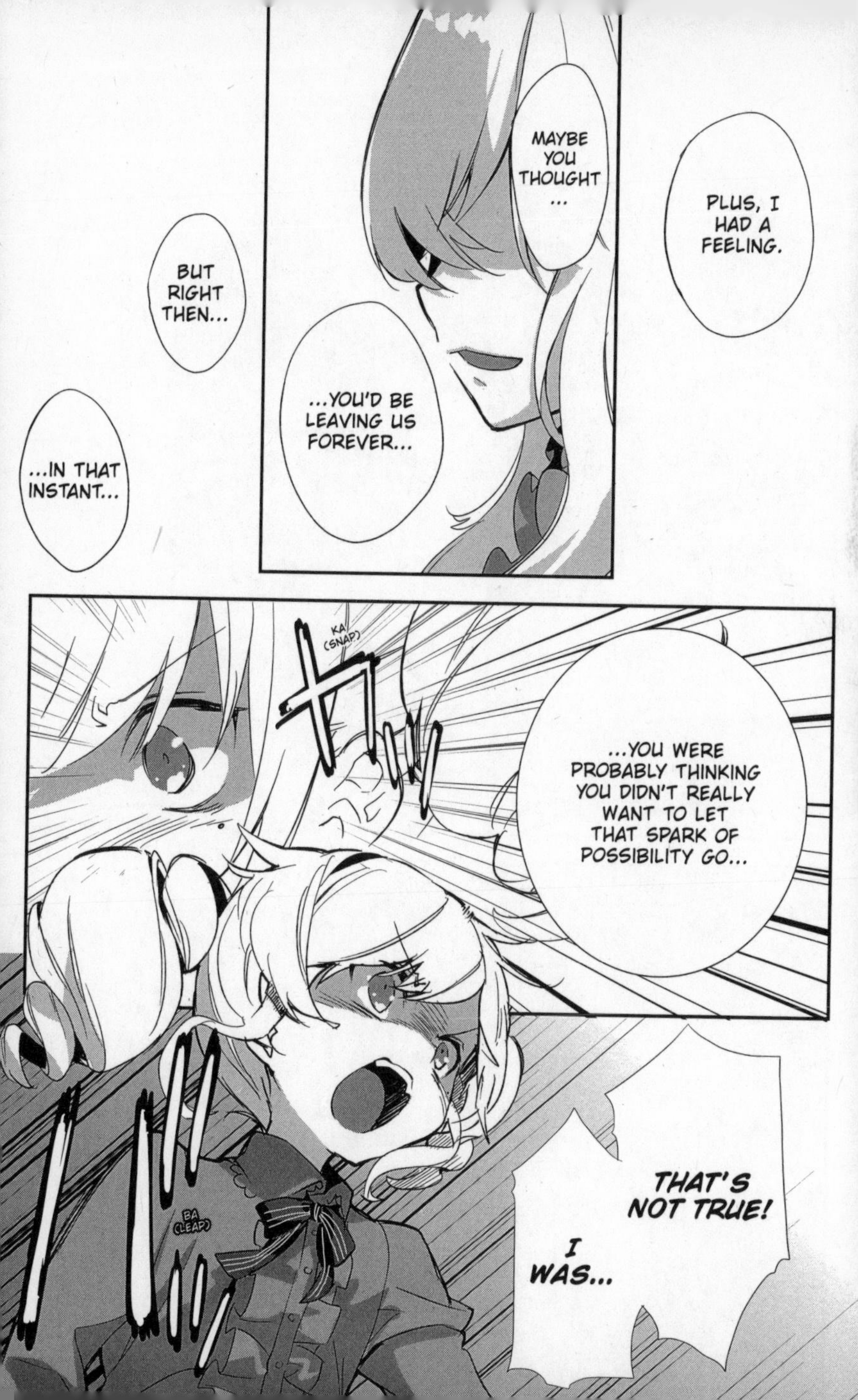
PLUS, I HAD A FEELING.
MAYBE YOU THOUGHT...
BUT RIGHT THEN...
...YOU'D BE LEAVING US FOREVER...
...IN THAT INSTANT...
KA (SNAP)
...YOU WERE PROBABLY THINKING YOU DIDN'T REALLY WANT TO LET THAT SPARK OF POSSIBILITY GO...
THAT'S NOT TRUE!
I WAS...
BA (LEAP)

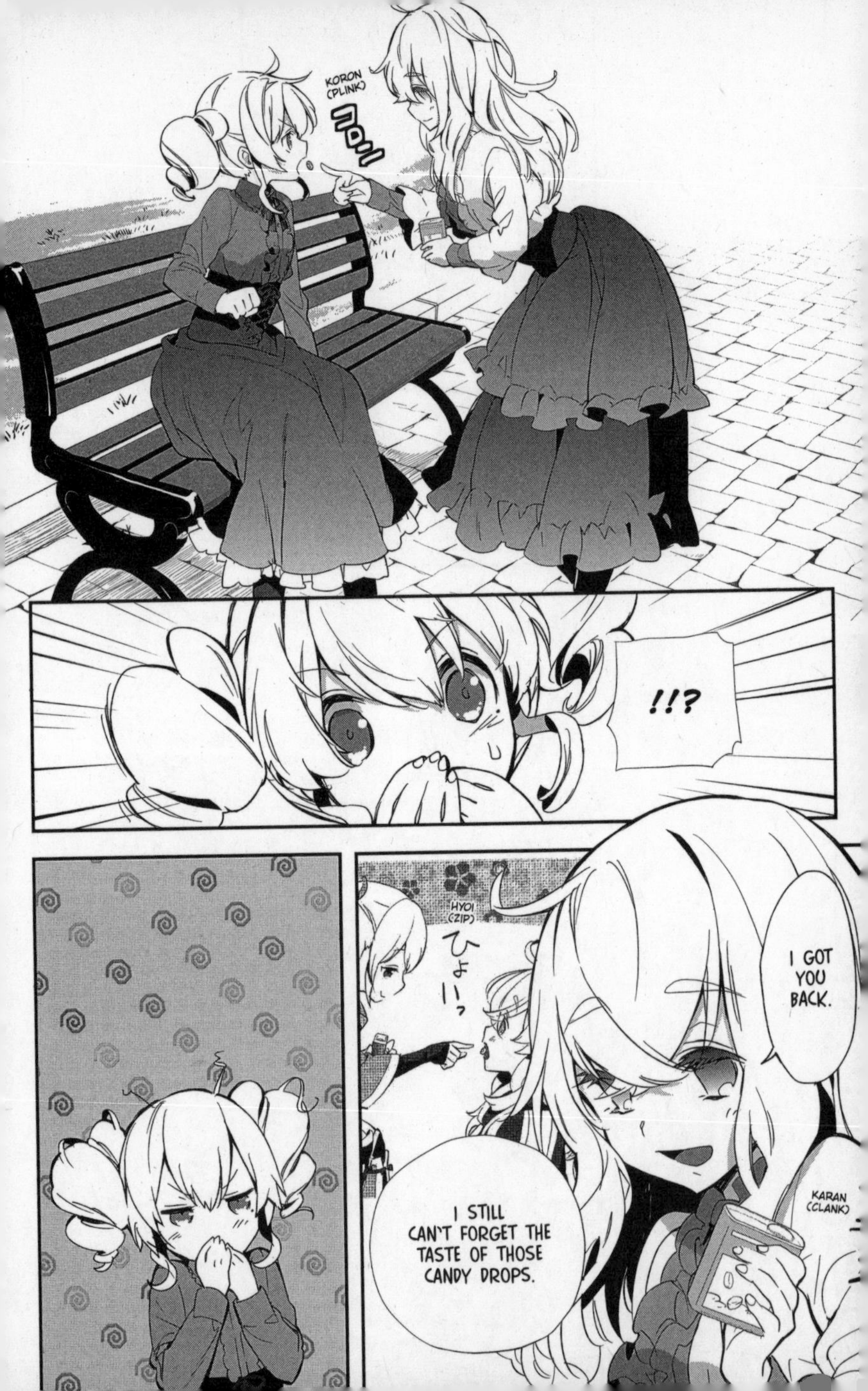
KORON (PLINK)
コロッ
!!?
HYOI (ZIP)
ひょいっ
I GOT YOU BACK.
KARAN (CLANK)
I STILL CAN'T FORGET THE TASTE OF THOSE CANDY DROPS.

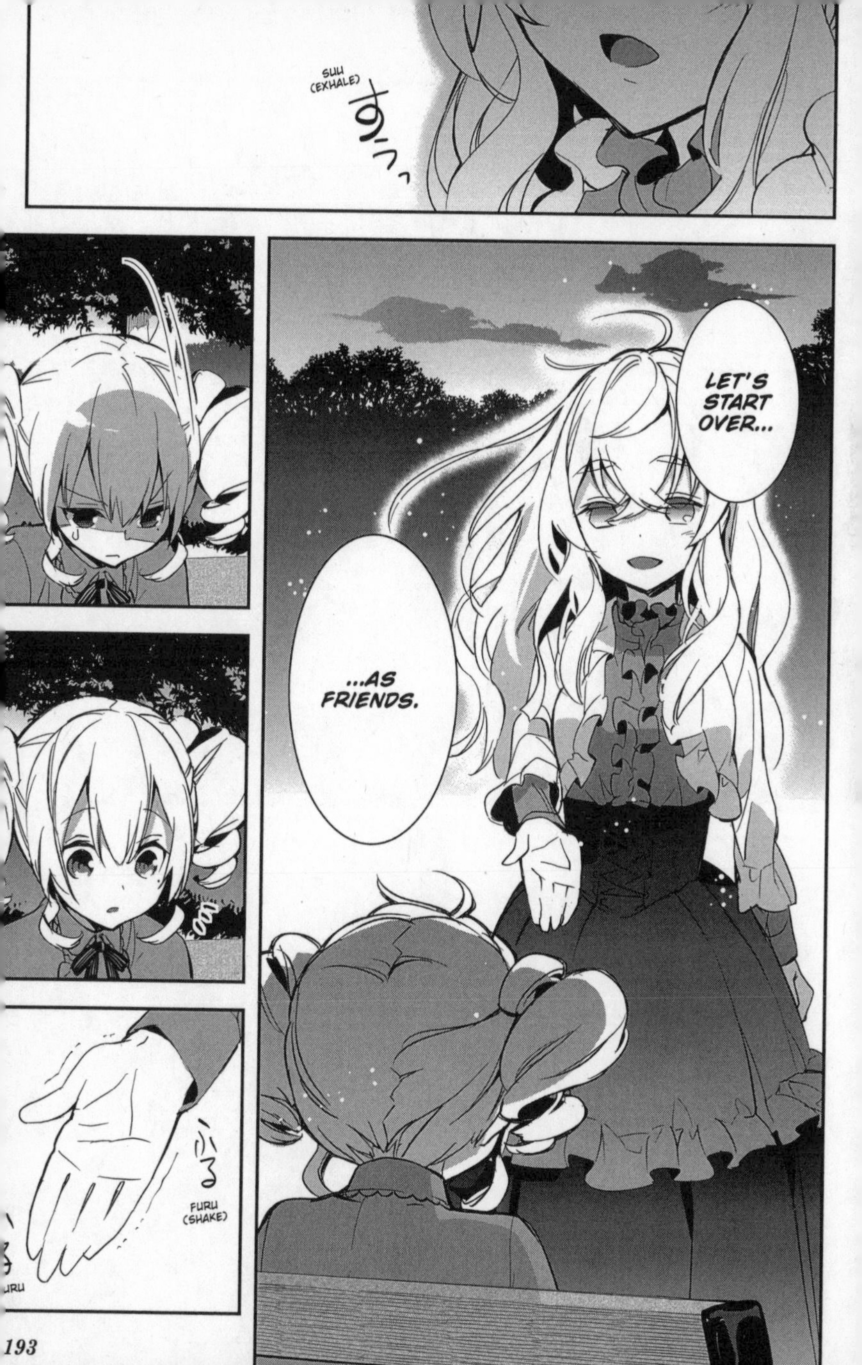
SUU (EXHALE)
すうっ
LET'S START OVER...
...AS FRIENDS.
ふる
FURU (SHAKE)
URU

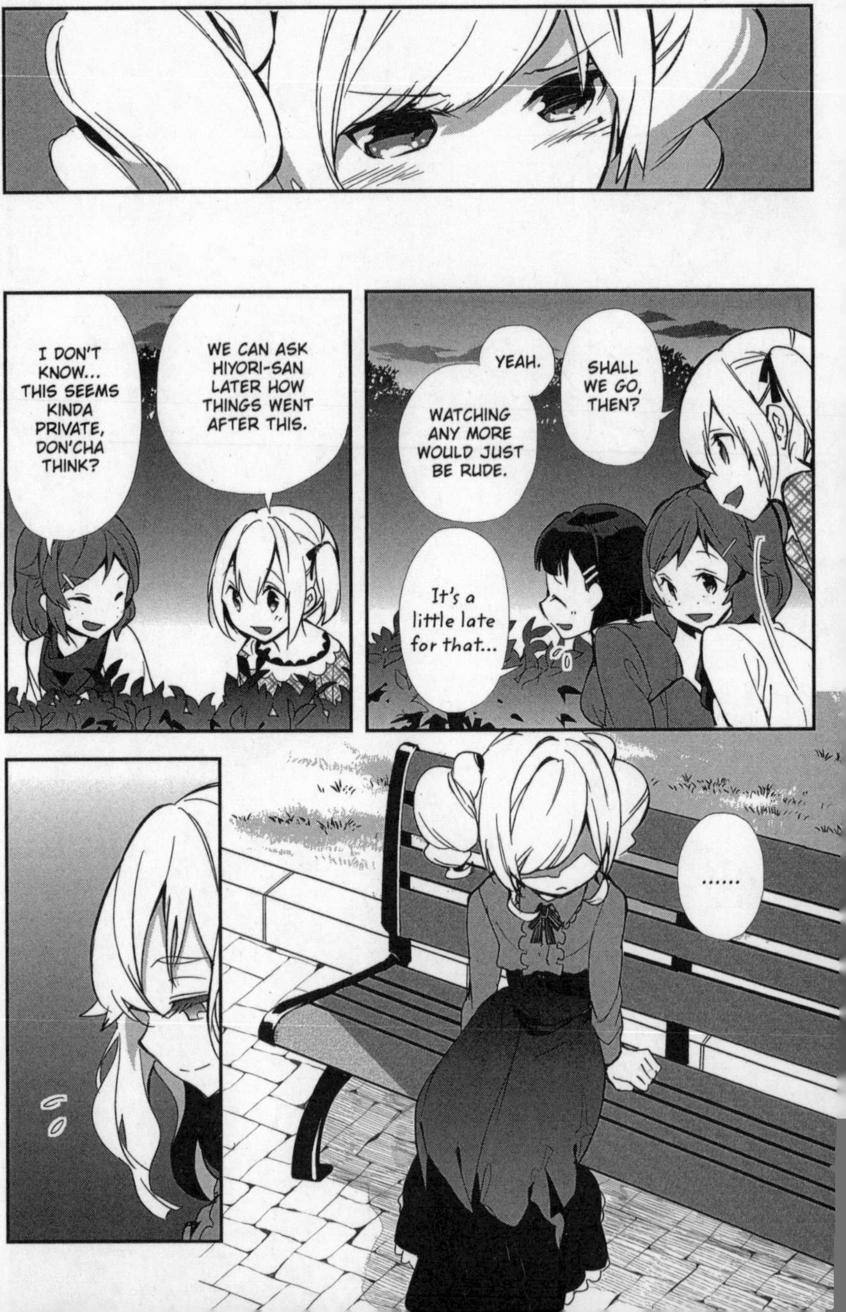
SHALL WE GO, THEN?
YEAH.
WATCHING ANY MORE WOULD JUST BE RUDE.
It's a little late for that...
WE CAN ASK HIYORI-SAN LATER HOW THINGS WENT AFTER THIS.
I DON'T KNOW... THIS SEEMS KINDA PRIVATE, DON'CHA THINK?
......

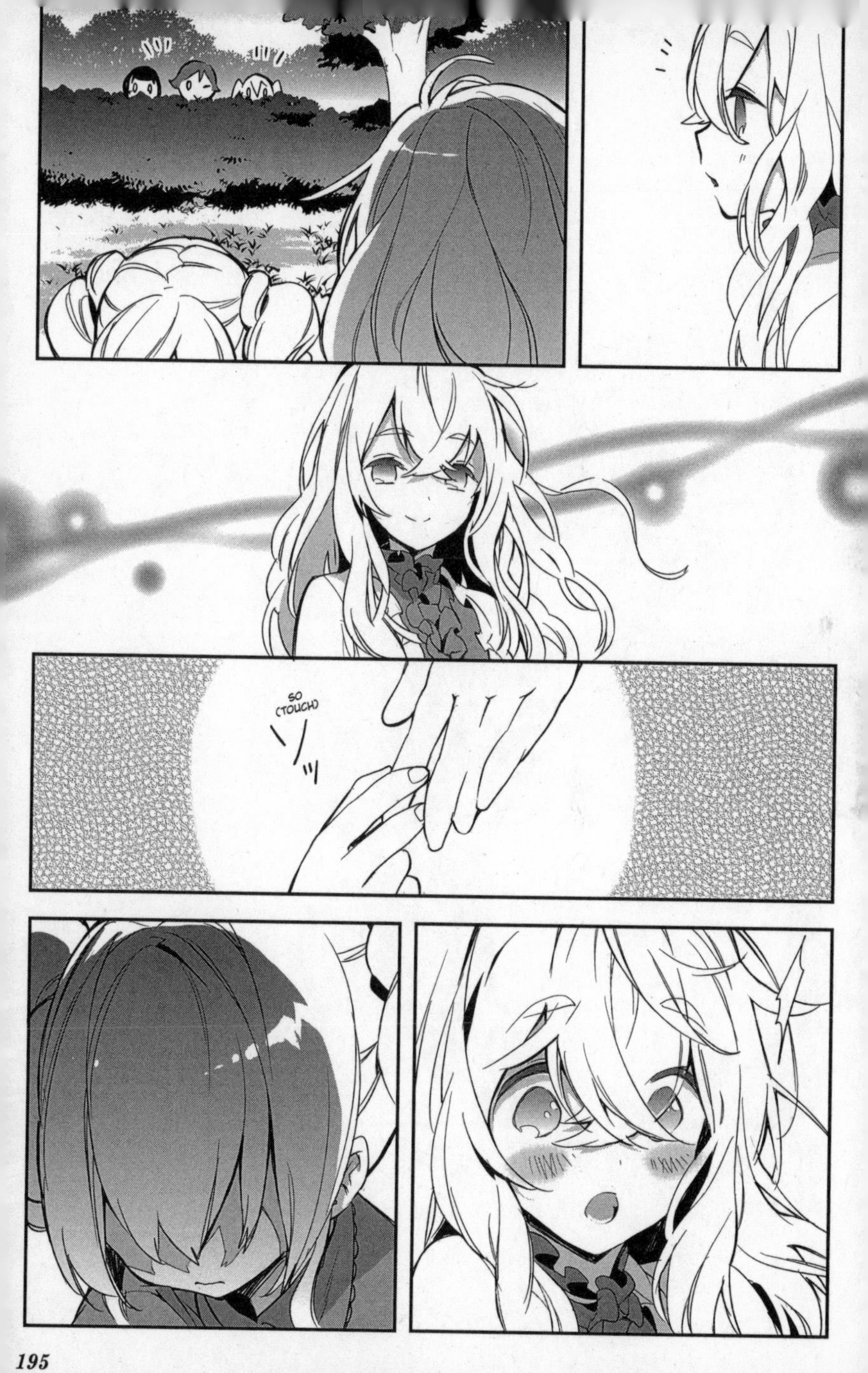
SO
(TOUCH)

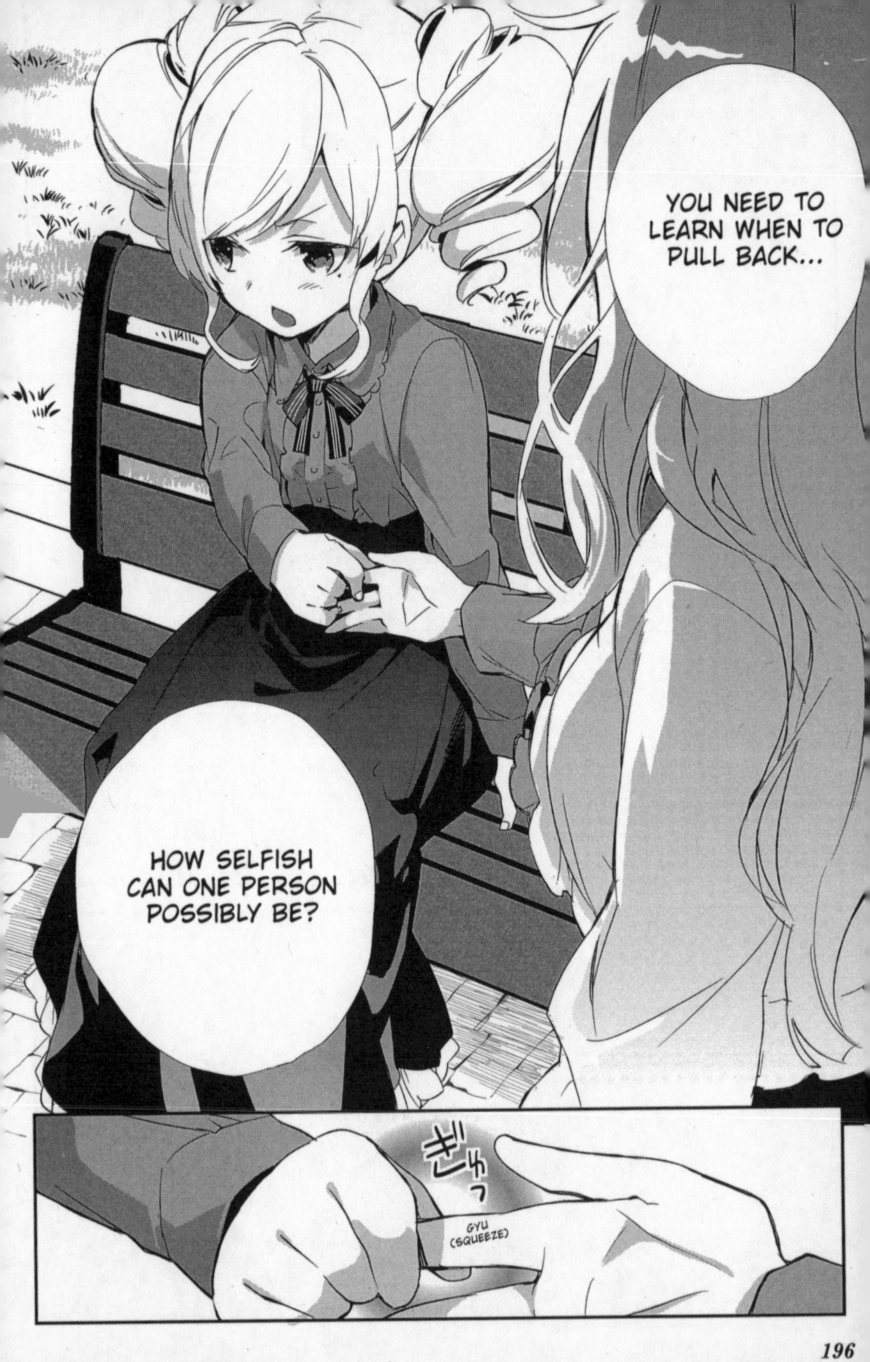
YOU NEED TO LEARN WHEN TO PULL BACK...
HOW SELFISH CAN ONE PERSON POSSIBLY BE?
ぎゅっ
GYU (SQUEEZE)

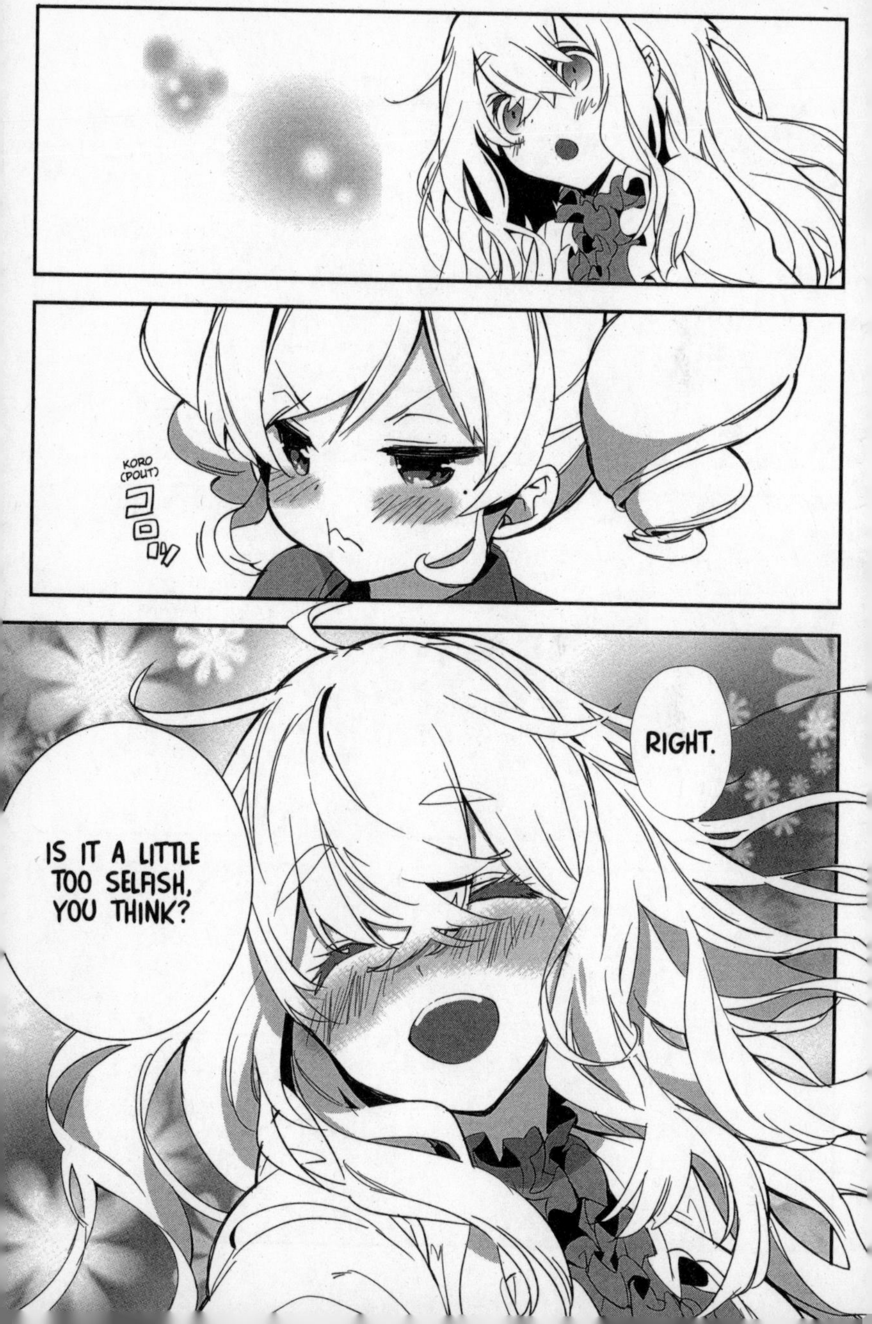
KORO (POUT)
コロッ
RIGHT.
IS IT A LITTLE TOO SELFISH, YOU THINK?

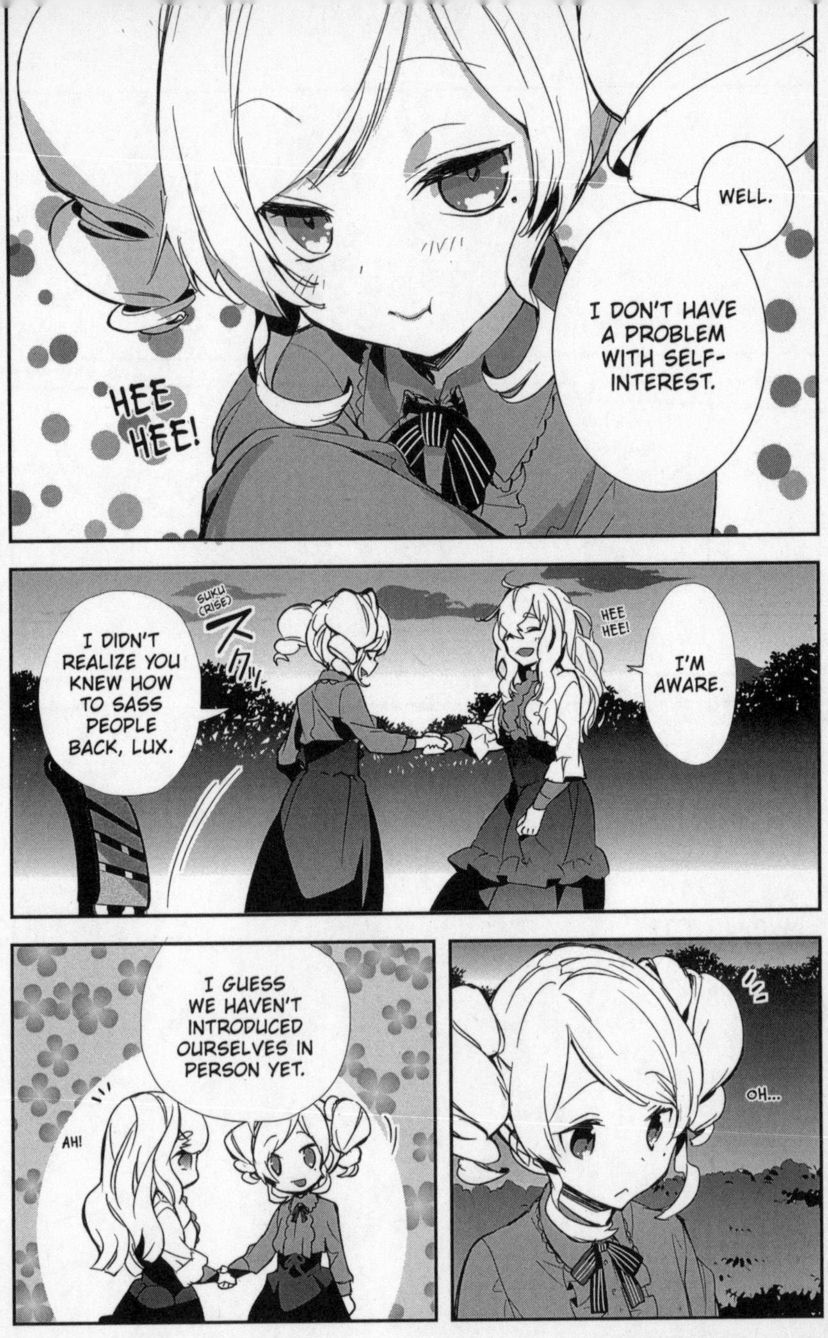
WELL.
I DON'T HAVE A PROBLEM WITH SELF-INTEREST.
HEE HEE!
HEE HEE!
I'M AWARE.
SUKU (RISE)
I DIDN'T REALIZE YOU KNEW HOW TO SASS PEOPLE BACK, LUX.
OH...
I GUESS WE HAVEN'T INTRODUCED OURSELVES IN PERSON YET.
AH!

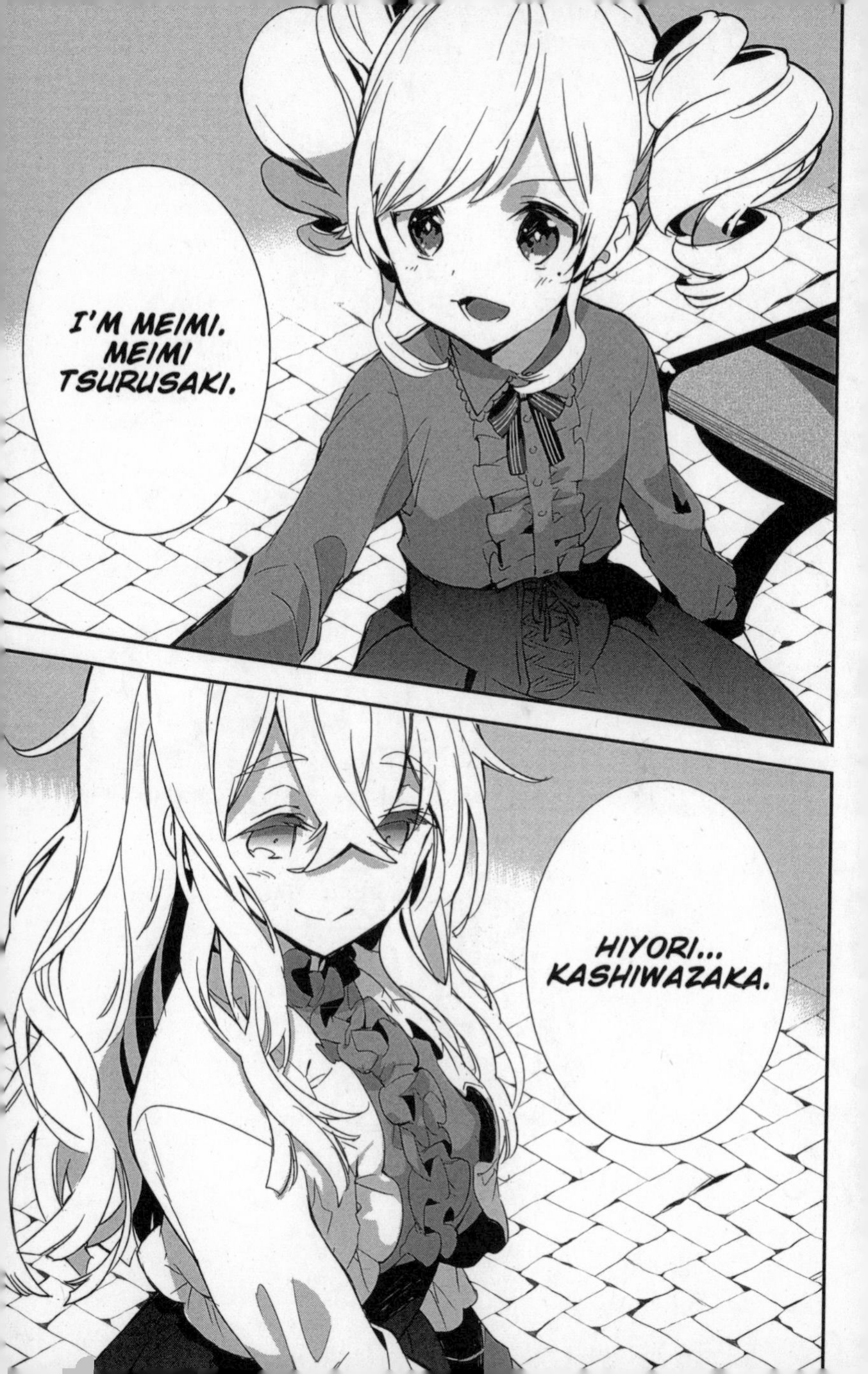
I'M MEIMI. MEIMI TSURUSAKI.
HIYORI... KASHIWAZAKA.

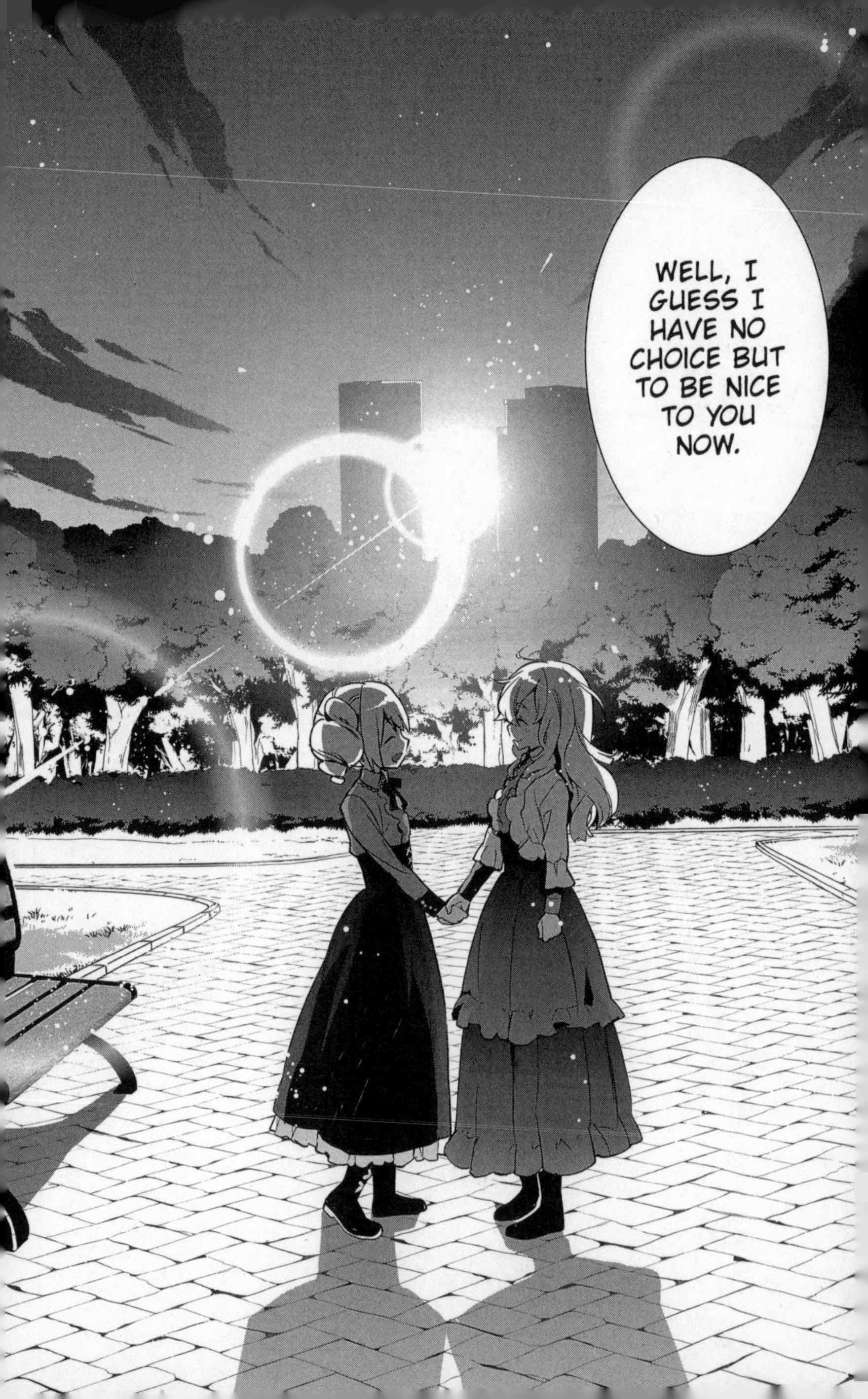
WELL, I GUESS I HAVE NO CHOICE BUT TO BE NICE TO YOU NOW.

SWORD ART ONLINE
GIRLS' OPS

SAO GIRLS
SLEEPING SERIES
MEIMI

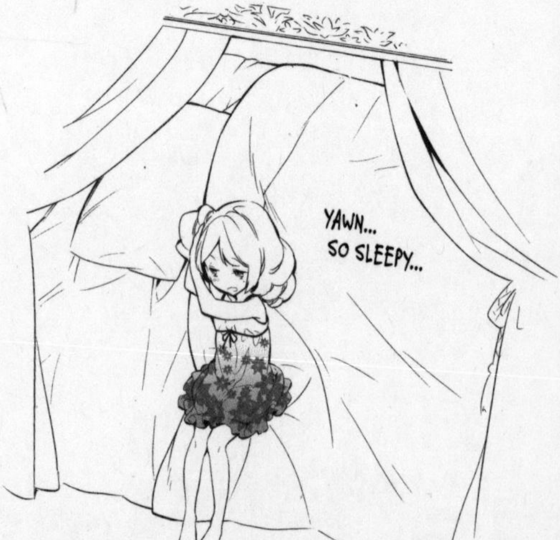
YAWN... SO SLEEPY...

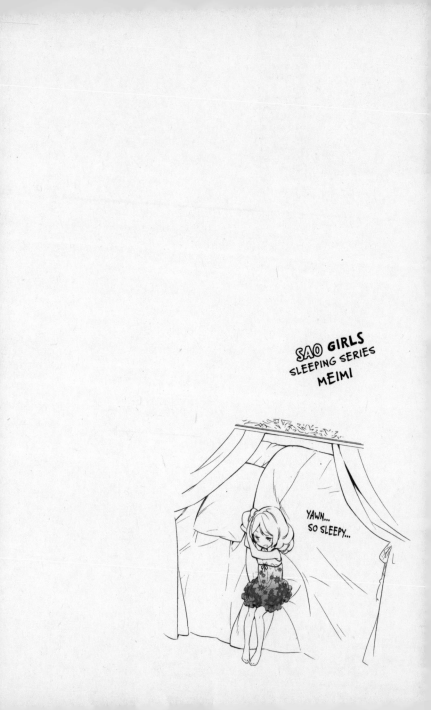

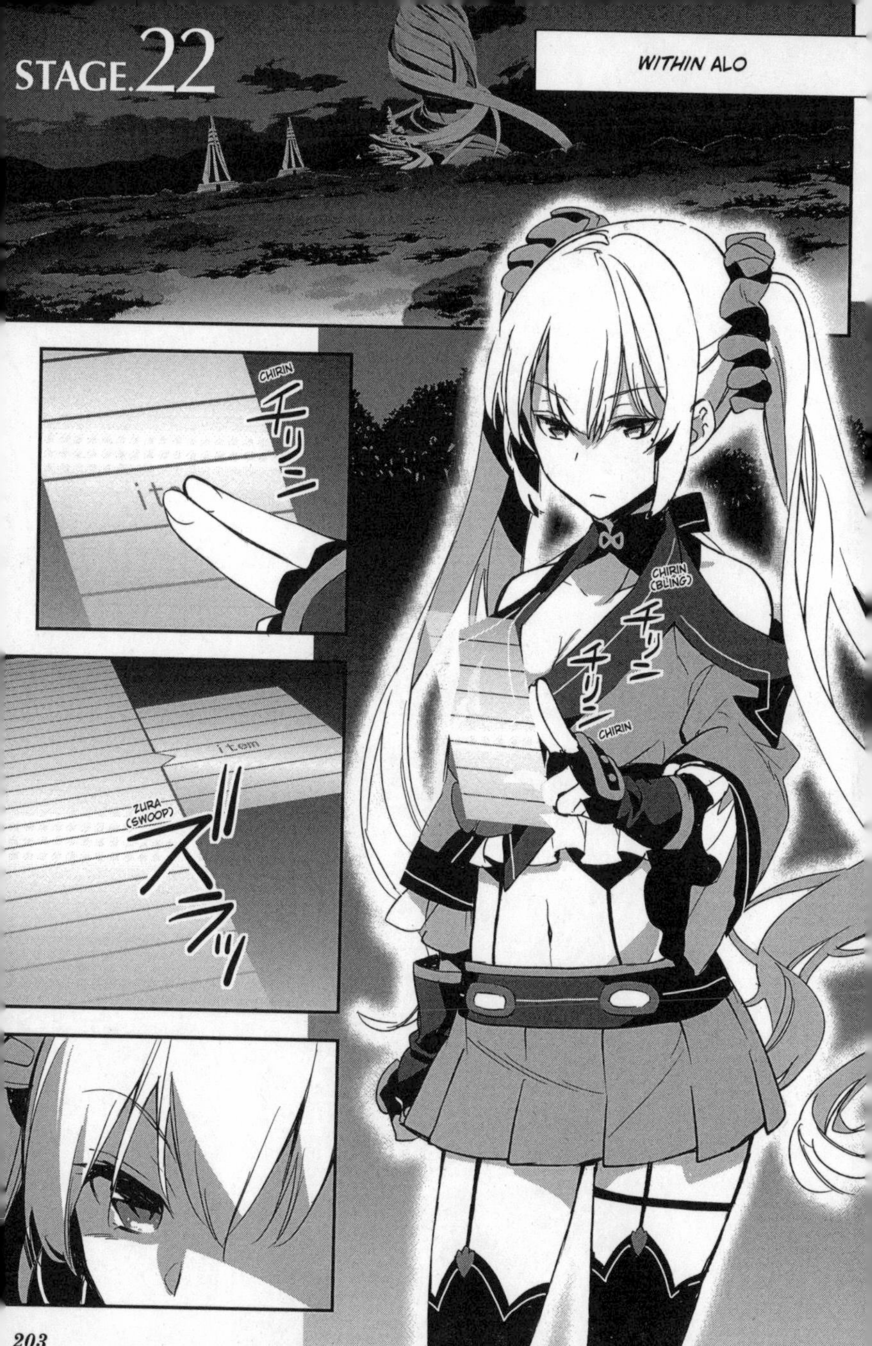
STAGE.22
WITHIN ALO
CHIRIN
チリン
item
CHIRIN (BLING)
チリン
チリン
CHIRIN
item
ZURA (SWOOP)
ズラッ

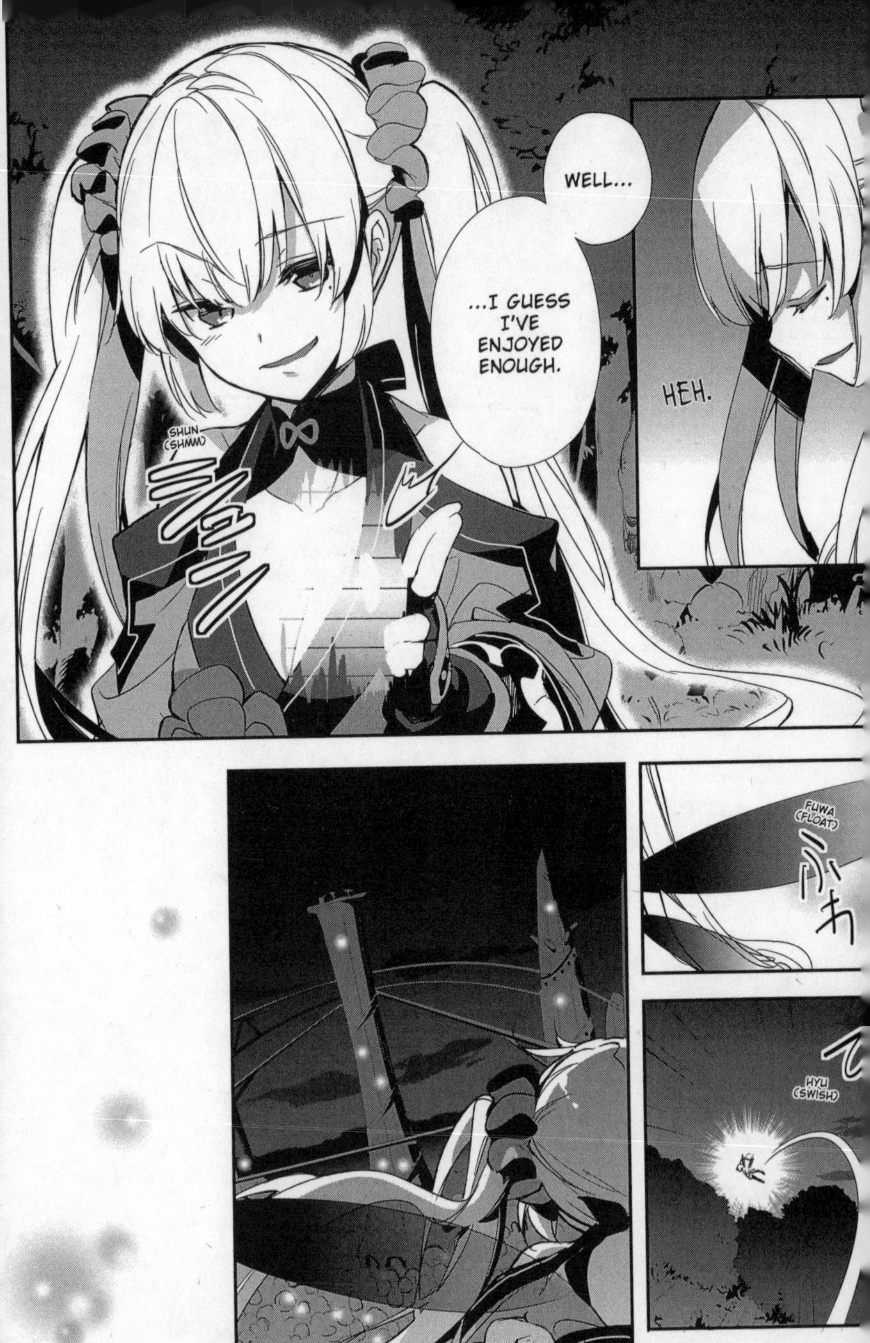
WELL...
...I GUESS I'VE ENJOYED ENOUGH.
HEH.
SHUN (SHMM)
シュン
FUWA (FLOAT)
ふわ
HYU (SWISH)

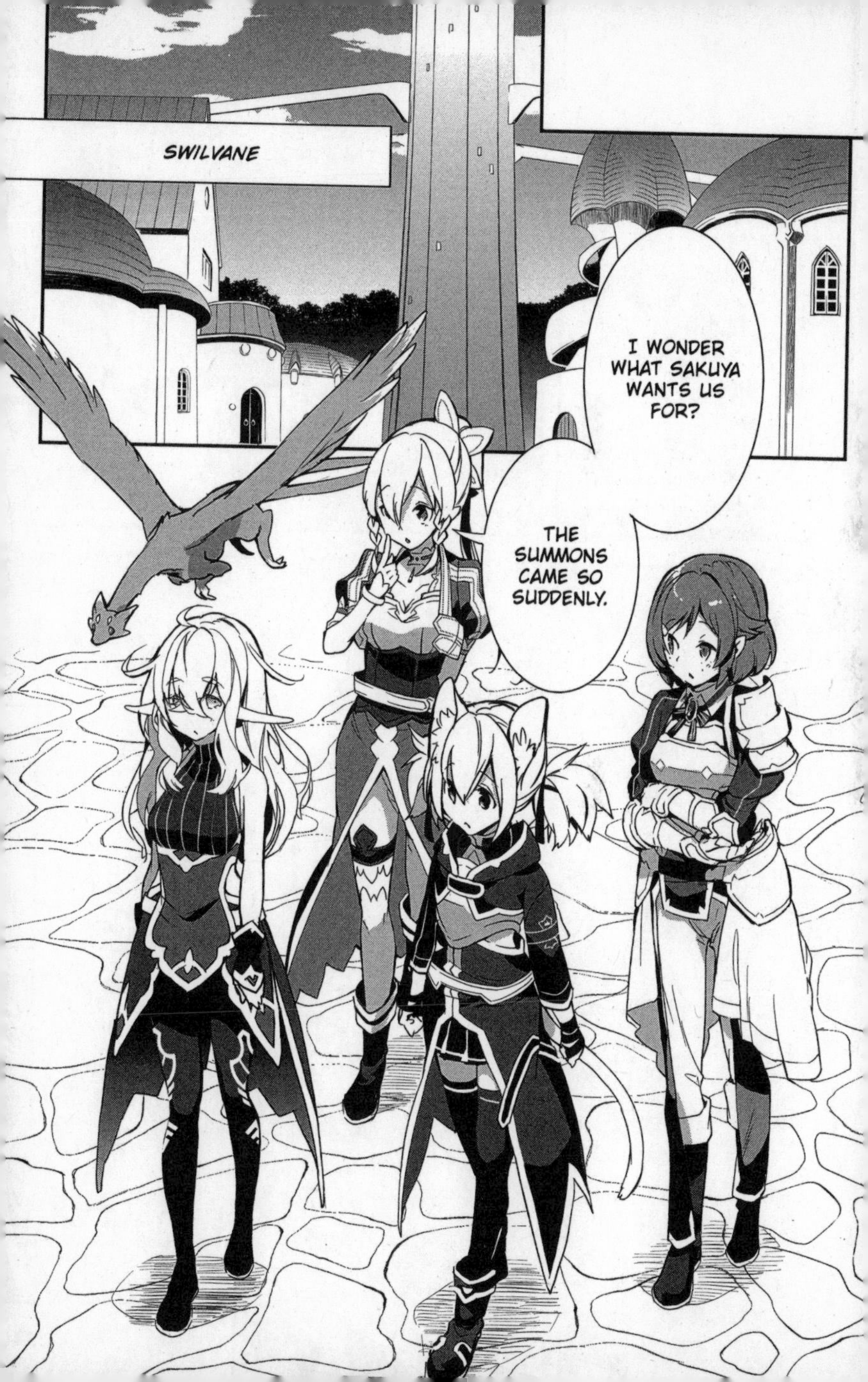
SWILVANE
I WONDER WHAT SAKUYA WANTS US FOR?
THE SUMMONS CAME SO SUDDENLY.

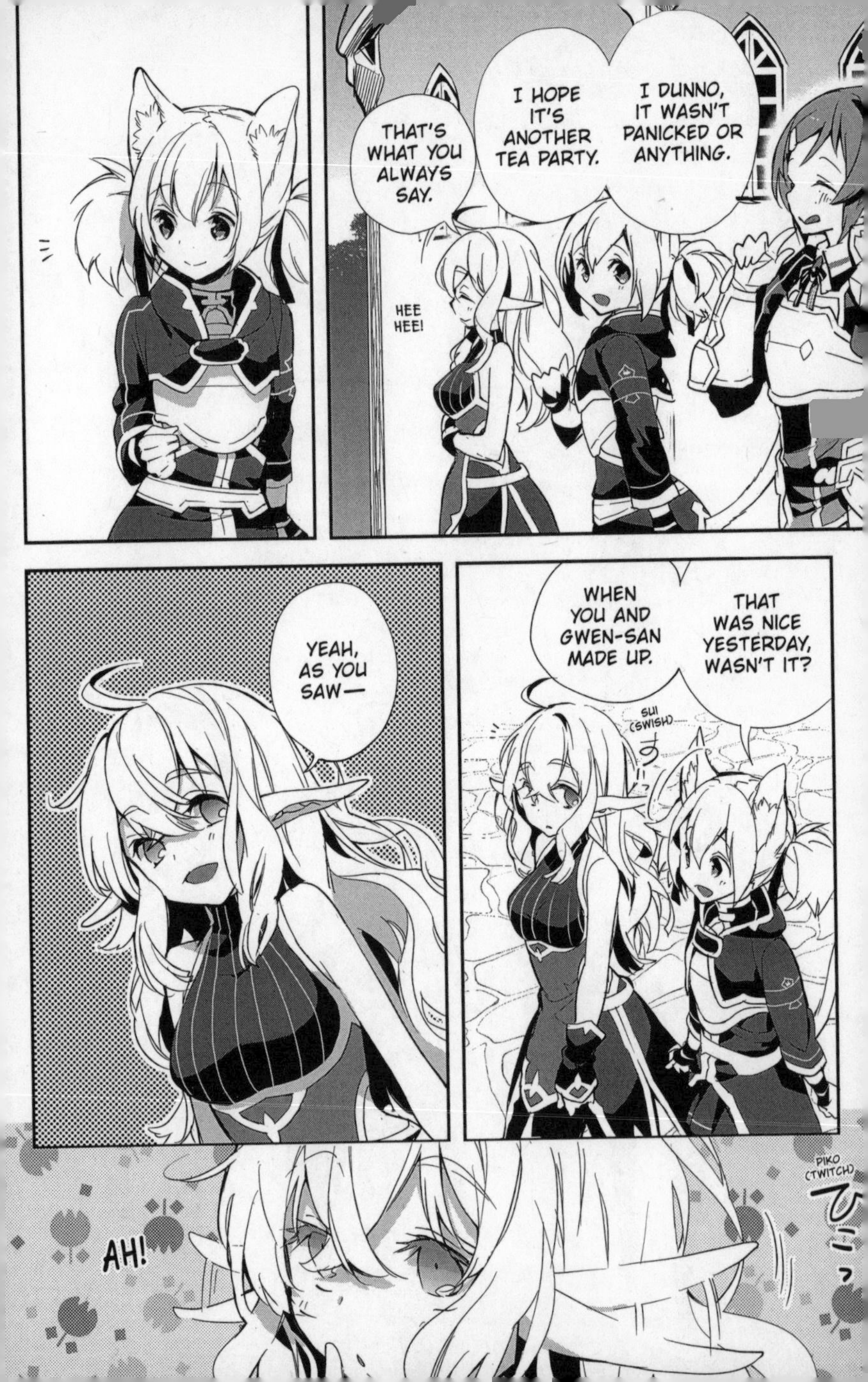
I DUNNO, IT WASN'T PANICKED OR ANYTHING.
I HOPE IT'S ANOTHER TEA PARTY.
THAT'S WHAT YOU ALWAYS SAY.
HEE HEE!
THAT WAS NICE YESTERDAY, WASN'T IT?
WHEN YOU AND GWEN-SAN MADE UP.
SUI (SWISH)
YEAH, AS YOU SAW—
PIKO (TWITCH)
AH!

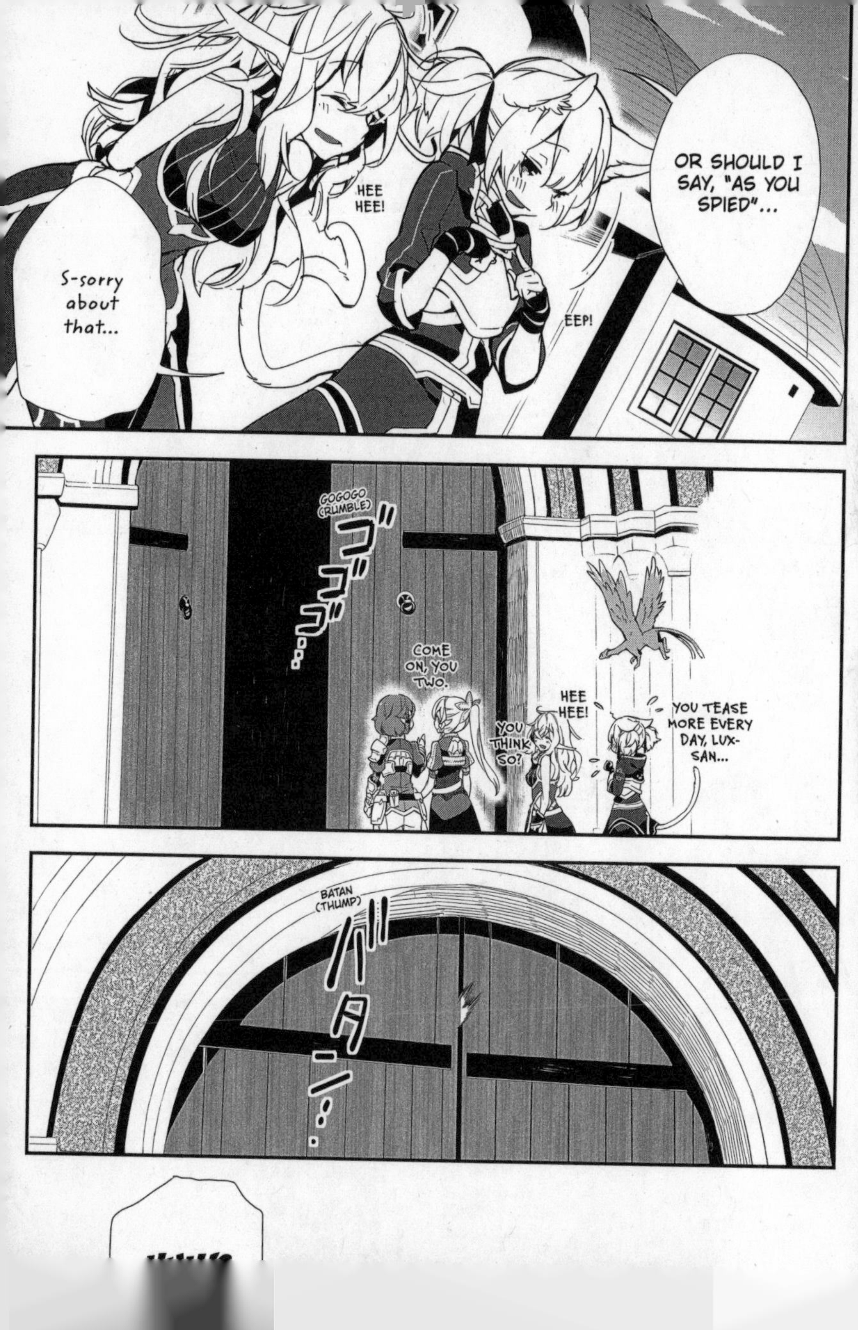
OR SHOULD I SAY, "AS YOU SPIED"...
EEP!
HEE HEE!
S-sorry about that...
GOGOGO (RUMBLE)
YOU TEASE MORE EVERY DAY, LUX-SAN...
HEE HEE!
YOU THINK SO?
COME ON, YOU TWO.
BATAN (THUMP)

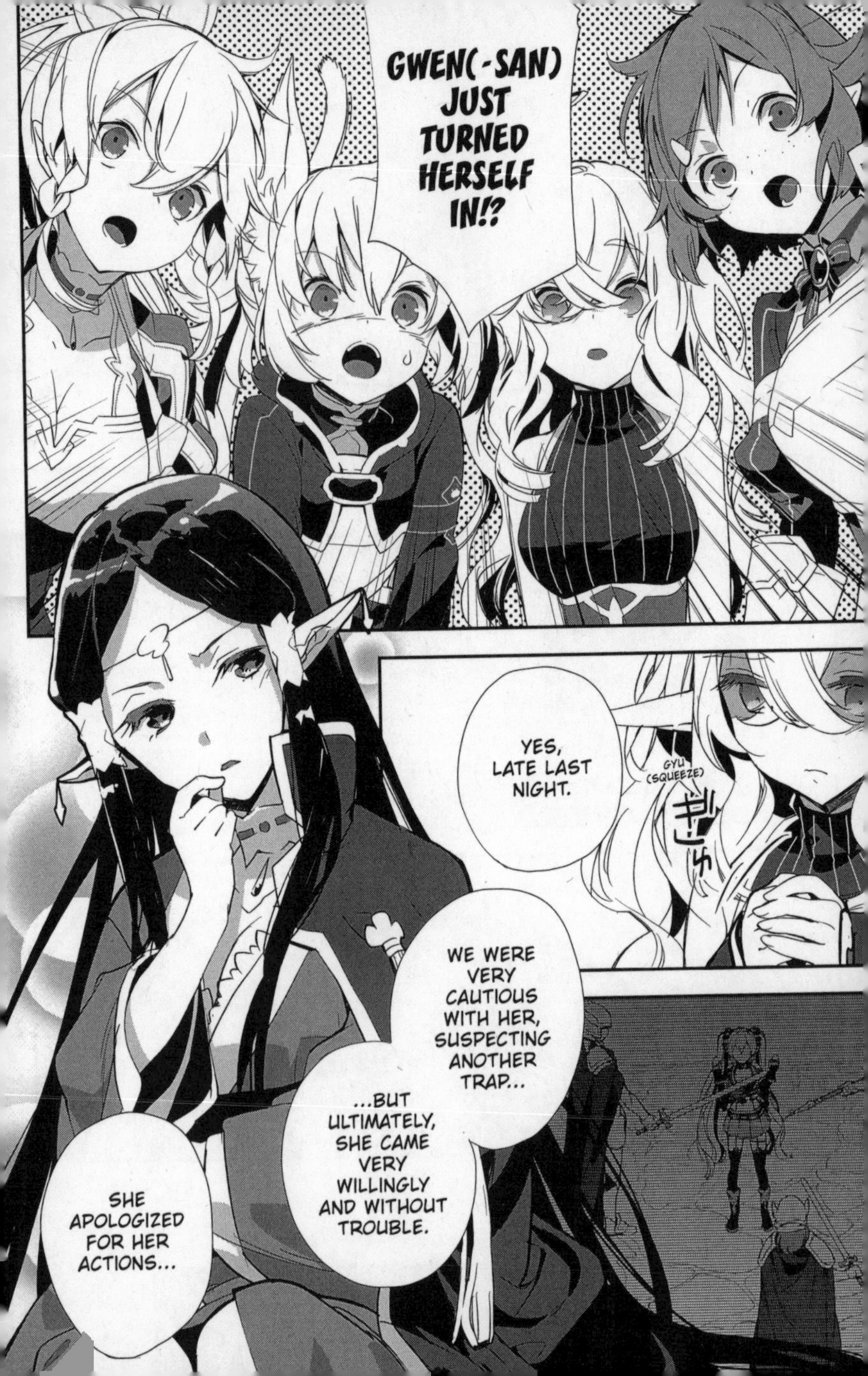
GWEN(-SAN) JUST TURNED HERSELF IN!?
YES, LATE LAST NIGHT.
GYU (SQUEEZE)
WE WERE VERY CAUTIOUS WITH HER, SUSPECTING ANOTHER TRAP...
...BUT ULTIMATELY, SHE CAME VERY WILLINGLY AND WITHOUT TROUBLE.
SHE APOLOGIZED FOR HER ACTIONS...

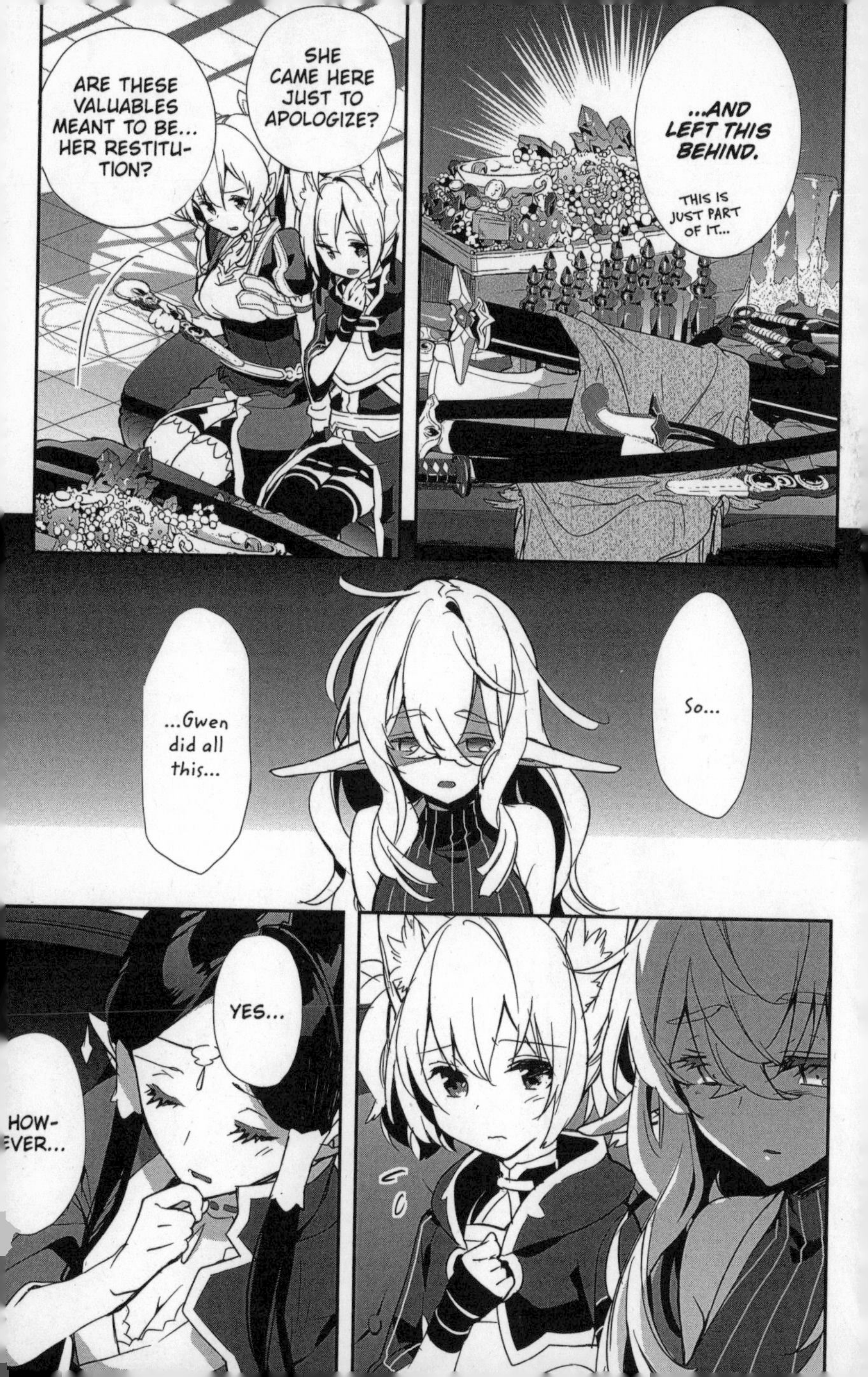
...AND LEFT THIS BEHIND.
THIS IS JUST PART OF IT...
SHE CAME HERE JUST TO APOLOGIZE?
ARE THESE VALUABLES MEANT TO BE... HER RESTITUTION?
So...
...Gwen did all this...
YES...
HOW-EVER...

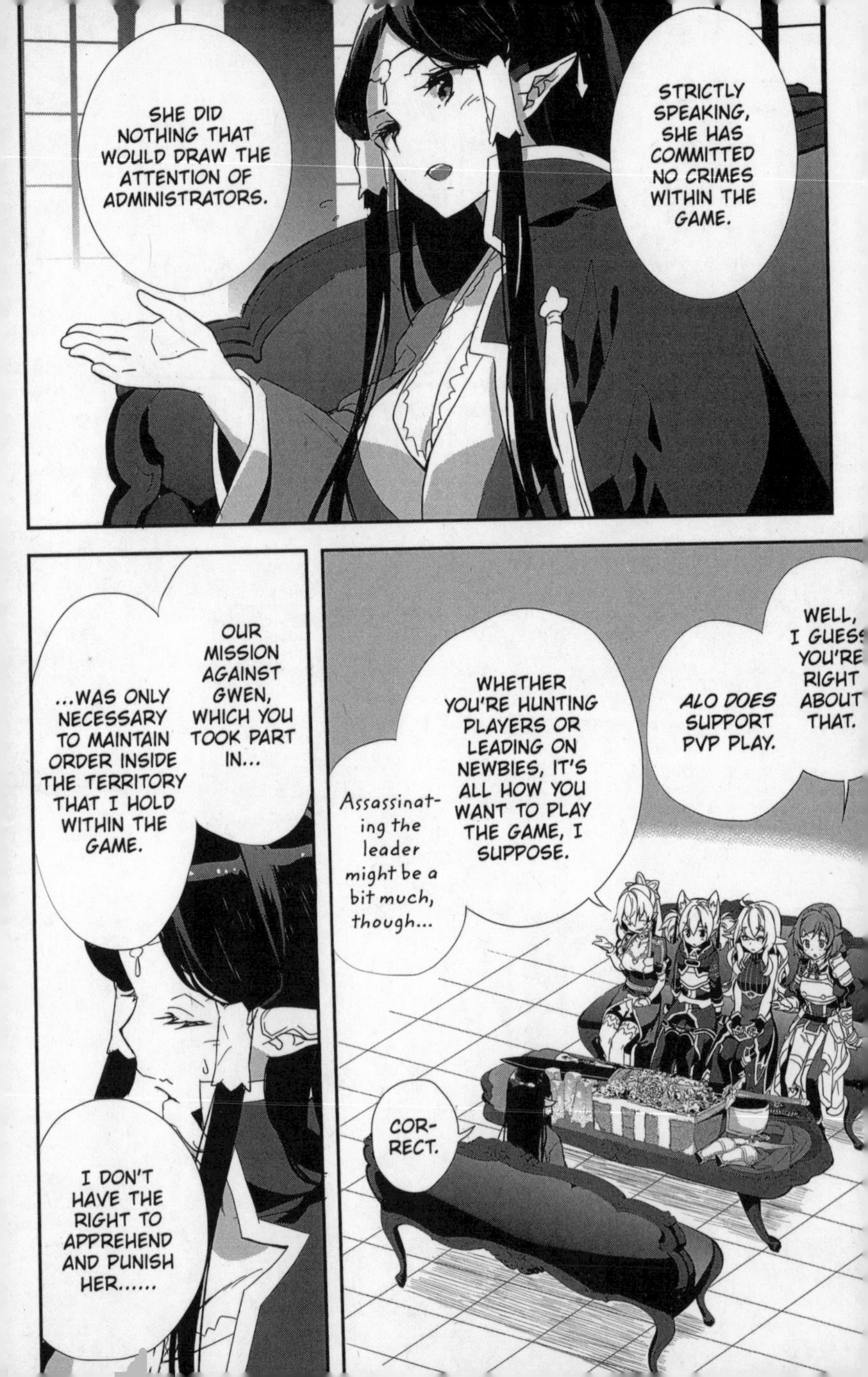
STRICTLY SPEAKING, SHE HAS COMMITTED NO CRIMES WITHIN THE GAME.
SHE DID NOTHING THAT WOULD DRAW THE ATTENTION OF ADMINISTRATORS.
WELL, I GUES YOU'RE RIGHT ABOUT THAT.
ALO DOES SUPPORT PVP PLAY.
WHETHER YOU'RE HUNTING PLAYERS OR LEADING ON NEWBIES, IT'S ALL HOW YOU WANT TO PLAY THE GAME, I SUPPOSE.
Assassinating the leader might be a bit much, though...
COR-RECT.
OUR MISSION AGAINST GWEN, WHICH YOU TOOK PART IN...
...WAS ONLY NECESSARY TO MAINTAIN ORDER INSIDE THE TERRITORY THAT I HOLD WITHIN THE GAME.
I DON'T HAVE THE RIGHT TO APPREHEND AND PUNISH HER......

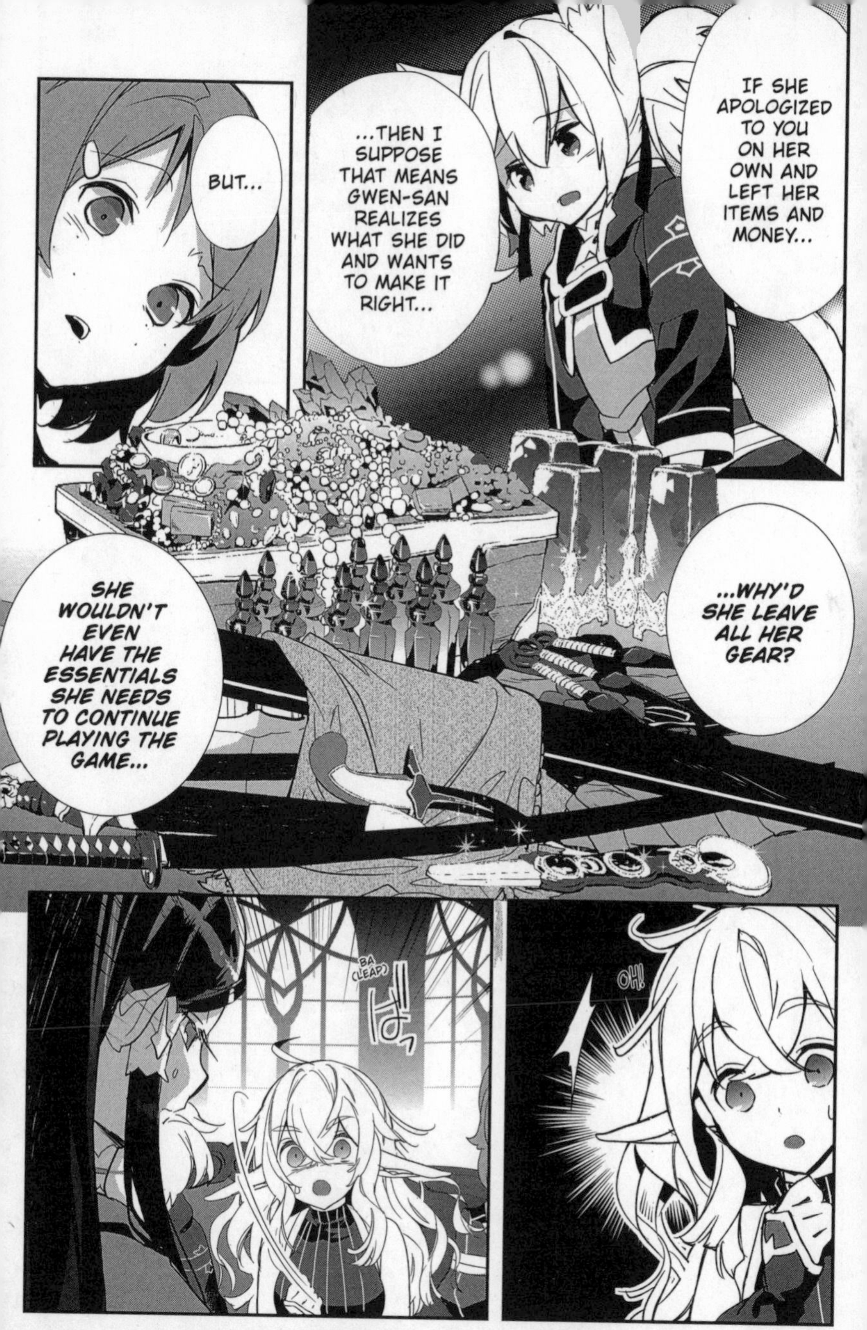
IF SHE APOLOGIZED TO YOU ON HER OWN AND LEFT HER ITEMS AND MONEY...
...THEN I SUPPOSE THAT MEANS GWEN-SAN REALIZES WHAT SHE DID AND WANTS TO MAKE IT RIGHT...
BUT...
...WHY'D SHE LEAVE ALL HER GEAR?
SHE WOULDN'T EVEN HAVE THE ESSENTIALS SHE NEEDS TO CONTINUE PLAYING THE GAME...
OH!
BA (LEAP)
ばっ

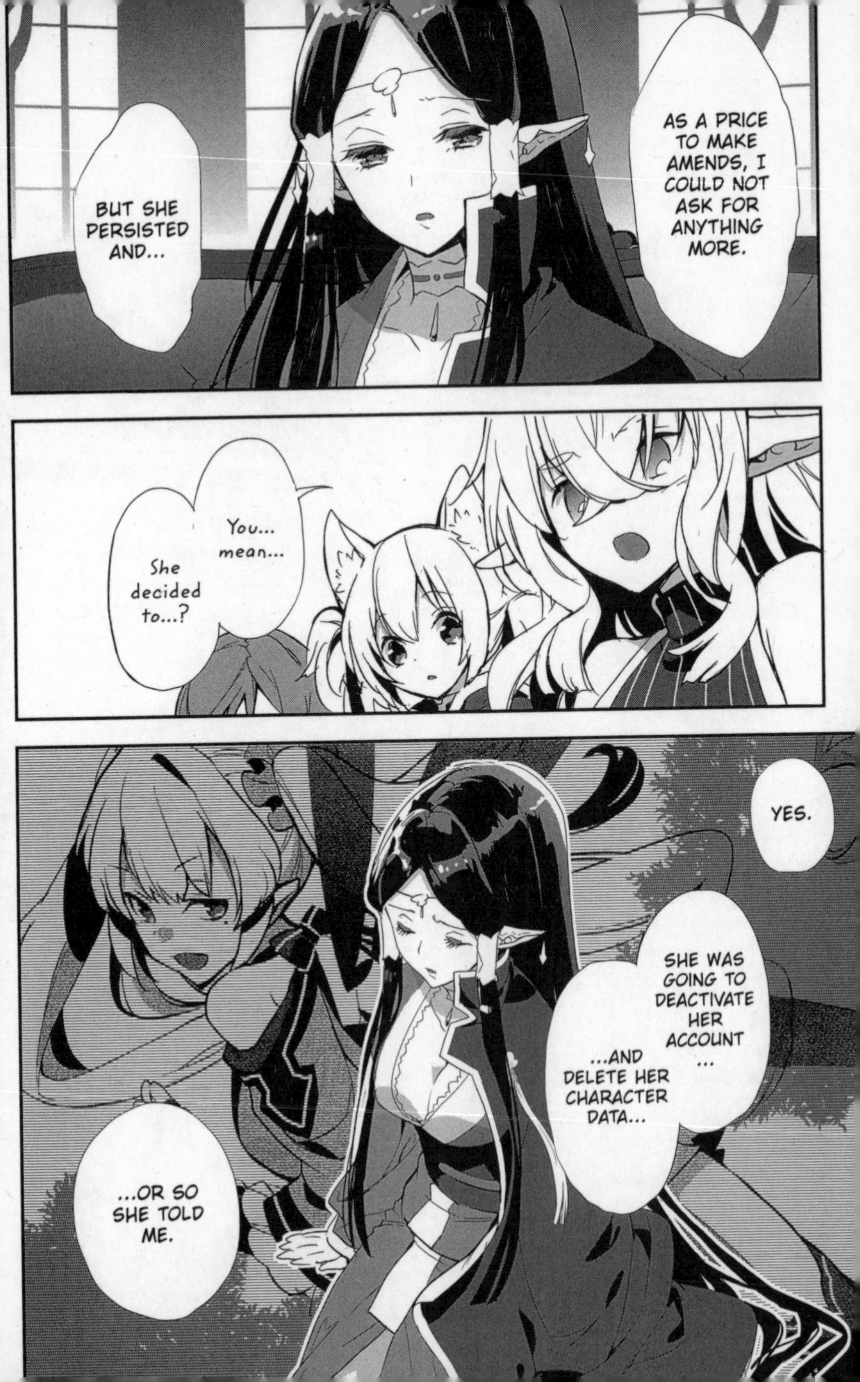
AS A PRICE TO MAKE AMENDS, I COULD NOT ASK FOR ANYTHING MORE.
BUT SHE PERSISTED AND...
You... mean...
She decided to...?
YES.
SHE WAS GOING TO DEACTIVATE HER ACCOUNT ...
...AND DELETE HER CHARACTER DATA...
...OR SO SHE TOLD ME.

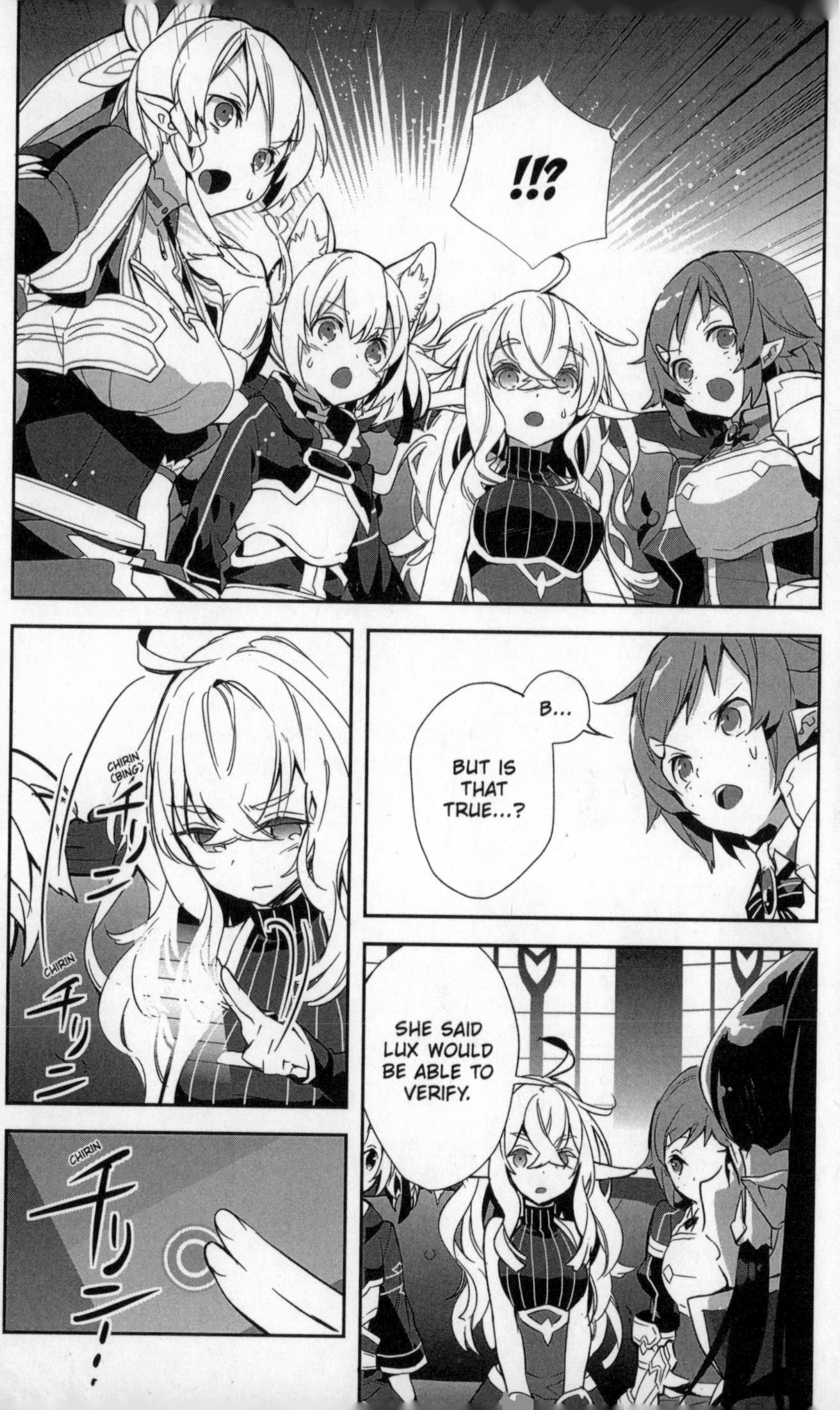
!!?
B...
BUT IS THAT TRUE...?
CHIRIN (BING)
チリーン
CHIRIN
チリーン
SHE SAID LUX WOULD BE ABLE TO VERIFY.
CHIRIN
チリーン…

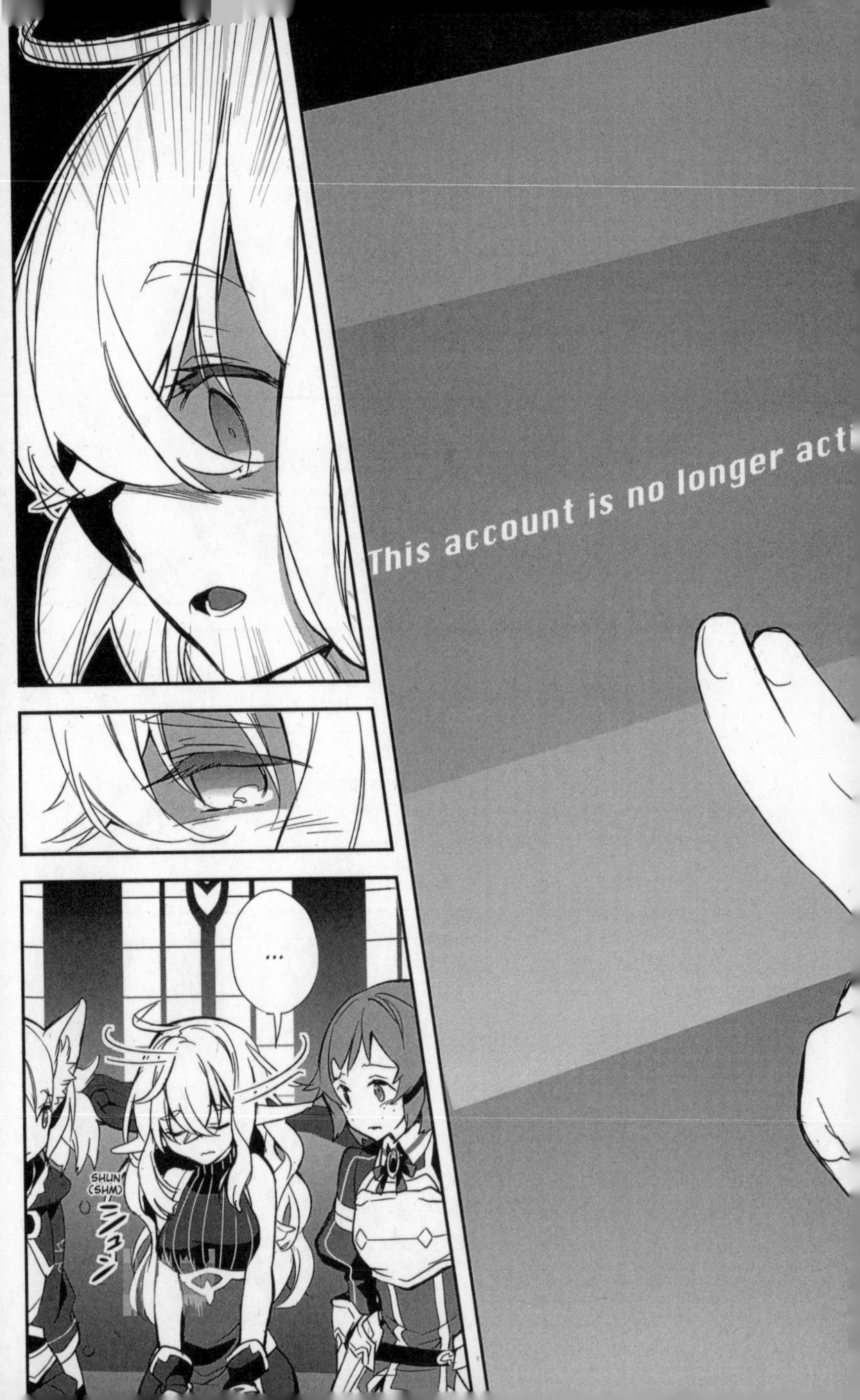

This account is no longer acti
...
SHUN (SHM)

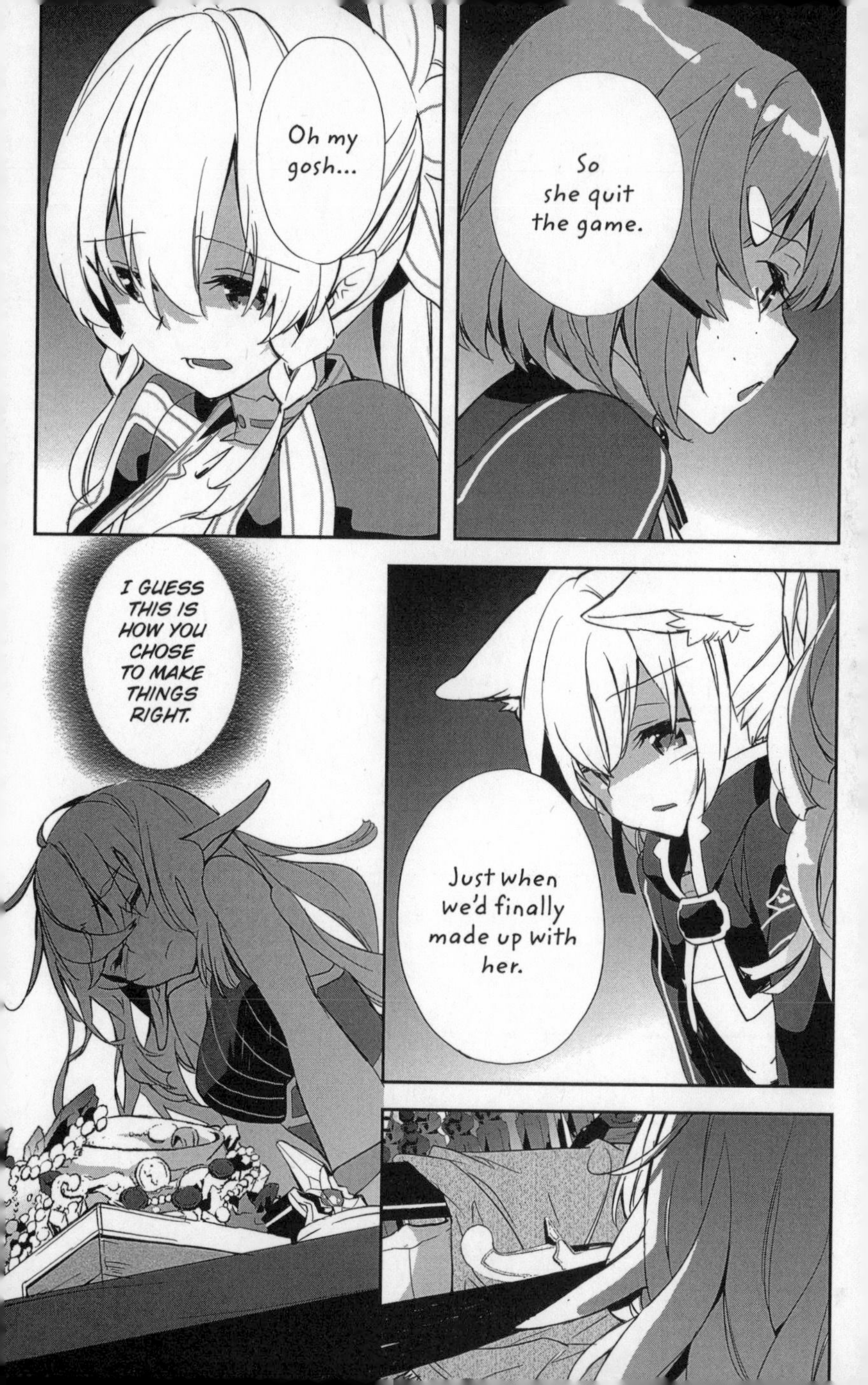
So she quit the game.
Oh my gosh...
Just when we'd finally made up with her.
I GUESS THIS IS HOW YOU CHOSE TO MAKE THINGS RIGHT.

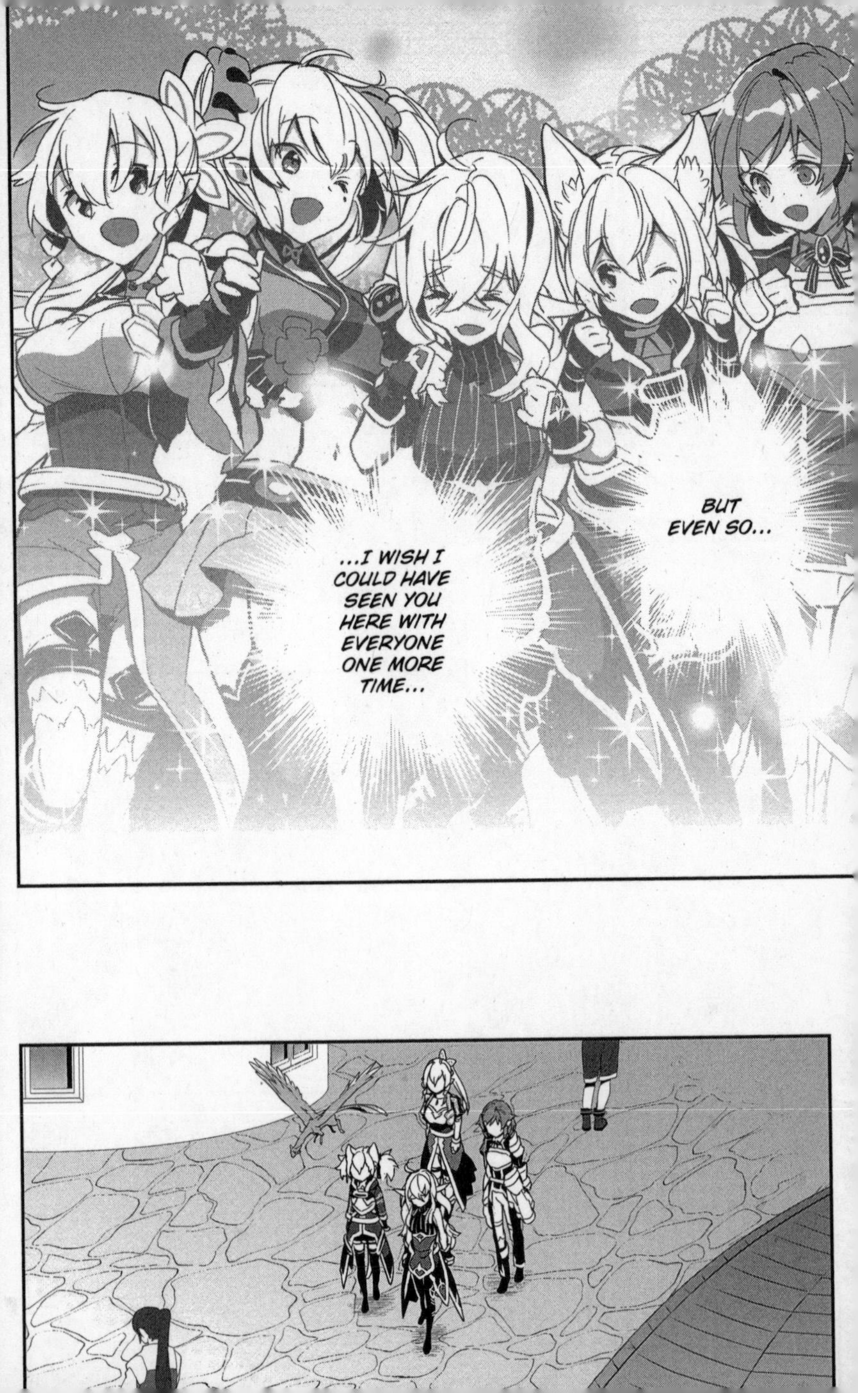
BUT EVEN SO...
...I WISH I COULD HAVE SEEN YOU HERE WITH EVERYONE ONE MORE TIME...

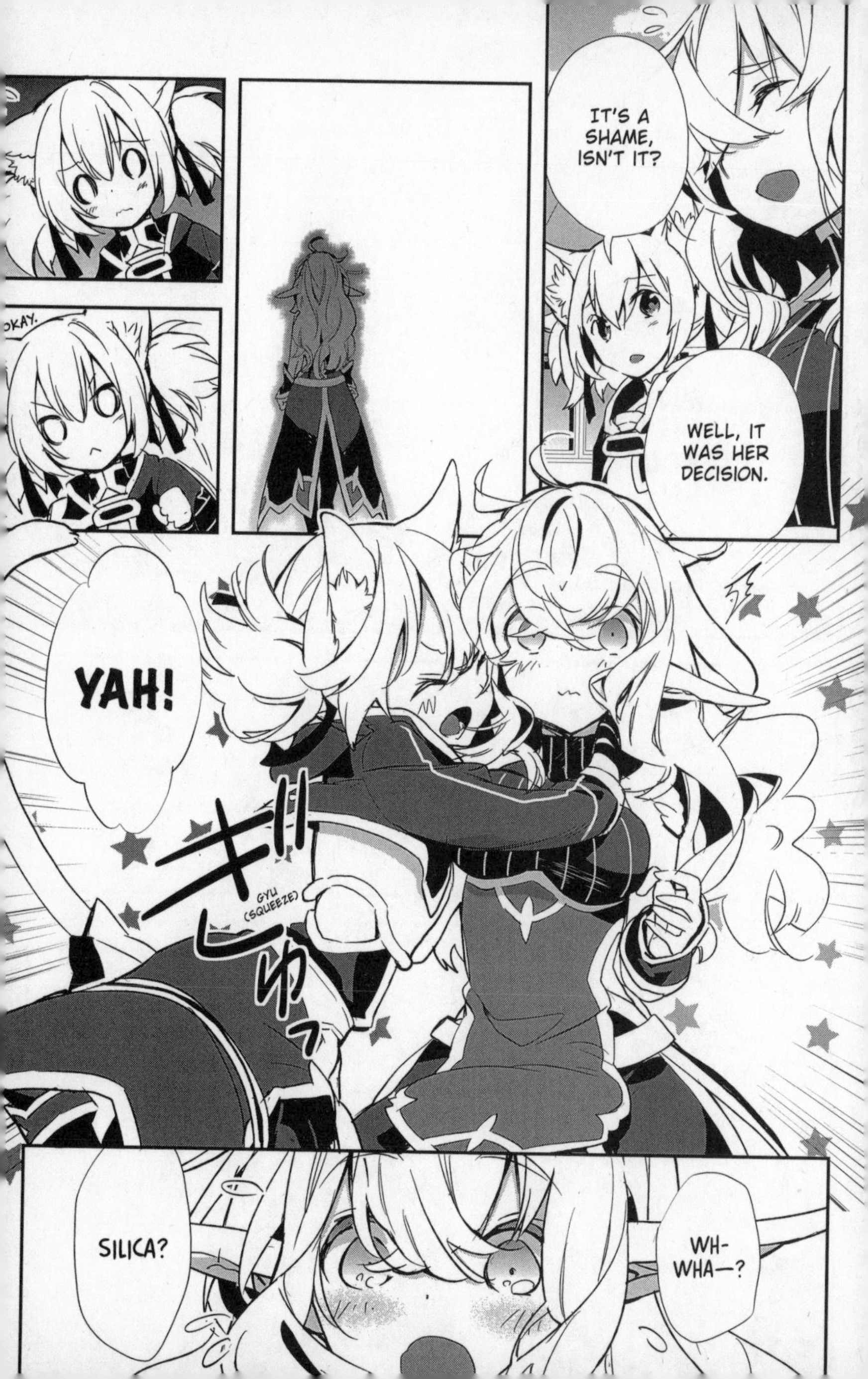
IT'S A SHAME, ISN'T IT?
WELL, IT WAS HER DECISION.
OKAY.
YAH!
GYU (SQUEEZE)
WH- WHA—?
SILICA?

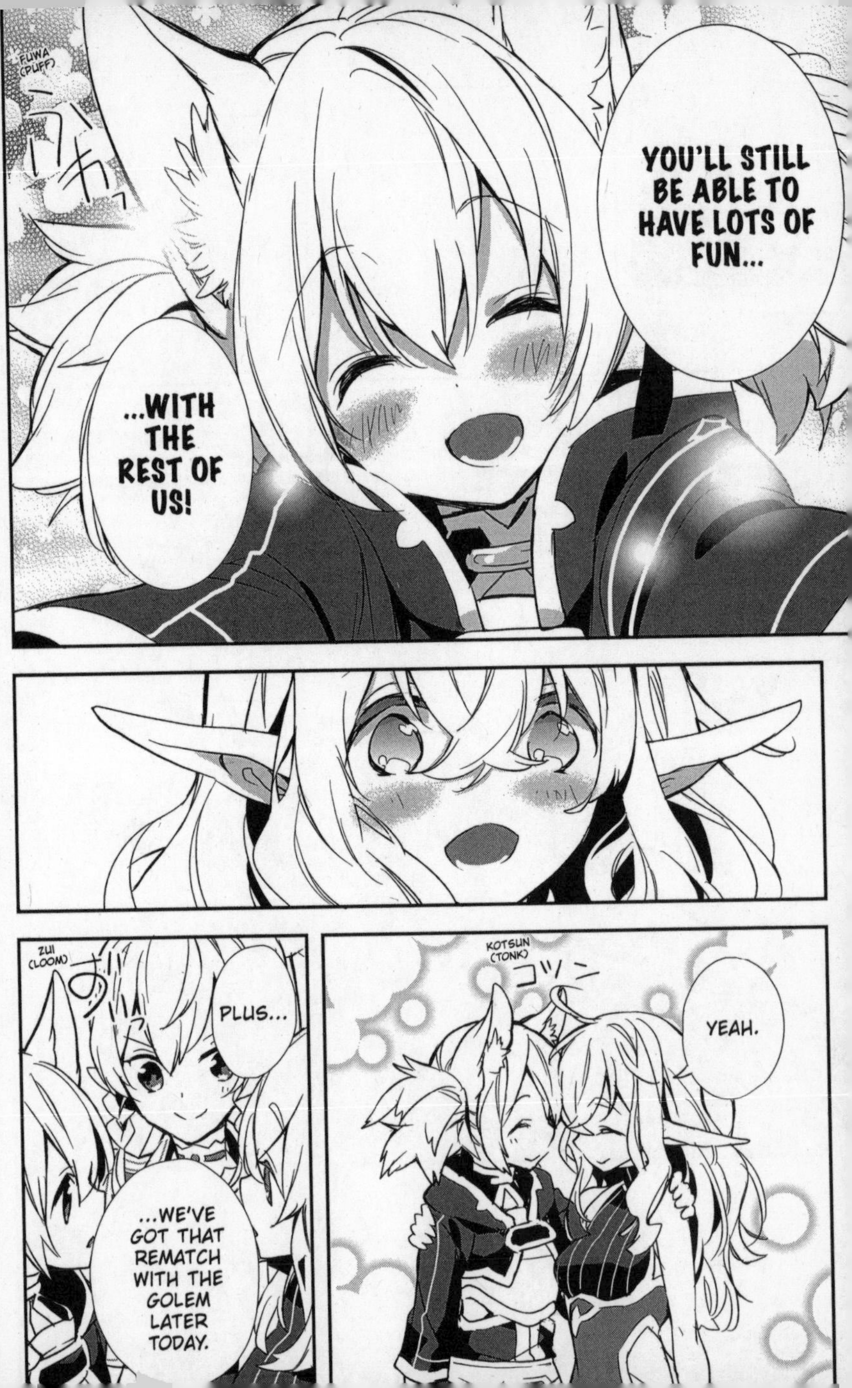
FUWA (PUFF)
YOU'LL STILL BE ABLE TO HAVE LOTS OF FUN...
...WITH THE REST OF US!
KOTSUN (TONK)
YEAH.
ZUI (LOOM)
PLUS...
...WE'VE GOT THAT REMATCH WITH THE GOLEM LATER TODAY.

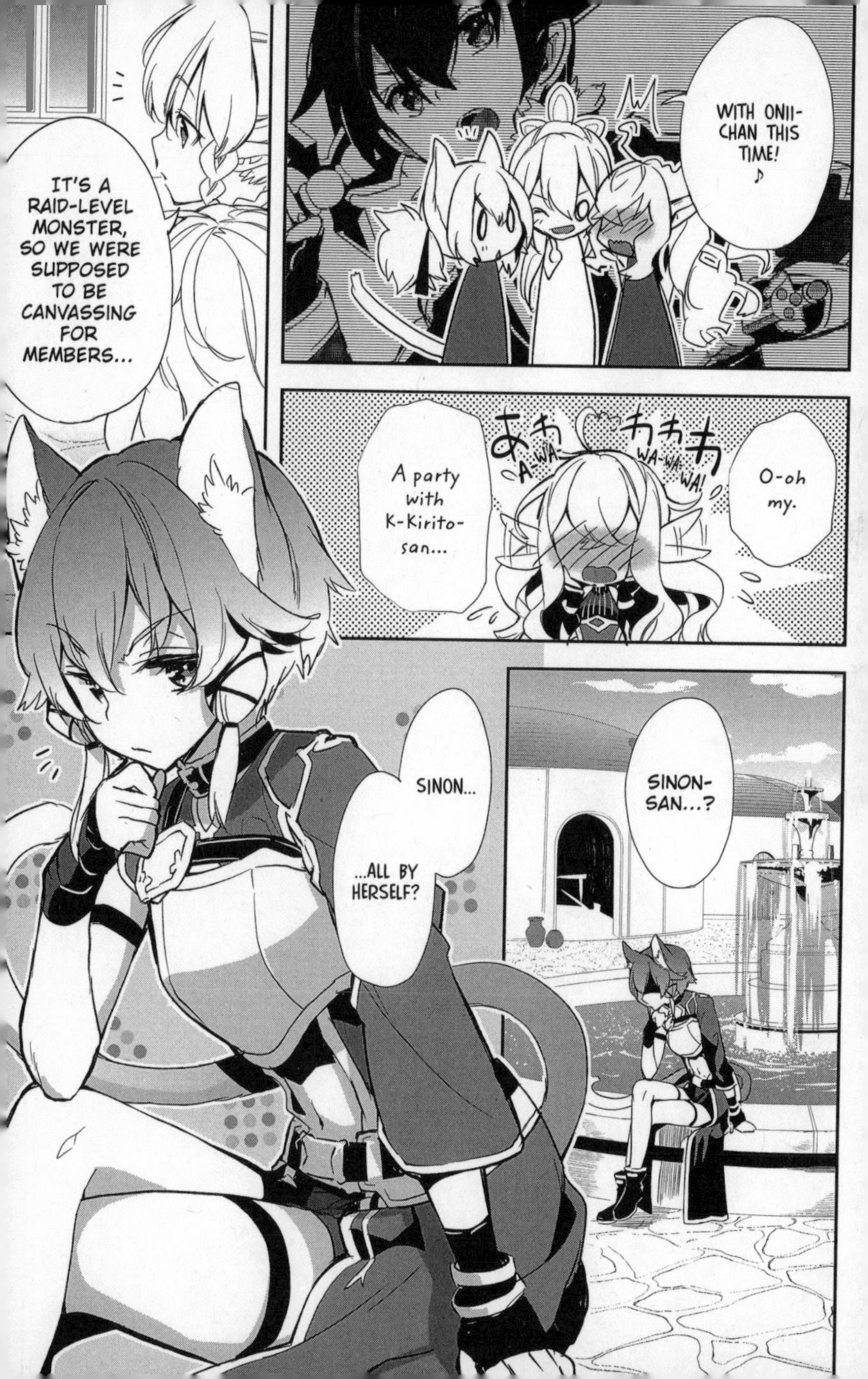

WITH ONII-CHAN THIS TIME! ♪
IT'S A RAID-LEVEL MONSTER, SO WE WERE SUPPOSED TO BE CANVASSING FOR MEMBERS...
O-oh my.
A-WA
WA-WA-WA!
A party with K-Kirito-san...
SINON-SAN...?
SINON...
...ALL BY HERSELF?

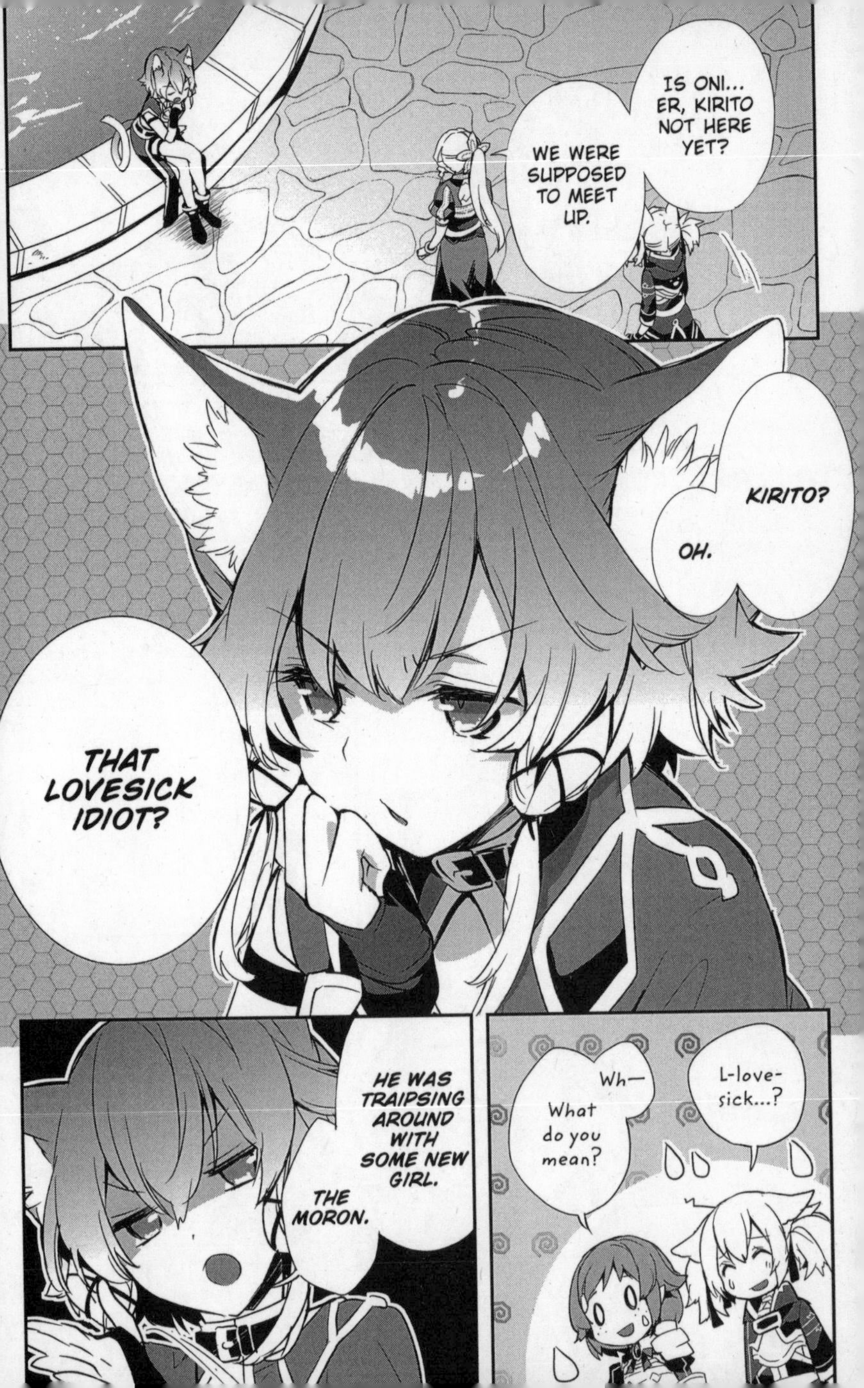
IS ONI... ER, KIRITO NOT HERE YET?
WE WERE SUPPOSED TO MEET UP.
KIRITO?
OH.
THAT LOVESICK IDIOT?
L-love-sick...?
Wh—
What do you mean?
HE WAS TRAIPSING AROUND WITH SOME NEW GIRL.
THE MORON.

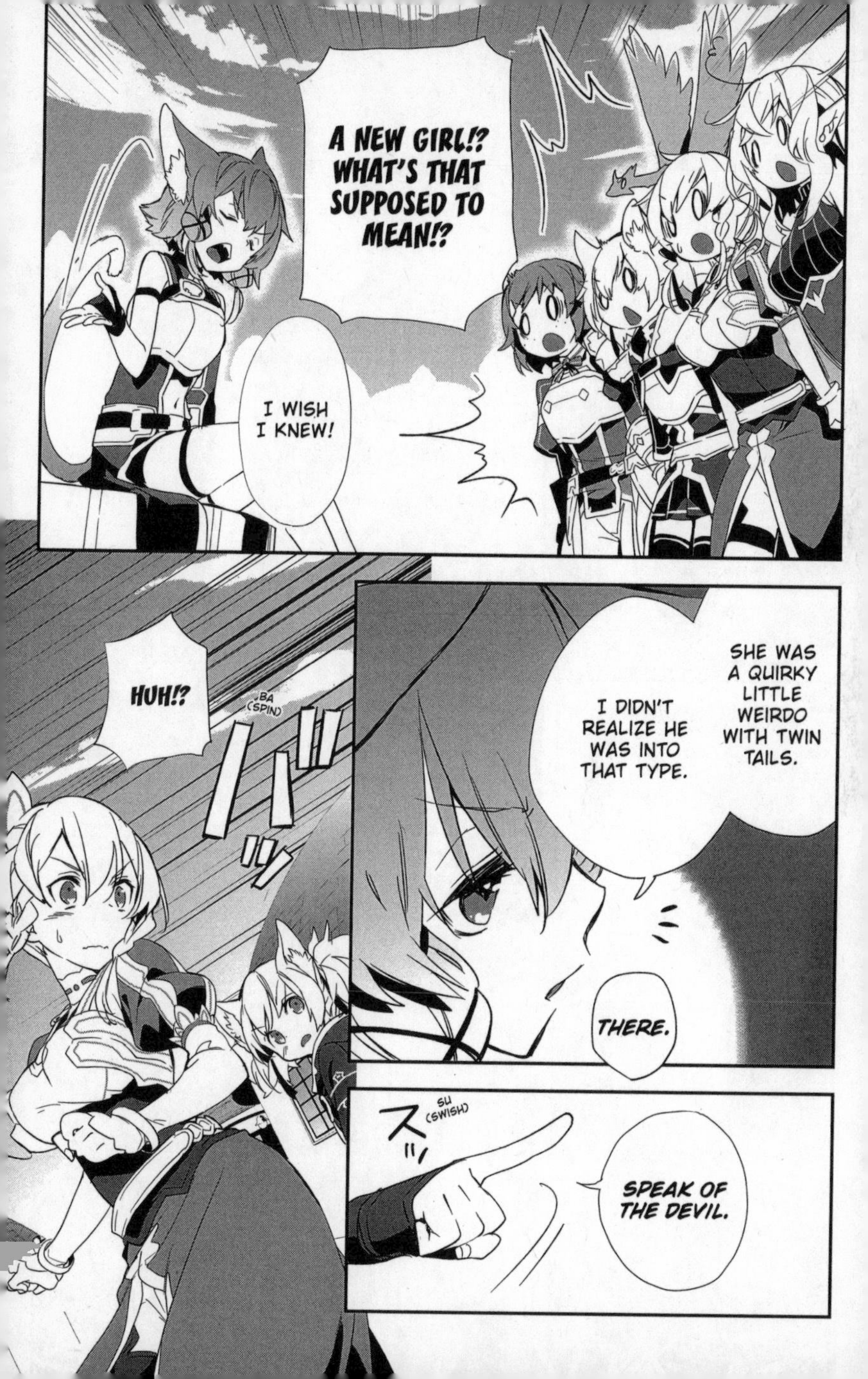
A NEW GIRL!? WHAT'S THAT SUPPOSED TO MEAN!?
I WISH I KNEW!
SHE WAS A QUIRKY LITTLE WEIRDO WITH TWIN TAILS.
I DIDN'T REALIZE HE WAS INTO THAT TYPE.
HUH!?
BA (SPIN)
THERE.
SU (SWISH)
SPEAK OF THE DEVIL.

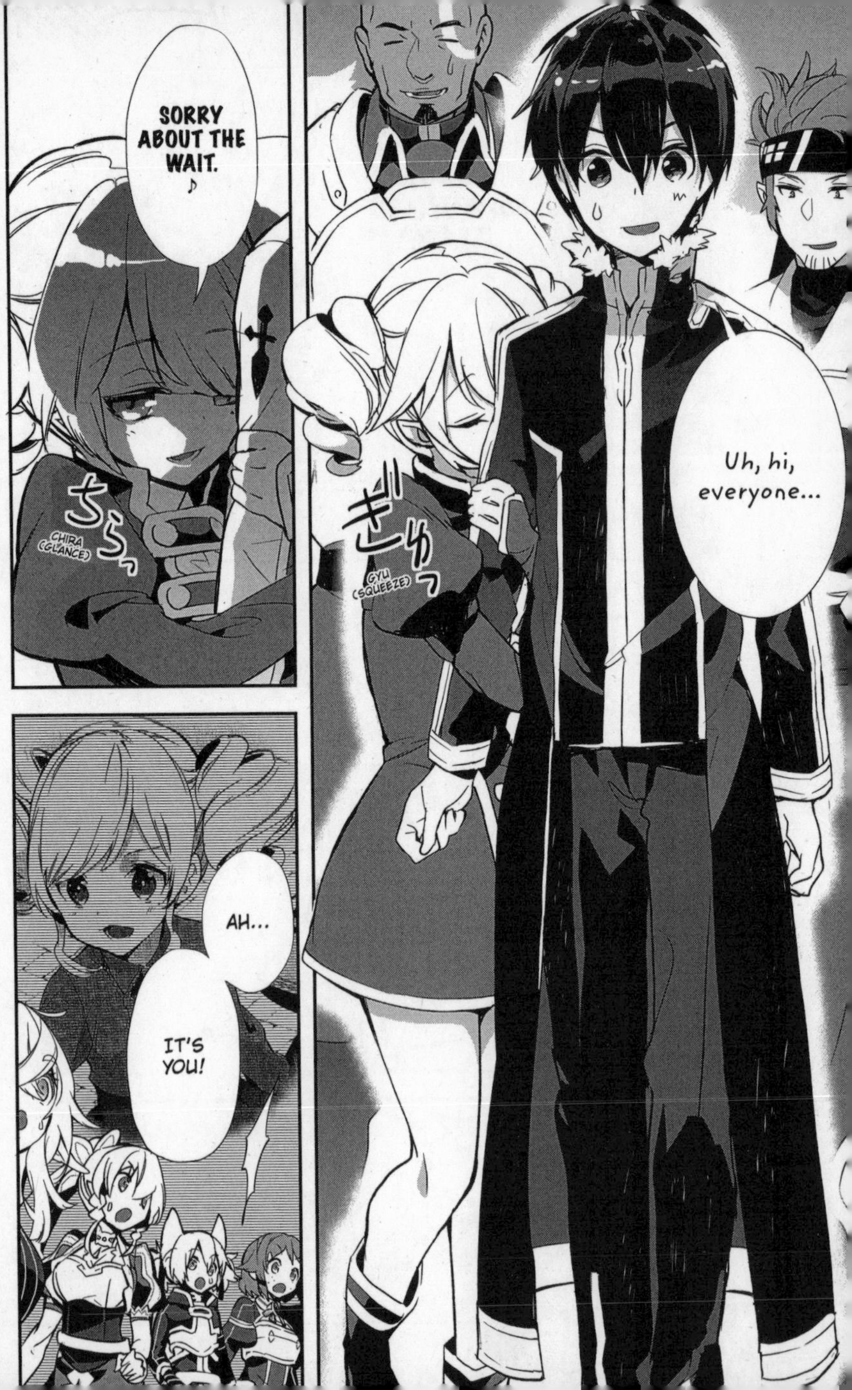
Uh, hi, everyone...
ぎゅっ
GYU (SQUEEZE)
SORRY ABOUT THE WAIT. ♪
ちらっ
CHIRA (GLANCE)
AH...
IT'S YOU!

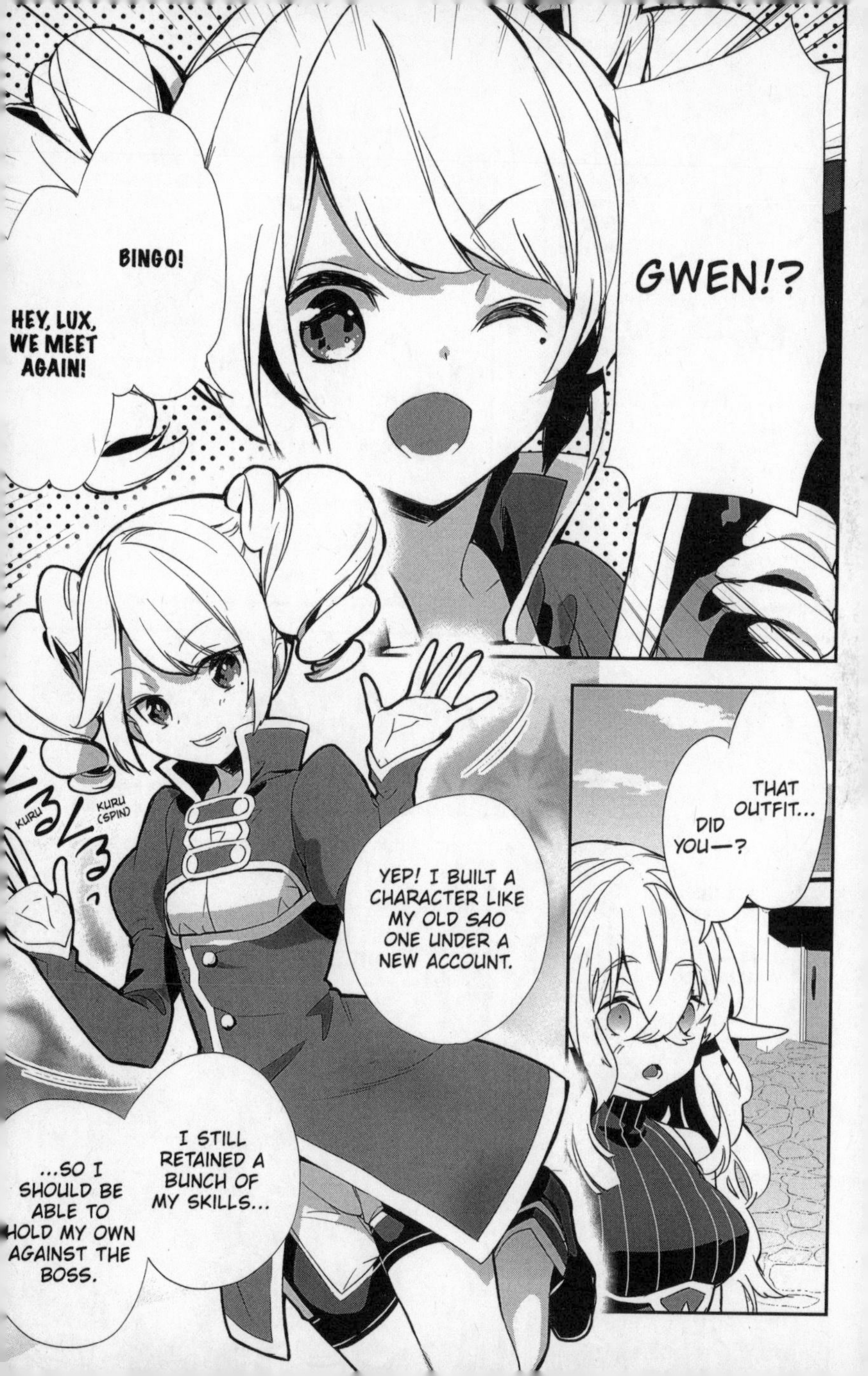
GWEN!?
BINGO!
HEY, LUX, WE MEET AGAIN!
THAT OUTFIT... DID YOU—?
YEP! I BUILT A CHARACTER LIKE MY OLD SAO ONE UNDER A NEW ACCOUNT.
KURU (SPIN)
KURU
I STILL RETAINED A BUNCH OF MY SKILLS...
...SO I SHOULD BE ABLE TO HOLD MY OWN AGAINST THE BOSS.

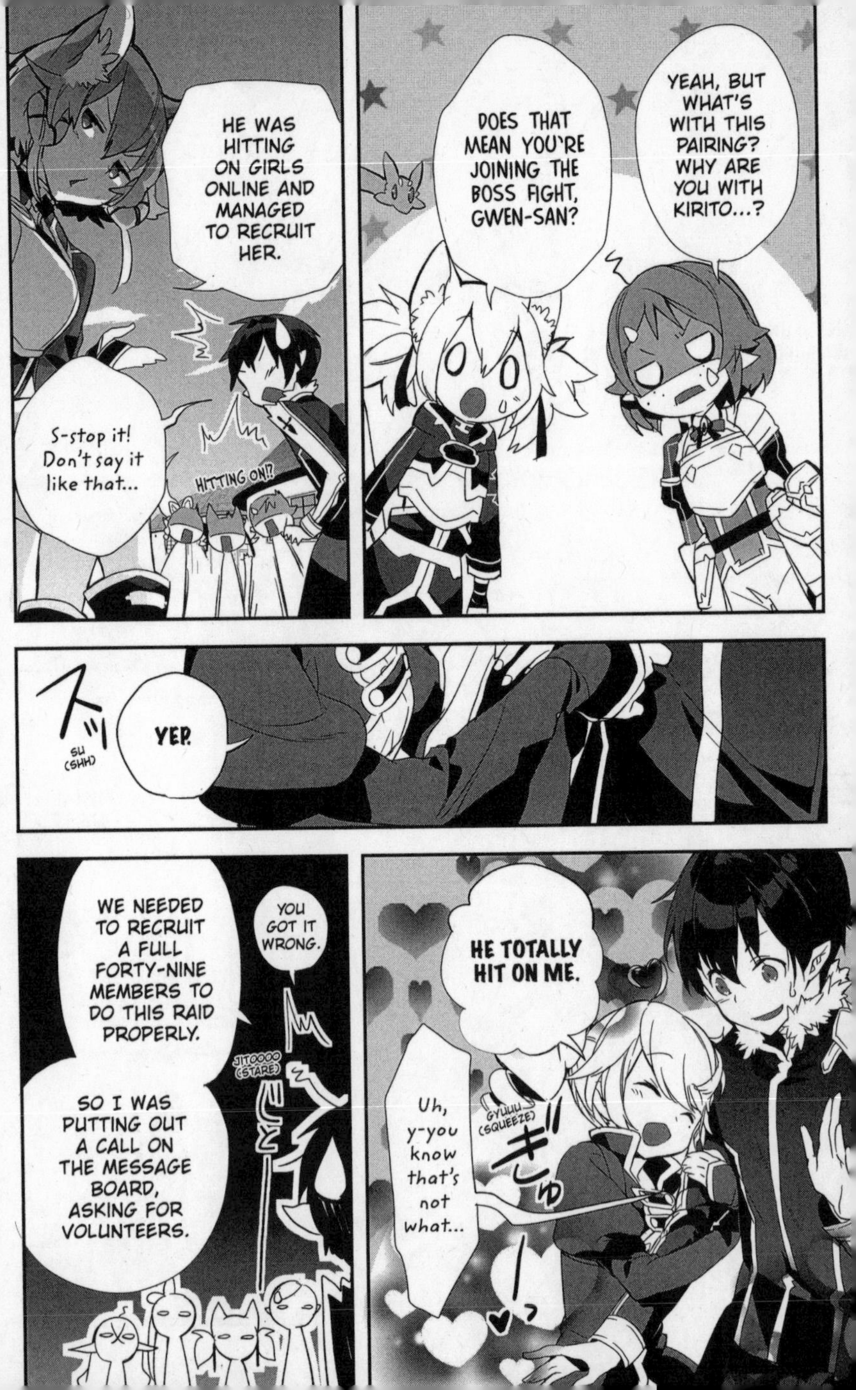
YEAH, BUT WHAT'S WITH THIS PAIRING? WHY ARE YOU WITH KIRITO...?
DOES THAT MEAN YOU'RE JOINING THE BOSS FIGHT, GWEN-SAN?
HE WAS HITTING ON GIRLS ONLINE AND MANAGED TO RECRUIT HER.
S-stop it! Don't say it like that...
HITTING ON!?
YEP.
SU (SHH)
HE TOTALLY HIT ON ME.
GYUUU (SQUEEZE)
Uh, y-you know that's not what...
YOU GOT IT WRONG.
WE NEEDED TO RECRUIT A FULL FORTY-NINE MEMBERS TO DO THIS RAID PROPERLY.
SO I WAS PUTTING OUT A CALL ON THE MESSAGE BOARD, ASKING FOR VOLUNTEERS.
JITOOOO (STARE)

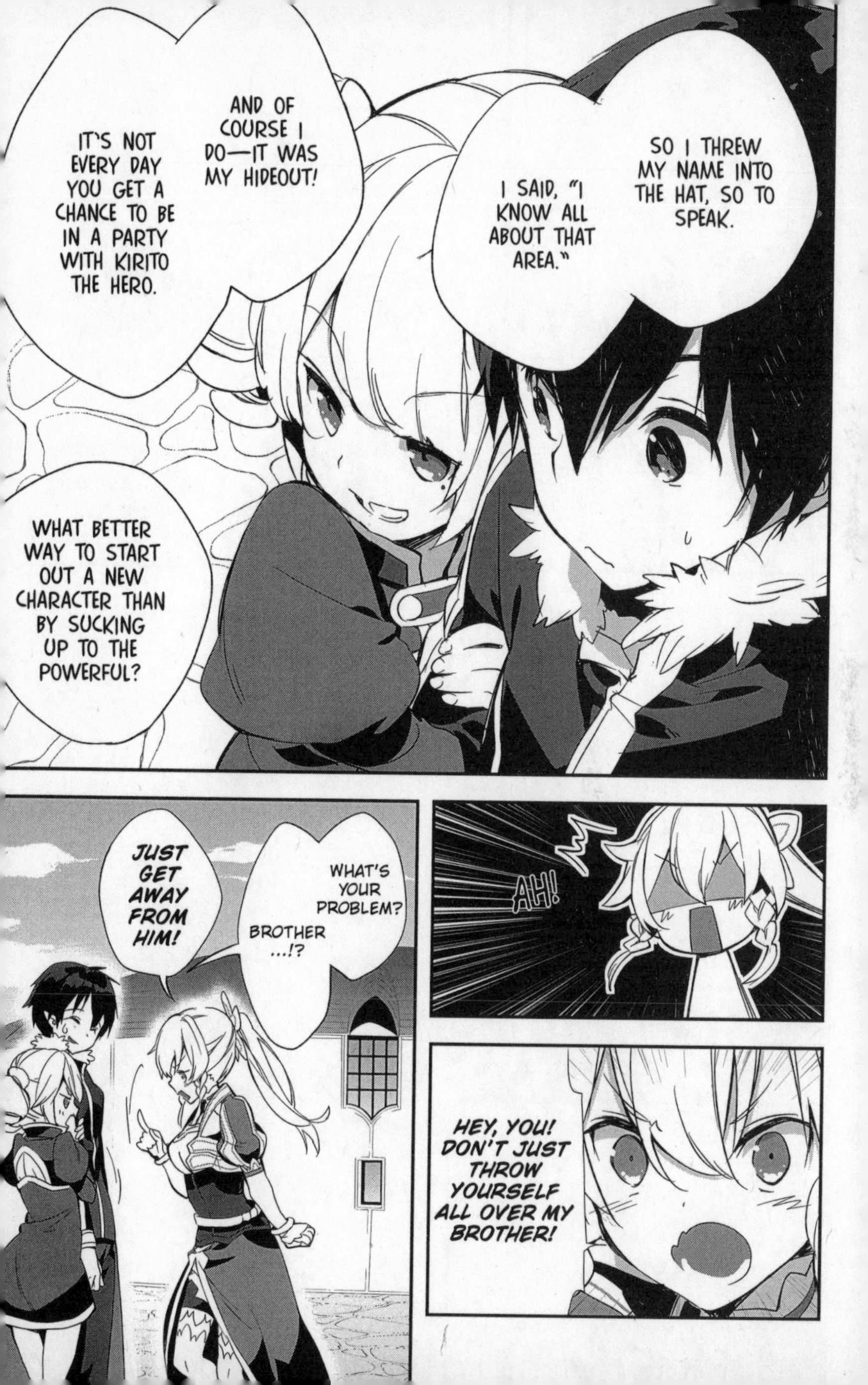
SO I THREW MY NAME INTO THE HAT, SO TO SPEAK.
I SAID, "I KNOW ALL ABOUT THAT AREA."
AND OF COURSE I DO—IT WAS MY HIDEOUT!
IT'S NOT EVERY DAY YOU GET A CHANCE TO BE IN A PARTY WITH KIRITO THE HERO.
WHAT BETTER WAY TO START OUT A NEW CHARACTER THAN BY SUCKING UP TO THE POWERFUL?
AH!
HEY, YOU! DON'T JUST THROW YOURSELF ALL OVER MY BROTHER!
WHAT'S YOUR PROBLEM?
BROTHER ...!?
JUST GET AWAY FROM HIM!

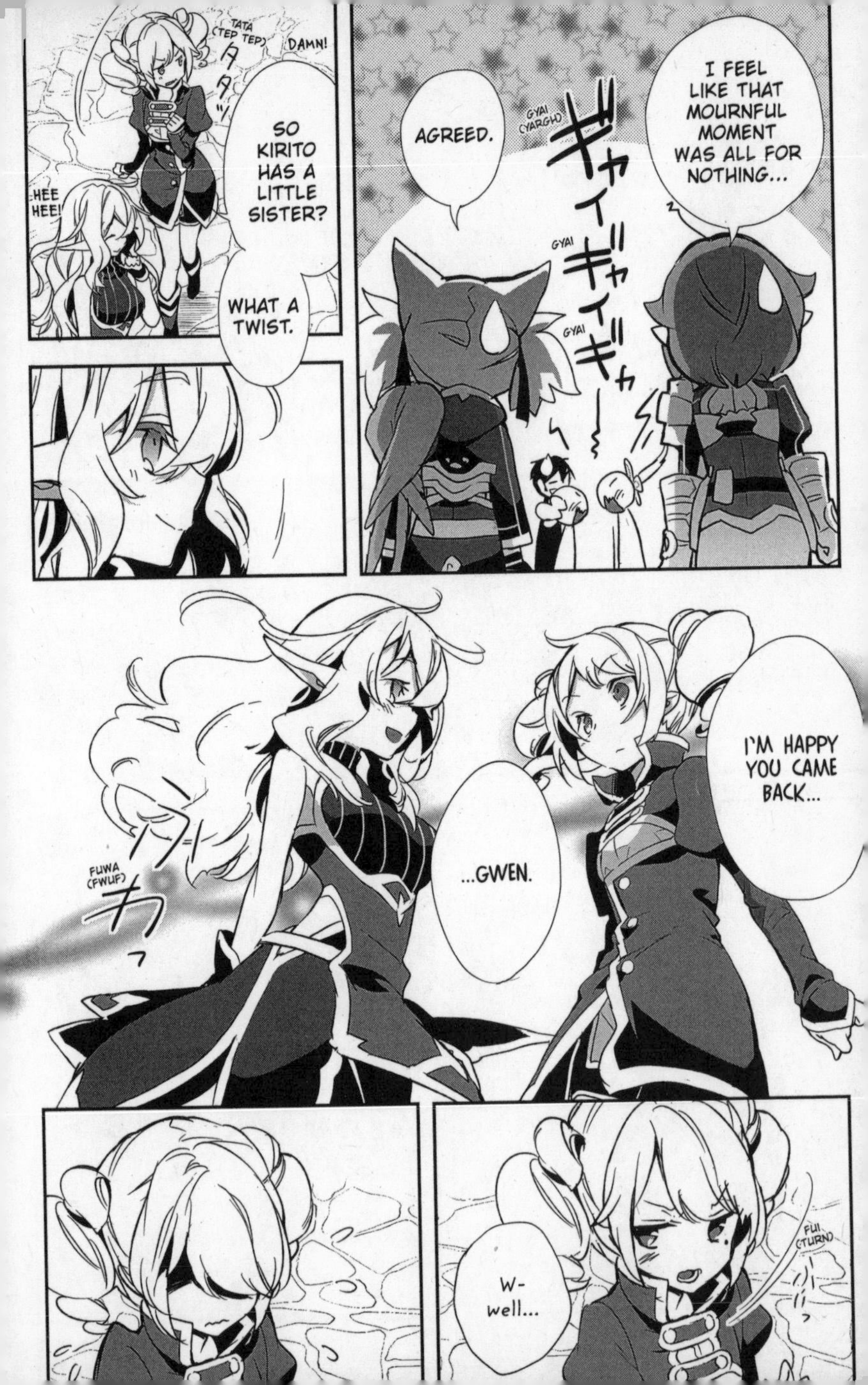
I FEEL LIKE THAT MOURNFUL MOMENT WAS ALL FOR NOTHING...
AGREED.
GYAI (YARGH)
GYAI
GYAI
TATA (TEP TEP)
DAMN!
SO KIRITO HAS A LITTLE SISTER?
HEE HEE!
WHAT A TWIST.
I'M HAPPY YOU CAME BACK...
...GWEN.
FUWA (FWUF)
FUI (TURN)
W-well...

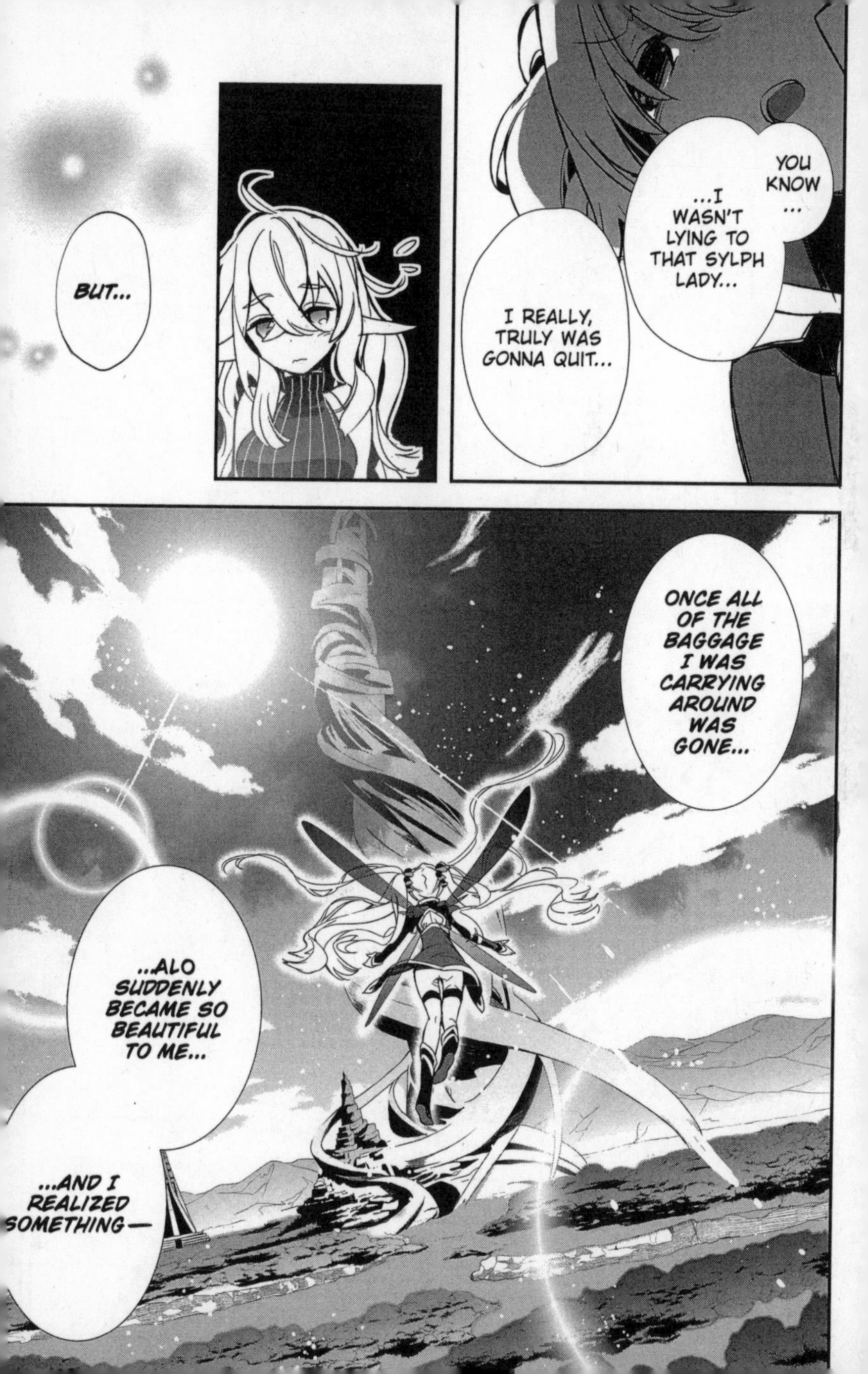
YOU KNOW...
...I WASN'T LYING TO THAT SYLPH LADY...
I REALLY, TRULY WAS GONNA QUIT...
BUT...
ONCE ALL OF THE BAGGAGE I WAS CARRYING AROUND WAS GONE...
...ALO SUDDENLY BECAME SO BEAUTIFUL TO ME...
...AND I REALIZED SOMETHING—

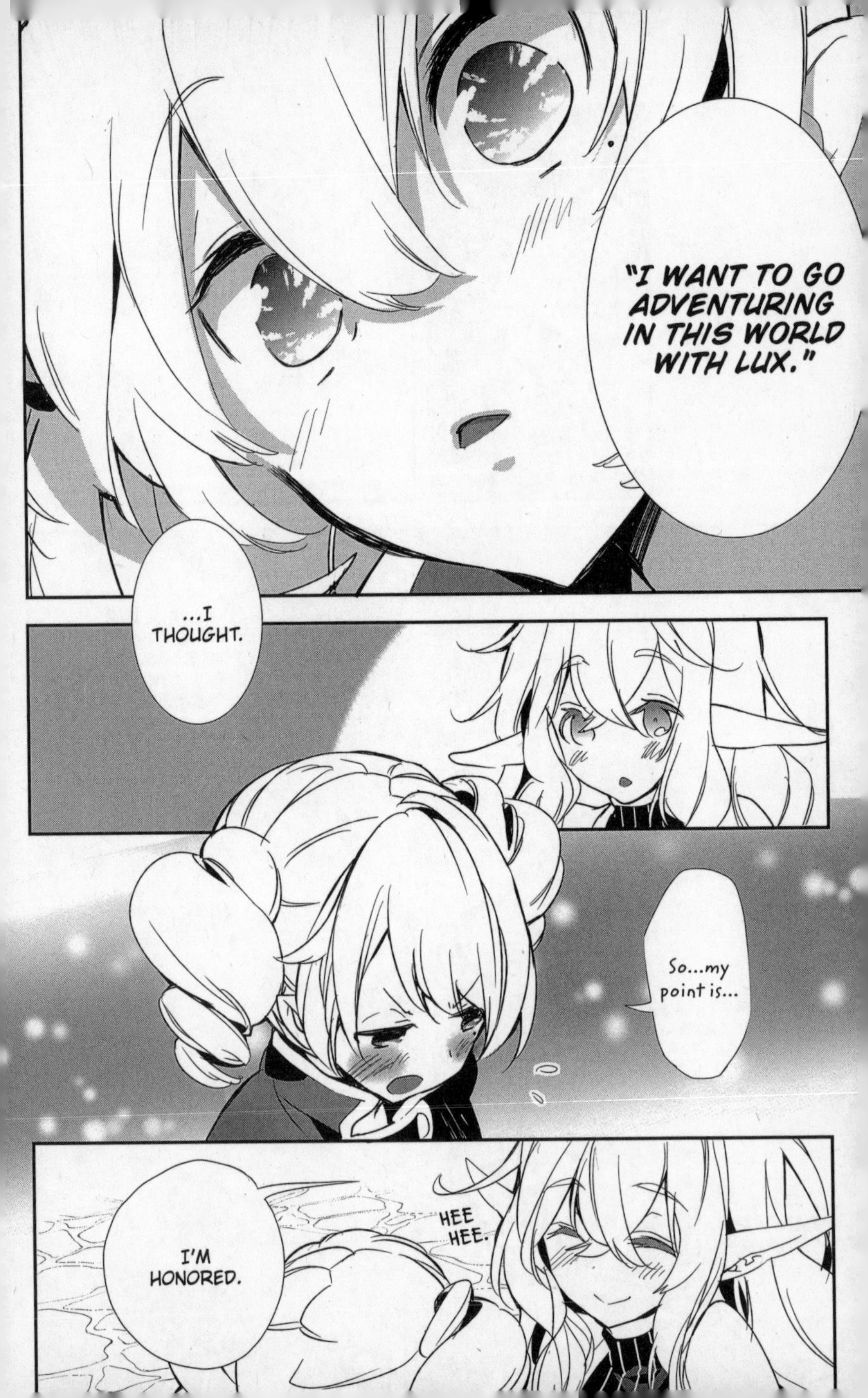
"I WANT TO GO ADVENTURING IN THIS WORLD WITH LUX."
...I THOUGHT.
So...my point is...
HEE HEE.
I'M HONORED.

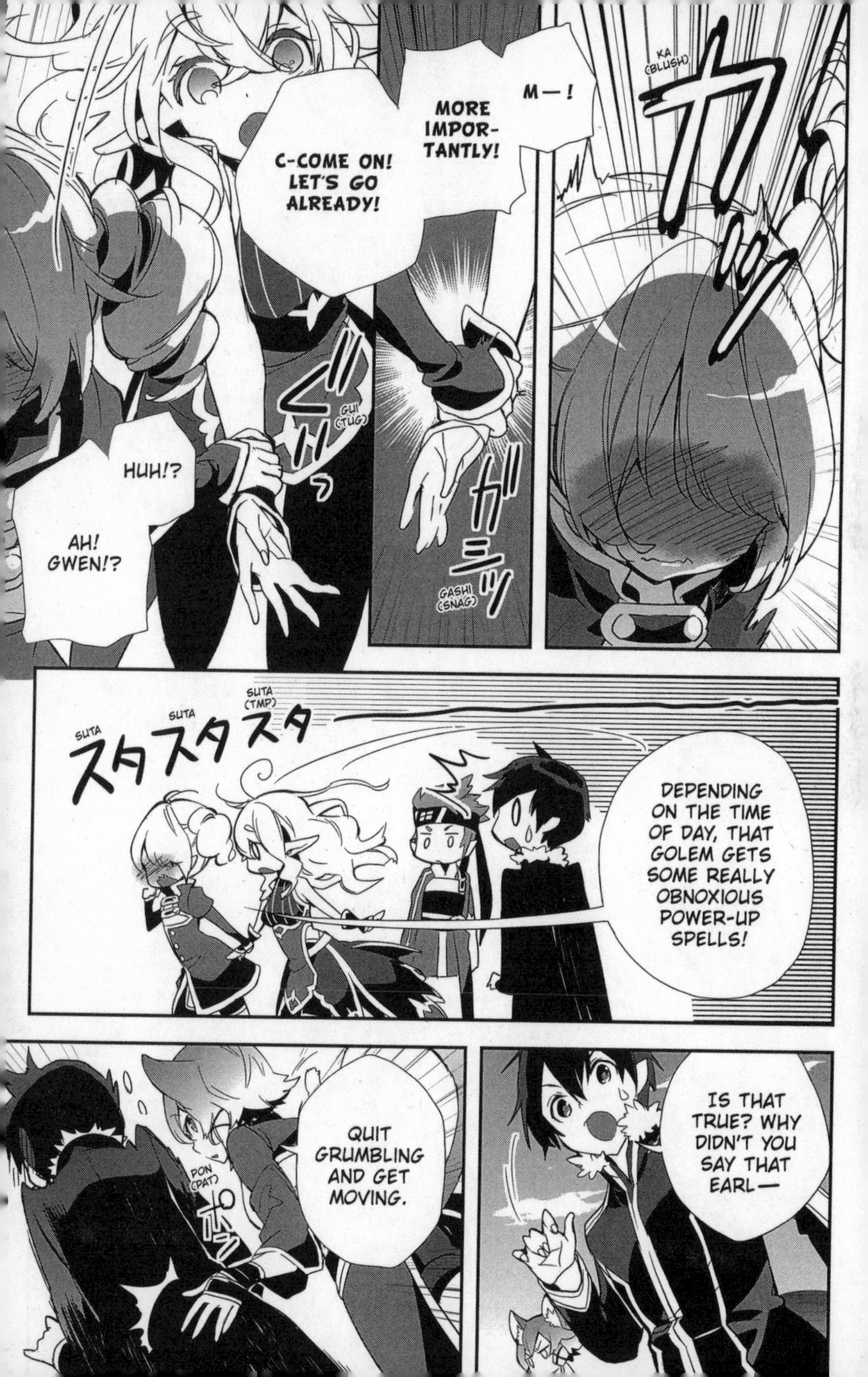

KA (BLUSH)
カッ
M—!
MORE IMPORTANTLY!
GASHI (SNAG)
ガシッ
C-COME ON! LET'S GO ALREADY!
GUI (TUG)
ぐいっ
HUH!?
AH! GWEN!?
SUTA SUTA SUTA (TMP)
スタスタスタ
DEPENDING ON THE TIME OF DAY, THAT GOLEM GETS SOME REALLY OBNOXIOUS POWER-UP SPELLS!
IS THAT TRUE? WHY DIDN'T YOU SAY THAT EARL—
QUIT GRUMBLING AND GET MOVING.
PON (PAT)
ポン

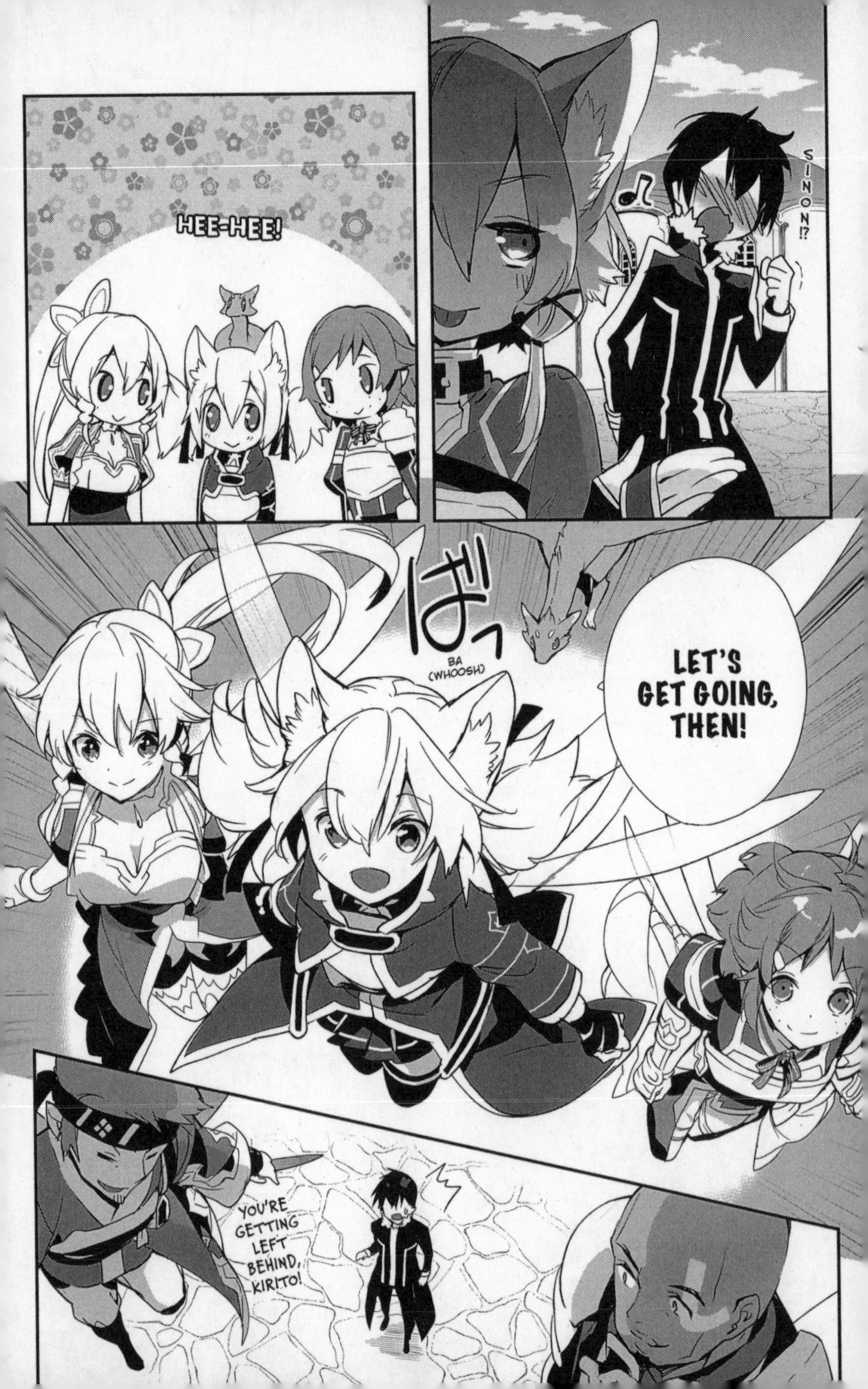
SINON!?
HEE-HEE!
LET'S GET GOING, THEN!
ばっ
BA (WHOOSH)
YOU'RE GETTING LEFT BEHIND, KIRITO!

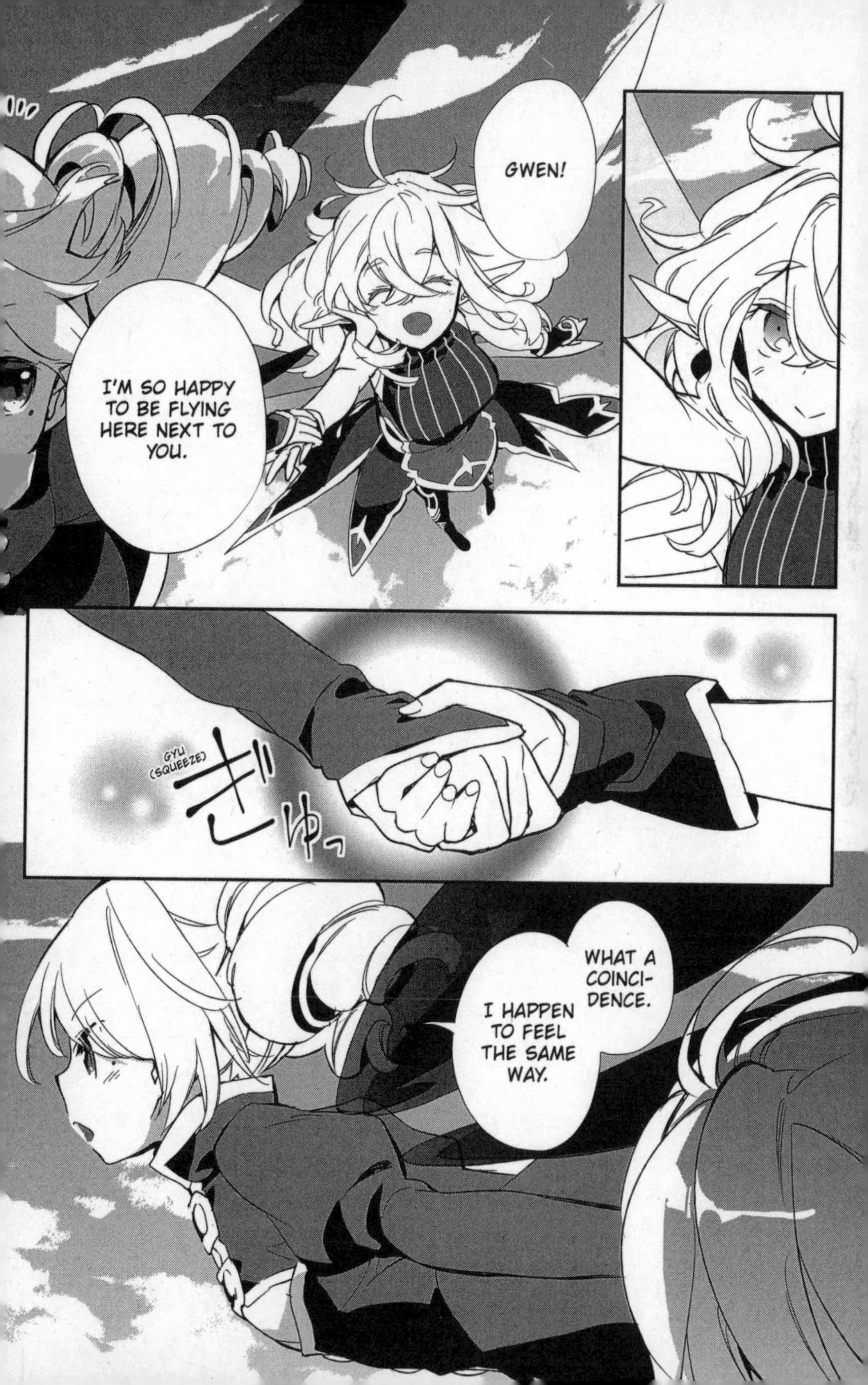
GWEN!
I'M SO HAPPY TO BE FLYING HERE NEXT TO YOU.
GYU (SQUEEZE)
ぎゅっ
WHAT A COINCIDENCE.
I HAPPEN TO FEEL THE SAME WAY.

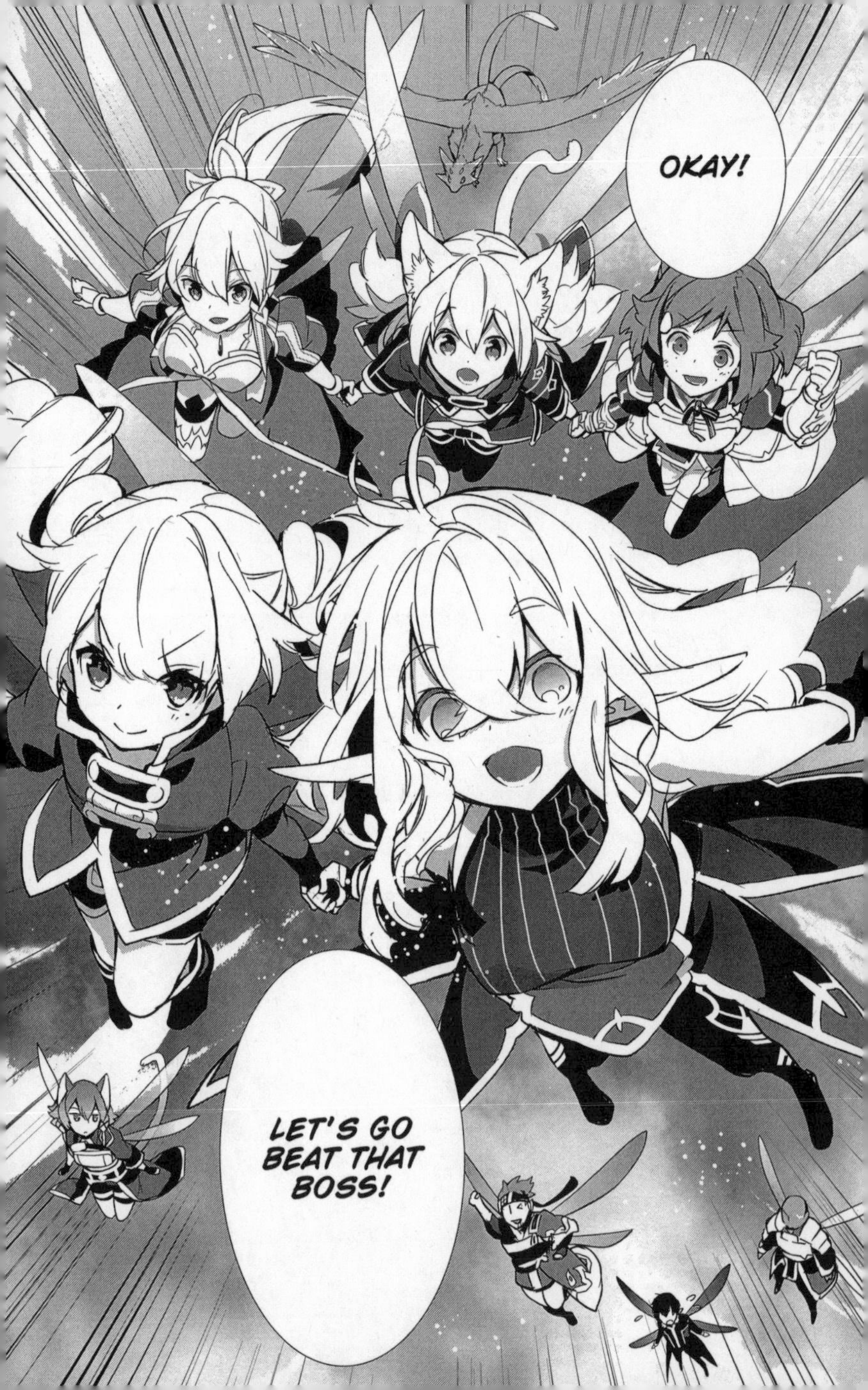
OKAY!
LET'S GO BEAT THAT BOSS!

SWORD ART ONLINE
GIRLS' OPS

SWORD ART ONLINE
GIRLS' OPERATIONS

To be continued in the next volume!

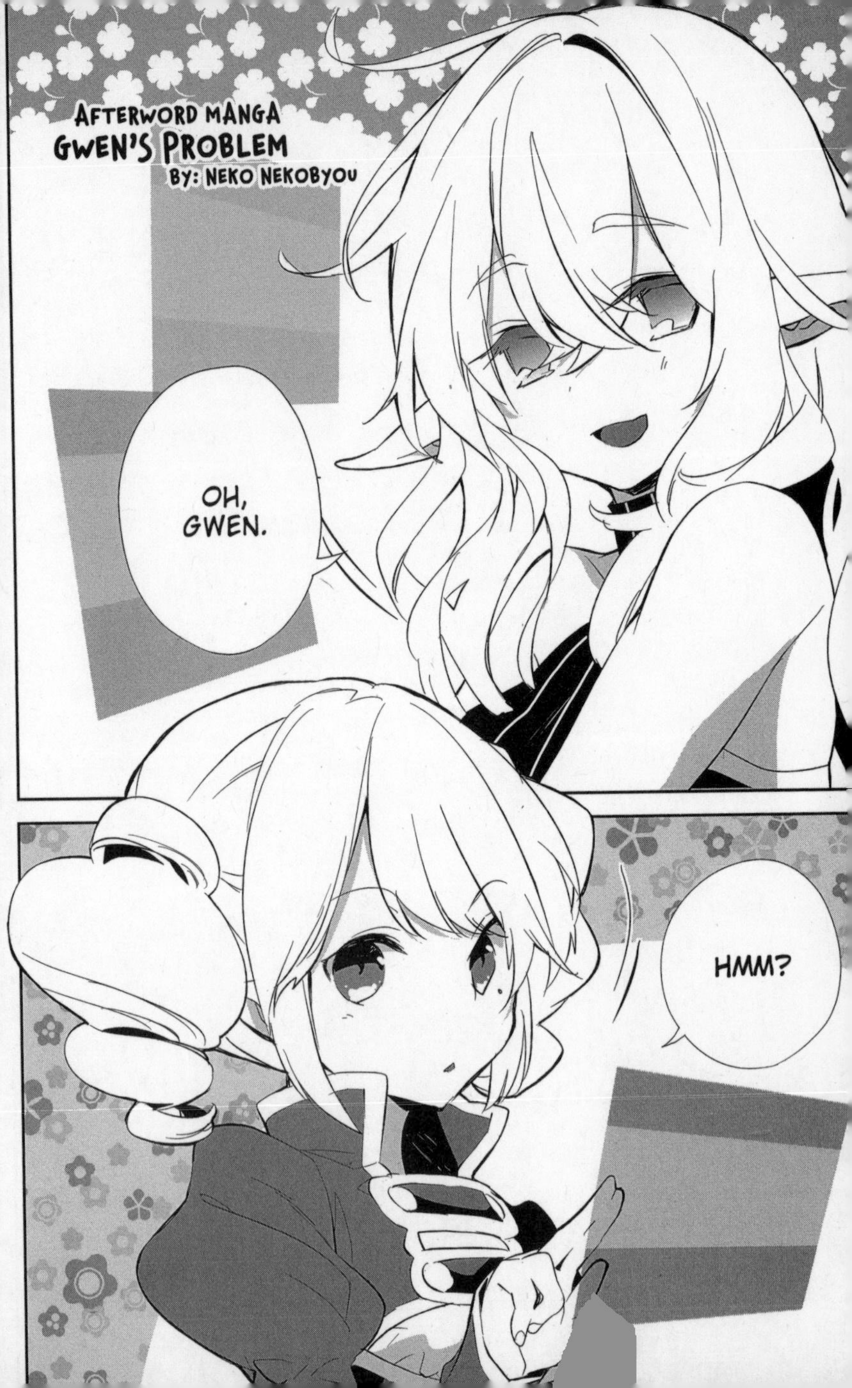
AFTERWORD MANGA
GWEN'S PROBLEM
BY: NEKO NEKOBYOU
OH, GWEN.
HMM?

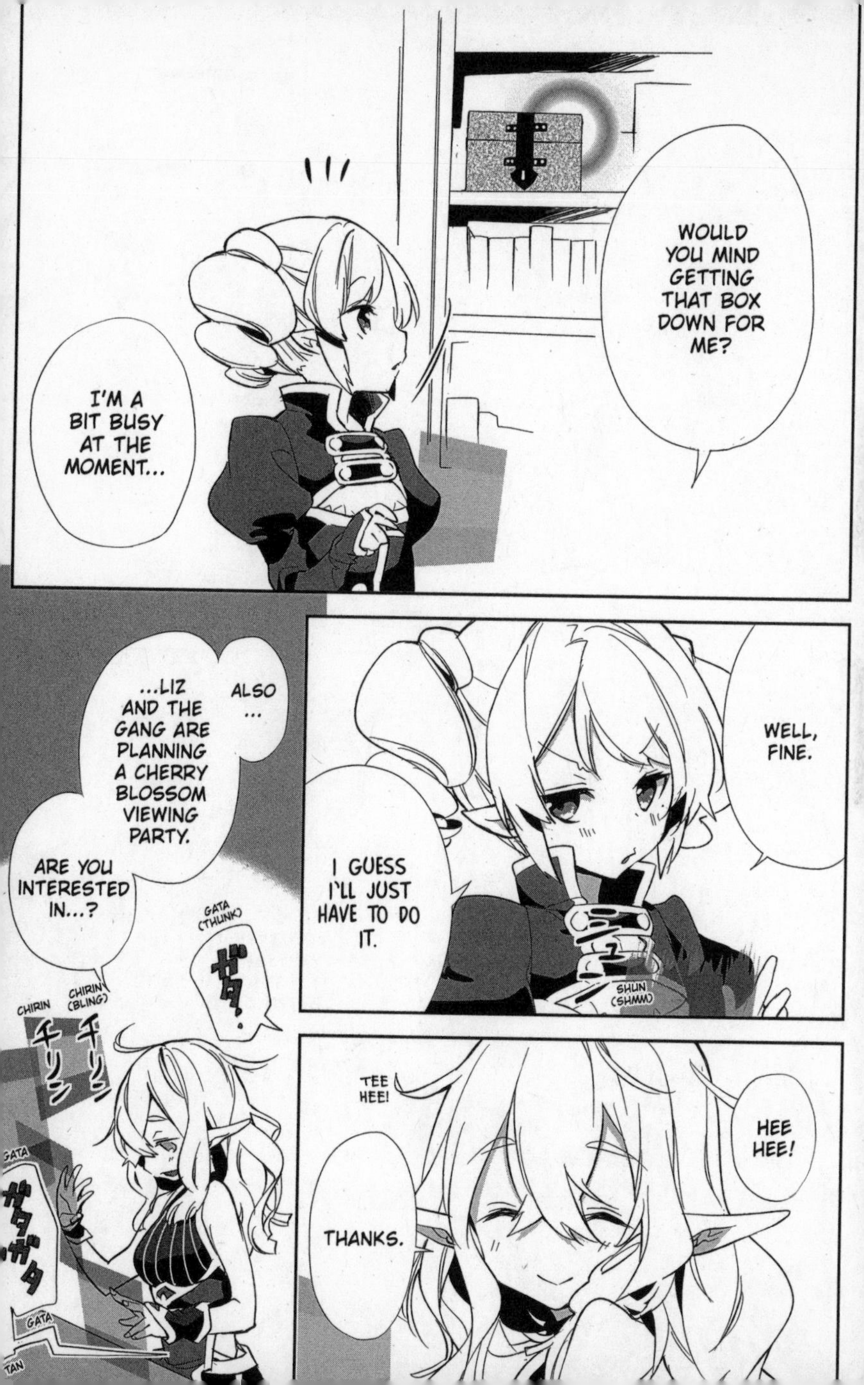
WOULD YOU MIND GETTING THAT BOX DOWN FOR ME?
I'M A BIT BUSY AT THE MOMENT...
WELL, FINE.
I GUESS I'LL JUST HAVE TO DO IT.
SHUN (SHMM)
ALSO ...
...LIZ AND THE GANG ARE PLANNING A CHERRY BLOSSOM VIEWING PARTY.
ARE YOU INTERESTED IN...?
GATA (THUNK)
ガタ。
HEE HEE!
TEE HEE!
THANKS.
CHIRIN (BLING)
チリン
CHIRIN
チリン
GATA
ガタガタ
GATA
TAN

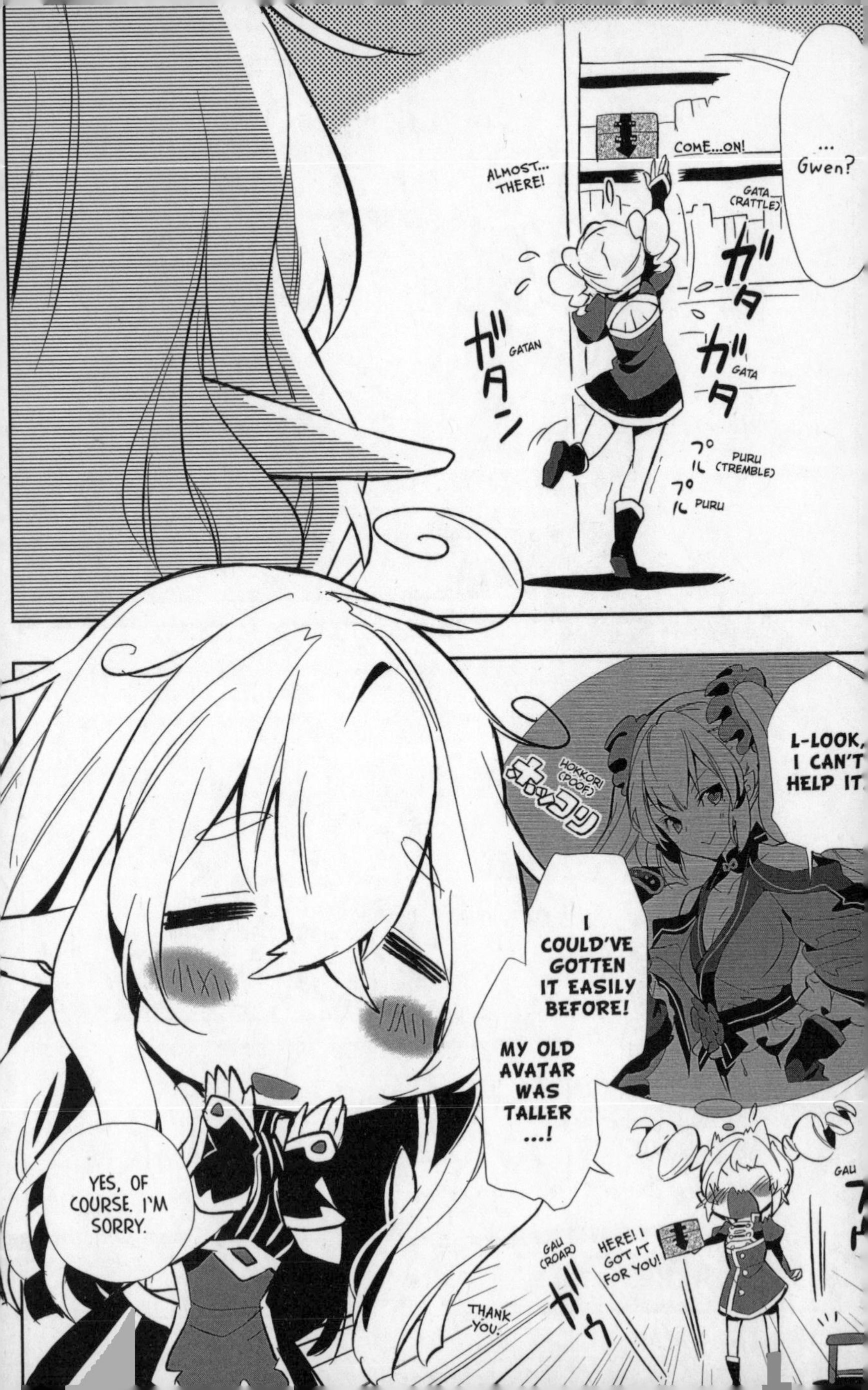

... Gwen?
COME...ON!
ALMOST... THERE!
GATA (RATTLE)
ガタ
ガタ
GATA
ガタン
GATAN
プル
PURU (TREMBLE)
プル
PURU
L-LOOK, I CAN'T HELP IT.
HOKKORI (POOF)
I COULD'VE GOTTEN IT EASILY BEFORE!
MY OLD AVATAR WAS TALLER...!
GAU
HERE! I GOT IT FOR YOU!
GAU (ROAR)
ガゥ
THANK YOU.
YES, OF COURSE. I'M SORRY.

Special Thanks!!

YAJI

REKI KAWAHARA-SENSEI

ABEC-SENSEI

SHINGO NAGAI-SENSEI

KAZUMI MIKI-SAMA

TOMOYUKI TSUCHIYA-SAMA

EVERYONE WHO READ THIS BOOK!

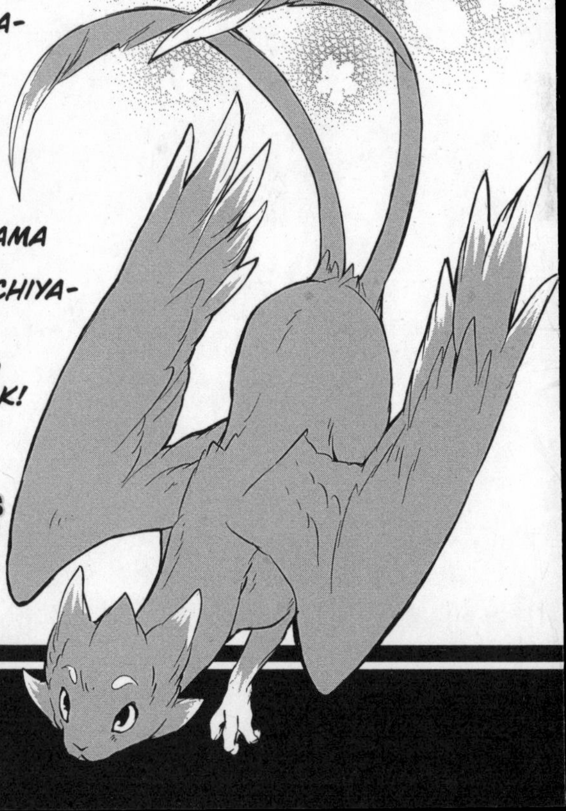

THE GIRLS' OPS SERIES WILL CONTINUE! HOPE YOU STICK AROUND!

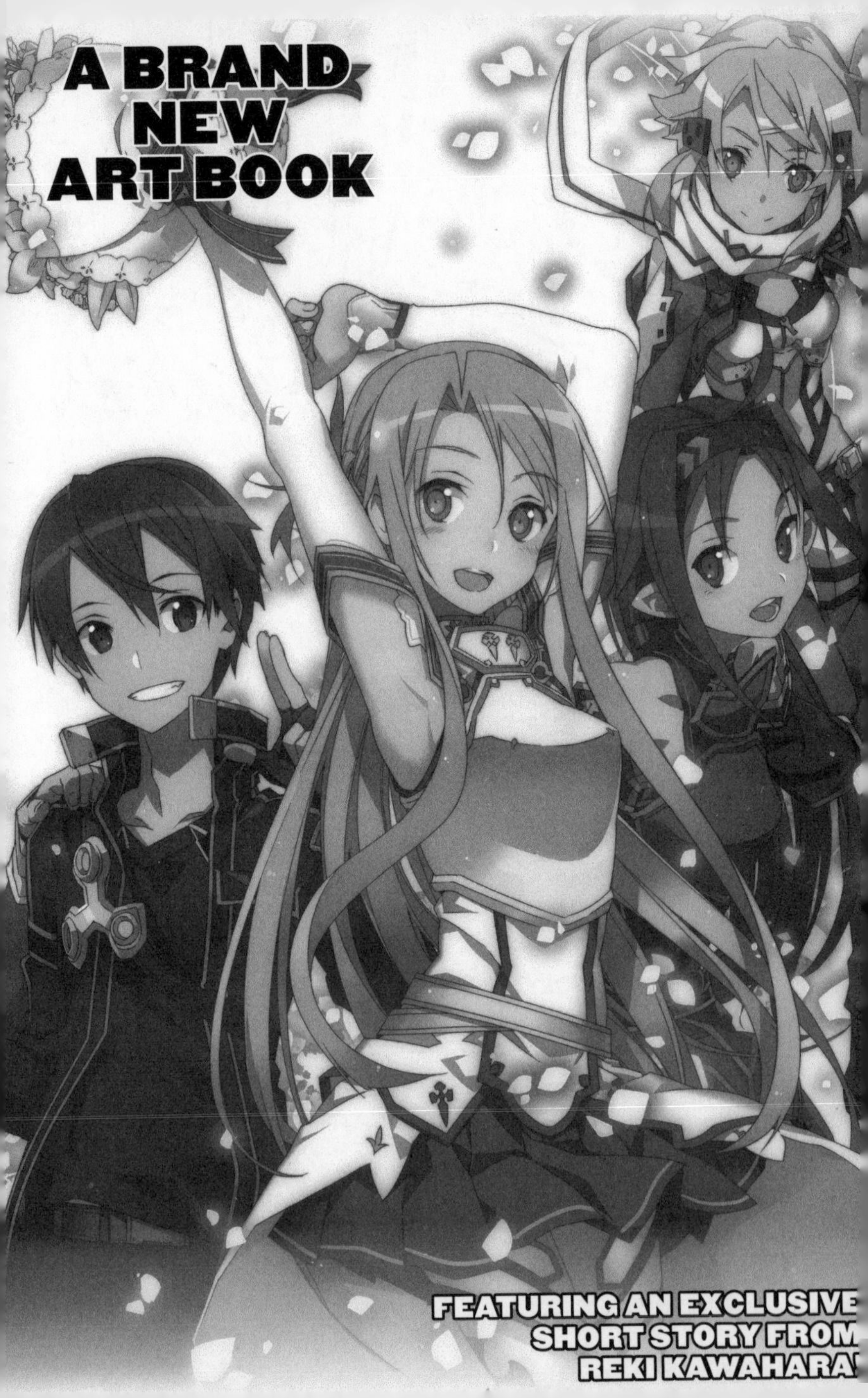
A BRAND NEW ART BOOK
FEATURING AN EXCLUSIVE SHORT STORY FROM REKI KAWAHARA!

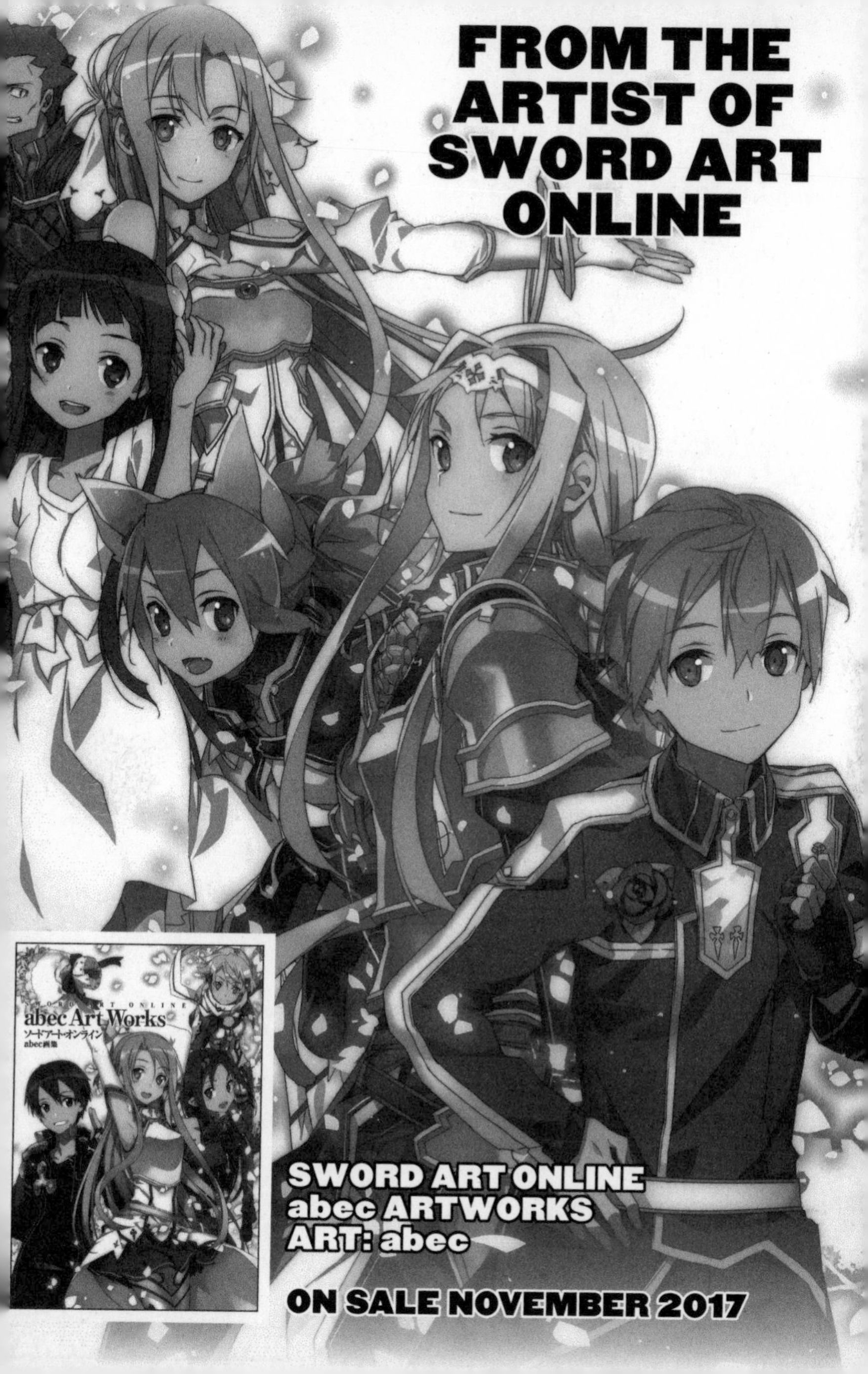
FROM THE ARTIST OF SWORD ART ONLINE
abec Art Works
ソードアート・オンライン
abec画集
SWORD ART ONLINE
abec ARTWORKS
ART: abec
ON SALE NOVEMBER 2017

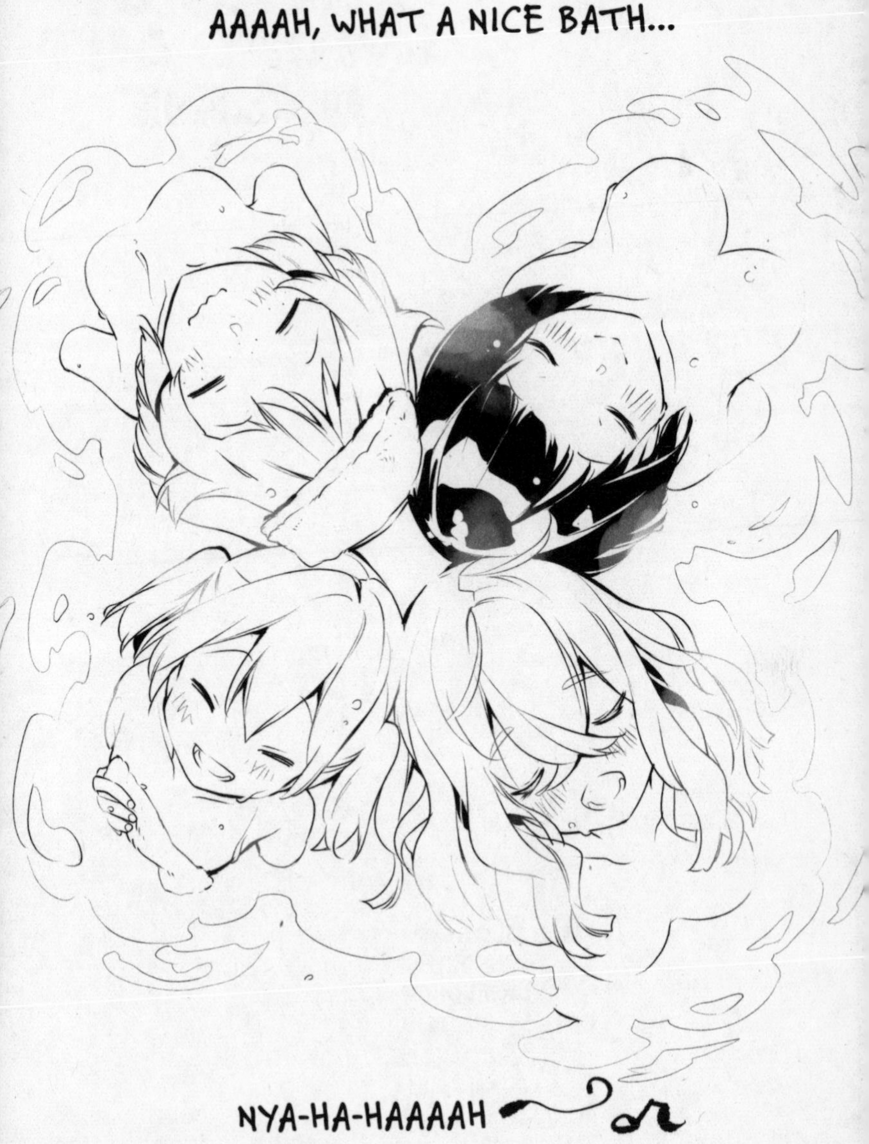
AAAAH, WHAT A NICE BATH...
NYA-HA-HAAAAH ♪

OKAY, LET'S GO!

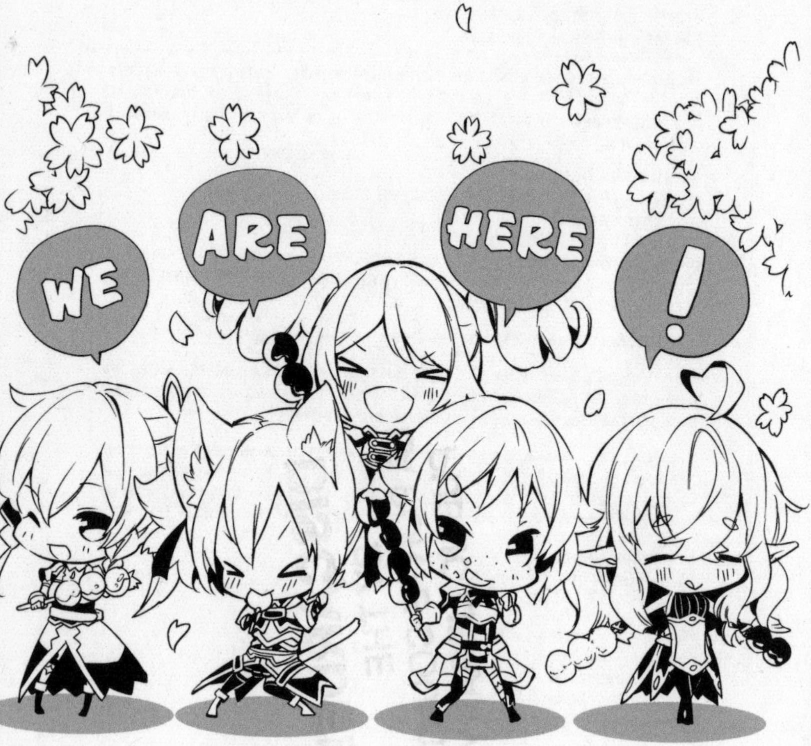
WE
ARE
HERE
!

CHERRY BLOSSOM VIEWING!
THESE GIRLS PREFER DANGO
OVER FLOWERS...

SWORD ART ONLINE: GIRLS' OPS 4

ART: NEKO NEKOBYOU
ORIGINAL STORY: REKI KAWAHARA
CHARACTER DESIGN: abec

Translation: Stephen Paul
Lettering: Brndn Blakeslee

Edited by ASCII MEDIA WORKS
First published in Japan in 2017 by KADOKAWA CORPORATION, Tokyo.
English translation rights arranged with KADOKAWA CORPORATION, Tokyo, through Tuttle-Mori Agency, Inc., Tokyo.

Yen Press
1290 Avenue of the Americas
New York, NY 10104

Visit us at yenpress.com
facebook.com/yenpress
twitter.com/yenpress
yenpress.tumblr.com
instagram.com/yenpress

First Yen Press Edition: October 2017

Yen Press is an imprint of Yen Press, LLC.
The Yen Press name and logo are trademarks of Yen Press, LLC.

The publisher is not responsible for websites (or their content) that are not owned by the publisher.

Library of Congress Control Number: 2015952589

ISBNs: 978-0-316-44197-1 (paperback)
978-0-316-44198-8 (ebook)

10 9 8 7 6 5 4 3 2 1

BVG

Printed in the United States of America